# BROWN TIDE RISING

# BROWN TIDE RISING

Metaphors of Latinos
in Contemporary
American Public Discourse

*Otto Santa Ana*

Foreword by Joe R. Feagin

 University of Texas Press, Austin

Publication of this book has been assisted by a challenge grant from the National Endowment for the Humanities.

First edition, 2002

Library of Congress Cataloging-in-Publication Data

Santa Ana, Otto, 1954–
Brown tide rising : metaphors of Latinos in contemporary American public discourse / Otto Santa Ana.— 1st ed.
      p.      cm.
Includes bibliographical references and index.
ISBN 0-292-77766-3 (alk. paper) —
ISBN 0-292-77767-1 (pbk: alk. paper)
1. Hispanic Americans—Public opinion.   2. Hispanic Americans and mass media.   3. Discourse analysis—United States—Psychological aspects.   4. Discourse analysis—Political aspects—United States.   5. Hispanic Americans—Politics and government—Public opinion.   6. Immigrants—United States—Public opinion.   7. Public opinion—United States.
8. United States—Ethnic relations—Psychological aspects.
9. United States—Race relations—Psychological aspects.
I. Title.
E184.S75 S268   2002
305.868073—dc21                              2001052227

092402-484058

*To Thelma, my morning light*

Oppressive language does more than represent violence; it is violence; does more than represent the limits of knowledge; it limits knowledge. Whether it is the obscuring state language or the faux language of mindless media; whether it is the proud but calcified language of science; whether it is the malign language of law-without-ethics; or language designed for the estrangement of minorities, hiding its racist plunder in its literary cheek—it must be rejected, altered, and exposed. . . . [A]ll are typical of the policing language of mastery, and cannot, do not, permit new knowledge or encourage the mutual exchange of ideas.

*Toni Morrison*
From Morrison's lecture upon receiving
the 1993 Nobel Prize for literature

# Contents

# Foreword

*Joe R. Feagin, University of Florida*

In the year 2000 the U.S. Census counted 35 million Latinos, marking a substantial increase since the previous census. The Latino population is increasingly dispersed, and Latinos are now the neighbors of other Americans in every region. Many are immigrants who work hard under difficult conditions and for little pay. They harvest crops, build and clean houses, dig ditches, cut lawns, cook, and wash dishes for other Americans. Yet, they and their native-born relatives are often treated as unwanted or hated outsiders.

Across the United States today, growing numbers of Latinos report housing, policing, and other discrimination, usually at the hands of white neighbors. For example, the village of Mount Kisco in New York agreed, under a consent decree with the federal government, to stop using building codes and park regulations to discriminate against Latino laborers. Last year this consent decree was extended because of continuing complaints that a housing ordinance was being used to discriminate against Latino immigrants.

Sometimes the anti-Latino hostility is expressed violently. Some Mexican immigrants have been killed near the U.S.-Mexican border, apparently by white vigilantes. In Bloomington, Minnesota, a Latino worker was badly beaten for speaking Spanish at his workplace. In Farmingville, New York, a "quality of life" group has been formed, apparently to help keep Latino immigrants out of the town. The beating of two undocumented immigrant laborers by tattooed white supremacists there in late 2000 has not yet spurred significant state action against such anti-immigrant violence.

On their Internet Web sites and in their videos and books, members of white supremacist groups often refer to Latino/a immigrants as a "cultural cancer," as a "wildfire," or as a "gang of illegals" that is making "America less beautiful," as people with a plan to "reconquer" the United States. Similar verbal attacks on Latinos can be found in all parts of the country. Recently, homeowners in a heavily white Bronx village received letters warning residents that their area was being overrun by Latino immigrants, who were described as "forces of evil" and "low-income trash."

Clearly, those whites who control the nation's mass media and its reporting on immigration issues would condemn violence against Latinos and would reject the more stridently racist language used by white supremacists against Latino immigration.

Yet, as the pioneering linguist Otto Santa Ana clearly demonstrates in this pathbreaking book, the "liberal" stalwarts of the mass media sometimes collude in such attacks on immigrants by using metaphorical language that is similar to that asserted by the white supremacists. A negative metaphorical language is commonplace in newspaper discussions of Latino immigrants across the United States. Santa Ana's examination of articles, from a distinguished national newspaper, on undocumented immigrants around the time of the Proposition 187 vote finds that the dominant metaphors are of immigrants as animals or immigrants as invaders and other disreputable persons. Numerous articles speak of public programs being "a lure to immigrants," of the electorate's appetite for "the red meat of deportation," of INS agents catching "a third of their quarry," of Proposition 187 supporters who "devour the weak and helpless," or of the need to "ferret out illegal immigrants." Other articles portray the process of immigration as dangerous or threatening—as a burden, dirt, a disease, an invasion, or waves flooding the nation. The impact of this metaphorical language, as Santa Ana so well demonstrates, is to reinforce a negative public view of the immigrants and to hide the individuality and humanity of these human beings, people who are seeking only to make better lives for themselves and their families.

Clearly, the language and metaphors of this mainstream reportage are not as consistently strident as the language of the aforementioned white supremacists, and this metaphorical reportage is not linked to overt racist diatribes against immigrants. Yet, there is still significant overlap with those more disreputable sources in the mainstream media's metaphorical representation of immigrants, especially the latter's representation of immigrants as threatening, dangerous, animal-like, an invasion, or a disease attacking the nation.

While the mainstream media reporters and editors may editorialize against the white supremacist groups, and even against anti-immigrant legislation, their language and metaphors are similar to those used by the white supremacists, which suggests that at some level they may also share some of the supremacists' views on immigrants and immigration. A number of researchers, such as James Ridgeway, have shown that the white supremacy movement is not an aberration but rather broadcasts racist views about people of color that overlap to some degree with some mainstream white views in the mass media and in politics. The difference between the mainstream language and metaphors of some media people and some major politicians on race or immigrant matters, and the language and metaphors of the white extremists, often seems to be one of degree and not of kind.

Perhaps more importantly, the negative language and metaphors targeting Latino immigrants have serious action implications. Once a group of people is defined as somehow not fully human, as animal-like, or as a disease or national burden, then it is easier to treat such individuals like debased people or animals. This is not just a theoretical proposition, for such a connection can be seen in the numerous recent cases of anti-Latino violence and overt discrimination, the latter in areas such as housing code enforcement. Anti-immigrant groups in California forced Proposition 187 onto the California ballot, which passed with a substantial majority in 1994. Proposition 187 attempted to sharply restrict the access of undocumented immigrants to public services, including schools and hospitals, and to reduce them to a very debased status. Across the country, immigrant-bashing has been common among some business leaders and politicians since that time.

In California, the anti-immigrant and anti-Latino public sentiment did not end with Proposition 187. In 1996, California voters, the majority of whom were Anglo whites, passed Proposition 209, ending affirmative action in California's educational institutions. Santa Ana shows that the opponents of affirmative action cleverly appropriated the traditional civil rights discourse about racism by framing affirmative action as itself racist and thus promoting Proposition 209 as an anti-racist measure, even as the "California Civil Rights Initiative." In this way they destroyed one of the few remaining government programs aimed at remedying centuries of discrimination against Americans of color. Santa Ana also examines public discourse around the 1998 California Proposition 227, which ended bilingual education for 1.3 million non-English-speaking children. Using the tools of the linguist, Santa Ana explains how the uninformed electorate was convinced to accept the referendum, which again was cleverly described as insisting on "English for the children." Yet, in reality, this referendum was an attack on non-English-speaking children which put them at even greater risk of educational failure.

Today, the United States is becoming ever more multiracial and multicultural. Major challenges to white control and domination are arising from population and political changes. European Americans are a decreasing proportion of the U.S. population; they are a statistical minority in many of the largest cities and in the states of New Mexico, Hawaii, and California. If current migration and birth rates continue, about 2004, whites of European background will be a minority of the Texas population; between 2015 and 2040, they will be a minority of the population in many other states; and by the 2050s, they will be a minority of the U.S. population. White Americans, who have been used to being the unchallenged group demographically, economically, and politically in the United States, are increasingly facing the challenge of living up to their long-asserted ethic of "liberty and justice for all" and of helping, with Americans of color, to build a true democracy in a nation of people of highly diverse backgrounds and cultures. At this point in U.S. history, it is not clear whether the majority of white Americans will join in that effort to build a multiracial democracy, or will instead retreat into a new American apartheid.

In this original book Otto Santa Ana presents important empirical data and an innovative theoretical perspective on the dominant public discourse that legitimates public policy in regard to such critical societal issues as immigration, bilingual education, and affirmative action. Santa Ana asks us to listen with new ears to the apparently balanced debates between conservative and liberal commentators and policymakers. With a unique combination of empirical data and theory, Santa Ana helps us to raise, and often to answer, some of the critical questions about the present realities and possible futures of this increasingly troubled and conflict-ridden society.

# Preface

When I moved to California in 1994, Proposition 187 was the inescapable topic of conversation. This referendum would have prohibited state and local governments from providing education, health care, and other social services to undocumented immigrants and their children. Its backers, the "SOS" (Save Our State) Committee, were conducting a massive campaign. They were met by a vigorous countercampaign. I was startled by the language used and reported in the news, as well as in heated discussions which I heard everywhere. As a newcomer, I had not been desensitized to the public discourse, which was extraordinarily adverse toward immigrants, as well as toward Latinos, who were readily equated with immigrants. A general anxiety about immigration to the state was palpable in almost all discussions of the period, even among people who found the actual referendum to be reprehensible.

For instance, the *Los Angeles Times* published a number of scathing editorials against the referendum, calling Proposition 187 "half-baked," "ridiculous," and "wrong morally . . . wrong politically." In spite of such commentary, the *Times* texts also resonated fear and anger. This made me wary. I undertook a routine content analysis of the newspaper to test my suspicions. I was surprised to find little or no bias, by the typical measures of content analysis. The *Times* aims at the highest current standards of journalism. As a partisan who knew to my dismay that California's voters would ultimately approve Proposition 187, I wondered whether I was somehow conjuring a phantom.

Still, certain phrases stayed in my mind for days after I read or heard them—*massive northward influxes, great waves of immigration, a sea of brown faces,* and so on. At first, I scoffed, until the implications of such public discourse metaphors became clear. Cognitive science instructs us that human thinking, at base, is not mathematical code or logical expression. Human thought is constructed with images that represent reality. These images are metaphors. We first invent, and then rely almost exclusively on, metaphors to make sense of the world we live in. To the extent that this finding of cognitive science is the case, it follows that with a turn of phrase, such as *foreigners flooding the country,* the Latino community was portrayed as a force that is destroying California. Yet, this fear-provoking message was being transmitted by means of an only seemingly harmless figure of speech that is never examined in journalism, and only rarely in academic discourse analysis. As will unfold in the course of this book, metaphor is the mental brick and mortar with which people build their understanding of the social world.

Accordingly, in this book I examine the metaphors used in American public discourse in the last years of the twentieth century. These metaphors are not merely rhetorical flourishes, but are the key components with which the public's concept of Latinos is edified, reinforced, and articulated.

For forty years, Mexicans in the United States were characterized as a Sleeping Giant. During that long period of time, the community was viewed as an immense, and inert, population. In 1993 the metaphor changed. When this discourse changed, so too did the public's perception, and its electoral responses to this population. In 1994 Proposition 187 was overwhelmingly approved by California voters because the public discourse reaffirmed historic dominance relations at a time when the largely Anglo-American electorate felt threatened. The key to this change in public discourse was the commonplace, unobtrusive prose metaphors of immigrant, citizen, immigration, and nation.

During the 1990s the passage of two additional anti-Latino referenda eliminated both affirmative action and bilingual education in California. To make sense of the anti-affirmative-action referendum, Proposition 209, I analyze the metaphors used to construct racism and its legal remedies at two points in time: in the 1960s, when affirmative action was instituted, and in the mid-1990s, when it was outlawed in the state. Cognitive science provides an explanation of the electorate's consistent approach in these two periods, which led to diametrically opposed responses to the use of race to remedy institutional discrimination. The difference: how racism was metaphorized.

As for the anti-bilingual-education referendum, Proposition 227, I examine the public discourse on U.S. public education and, from this cognitive science frame of reference, the public's understanding of how children learn, and how teaching takes place. On these latter counts, the public continues to be informed by hoary nineteenth-century metaphors. Because the public understands education in terms of these outmoded metaphors, it can only act to sustain the current antiquated system, which is particularly detrimental to language-minority students. Metaphor theory provides a new account of why the nation fails to build innovation into its public school system.

Thus, focusing the lens of cognitive science on everyday American public discourse is very revealing. In this book, the emphasis is on contemporary public representations of Latinos. However, this combination of theory and method can open a new window of insight onto social trends and policy prospects across the panorama of national current events.

As I write this preface, the United States is experiencing a remarkable moment of domestic ease, as the economy surges to its greatest output in thirty years. The country is content, in contrast to the anxious times of the mid-1990s. As a result, nativist anxieties about the brown population of the United States have also subsided. This economic bubble, however, may burst at any time. History teaches that when hard times return, Latinos and immigrants will again be falsely blamed. Thus it is worthwhile to study the public discourse of the agitated Anglo-American electoral majority when it lashed out at the Latino communities in the 1990s.

OSA
December 1999

# Acknowledgments

The book in your hands is the fruit of steady institutional support, the hard work and creativity of my students, and the indispensable love of my friends and family.

I would like to express my appreciation to the National Research Council and Ford Foundation for a 1997 postdoctoral fellowship which offered me an uninterrupted year to work on this book. Moreover, as a brother of the family of Ford Fellows, I was unconditionally supported as a scholar; their fellowship is as spiritual as it is intellectual.

Further financial support during 1997–1998 was offered by key UCLA administrators: Scott Waugh, Dean of the School of Letters and Sciences, and Raymund Paredes, former Associate Vice Chancellor for Academic Development (now Director of the Creativity and Culture Program of the Rockefeller Foundation). During this year I was encouraged and supported by my departmental colleagues, the César Chávez Center for Chicana and Chicano Studies, and its interim director, Raymund Paredes. The work on the book began before the Fellowship year, and was not completed until late 1999. For that reason, I can happily thank many more people.

I received a 1996 Latina/Latino Policy Research Award from the California Policy Seminar, which permitted extensive data analysis. I would like to thank CPS Director Andrés Jiménez and the CPS review board for their faith in my unconventional policy proposal, as well as their forbearance concerning my delayed final report. Additionally, I secured two UCLA Academic Senate Grants in connection with this book, for which I am grateful.

In 1997 I received financial support from the Language Minority Research Institute at the University of California Santa Barbara, through the good offices of then-LMRI Director Reynaldo Macías. Reynaldo also served formally as my Ford mentor during the Ford Fellowship year; I am especially grateful that he has forgotten that twelve months make up a year, since I will not be able to learn in a dozen years all he has freely shown me.

The members of the UCLA Chicano Studies Research Center, and notably its director, Guillermo Hernández, have offered me financial support, intellectual encouragement, and friendship since my arrival at UCLA. Guillermo, a scholar always brimming with ideas, fiercely criticized my thesis very early on with so much compassion that I could only be inspired. It didn't hurt that he provided a key to unlock a quandary he himself noted.

I have received critique and support from the UCLA Communication Forum, and thank its director, Neil Malamuth, who invited me to present my early work to Forum members. I count as friends and supportive critics across the country Terrence Wiley, John Baugh, Richard Cameron, Richard Anderson, and Colleen Cotter. Pivotally, Rosina Lippi-Green first encouraged me to write this book, Ricardo Stanton-Salazar convened our auspicious book writers club, and my *concuño* Michael D'Andrea formulated the book's title and worked with me on the prose of Chapter 2. Eduardo Hernández-Chávez is also due for special thanks. Also, I wish to thank UCLA Research Librarians Norma Corral and Miki Goral, who helped secure a CD-ROM subscription to the *Los Angeles Times*, which made the systematic analysis of this newspaper possible.

From our first meeting, I received steady support for this book from Theresa May, Editor-in-Chief of the University of Texas Press. A detail of "La Memoria de Nuestra Tierra," a recent mural by my friend Judith Baca, graces the book's cover. Judy creates veritable theaters of art that bear witness to the full range of histories of this country. Joe Feagin has honored me with the book's foreword. The encouragement of this major contemporary scholar on American racial/ethnic relations, racism, and social justice and two-time winner of the Gustavus Myers Human Rights Book Award is inestimable.

I am honored to work closely with very fine undergraduate scholars at UCLA. In our study of public discourse and metaphor, they served as independent judges of metaphor interpretation (which allowed intersubjective labeling) and as library and computer workers, and were first architects of insurgent metaphors. The Wordsmiths, whose creative energy made this book possible, were: Cynthia Sánchez, Cristina Fernández, Enrique Covarrubias, Elva Córtez, Valente Guzmán, Luis Garibay, Felipe López, Elías Serna, Pamela Alcoset, Monica Villalobos, Pedro Jiménez, Jr., Ramona Ortega, María-Carmen Íñiguez, Christina Torres, David Zamora, Rubén García, Patricia Loo, Elizbeth Espinoza, René González, and Roseanna Guzmán. Three Wordsmiths—Juan Morán, Eduardo Rivas, and Érika Villegas—must be recognized for their estimable conceptual contributions and dedication to our project. Each became a full research partner for a time during this intellectual enterprise. Special thanks go to Wayne Lewis, for acute interpretation of metaphor, expertise with exasperating software, and admirable intellectual integrity, which led me to articulate more fully the principles underlying my judgments. This book is far richer because of all of these young scholars.

I want to thank my two families. The Santa Annas have supported me long-distance for over three decades. Los Meléndez envelop me *en familia* each day and especially on Sunday afternoons. I have been sustained by their love, laughter, affection, as well as their *mole poblano, lasagna alla casareccia, ensalada de nopal,* and peanut butter cookies.

———

I dedicate this book to my morning light, Thelma Meléndez de Santa Ana. My day dawns upon her smile; my words begin to breathe upon her breath. Without her, I am a sounding brass or a tinkling cymbal.

———

As a matter of policy I declare that the views and opinions expressed here are my own and do not necessarily represent those of the California Policy Seminar or the Regents of the University of California. I am responsible for all misstatements.

## CHAPTER ONE

# Why Study the Public Discourse Metaphors Depicting Latinos?

The Mexican Sleeping Giant never woke up. It died in its sleep in the summer of 1993. At this time, the image of Mexicans and other Latinos maintained by the public in California and the rest of the United States changed, seemingly almost overnight. For fifty years, the Sleeping Giant image sustained the general view that Mexicans posed no threat to the Anglo-American hegemony in the United States.[1] During this same period, on the other hand, what Anglo-Americans did greatly affected their Latino compatriots. Before the 1990s, far-ranging injustices were visited upon Mexican Americans, notably during the Great Depression the unjust deportation (dubbed "repatriation") of thousands of U.S. citizens of Mexican descent; during World War II the officially sanctioned attacks by U.S. soldiers on Mexican American citizens (and soldiers) just because they wore the fashion statement of the day; during the mid-1950s the disgraceful actions of the Immigration and Naturalization Service (INS) when it conducted its crudely named "Operation Wetback"; during the twenty years ending in the mid-1960s, when the government and agribusiness often colluded in the abuse of Mexican workers participating in the Bracero Program; during the 1970s police repression of Chicanas/os protesting the Vietnam War and social injustice; and continuing into the 1990s, when agribusiness obstructed the peaceful farmworkers' search for a living wage and humane working conditions. However, these were only the most notorious public examples of a majority bullying a minority population. The daily personal tragedies inflicted by U.S. institutions on Mexicans and other Latinos must also be noted. Consider, for one, the wretched treatment of Mexican American students in U.S. public schools over the twentieth century. Correspondingly, this minority population responded with significant acts of resistance.[2] Mexicans and other Latinos built energetic social, syndical-

ist, and legal organizations, such as the League of United Latin American Citizens (LULAC), the United Farm Workers (UFW), and the Mexican
American Legal Defense and Education Fund (MALDEF). Mexicans and
Latinos participated in mass actions, such as the Chicano public school student Blow Outs, nationwide grape boycotts, the Chicano Moratorium, and
many marches and demonstrations. Likewise, we witnessed individual acts
of courage, such as the celebrated hunger strikes by César Chávez. Still, there
are many others who remain less familiar to the public. In the realm of education, we can point to the activist scholarship of George I. Sánchez, who publicly contested the prevailing view of U.S. social science of the 1930s, which
postulated that the intellectual ability of Mexican American students was inferior to that of Whites.[3] Another paragon is Don Ernesto Galarza, who for
over forty years wielded the sword of scholarship with the force of ethical
conviction to defend both Bolivian tin miners in the 1940s, and Mexican Braceros in the 1950–1960s, from exploitation due to U.S. government/business
collusion and, among many other issues, promoted the education of Mexican American students in the 1960s, appealing for cultural sensitivity and
pedagogic skill training of teachers, as well as advocating for high-quality
bilingual education.[4] Then there is Sal Castro, a high school teacher, who
supported his Chicano students in their public challenge of the Los Angeles Unified School District's racist policies. In the ensuing "Blow Outs" of
March 1968, ten thousand students and their supporters demonstrated for
educational equality for Mexican American students. Castro and his student
leaders were arrested, and in turn took the LAUSD to court demanding educational reform.[5] Yet an indifferent white majority—all the while benefit-
ing from institutionalized inequity based on race—was unconcerned. The
Latino communities were for the most part off their radar screen.

    For the U.S. public, no matter how large the Mexican Sleeping Giant
was, it simply could not menace the Anglo-American way of life any more
than could the Jolly Green Giant. Anglo-America has a history of dismiss-
ing this population as inconsequential. Although by the late 1990s Latinos
would be the largest minority group in the United States,[6] the U.S. public still tended to see Latinos as the silent servants who made its beds or
bussed its tables, the humble gardeners who pruned overgrown shrubs in
the backyard, and those uniformed parking attendants who rushed to open
the car door. These brown people were expected to perform their menial
roles quietly, efficiently, and without dissent. While white Americans came
into contact with lowly Latino service workers, or quite anglicized Mexi-

can Americans, the preponderance of the Latino population was invisible. In California and elsewhere in rural areas they worked in fields out of sight. In urban areas, they had been redlined into residential isolation. The greater part of their children attended highly segregated public schools. And their brown faces never appeared in national news or entertainment media, except in safely circumscribed ways.

In 1993 this all changed. As it had during the national debates leading to the Immigration Acts of 1921 and 1924, the racial character of the nation in the twenty-first century has become a source of consternation for the U.S. public, and a wellspring for exploitation by politicians and nativists. Anxiety as well as interest about Latinos increased. Pundits of various political stripes predicted parallel scenarios for the twenty-first century. Some saw a gentle browning of America, others foresaw the dilution of U.S. culture and subversion of its politics, while a few anticipated the outright reconquest of the U.S. Southwest by Mexican multitudes. Everyone expected significant change; the only difference resided in the commentator's comfort with change.

For a few Latinos, times have never been better. However, relations with the white majority turned particularly sour during this decade for the greater portion of the Latino communities, as demonstrated by three anti-Latino political initiatives that were ratified in California. Consequently, many in these ethnic communities recognized, as the century drew to a close, that they were experiencing greater racialization in a society which continues to alienate them, rather than adapt to incorporate them. In this book, the public image of Latinos during the 1990s will be explored.

## Section 1: The Hispanic Decade

At the end of the era of the Civil Rights and Chicano Movements, *Time* magazine ran a 1978 cover story entitled "It's Your Turn in the Sun," which played up the future of this growing ethnic group. The 1980s would be the Decade of the Hispanics.

> The Hispanics' very numbers guarantee that they will play an increasingly important role in shaping the nation's politics and policies. Just as black power was a reality of the 1960s, so the quest for latino power may well become a political watchword of the decade ahead.[7]

Rather than documenting structural change, the bulk of the magazine's coverage highlighted points of concern, including a serious undercount of the federal census, high poverty levels, and low educational attainment. Special attention was given to the need for bilingual education for eligible students, the lack of representation in elected posts and the civil service, as well as the shadow lives of undocumented workers. However, the tone was upbeat, and "confidence is just one more proof, if another were needed," that the near future would be bright for Latinos.

This optimism was not well founded. At the end of the decade, Chicanos were poorer than at its start. Twenty-five percent of Latino families, nearly 25 percent of Latino elderly, and 35 percent of Latino children lived below the official income levels of poverty. In the 1980s, the earning power of Latino males declined, from 90 percent of the wages of white men with similar training, to 78 percent. Moreover, the prospects for the long term were not any better. In 1968, 50 percent of Latinos did not finish high school. In 1990, when a high school diploma was even more important, the figure had not budged at all.[8] This figure is unchanged in the first years of the new century.

In 1978, *Time* did not take into account the most important factors. The ascent of the Jolly Brown Giant depended on more than a political opening of U.S. society, in the spirit of the Civil Rights Movement. The tools that this movement fought for to create a more democratic society—affirmative action, bilingual voting ballots, unprecedented legal challenges to residential redlining and schoolhouse prejudice, and bilingual education—indeed presented a cheerful future, if viewed through a liberal lens. Economic and crucial social factors were not part of *Time*'s equation, however, which made the outlook less auspicious. For one, a portion of U.S. society would not share its present or future wealth with its nonwhite compatriots, particularly if this meant giving up its prerogatives.

Second, it was assumed that Latinos would assimilate as white European immigrants did at the turn of the century. Had Latinos been viewed as white, and come from far away, in limited numbers, over a short period of time, then the expected assimilation might have occurred. In this scenario, Latinos would have taken their place in the mainstream unobtrusively. But how could the immense population of Latinos leave nary a footprint, much less not shoulder some individuals to one side, as it took its proportionally prominent place in society? Assimilation did not work since Latinos did not come to the United States from a distant land; in many ways they never left their homeland. They have continued to move northward over the century in increasing numbers that give no indication of abating. And, they seemed much more reluctant to give up their Spanish and other aspects of their home culture than true immigrants, such as European-origin people.

Most important, *Time* writers did not acknowledge that Anglo-Americans continued to view their society through a racializing lens, which meant Latinos were not as white as Anglos.[9] The dominant Anglo-American majority saw Mexicans (and other Latinos) as inferior to themselves. *Time* did not note the racial project which continues to articulate a subordinated status for Latinos in the United States,[10] or acknowledge the policies which secured for white citizens an economic advantage in terms of race, policies which George Lipsitz terms Anglo-America's possessive investment in whiteness.[11] Soon the decade of the 1980s had run its course, and the Brown Giant scarcely stirred, much less moved to its feet.

## The Inciter

Pete Wilson dashed any hopes that the decade of the nineties would turn out to be the merely delayed Hispanic Decade. As the newly elected governor of California in 1991, Wilson had a reputation as a moderate Republican. He succeeded an archconservative governor. However, Wilson had the misfortune to take office at the end of the Cold War. California had relied heavily on defense industries since 1945 to sustain enviable economic growth. However, in the two years following the 1989 fall of the Berlin Wall, California lost 600,000 jobs. The state suffered an appalling $14.3 billion shortfall in its $42 billion budget.[12] At the recession's low point, in 1993, the state was forced to use promissory notes to "pay" its private contractors for essential services. As a result, Wilson's voter approval rating plummeted, and his re-election hopes appeared moribund as an engaging and articulate Democrat took aim at his office.

Two years later Wilson easily beat his rival. To win at the ballot box, he chose the political low road. He lashed out at immigrants—Mexicans and Latinos—advocating tough policies to switch off the "giant magnet of federal rewards" which provide "incentives to illegal immigrants to violate U.S. immigration laws." In August 1993, he published an "Open Letter to the President of the United States on Behalf of the People of California,"[13] in which he said:

> Massive illegal immigration will continue as long as the federal government continues to reward it. We must repeal the perverse incentives

that now exist for people to immigrate to this country illegally. To stem the flow, we must seal the border and turn off the magnet.

Wilson claimed that federal mandates to educate the children of illegal immigrants and provide these families emergency health care accounted for $1.75 billion of California's debt. The "perverse incentives" that Wilson proposed to abolish included those arising from federal laws that mandate public education and health services for immigrant families, as well as the Fourteenth Amendment of the U.S. Constitution, which grants citizenship to children born in the United States, regardless of the status of their parents. This baldly nativist rhetoric won Wilson roars of approval from recession-weary voters. Immigration became an emotionally charged political issue, as it had been in other recessionary times, and the mood of the dominant constituencies of California political life became perceptibly negative toward Latinos.

In California, the political bellwether of the country, Latinos took center stage—as targets of public outrage. Once the governor expressed anti-Latino sentiments, xenophobia was no longer confined to private discussions. It became the stuff of public discourse. Nearly all Californians will say that the greatest portion of Latino residents, citizens and noncitizens, work diligently for their daily bread. Most will admit, when presented with figures and other evidence, that Latinos had been unfairly relegated to the back of the line for the post–World War II economic benefits that they had earned. Nonetheless, Latinos were blamed for the bad times precipitated by the end of the Cold War.

Wilson's disingenuous remonstration of Latinos signaled a change in the public discourse of California. Within months of this notorious, highly publicized rebuke, an explicitly anti-Latino political referendum came before the general public. From its appearance, Proposition 187 enjoyed remarkable support. In spite of being a crudely written, socially divisive, and certifiably unconstitutional referendum, it was approved overwhelmingly by a largely white electorate in November 1994. Not unexpectedly, Pete Wilson was easily reelected on the same day.

In a twist of fate, soon after the election the recession released its grip on the state. Before his second term ended, Pete Wilson oversaw the largest state government surplus in California history, $4.4 billion. Nevertheless, the anti-Latino fever was far from abated. Proposition 187 led to other referenda. In 1996 the "California Civil Rights Initiative," Proposition 209, ended the use of affirmative action principles in all state hiring and promotion. Two years later, Proposition 227, the initiative dubbed "English for the Children," eliminated bilingual education from California public schools for 1.3 million non-English-speaking schoolchildren. Thus it must be recognized that economics was not the real source of the anger of the white electorate toward Latinos. In hindsight, the 1980s was not the Decade of the Hispanic. With no little sarcasm, the 1990s was the Decade of the Hispanic—as dupe.

## Section 2: The Discourse on Latinos

This book was not written to reproach Pete Wilson. Politicians who do not aspire to statesmanship commonly cast false aspersions to prolong their personal careers. Rather, this is an inquiry into how the general public so readily accepted his irrelevant viewpoint. This book does not center on history or ethics, but on language. Attention is focused on the language of the public rebuke that Latinos suffered in the 1990s.

Wilson retold an old story. Why and how did this message, as language and discourse, resonate so well with his audience? In brief, during this period, the greatest part of public discourse reaffirmed conventional views of the American nation. The message articulated the traditional relationship that Mexicans (and by extension, other Latinos) had to the body politic. In coarse terms, the public was reminded to put Mexicans in their place. Crucially, it will be shown that the traditional pecking order was expressed by way of a particular set of textual images; Latinos were debased in terms of metaphors used in everyday speech. A few tokens from the Proposition 187 period will illustrate:

> *awash under a brown tide . . .*
> *the relentless flow of immigrants . . .*
> *like waves on a beach, these human flows are remaking the face of America . . .*

By way of such metaphors, the current image of Latinos in the public's imagination took hold. These metaphors, along with thousands of others, form the basis of this empirical study of contemporary public discourse about Latinos. The change in the political discourse about Latinos in the 1990s, based on the metaphoric characterizations of the population, occurred at a time when a significant social reorientation was taking place, and momentous political decisions concerning Latinos were being debated. Such metaphors shaped public opinion about Latinos. In California these images prompted crucial social and political changes. More generally, the linguistic claim is that such metaphors constantly shape the public's worldview.

The public discourse encompassing California's three anti-Latino referenda of the 1990s is the focus of this study, based on the assumption that such discourse constitutes public opinion and worldview. *Discourse* is a term used in several ways. It means the way we converse about things, in this case, Latino political issues. More specifically in this book we will be concerned with the "material content" of discourse. This linguistic material consists of quantifiable pieces of verbal text that are expressed in speech or print. A third, academic use of the term discourse refers to highly abstract social behavior. This last use of the term will be avoided when possible, since theory based on such amorphous conceptualizations of discourse has proven to be susceptible to empirical criticism.

In this study, two rarely associated ways of studying language have been brought together. First, methods developed to investigate natural language, best exemplified in the empirical linguistic work of William Labov, are adapted to catalog the record of contemporary American public discourse about Latinos. The public discourse promulgated in hundreds of articles from an important print media source, the *Los Angeles Times,* among other sources, is comprehensively sampled for Latino topics. Second, the interpretation of the newsprint data is made in light of cognitive science theories about how humans understand the world. In brief, the claim is that people do not principally make sense of their surroundings in terms of linear thinking and logical syllogism. Instead, image formation is a central process of human thought. Humans build their concepts of the world in terms of images. In text, this function is expressed by means of metaphor. George Lakoff is most responsible for developing this theory into a full epistemological account over the last fifteen years. This book applies contemporary cognitive metaphor theory to current political issues on the basis of an abundant natural language data set.

As a result, this study goes beyond a simple description of Latinos in terms of public discourse. Because its analysis is conducted in terms of an independently motivated cognitive theory of metaphor, it offers a principled explanation of why the electorate responded to political discourse about Latinos as it did in the 1990s. Thus metaphor in discourse is a window on the ways that Americans frame their domestic worldview, and on their underlying political and social values. Indeed the metaphor in the book title captures the dynamic, potentially threatening images with which Americans now conceptualize Latinos. Today's metaphors for Latinos diverge from the immobile Sleeping Giant of previous generations. With these methods and theories, we can investigate the public's perception of Latinos and Latino political issues, as well as the public's view of the nation itself.

## Section 3: Synopsis

The present chapter sets the stage for the book's three subsequent parts. Part I is made up of one chapter and explains the theories and methods employed in the study. Part II, which is the body of the book, consists of analyses of the principal metaphors that frame the political concepts surrounding the debates about Latinos in the 1990s in California. In Part III, two types of conclusions are offered.

Part I's consideration of theory and method is taken up in Chapter 2. As stated above, in this study cognitive linguistic theories (developed by way of introspection) are wed to principles of research that allow the empirical study of naturally occurring language. This marriage of theory and method is presented here. Furthermore, an argument is made against the position that language is fundamentally code and form. One consequence of such a restrictive view is that meaning in metaphor derives from literal expressions. In contrast, for the purposes of the present study, language is basically figurative. The metaphors in the material content of sentence strings and longer discourses cannot be derived from nonmetaphoric language. The view expressed in this chapter is bolstered by cognitive science evidence for the centrality of metaphor across the whole spectrum of human thought, from scientific theorizing, through organizational and institutional discourse, to ways of conceptualizing everyday life. The key finding of this survey of cognitive science research is that public perception of the social world is constructed in terms of metaphor. One conclusion to be drawn is that common metaphor, as expressed in public discourse, can be studied as the principal unit of hegemonic expression. However, in order to apply these theories to real-world issues, methods must be used to avoid sampling and other bias as well as the hazards of idiosyncratic interpretation. Instead, reproducible ways to sample and interpret public discourse which were employed in this study are described. The assumptions and procedures of empirical linguistic principles used for this study of public discourse as naturally occurring language are presented in detail. Chapter 2 is not indispensable to make out the findings of the chapters which follow; it spells out the author's theoretical bases and the reasoning behind his practices.

In the course of the 1990s, the California electorate was called on to vote on three important referenda, Propositions 187, 209, and 227. Each was designed to impose fundamental restrictions on 31 percent of the state's population, its Latino community. Latino voters rejected each measure. Nevertheless the measures were ratified by the more numerous white electorate. Analyses of the predominant metaphors surrounding these referenda make up Part II of the book. This begins with Chapter 3, which covers the public discourse and debate surrounding Proposition 187, the anti-immigration referendum. The questions that are evaluated in terms of the predominant metaphorization of political issues in this chapter include: What distinguishes a citizen from an immigrant? and What is immigration?

Chapter 4 deals with the public discourse, both in the 1960s and the 1990s, on affirmative action, which was at issue in Proposition 209. This referendum expunged affirmative action in California state and local government and education in 1996. The metaphorizations of American beliefs about race and racism are brought to light in this chapter.

Proposition 227, a referendum that eliminated bilingual education for immigrant children in California public schools, was discussed in public forums from 1996 to 1998, the year it passed. Two issues turn out to be distinguishable: What constitutes education? and What is bilingualism? Chapter 5 characterizes the metaphors that govern the layperson's understanding of education, while Chapter 6 reveals the commonplace beliefs about English and other languages in the United States.

Part III of the book has two chapters. An important finding of the foregoing study of the California referenda of the 1990s is that the widely disparate discourses on immigrants, citizens, race, racism, education, and language are conceptually coherent and congruent. The metaphors that shape these discourses in turn are delimited by two dominant "umbrella" metaphors of the nation. This is the topic of Chapter 7. In this summary chapter, the implications of the dominant metaphors which constitute the public's view of Latinos and their social issues are developed. In brief, contemporary public discourse reveals a dismal portrayal of Latinos in today's society. Latinos are not integrated into their nation. In public discourse, to put it bluntly, Latinos are never the arms or heart of the United States; they are burdens or diseases of the body politic. Likewise Latinos are characterized as foreigners invading their own national house.

In the decade of anti-Latino politics, Latinos were unable to effectively contest this public discourse. Latinos vainly tried to challenge the neoconservative rhetoric which blamed immigration for the end of the Cold War, which indicted affirmative action as the last source of racial discrimination in the United States, and which imputed to a child's home language the failure of public schools to educate our children. One reason for the inability to effectively contest the xenophobic discourse was the matter of media access. Another was creativity. Latinos did not articulate a viable alternative discourse which would successfully challenge the mainstream worldview. This issue is taken up in Chapter 8.

The importance of discourse is its role in creating and sustaining a worldview and a social order, for as Michel Foucault declares:

> As history constantly teaches us, discourse is not simply that which translates struggles or systems of domination, but is the thing for which and by which there is struggle. . . . Discourse is the power which is to be seized.[14]

Insofar as discourse is power, contemporary U.S. public discourse on minority communities is oppressive. Nonetheless, metaphor has a saving grace. The socially divisive metaphors, which are common currency today, are by no means natural. Nor are they the only way to conceptualize Latinos and their political issues. Alternatives can be developed. Renegade metaphors can be constructed and disseminated to replace ones that produce intolerant attitudes. A well-articulated, insubordinate political posture can be formulated which is both faithful to the principles of social justice and appealing to the wider electorate. In Chapter 8, the means to develop insurgent political metaphor are presented.

# PART I

# Theory and Method

## CHAPTER TWO

# How Metaphor Shapes Public Opinion

In the late twentieth century, Latinos were represented by thoroughly negative and derogatory images in contemporary American public discourse. These were not petty aggravations that could be swept away with amended media practices of political correctness. Nor were they harmless remnants of the blatantly racist public discourse prevalent in the earlier part of the century. These prejudicial representations were and continue to be indices of the operative social values of American society.

By representations, I mean the constructs in public discourse with which Americans build their commonplace understanding of the Latino community.[1] These demonstrate that foundational racism against Chicanos and other Latinos has persisted since the late nineteenth century. The bases of this racism have not fundamentally changed. All that has changed is its expression, which has become ostensibly "benign," or more accurately, "sanitized."[2] Chicana/o social critics have stated this from a variety of stances.[3] This claim is presently being made on the basis of a data-rich empirical study of a southern California newspaper and developed with the help of theories and methods drawn from discourse analysis, cognitive science, and mass media studies.

Section 1 describes the overarching theoretical framework of the study, while Section 2 explores the notion *discourse*. Section 3 provides a critique of two widely held rival theories of metaphor to set the stage in the following section for the cognitivist theory of metaphor. Presenting the theory grounding this work, Section 4 is detailed, and marshals a wide range of supporting evidence. Various critiques that have been leveled against this cognitive theory of metaphor wrap up the discussion of theory in Section 5. Issues of method are taken up in Section 6, where mass media are addressed. The actual procedures to study metaphor in public discourse are presented in Section 7, followed by a brief summary section.

## Section 1: Critical Discourse Analysis

In this chapter the assumptions, methods, and findings of the principal theory that will be used will be presented. The full complement of theories and methods invoked has distinct disciplinary sources. In order to organize these disparate theories and methods, a unifying research framework, critical discourse analysis, is employed.[4] Like other branches of discourse analysis, it is multidisciplinary.[5] It is a self-critical framework of language-based research which aspires to the highest standard of scientific adequacy.[6]

*Socially Engaged Social Science*

Critical discourse analysis places emphasis on the study of discourse in action rather than its structural character. Drawing on the work of Antonio Gramsci and the tradition of the Frankfurt School, it interweaves several interests. It is concerned with the possibility of knowledge, making "common sense" and "reason" the objects of study. It also focuses attention on the operations of discourse that conceal unjust social practices that reinforce inequalities of wealth and power. Critical discourse analysis also has an explicit normative component.[7] Critical theorists reject positivism, which accedes to the view that social science can employ the objectifying precept of natural science. Most importantly, while social activism is not a relevant consideration within the great part of linguistic research—no wider social purpose is served in discovering the structure of relative clauses in Icelandic or critiquing alternative analyses of the causative constructions in Kanien'kehaka—research in critical discourse analysis should have a bearing on the lives of people.

What makes discourse analysis critical is its focus on real-world problems of injustice, rather than on theoretical issues of discourse that only incidentally involve issues of social concern. Critical theorist Teun A. van Dijk characterizes the central issue of critical discourse analysis as the role that discourse plays in reproducing societal dominance: how hierarchical social relations are enacted, sustained, and legitimated through discourse.[8] Thus its unabashed attention to inequitable societal relationships and their remediation separates critical discourse analysis from other discourse analyses, whose topics are chosen in large part to further the theories of the nature of human discourse. Placing justice at the center of the research agenda creates socially engaged scholarship. In such an enterprise, at minimum, injustice can be addressed through a scientifically principled research agenda that leads to deeper understanding. As critical theorist Norman Fairclough states, consciousness is the first step toward emancipation.

## Section 2: Discourse

*Discourse* is as encompassing a concept as "culture," "action," or "mind." The notion of discourse is taken in two related senses. It is understood to be the components of connected expressions of language, both verbal and written. As such, the communication events of everyday life that are studied under discourse analysis include, among many others, conversation; newspaper genres such as news reports, editorials, and so on; legislative debating; novels; advertising; scientific expression in journals and textbooks; and film. Van Dijk lists the following kinds of linguistic elements and the layers of analysis of this interdisciplinary enterprise: phonetic and intonational expression (speech); graphic expression (writing); syntactic and lexical structure; semantic structure within a sentence, across an extended text, or of a semantic domain; the social actions that are enacted via talking (illocutions), politeness, and other pragmatics functions; metaphoric, stylistic, and other rhetorical processes; narrative and text analyses such as text composition studies of essays or the argument structure of editorials; institutional discourse analysis, as of the language of the courtroom or classroom; conversation and talk interaction studies; talk participant and talk event studies; and studies of cognitive processes of talk, e.g., memory, learning, production, and so on.[9] This is discourse in its linguistic material sense, the warp and weave of the communicative fabric that has a richly patterned texture. As such, one can imagine an exhaustive study of a brief and eloquent discourse, such as Martin Luther King, Jr.'s "I Have a Dream," would fill volumes.[10]

Yet the material content tallied in this book can also be considered the mere product of the process of discourse. In the second sense, discourse is the language-based subset of social practice. In fact, historicist Michel Foucault refers to linguistic and nonlinguistic practice as discursive formations. Fairclough's interpretation of Foucault's abstract theory of practice for language-centered analyses will be employed in this study.[11] Fairclough, the critical discourse analyst, focuses on the material content of discourse. In Fairclough's formulation, discourses are types of social practices within social orders that are expressed by individuals. People, as subjects, function within a subject "space," or position, that is defined within the encompassing social order in terms of particular discourses/practices. These subject positions confine the subject, that is, each individual person, in terms of his or her knowledge and beliefs, social relationships, and subjecthood (social identity). Such discourse practices embody unreflected and naturalized ideological assumptions about the subject space, and are the focus of critical discourse analysis since they are reproduced, and their ideological assumptions are reaffirmed, when the discourse practices are enacted by the subject. As people live their lives as subjects, the institutional practices that sustain and legitimize existing power relations through the association of discourse and subject position inculcate them to acquiesce unreflectingly to the ideology of the standing social order, including relations which enact the social inequities associated with minority status.

These power-defining discourse practices become so automatic that people do not notice them as they go about their everyday lives. As a subject, everyone functions within a range of social positions without much attention to the attendant discourses of each position, and with even less mindfulness of the ideological content embodied and rearticulated in the practice of these discourses. To amend Pierre Bourdieu's pithy phrasing, "strictly speaking, subjects do not know what . . . they do [or say] has more meaning than they know."[12]

Ideology is the articulated social order to which people are normally oblivious. It is usually taken for granted as individuals go about their everyday lives and fulfill their various tasks and habitual actions. Those contingencies that are never questioned, such as the background understanding about their social space, social beliefs, relationships, and identities that are established in the day to day, are also products of the discursive process of ideology. When, for example, it is just "common sense" that "illegal aliens" have fewer rights than citizens, or it is only "natural" that students have to disregard or deny their home world in order to be taught things by their teachers, or that only the "very best" students, who happen to be members of a privileged class, go to the best colleges, then we are operating within the ideological assumptions of the U.S. social order. Fairclough argues that four kinds of products of discourse become naturalized by dint of repetition. One is the definitions of words, such as the key concepts in this study of Latinos, including race, language, and citizen. The second, borrowing Ervin Goffman's theater metaphor, is the stage directions of social interaction. By way of illustration, consider how teachers and administrators control the interaction with Latino parents when discussing their children.[13] Third is the way that the stage is bounded, so that, for example, access to the preserve of the top echelons of higher education is limited to certain types of young people. Fourth is the social actor's identity. To illustrate this discourse product, subjecthood, one can ask what it takes to be a white person, or a person of color, in the United States today. The definition of key terms and subjecthood for Latinos in today's America is developed in the course of the present study.

Surprisingly, the macro-level research engaged in the study of discursive practice rarely scrutinizes the linguistic material of discourse. In spite of the general enthusiasm nonlinguists have expressed over the "linguistic turn" in social theory, language material does not figure prominently in many discussions of discourse as practice.[14] Likewise, many linguists and discourse analysts (while maintaining a safe "scientific" distance from social theory in their own micro-level work) reel at the liberties taken by theorists who talk about the practice of discourse without solid control of its material.

While noting Foucault's provision, namely that "discursive practices cannot be reduced to the demands of logic or linguistics,"[15] this study will scrutinize the actual micro-level material of discourse practice, in order to illuminate how unjust dominance discourse at the macro level is perpetuated. Some would say that efforts to empiricize Foucault's theory of discursive formation for the purposes of the study of the material content of discourse are bound to be unprofitable. Ernesto Laclau states that while linguists are bound by the structuralist logic of the sign, Foucault is not. His very macro-level notion of discourse does not have a linguistic material basis. Rather than attempting to analyze discourse as linguistic material, Laclau continues, Foucault endeavored to "isolate the totalities within which any production of meaning takes place." This "quasi-transcendental" move begins at "second-level phenomenology." Likewise, Foucault's unit of a discursive formation is the *episteme,* which is defined as "the total set of relations that unite, at a given period, the discursive practices that give rise to epistemological figures, sciences, and possibly formalized systems." The epistemes of the ages, existing at a very abstract stratum, are the Classical Age, the Renaissance, and Modernity. Laclau notes that Foucault, in the later part of his career, realized that discursive formation as he had formulated it was so heterogeneous that the notion of the episteme was not serviceable.[16] In spite of all this, critical discourse analysis can adapt the notion of discursive formation, identifying it in concrete linguistic content, to pursue its own brand of critical theory. For these reasons the present study of the discourse processes that sustain today's representations of Latinos and Latino political issues is based in large part on the discourse material, namely mass media texts, of the *Los Angeles Times,* as will be elaborated in Section 7 of this chapter.

But before turning to these texts, in Section 3 distinct metaphor theories will be critiqued and rejected, so the cognitivist theory of metaphor can be offered instead. It is herein proposed that a long-sought theory-based unit of analysis for the critical discourse analysis project can be located on the basis of cognitivist theory. Teun van Dijk, whose compendium of discourse elements and analytic levels was cited above, has called for such a unit of analysis. All the linguistic subsystems of material discourse compose the seamless and patterned texture of dominance relations that is woven into natural language expression. The tenets of critical discourse analysis indicate that there should be specific elements of discourse which are central to the hierarchical structuring of society. However, an endless series of studies which do not share a unit of analysis may not advance the research enterprise. The utility of the critical discourse analysis enterprise will be undercut if no principled linguistic element can be hypothesized. If any element of material discourse can be shown to participate in the enactment of social position, then it could be postulated that there are no governing principles in linguistic discursive formation.[17] In keeping with this search, van Dijk's call for a theoretically based unit of analysis is meant to advance the research enterprise.[18]

I propose that metaphor is the unit of analysis in discursive practice. Much of the rest of the chapter is a discussion of George Lakoff's theory of metaphor, which is informed by his rationalist studies within the cognitive linguistics framework, and by his epistemology, Experiential or Embodied Realism. This conceptualization of metaphor is based in a constructivist linguistic paradigm, as will be detailed in Sections 5 and 6 of this chapter, which stands in opposition to the dominant positivist paradigm. Again, everyday metaphor, as boldfaced in the following example, weaves the patterns of social relations into natural language expression.

> At a mayoral candidates' forum, a member of the audience asked a question about illegal immigrants. One of the candidates . . . said that while "I am a very strong supporter of legal immigration, what I am not a supporter of is illegal aliens. What I am not a supporter of is continuing to provide ongoing benefits. . . . it's like **overloading the lifeboats of a sinking ship.**"[19]

The ship mentioned in this excerpt from the *Los Angeles Times* is a single instance of the productive metaphor for the United States, NATION AS SHIP, and is often referred to as the *ship of state*. Everyday metaphor, as it is casually used in commonplace public texts, is a crucial measure of the way that public discourse articulates and reproduces societal dominance relations. Even though many scholars continue to assume that such metaphoric expressions are only rhetorical frills, cognitive theorists now argue vigorously for metaphor's central role in the construction of the social order. In fact, the view that metaphor is merely ornamentation results from the belief that metaphoric understanding is derived from literal expression, and that metaphor is consequently a marginal element in the material of discourse. Variations of the view that metaphor is a central element in mental representation have been promulgated by linguists such as Lakoff, Gilles Fauconnier, and Ronald Langacker, and cognitive psychologists such as Raymond Gibbs. The principles underlying such a constructivist paradigm have been supported by scientists and philosophers of remarkably dissimilar styles and temperaments, such as Jerome Bruner, Jacob Bronowski, Edward O. Wilson, Stephen Jay Gould, Donna Haraway, and Thomas Kuhn.

## Section 3: Rival Metaphor Theories

As will be elaborated in the following section, the theory of metaphor based in the cognitive science paradigm claims that the conventionalized everyday metaphor constitutes the social values of people who use these ways of speaking. Metaphors provide the cognitive framework for worldview. Metaphor, and other associated figurative language used in the daily discourse of social issues, can be studied to reveal the values underlying social order. Consequently prose metaphor is a crucial discourse element that makes such historically contingent dominance relations seem natural. People's ways of interacting with one another may seem natural and based on intrinsic characteristics, but in fact the social structure that is taken as intrinsic to humankind is almost entirely constituted by human agency. It is reconstituted moment by moment in daily interactions, including the way we talk about things.

In order to place the cognitivist theory of metaphor in a disciplinary context, this section follows Lakoff as he compares it to two other linguistic theories which dispatch metaphor to the periphery.[20] The first, literalist theory, holds that metaphor should be strictly interpretable by means of linguistic structure and lexical meaning systems alone.[21] The second, pragmatics theory, is a prominent view that metaphor is properly understood to be a communication phenomenon involving only the information that can be deduced from the linguistic string and certain defined principles about the way interlocutors interact.[22] Crucially, both these theories hold that interpretation of metaphor is merely derived from the corresponding literal linguistic strings. Thus these theories are inimical to conceiving of discourse as practice. Much of the following discussion will be a comparison of the merits of these views. It should be noted that individual semanticists and cognitive linguists work within research modes that draw from both positivism and constructivism, and most assuredly hold more nuanced theories of metaphor and meaning than can be introduced in this boiled-down synopsis. The strongest versions of these views are posed here. On the arguments and evidence against views that take metaphor to be derived from the literal, a case is built that metaphoric thinking not only reflects, but constitutes, the social domains of science, law, and most aspects of everyday life. The purpose of this section is to provide sufficient evidence of the ubiquity and productivity of the comprehension of the social world by way of metaphor, so that the ensuing analysis of Latino representation in the public discourse can center on this key element of discourse material.

*Literalist Theory*

A comparison of the contending theories is a microcosm of the differences underlying constructivist and positivist paradigms of social science. Linguistics, as with other sciences, has both constructivist and positivist streams of research. Constructivism, which encompasses both critical discourse analysis and cognitive metaphor theory, is based on the assumption that cognition is a mental construction.[23] Its tenets contrast with those of the positivist paradigm.

Within the positivist point of view, the social world is made up of things that are independent of human thinking and have constitutions unaffected by human interaction. Consequently these things fall into apparently natural groupings. When people turn their attention to them, the "natural" categories of these social objects may be discovered, and statements can be made that mirror these discoveries. One linguistic goal within the positivist paradigm is to provide the means to accurately transmit these statements about the so-called immanent order of the world. These are stated in terms of logically consistent propositions that correspond to the real world. Emphasis in positivist theories is placed on the expression of facts. Ways of expression that are figurative (nonfactual) are less important. It is an easy step to presume that literal sentences are normal and unmarked, while nonliteral expressions such as metaphor are derived from, and can only be understood by means of, literal ones. In order to understand the expression *Truth is the daughter of Time,* the positivist holds that one must invoke a corresponding literal expression, such as *Transcendent facts are gleaned from perspectives gained over a period of time.* Since, in this view, the interpretation of metaphor is dependent on a corresponding literal expression, metaphor is believed to be an incidental and relatively unimportant aspect of language. This, of course, conflicts with the constructivist paradigm. To various degrees constructivists have imputed a major role in humankind's way of making sense of the world to metaphor and other nonliteral language behavior.

Much positivist language research in the last two centuries was directed toward the development of a so-called perfect language, made up entirely of logical expressions that could be transmitted with no loss of information. Given the scientific enterprise that developed since the European Enlightenment, with its focus on reductionist logic, if the sentence is the unit of communication, the vehicle for transmission of literal expressions in logical form, then its optimal study should be in terms of a decontextualized literal sentence presented in isolation in which its meaning is unambiguous and essential. For positivists, what goes on in everyday human talk, that is to say, contextualized communication interchange about the mundane, the vague, and the momentary, is immaterial. The key question for much of positivist linguistics became how literal sentences are decoded, rather than how people make meaning via language.[24] Thus the comprehension of nonliteral and otherwise so-called imperfect communication, including metaphor, was taken to be parasitic on literal sentences. For example, the esteemed linguist Ray Jackendoff stated that the inclusion of metaphor systems "debases" his theory of grammatical and semantic relations.[25] Positivism remains strong in mainstream linguistics today. The great majority of present-day linguistic research is conducted with little or no regard for aspects of language which are the object of focus in the constructivist paradigm.

## Pragmatics Theory

Similarly, another positivist approach to metaphor is the widely held pragmatics (or language use) model. In this model, the interpretation of metaphors can take in more information than just the linguistic features of the sentence itself. Thus pragmatics can attempt to interpret a real-world sentence that comes from the *Los Angeles Times* in the period when Latino immigration became a political issue, such as: Pete Wilson *"found two dogs that hunt: immigration and crime."*[26] For pragmatists, language is used by interlocutors, and with certain limited types of knowledge based on what speakers do, a model of metaphor interpretation is set up.

The pragmatics view requires the listener to undertake a three-step procedure upon hearing a literally implausible statement, like the foregoing example. At step one, the listener cannot make literal sense of the statement, since immigration, which is a demographic process involving people, cannot literally be a dog. Nor is crime a barking quadruped. However, within the pragmatics model, since it is presumed that the speaker's proper intention in communication is to be cooperative in the talk exchange,[27] the listener takes the second step and supposes that a nonliteral message is being transmitted. In the third step the listener constructs a contextually plausible meaning to make sense of the sentence by referring to background information known through life experience, or provided in the *Los Angeles Times* article, specifically, this nonliteral statement was made by a political analyst upon noting the growing support for Wilson among a majority of potential voters in recent polls. The analyst also cited a new stump speech. In it, Wilson employed two tactics. He vilified undocumented workers, and denounced inner-city crime. Thus the two dogs mentioned are metaphors for the political issues that Wilson cynically exploited in his reelection bid.

Experimental psychological studies of cognition provide counter-evidence to the pragmatics theory of metaphor and offer clinical evidence for the cognitivist approach. These studies have been adeptly summarized by Raymond Gibbs. The majority of the experimental psychology studies which investigate metaphor employ a reaction-time format. Previous reaction-time research has established that more time is needed to comprehend linguistically complex sentences than simple sentences. Classical comprehension studies have consistently demonstrated that the passive sentence *Thelma was kissed by Otto* takes readers about one-half second (500 milliseconds) more time to comprehend than the corresponding linguistically simpler active sentence, *Otto kissed Thelma*. Likewise an affirmative sentence such as *John-Michael smiled at Luc Patrick* is consistently processed more rapidly than the negative, *John-Michael did not smile at Luc Patrick*. Consequently, experimental psycholinguists performed reaction-time studies, following the assumptions of this format, comparing sentences involving metaphors and corresponding sentences that did not have metaphors.

The pragmatist would expect that reaction time is greater for the sentences involving metaphors, since the three-step procedure would be required. Further, since no special procedure should be necessary for the non-metaphor sentence, it should be processed more rapidly. However, studies of metaphor-bearing sentences and their literal equivalents (within an appropriate context for interpretation) found no significant reaction-time differences.[28] These findings provide no evidence to privilege literal sentences, nor do they furnish evidence for the three-step procedure to interpret metaphor. Moreover, Gibbs reports on additional studies which indicate that readers process metaphors, even when directed to focus their attention only on the literal portion of a sentence. In short, while there is a great deal more to learn about language processing in general and metaphor processing in particular, little evidence exists that we comprehend a metaphoric expression by analyzing its literal content. More generally, it is increasingly evident that human thought patterning does not follow the classic syllogistic lines presumed in positivist projects of social science.

## Section 4: Cognitivist Theory

While the positivist paradigm of linguistic science has been and remains predominant, the constructivist view has a long history.[29] With it comes the observation that figurative language gives structure to humankind's worldview. In a rewarding review,[30] James W. Fernandez describes historical figures such as Giambattista Vico (1668–1744), whose catch-phrase was *Homo non intelligendo fit omnia*. The following quote may elucidate Vico's thinking:

It is noteworthy that in all languages the greater part of expressions concerning inanimate things are created by metaphors drawn from the human body and its parts, and from the human senses and emotions. For example "head" for top or beginning; the eye of needles and potatoes; "mouth" for any opening; the lip of a cup or pitcher; the teeth of a rake, a saw, a comb; the beard of wheat; the tongue of a shoe; the gorge of a river; a neck of land; an arm of the sea; the hands of a dock; "heart" for center. . . . All this follows from the axiom that "when man is ignorant he makes himself the measure of the universe," since, in the examples brought forward, he has made himself an entire universe. [While] rational metaphysics teaches that *homo intelligendo fit omnia* (man becomes everything through understanding), [in contrast] imaginative metaphysics states *homo non intelligendo fit omnia* (failing to understand, man becomes [the model for] everything). There is perhaps more truth in the latter statement than the former. For man unfolds his mind by understanding things, but by failing to understand, he fashions these things [on the model] of himself. . . . He has made an entire world [in his own image].[31]

Note that Vico's rational metaphysics and imaginative metaphysics correspond to positivist and constructivist orientations.

While the ancient discipline of rhetoric has been the central arena for the study of metaphor over the past millennium, this state of affairs changed in the late twentieth century. William M. Purcell describes an order-of-magnitude increase in the interest in metaphor in the 1970s.[32] Max Black notes the expansion, citing a single bibliography of nearly three hundred pages containing over four thousand references on metaphor.[33] All this occurred before the milestone book by Lakoff and Johnson stimulated even greater interest after 1980. Cognitive science studies show how metaphors shape commonsense thinking, and although their methods are vastly different, they share this object of study with critical studies of discourse processes.

Metaphor is more than poetic color and superficial ornamentation. It shapes everyday discourse, and by this means it shapes how people discern and enact the everyday. Cicero stated that metaphor occurs "when a word applying to one thing is transferred to another, because the similarity seems to justify the transference."[34] In the intervening two thousand years the definition has not changed much. To use the terminology of Lakoff and Johnson, a metaphor is a conceptual mapping from a semantic source domain to a different semantic target domain. The source domains often, but not always,[35] are those things humans can easily think about, the parts of the human physical world which are handy and familiar. The target domains are most frequently conceptual ones, hidden from the five human senses or otherwise unknown to them. People borrow the conceptual structure of the familiar to "get a handle on" or, as will be described, to "embody" the target domains.[36] Then the borrowed structure is used extensively, even exclusively, with no more thought about the target domain.

For example, Lakoff and Johnson cite a set of conventionalized English expressions that stem from metaphors used to talk about the target domain of love.[37] These include: *I could feel the electricity between us; There were sparks; The atmosphere was charged; I'm crazy about her; She drives me out of my mind;*

Metaphoric Mapping of LOVE AS MADNESS:

| Semantic Source Domain of MADNESS | → | Semantic Target Domain of LOVE |
|---|---|---|
| (a) loss of self-control | ⇒ | (a) loss of self-control |
| (b) externally imposed | ⇒ | (b) externally imposed |
| (c) irrational actions | ⇒ | (c) irrational actions |
| (d) further semantic structure | ⇒ | (d) identical to semantic structure of source domain |
| ⋮ | | ⋮ |

Text instances of LOVE AS MADNESS:

*I'm crazy about you.*
*He flipped out when she arrived.*
*She couldn't help herself in Elton's presence.*
*She drives me out of my mind.*

**Figure 2.1. Metaphors as mapping and as text**

*He constantly raves about her; She fought him off, then she fled from his advances; She is besieged by suitors, she has to fend them off,* etc. Scores of similar sentences can easily be compiled. Lakoff and Johnson grouped them into three metaphors for love, namely, LOVE AS A PHYSICAL FORCE, LOVE AS MADNESS, and LOVE AS WAR.[38] These collocations of words and many more can be analyzed and hierarchized with knowledge of American English and U.S. culture to delineate for Lakoff and Johnson a cognitive model of the target domain, LOVE, of which these three metaphors form a part. A central metaphor characterizes the physiological effects pertinent to the prototypical model, or scenario. For Lakoff and Johnson such metaphoric mappings are a major process of human understanding. Of course the mappings are not the only cognitive process. Nevertheless, such a claim is not only interesting as science. It also has important social implications.

## Constructivist Claims

In the constructivist view, certain assumptions are maintained. For one, the neurological processing of language is not assumed to be fundamentally different from other cognitive processes, as has been argued at times by formal linguists. In the absence of evidence of distinct hardwiring of human brains corresponding to different thinking processes, constructivists assume that there is cognitive uniformity across linguistic and nonlinguistic processes. Thus visual metaphor presumably operates in the same way as verbal metaphor. Metaphor and other tropes in this sense are at least reflections of the way human beings comprehend the social world. This move demotes the literal sentence from privileged to common status. It requires greater attention on the part of linguists to the contextualization of natural language use. Also, it opens the way for language studies of discourse as social practice.

As for the study of metaphor in particular, this change of perspective is significant. As Lakoff notes, the positivist and the cognitivist analyses are evaluated for adequacy by fundamentally different criteria.[39] For the former, since metaphor interpretation is presumably derived from the literal, the adequacy of analysis is judged on the precision of the plotting from the literal sentence to the figurative metaphor. This plotting becomes the basis for, and often the end of, any further interpretation. In the cognitivist theory of metaphor, on the other hand, an analysis is judged to be more adequate on two criteria, which in this book will be called coherence and congruence. Insofar as there is greater coherence, namely, more semantic precision in the mapping between the semantic domains of the metaphor, the analysis will be considered more satisfactory. Second, greater congruence, in other words more encompassing consistency between the linguistic expressions of a metaphor and the wider uses of this imagery, will be a measure of the utility of the analysis. The literal sentence does not have a central place in such analysis. In practice the literalist approach proves to be quite restrictive of figurative language study. To the literalist, on the other hand, the goals of the cognitivists appear to be outsized and dismissive of the fundamentals. Nevertheless, there are certain arguments and substantial empirical evidence that support the cognitivist assumptions and consequently support the enterprise undertaken in this book.

*Evidence for the Cognitivist Perspective*

Lakoff noted that in the literalist view of metaphor, each individual metaphoric expression in the following set of sentences can only be seen as unrelated: *He's crazy about her. He flipped his lid when she walked in. He couldn't help himself in her presence. With one smile he went positively batty. He was mad about her,* etc. For the literalist, this set of sentences only accidentally shares a meaning "to be in love." This is to say, no evidence can be adduced from the individual sentences to believe that the different expressions of being in love are anything more than chance coincidences. Recall that in the strictest version of the literalist approach only linguistic information that can be extracted from the sentence itself can be used for interpretation. In order to demonstrate in literalist terms that these various example sentences invoke the same source domain, the literalist must first find sufficient information in the linguistic material of each sentence to make sense of the metaphor in terms of its presumed literal correspondent, if at all possible. Then a comparison of the literal propositions of each sentence might be attempted. In the cognitivist view, in contrast, this comparison is not a problem. This is not a random set of sentences; the sentences, instead, are correlated instances of a single ontological correspondence (metaphoric mapping).

It should be noted that the cognitivist focus of attention is not on individual sentences (see Figure 2.1). The object is not any particular linguistic expression of a metaphor, but the metaphoric mapping between two semantic domains. The mapping is labeled, in this case, as LOVE AS MADNESS. Each linguistic expression of this grouping is a variation that reflects the single conceptual mapping of one semantic domain, MADNESS, to a second semantic domain, in this case LOVE. Since noncognitivist explanations of metaphor have not captured the obvious relation among the examples, this constitutes support for the model of metaphor that does.

Another linguistic advantage of the cognitive model of metaphor that Lakoff noted is its built-in capacity to explain why particular words, such as *loony,* and idiomatic expressions, such as *goo-goo eyed,* are used to express notions about love.[40] A semantic domain mapping explanation for such patterning is evidence for the constitutive role of metaphor in organizing the world. This feature of the cognitivist model is not shared by its competitors.

Additional linguistic support for the cognitivist enterprise comes in the creation of novel text instances of metaphors. Again these are not arbitrary collocations of words, but are motivated constructions, new instances of a productive conventional mapping across semantic domains. If one checks out the titles of the *Billboard* #1 hits over the last twenty years, it is clear that songwriters apply new twists to the ever-handy LOVE AS MADNESS metaphor. By way of illustration, the reggae tune "Can't Help Falling in Love" took UB40 to the top of the charts; "Crazy for You" was a crossover ballad for Madonna; the *Flashdance* movie emblem, "Maniac," was written by Michael Sembello. Originally a country music tune, "I Can't Stop Loving You" became a romantic pop classic as sung by Ray Charles; "She Drives Me

Crazy" was recorded by the Fine Young Cannibals; and, among many other MADNESS hits, "I Almost Lost My Mind" was crooned by the never-wild-and-crazy Pat Boone.[41] These titles demonstrate the productivity of this conventional metaphor. LOVE AS MADNESS is as venerable as it is popular. It appears in Plato's dialogue *Phaedrus,* appropriately enough as the common-sense understanding of love as an affliction in which lovers are not in their right mind.

Again, what is consequential about the cognitive enterprise of metaphor is the conceptual mapping, not any particular string of words. The mappings of LOVE AS WAR, AS MADNESS, and AS A PHYSICAL FORCE are conventional metaphors, which is to say they are an established part of the conceptual system of English speakers. This implies that there is a retrieval system of mappings that constitute the conceptual elements that people invoke to make sense of the social world, all through the metaphors they commonly use.

Apart from metaphor's being a key element in the way that pop musicians conceptualize LOVE, another argument based in linguistic material provides evidence that metaphor and other figurative language are not rare, but common. Metaphor and metaphoric thinking permeate many aspects of human life. Eve Sweetser demonstrated metaphoric influence in the changing of meanings of words and the growth of the lexicon throughout recorded time and in prehistory.[42] Combining the insights of cognitive linguistics with the tools of traditional historical linguistics, Sweetser focused on the origins of polysemy, namely, homonyms that have distinct meanings. Within the cognitivist enterprise, polysemy can be understood to be lexical expansion of productive metaphoric mappings. The word *over,* for example, has about one hundred distinct, but metaphorically related, meanings.[43] Polysemous words are among the most frequent ones used in everyday talk.[44] Within the literalist account of meaning, no matter how ubiquitous and productive, polysemy is incidental and haphazard, and is generated on the basis of analogy. But analogy is a description, not explanation. In the cognitive account, in contrast, each new meaning is explained as a new variant generated on the basis of a productive ontological correspondence, that is, a metaphor. Sweetser's analysis of the development across time of change in the meanings of English modals, conjunctions, conditionals, and perception verbs incorporates metaphoric and cultural aspects of cognitive structure in order to explain the changes in meaning of some words, and the multiple meanings of these and related words. Across thousands of years among the Indo-

European languages, perception words like *see* have often come to acquire extended meanings equivalent to "to know." Using established comparative linguistic methods, Sweetser found evidence of an ancient metaphor, TO KNOW IS TO SEE, which captures a pattern across these languages. This metaphor is part of a more encompassing prehistoric metaphor, MIND AS BODY, which also has reflexes across the range of Indo-European languages. Thus there is a well-developed explanation in metaphor theory about how new words are created. Any analysis of these semantic changes which does not incorporate metaphor mappings into its account fails to account for the attested pattern of the multiplication of words across the Indo-European languages.

Another indication of the pervasiveness in everyday life of metaphoric thinking can be seen in the turns of phrase that have a metaphoric origin, but which have over time become literal for all practical purposes. In the previous example, *He couldn't help himself when she's around* expresses "to be in love" in a turn of phrase that employs madness as its source domain. Note that this sentence does not, strictly speaking, involve a metaphor. The proportion of everyday talk that is made up of such collocations of words is remarkable. Most of these are so common that they are transparent, that is to say, they do not draw attention to themselves. They are thoroughly integrated into everyday speech. Yet just as linguistic expressions are verbalized instances of conceptual mappings of a source semantic domain to a target domain, so these conventionalized expressions are reflections of metaphoric thinking. Thus there are traces of metaphoric thinking in most parts of everyday speech, from metaphors, certain idiomatic expressions, metonymy and other tropes,[45] as well as the conventionalized literal expressions. And for the purposes of this book, an independently formulated theory can be employed to explain the analysis of discourse material. The analysis aims to understand the discourse practices employed in the reproduction of the social order that maintains unjust hierarchical relationships. As will be touched upon in the following, there is further theoretical evidence within the cognitive theory of metaphor for an important role for metaphor and metaphoric thinking in establishing ideology.

*Foundational Metaphor*

In the cognitive theory of metaphor the mappings are seen to be invariant linkages which are invoked, or "commented on in different linguistic expressions."[46] In the course of twenty years of research, the semantic domains that have been found to be metaphoric give order to every aspect of daily life, and not merely odd cultural peculiarities of LOVE and NATION. They also include some of the most foundational aspects of human life. These include the everyday way of dealing with time, orientation in space, human emotions, what constitutes an event in human experience or in human imagination, how people think they understand things, and how they talk about the very ideas that they come up with, among other conceptual keystones.[47]

These foundational metaphors are not haphazardly distributed through the semantic fields of English. The basic metaphors lay a cognitive foundation for higher-level everyday human understanding. As infants, we have particular preconceptual experiences, such as "body movements, our ability to move objects, to perceive them as wholes and retain images of them; and certain image-schemata which recur in our everyday bodily experience, e.g., containers, paths, balance, up and down, part and whole, front and back."[48] Lakoff and Johnson's hypothesis is that our preconceptual physical experiences as gravity-bound bipeds give rise to most abstract concepts by metaphorical projection.

Lakoff has demonstrated the existence of a hierarchical structure that organizes metaphors at distinct levels of abstraction, from the most foundational and cognitive to more conceptual and cultural ones.[49] For example, Lakoff has delineated the topology of one semantic domain of human experience, the event.[50] That is to say, each and every occurrence of an event — whether a minor incident, a single episode in the course of a progression, a particular circumstance within a forgettable act, or a happening of greatest importance — all have been mapped out in terms of the semantic elements that are automatically drawn upon to interact with the world. This fundamental part of people's way of talking about and constructing their world is most certainly conceptualized metaphorically, inasmuch as its elements (state, change, process, action, cause, and purpose) are understood in terms of space, motion, and force. The mappings of the event metaphor in turn become the basis for other conceptual and higher-level cultural metaphors. Figure 2.2 is an adaptation of Gibbs's depiction.[51]

Gibbs elaborates the relationship among these metaphors at some length. In short, in the same way that the conceptual structure of the source domain is transferred onto the target domain in a simple linguistic expression of a metaphor, so are the conceptual organization and its various and significant structures of the event structure metaphor "inherited" by the conceptual metaphor LIFE IS JOURNEY. These structures in turn are inherited

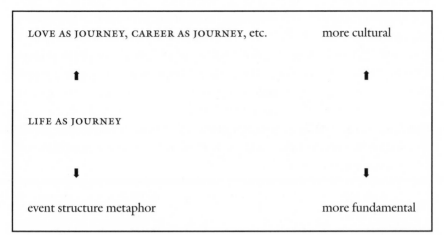

| | |
|---|---|
| LOVE AS JOURNEY, CAREER AS JOURNEY, etc. | more cultural |
| ↑ | ↑ |
| LIFE AS JOURNEY | |
| ↓ | ↓ |
| event structure metaphor | more fundamental |

**Figure 2.2. Hierarchies of mappings**

by higher-level metaphors. Thus the congruence of metaphoric thinking is due in part to its basis in foundational human experience. The validity of the source domain experience, namely space, motion, and force, is beyond question. It is the embodied knowledge which people employ in daily life. As Lakoff states, we first learned it as infants in our life experience in our little bodies. And the source domain experiences that we learn as infants are reinforced in daily living in these same, if somewhat larger, bodies.[52] Hence Lakoff's epistemology is termed Embodied Realism. As space, motion, and force notions are invoked in metaphoric thinking, these corporeal verities provide a comprehensible and generally unquestioned basis for higher-level linkages, including dominance relations that make up part of the social order.

*Metaphor in Science*

Metaphoric thinking is pervasive, not only in foundational conceptualization, but also in high-level cognitive activities such as scientific thinking. While the positivist position, with its Enlightenment presumptions, takes for granted a significant difference between a scientist's and layperson's way of thinking about the world, the cognitivist sees little evidence to suggest a qualitative difference between everyday thinking and scientific thinking. At base both are metaphorical. In the nineteenth-century positivist view, metaphorical thinking was considered the sign of a juvenile science, and as the science matured its dependence on indeterminate metaphor would give way to a purportedly more perfect language, culminating in the use of mathematical formulations. This belief has been superseded. Twentieth-century historians of science have demonstrated that model-building, one of the primary activities in science, is chiefly a search for more encompassing and appropriate metaphors. Succeeding generations of researchers replace once-apt, but now antiquated, models (metaphors) with more satisfactory ones. As an example, Edward O. Wilson quotes a Nobel Prize winner in physics, Hideki Yukawa, as he describes the method he used to advance his understanding of the binding forces of the atom:

> Suppose there is something which a person cannot understand. He happens to notice the similarity of this something to some other thing which he understands quite well. By comparing them he may come to understand the thing which he could not understand up to that moment.[53]

These metaphors provide new ways of talking and thinking about a phenomenon. Scientific paradigm shifts are the exemplars of such metaphoric revolutions of scientific understanding.[54] This process takes place at all levels of scientific thinking. Thomas Kuhn provides examples of how nineteenth-century metaphorical models in physics, such as ATOMS AS SOLAR SYSTEMS, were replaced with the early-twentieth-century NUCLEI AND ELECTRONS AS BILLIARD BALLS:

> I . . . would . . . draw attention to the way in which metaphors like that relating atoms and solar systems are replaced. Bohr and his contemporaries supplied a model in which electrons and [the] nucleus were represented by tiny bits of charged matter interacting under the laws of mechanics and electromagnetic theory. That model replaced the solar system metaphor but not, by doing so, a metaphorlike process. Bohr's atom model was intended to be taken only more-or-less literally; electrons and nuclei were not thought to be exactly like small billiard or Ping-Pong balls; only some of the laws of mechanics and electromagnetic theory were thought to apply to them; finding out which ones did apply and where the similarities to billiard balls lay was a central task in the development of quantum theory. Furthermore, even when that process of exploring potential similarities had gone as far as it could (it has never been completed), the model remained essential to the theory. Without its aid, one cannot even today write down the Schrödinger equation for a complex atom or molecule, for it is to the

model, not directly to nature, that the various terms in that equation refer. . . . I would hazard the guess that the same interactive, similarity-creating process which Black has isolated in the functioning of metaphor is vital also to the function of models in science. Models are not, however, merely pedagogic or heuristic. They have been too much neglected in recent philosophy of science.[55]

In his fascinating book on the figurative basis of the human mind, Gibbs amassed the views of a good number of other scientists and philosophers of science who now argue that rather than being merely incidental, metaphoric thinking constitutes a central part of scientific theory and practice.[56]

In the history of the social sciences, a procession of successively more adequate metaphoric imagery is also found. One example is the recently promoted and increasingly obsolete MIND AS COMPUTER metaphor. This metaphor was preceded by the MIND AS ANIMATE BEING metaphor,[57] which arose in the recent decades in psychology. In fact, John Searle notes that thinkers across history have appealed to the "latest technological device" to conceptualize the brain. Thus in Searle's own youth, the brain was describe as a "telephone X-bar system." Much earlier, in the nineteenth century, some referred to the brain as a telegraph system. Searle states that a distinguished British neurobiologist metaphorized the brain as a Jacquard loom, which was the first automatic weaving machine able to produce highly intricate patterns. In the eighteenth century we can also find a more general form of this metaphor, namely MIND AS MACHINE, prompted by Julien Offray de La Mettrie's influential book entitled *L'homme Machine* (Man a Machine).[58] The most complicated technology in the seventeenth century, the mill, was Leibniz's metaphor. Searle even notes that ancient Greeks described the workings of the brain as a catapult.[59]

*Inertia of Conventional Metaphors*

All these examples involving change in the metaphor in scientific thinking should not be taken as indicating that there is no resistance in the turnover of scientific models. Nothing could be further from the truth. Replacement of a dominant metaphor involves overcoming a great deal of inertia, particularly when the metaphor also constitutes everyday aspects of human lives. In these cases people are extremely resistant to changes, and often will not even temporarily entertain alternative perspectives. This intractability is associated in part with the metaphoric framing process itself.

In a pioneering piece of research, Michael Reddy demonstrated that metaphor frames a basic element of how people, even linguists, think about communication and language. Thus the very means by which people communicate is conceptualized metaphorically, and much turns on this way of talking about talking.[60] One metaphor, which is commonly expressed in conventional words and turns of phrase, is shown by Reddy to be linked to a particular way of conceptualizing human communication, for the linguistic scientist and for the layperson. The image that frames communication for both is what Reddy calls the conduit metaphor.

Reddy argues that by way of this thoroughly inaccurate but altogether commonplace metaphor, linguists and nonlinguists alike talk as if language itself were a self-contained carrier of ideas, and as if sentences were the receptacles for concepts which are packed into a sentence to be *submitted, imparted, sent, conveyed, delivered, passed on, expressed, transmitted,* and so on. People further speak as if all that is needed to understand an utterance is for a hearer/reader to unpack the sentence. The listener's creative processing, interpreting strings of words with their visual and aural context into sensible propositions, is entirely lost with the conduit metaphor. If given a moment to think, people might recognize that the decontextualized sentence is not rich enough to serve all simple and normal communication functions, and that this model conforms to the positivist views about language which separate communication and its material from other social practices which construct meaning. However, people commonly speak as if it were as simple as packaging a sentence with meaning and sending it to the recipient. So they accept the expressions *putting each idea into words, capturing a thought in an apt phrase, his words were filled with emotion,* and *that message rings hollow* as literal. To see how deeply ingrained this way of thinking and speaking about communication is, the reader should attempt the surprisingly difficult exercise of speaking about discourse with expressions that integrate the material and practice aspects of discourse.

*Backgrounding and Foregrounding in Conventional Metaphor*

Metaphors are specific mappings between two particular semantic domains. Each metaphor establishes a mapping which is a distinct association which foregrounds certain semantic features and backgrounds other features. For example, in the LOVE AS WAR metaphor, conflict (leading to a surrender of one party to the victorious other party) is foregrounded. Other elements of the experience of love that are quite important are backgrounded, or completely passed over, with this metaphor. In contrast, an alternative metaphor, such as LOVE AS MADNESS, foregrounds the psychological state of the individual and backgrounds the interaction between the parties.

Likewise, profound consequences follow the framing of communication by means of the conduit metaphor. For one, if the communication message is taken for granted to be self-contained, the uncontextualized sentence can be settled on as the one true unit of analysis. The framing of the conduit metaphor dismisses segments of language larger or smaller than a sentence which may be important in human communication. More importantly, the focus on transmission of the self-contained message passes over the entire social interactional process by which communication takes place. That is to say, a conceptual demarcation between the code of communication and the process of communication is introduced. Although this analytic distinction has proven to be useful for rationalist linguistic inquiry, this artificial divide cleaves the discursive process. As Fairclough noted, there is a tendency among linguists and nonlinguists to discuss the relationship between language and society as existing between "external" entities, whereas an "internal and dialectical" unity is involved.[61]

The consequences of thinking in terms compatible with the conduit metaphor are profound. For the science of language, the gestalt of contextual real-world communication has been passed over in favor of the stripped-down skeleton of talk, the sentence in isolation. On the broader social canvas, language has been readily segregated from other human behavior. Language is integral to society, with linguistic phenomena a special case of social phenomena. Thus in the conduit metaphor, the constitutive aspects of language are backgrounded. Some linguists, other social scientists, and philosophers of language continue to be influenced by the presuppositions of this conventional metaphor.

## Shifting Metaphors in Science and in Everyday Life

Scientific models are sustained as long as the empirical evidence about the phenomenon continues to conform to the model. In the critical and skeptical atmosphere of science, the search is always on to extend and to test the current model, and as evidence accumulates that does not fit, criticism increases, until another, more apt and explanatory model/metaphor is discovered to replace it. However, this is not the case for everyday models of reality which are sustained and reinvoked regularly, irrespective of their inaccuracy and inadequacy. One such commonplace concept is communication.

The stories English speakers tell about communication are largely determined by semantic structures of the language itself. This evidence suggests that English has a preferred framework for conceptualizing communication, and can bias thought process[es] toward this framework, even though nothing more than common sense is necessary to devise a different, more accurate framework. . . . My own belief is that this frame conflict has considerable impact on our social and cultural problems.[62]

Reddy pointed out the obstinate pervasiveness of the conduit metaphor both in the scientific and commonplace references to language. Fortunately, he also pointed out the saving grace of higher-order metaphors, namely, they are not immutable. As follows from the hierarchical structuring of metaphors, there are various levels of conventionalization of metaphors, from fixed to fluid. For cultural, scientific, and political metaphors, deficient mappings ultimately can be replaced with better alternatives. Reddy offered an alternative framing metaphor, LANGUAGE AS TOOLMAKER, that does not have the liabilities of the CONDUIT metaphor.[63] Metaphor, as a cardinal means of human cognition, curbs people's view of the world. But it may also be used to reconceptualize worldviews. Reddy indicates that novel, more accurate conceptual frames can and should be sought and promulgated to promote a more adequate view of the ideas of the social world.

*Caveat for the Study of Discourse Metaphor Research*

Across the full spectrum of studies of humanity, there has been an expanding awareness of the world-generating power of discourse. Historian Joanne Brown, writing in a recent compendium of social thought, recommends looking to the visual arts for a fuller understanding of the social world of discourse (to which she refers as "language"):

> By filling in the spaces between conventional objects of study, [language] maps the relations among them historically as well as socially. Historians need a vocabulary for language which captures this space-in-between, the interstitial, tense nature of language, in the way the painter Mornadi, or Caravaggio, or Vuillard, or Mary Cassatt captured the space in between and made it define, with exquisite sensitivity to the moment as well as to the object, the ostensible solid object of study of the work.[64]

There is a peril in this reflection on the power of discourse. Discourse practice can be overstated, particularly if one does not keep in mind the material constraints of discourse, as Paul Chilton reproves.[65] By way of illustration, in the same passage where she offers a well-turned evocation of the place of discourse in history, Brown indulges herself with a delirious array of images that is first bewildering, and ultimately disappointing:

> Language is no mere mirror, tool, weapon, that we can turn from, lay down, or bury at will. Language is our skin. It is the wind in our sails. It is a wave. It is the water in the river that was the rain. It is the fetus. It is the warp. It is the egg, before and after the chicken. It is the mouthful that builds strong bones. It is sticks and stones.[66]

## Metaphor in Institutions

Metaphors underlie the functioning of social institutions, such as the concepts of law in the judicial system. Stephen Winter argues that legal thinking is profoundly metaphorical.[67] It is commonly assumed by the legal community, for example, that the First Amendment to the U.S. Constitution is a set of doctrinal rules that are more-or-less deterministically applied to particular cases. Winter notes, as an instance of this kind of thinking, that Owen Fiss defines the Bill of Rights "as a charter of ideals and principles, and adjudication as the process by which we make those values real." Consequently, in Fiss's view, the Bill of Rights is a timeless and immutable ideal, and "the crux of modern free speech law is . . . a conflict 'over the mediating principle that gives fullest expression to that ideal.'"[68] Fiss continues: "Adjudication is one process by which these abstract ideals are given concrete meaning and expression and are thereby translated into rights."[69] Winter finds such a positivist notion of mediation from an ideal principle to a particular case "extraordinarily vulnerable" to criticism, since, for one, such absolute principles must correspond precisely to the world in order to work. Second, with echoes in Reddy's critique, the exercise of such principles requires perfect transmission of the logical proposition to its concrete application. In contrast, from the point of view of a constructivist critic, these principles are historically contingent; there is no mirroring of social reality in unchanging principles.

A more adequate characterization is that the First Amendment is practiced in terms of a metaphor. That is to say, jurists, from a local municipal judge to the Chief Justice of the Supreme Court, make decisions according to a metaphor defining the First Amendment which is contingent on a specific historical time frame. Winter points out the metaphors for freedom of speech have changed over time, and with it the way the legal profession thinks about a body of law, with weighty social consequences. In the seventeenth century, freedom of speech was described by John Milton in the following terms: "Truth is compar'd in Scripture to a streaming fountain." The earliest characterizations of the First Amendment implemented the flowing-water metaphor, and *free flow of ideas* was a conceptualization that emphasized progress toward essential truth. At this time the implications of such an understanding focused on limiting possible governmental interference in the flow of new ideas. However, once those ideas were expressed, and if they were deemed outmoded and an obstacle to the Truth, then they became quite vulnerable to governmental restriction. Winter provides a wealth of examples.[70]

By the twentieth century, however, Oliver Wendell Holmes, Jr., argued against the prevailing model of the First Amendment, and coined the *marketplace of ideas* notion of free speech. The semantic associations of this current metaphor include a quite different normative measure than that envisioned by the Founding Fathers. Whereas the seventeenth-century FLOWING WATER metaphor jealously safeguarded new ideas while allowing ideas to be squelched if they are seen as obsolete, the market metaphor forces an economic measure of the value of all ideas, whether old or new. Furthermore, in the earlier flowing-water metaphor, a single "Truth" was presumed. In contrast, multiple truths can be maintained in today's marketplace metaphor. Corresponding real-world consequences follow from the change of legal metaphor. For example, differential taxation of different forms of print media would not have been tolerable in the light of the previous metaphor, but is now an acceptable consequence of a marketplace norm for various print media.

Winter notes that while Holmes's metaphor is complex, it is far from novel. It is a conventional metaphor that incorporates culturally specific definitions and associations. Conventional metaphors set up relations that are deeply fixed in everyday thinking and are reconstructed from moment to moment as people talk. In time, and if there are no fitting options available, only one way to conceive the world is taken to be the case. Cognitive metaphor theory finds the foundational embodiment of the social world in metaphors that are hierarchically related. Semantic structures and presuppositions of more basic metaphors are said to be "inherited" by higher-level cultural metaphors like that of the marketplace. Thus people's thinking about society in terms of metaphor provides reasons both why there is such resistance at considering alternative metaphors of a social issue, and how paradigmatic change takes place.

## Metaphor in Social Policy

Since metaphor can describe the large-scale tendencies of social institution function across time, it can also begin to explain the function of social policy. Policy in the United States, as a site of negotiated action, is surprisingly immutable with regard to a range of social issues. Donald Schön, a public policy researcher, also argued that conventional metaphor is the key element in the way that social situations that require a policy response are conceptualized.[71] Using a line of thinking that should be familiar by now, he claimed that a society commonly and unreflectingly employs one framework to conceptualize a social situation. The "frame" of reference to the social issue then leads straightway to the kind of policy with which society will respond. "The essential difficulties in social policy have more to do with problem setting than with problem solving."[72] Furthermore he tied this strong normative posture to his metaphor theory. The single conceptualization of social issues is based on what Schön calls a "generative metaphor." Such a productive metaphor structures the way that individuals in a society, from the layperson to most policy experts, come to think about a given social situation. To use one of Schön's examples, low-income neighborhoods are regularly conceived in terms that are associated with one metaphor or another. Here the predominant metaphor is DISEASE, such as in *decaying inner cities.* Schön quotes a policymaker, William O. Douglas, who employed this metaphor:

> The experts concluded that if the community were to be healthy, if it were not to revert again to a blighted or slum area, as though possessed of a congenital disease, the area must be planned as a whole. . . . In this way it was hoped that the cycle of decay of the area could be controlled and the birth of future slums prevented.[73]

The use of the disease metaphor leads to semantic associations, judgments, considerations, and actions that can be attributed to the source notion of DISEASE. Importantly, from the point of view of the present study, these associations may or may not really be appropriate ways of thinking about low-income neighborhoods, are particular to the disease metaphor, and are automatically linked to the target of this metaphor. In this medical model, curing the disease may include *eradicating* the slum.

Schön pointed out that to establish a metaphor to characterize the "social problem" forestalls further alternative conceptualization on the topic. The social problem comes to be understood (within the mappings of the metaphor) to be unproblematic, and is soon taken to be a given.[74] It becomes the natural way of conceiving of the world. As the metaphor becomes naturalized (Schön used the term "conventionalized"), no alternative way of seeing the issue will be accepted. Public policy solutions for the social issue will typically take the form of solutions consistent with the conventional metaphor. Thus acceptable policy solutions will be those which are prefigured in terms of the metaphor, to the exclusion of other views.

An alternative conceptualization of this so-called *urban blight*, Schön indicated, would begin with the observation that residents of low-income neighborhoods demonstrate remarkable adaptability and creativity to develop their material circumstances and infrastructure without capital or governmental support. Schön asks us to reconceptualize the barrio and other inner-city ethnic enclaves, as have some policy thinkers, as "folk communities," rather than urban blight, which implies a medical solution requiring surgical removal or a cure. This emphasizes their strong informal and familial networks of support. Schön argued that policy responses to a nondisease metaphoric framing of the social issue can be potentially more effective. Moreover, the discussion of alternative metaphoric framings of the policy issue, in and of itself, promises greater breadth of understanding. Schön and Reim discussed how the use of such conceptual reframing is a powerful means to achieve alternative ways of comprehending society.[75]

Schön applied his research on metaphor-based framing of social policy issues to technological innovation, organizational behavior and homelessness, early retirement, and certain educational topics. He noted the public's resistance to reconceptualizing its view of the world, even in the case of repeated policy failure when the so-called urban *disease* does not respond to its self-evident *cure*. Schön's dictum is that conceptual conflicts are "immune to resolution by appeal to the facts. . . . New facts have a way of being either reabsorbed or disregarded by those who see problematic situations under conflicting frames."[76]

Schön's bold proposal does not sit well with policy and social science researchers coming from a positivist perspective. They are skeptical about the import of metaphor, and the power of discursive practice to organize social structure. From the positivist's point of view, metaphor does not constitute reality. In this view, referring to a slum as a disease simply summarizes a political position and is a prime element of persuasion. Though it certainly has the power to capture the attention of the electorate, in the positivist view, metaphor is nothing more than an oratorical device. The positivist describes metaphor's power as evocative, based on emotion and not sound reasoning, but certainly incapable of constructing and constraining public policy comprehension, as Schön claimed.

More generally, the positivists hold that language reflects social structure, and only trivially constrains social structure. All words have basically the same status, in the positivist view, and simply do not define human understanding. Another difficulty with Schön, following the line of these critics, is that he conflates technical and other precise scientific characterizations with commonplace everyday talk about a topic. The latter is replete with imagery that may be inaccurate and tends to be emotion-laden. For example, the skeptics say that any discourse on slums will tend to be negative—since ghettos and barrios are *eyesores* and *blemishes* on the urban landscape.

In his defense, Schön argues that the generative metaphor co-opts the thinking on a social issue for both the public and the specialists. Neither layperson nor expert is immune from the associative power of an apt and productive metaphor, since humans think in terms of metaphors. Metaphor is the unit of Schön's intriguing analysis, which again focuses on how society is constituted via everyday discourse. Schön and Reim point out numerous "intractable policy controversies" that are based on contending metaphoric representations of the social world.[77] Crucially for language-minority populations and for all concerned citizens, metaphor is central to the way people talk about themselves and their social world. As such it is the key element with which discourse constructs the social world.

## Summary

So far in this chapter, a progressive expansion has been made of the social domains in which there is evidence to argue that metaphor constitutes, to a good degree, society and its workings. Since the enterprise of the present book is explicitly political—how Latinos in U.S. society are constituted in public discourse—one question that may arise is how pervasive metaphoric thinking is in political action. For some readers, such thinking has long ago entered political spheres of social organization. As Stephen Winter affirms:

"The language of the law is not a surrogate for political discourse; it is a form of political discourse."[78]

## Section 5: Critiquing Cognitive Metaphor Theory

The study of metaphoric understandings of law and science, of everyday life and worldview, has been given substantive grounding with Lakoff's theoretical work on cognition. The boldness and scope of cognitivist metaphor theory, and its central place in Lakoff's encompassing epistemology, Embodied Realism, have been met with "sharp critical response as well as enthusiastic approval"[79] breaking down roughly along positivist/constructivist lines. As Patrizia Violi characterizes it, Lakoff ventures an answer to the question that has forever animated semanticists and flummoxed every parent of a curious four-year-old: "Where does meaning come from?"[80] Lakoff's answer is that core, basic-level concepts do not receive meaning from the external world. Rather, these basic concepts are inherently meaningful since they are directly associated with body experience, what Lakoff calls embodied knowledge. From this core set of concepts, as has been outlined above, a hierarchy of cognitive models (including metaphor) is structured which provides the basis for much of the human ways of understanding the world.

*Details, Labels, and Scope*

Three types of criticisms have been made of the cognitivist theory of metaphors of Lakoff and his colleagues. One which is central to cognitive science is that the particulars of the cognitive structure have not been worked out to the satisfaction of all semanticists and cognitive scientists. This is to say, the devil is in the details. We will not have occasion in this book to undertake the recitation of this argumentation.

The second kind of criticism, more important for the present enterprise, involves the adequacy of metaphoric map labeling to characterize a set of linguistic expressions. As James Hampton quips, "Lakoff's game is easy to play, and hard to test."[81] To use Jackendoff and Aaron's example, in one case a set of linguistic expressions is grouped by Lakoff and Turner with the LIFE AS FIRE mapping. Could a more general mapping, for example, LIFE AS SOMETHING THAT GIVES OFF HEAT, or a more specific mapping, such as LIFE AS FLAME, be a more adequate characterization? His critics say that Lakoff has not elaborated a clear labeling procedure.[82] However, following Eleanor Rosch's prototype theory (which Lakoff updates), a cognitive mapping will be characterized at a level of abstraction that permits a central type to which things apply if they are perceived similarly, as well as less central cases. Consequently the most adequate mapping should encompass both more general and more specific linguistic expressions.[83] Moreover, it should be kept in mind that labeling of a metaphoric mapping serves primarily as a mnemonic identification.[84]

Third is the criticism that Lakoff and his colleagues excessively expand what is traditionally understood to be a metaphor:

> Their overall characterization enlarges the scope of the term "meta-phor" well beyond the standard use of the term. While we think that many of their points are well taken, we believe their characteriza-tion obscures certain important distinctions and stretches the notion "metaphor" to a number of cases that should be understood in other terms.[85]

Jackendoff and Aaron wish to restrict the notion to "incongruous" map-pings between semantic domains, such that the sentence *Their relationship is at a dead end* involves a metaphor. Contrarily the following sentence would not contain a metaphor: *We haven't reached our goal of finishing this chap-ter.* In the former Jackendoff and Aaron approve of the RELATIONSHIP AS JOURNEY mapping and recognize an incongruity between personal relations and journey making, while in the latter, cross-domain mapping is judged not to be a metaphor but an instance of what Jackendoff has called thematic re-lations involving the language of space.[86] In the latter sentence they further note that "the incongruity of the mapping is acknowledged rather than de-nied, but its invocation seems beside the point."[87] In short, Jackendoff and Aaron want to slice up the cognitive phenomenon that Lakoff uniformly calls metaphoric. Jackendoff limits his use of the term "metaphor" to appli-cations of incongruous semantic mappings to particular sentences,[88] while Lakoff is far less interested in particular strings of words. Instead Lakoff at-tempts to embrace much more in his formulations. Notwithstanding the cri-tique, there is a shared vision. In their exacting review of his theory, Jacken-doff and Aaron state that Lakoff's

> thesis is not materially affected by the modifications to the theory of metaphor we have suggested here.[89]

Further:

if we point out the weaknesses in [Lakoff and Turner's] presentation, it is not with the aim of undermining their overall cognitivist approach, but rather to explore how a more convincing case could be constructed.[90]

In sum, for both Jackendoff and Lakoff, who are often seen as competing cognitive science theorists who "contrast sharply in the particular solutions they offer,"[91] the direction of cognitive theory is clearly moving away from a truth-conditional semantics toward a constructivist approach to cognition.

## Application

A final criticism deals with the application of metaphor theory to social issues. While there has been general acceptance of the insight of metaphoric constructions of orientational prepositions, change in the meanings of English modal verbs, conjunctions, conditionals, and perception verbs, as well as fixed conventional, structural, and ontological metaphors as well as metonymy, doubts have arisen in certain analyses of political domains.

We have already had occasion to review domains of knowledge and meaning in physical science, social science, and juridical history. These diachronic studies compare the metaphors of understanding of one period of time to another. In the case of science, they focus on the different conceptual models/metaphors of the periods, which lead researchers to pose distinct theoretical questions, to attend to certain aspects of a phenomenon and not other aspects, to advance correspondingly distinct hypotheses, and to develop distinct ways of talking and thinking about the phenomenon. Likewise in juridical studies, the pertinent case law, the kinds of compelling arguments, the structure of the precedents, and the subsequent legislative responses of different periods can be compared. Without a basis of comparison it would be harder to accept Winter's assertion, for example, about the existence of a commercial metaphor in current First Amendment case law application. In these studies the historical perspective provides a crucial point of view for analysis.

In contrast, synchronic studies of the contemporary metaphoric understandings of the present social order pose a distinct set of investigative problems, namely, questions of selection and validity. There are excellent studies of metaphor in discourse about the social order that have attended to these methodological concerns.[92] On the other hand, the principal innovator of metaphor studies, Lakoff, has undertaken certain so-called empirical studies of the metaphoric understanding of social phenomena that have not been as well received as his theoretical work.[93] By "empirical," Lakoff means investigations which derive from observations that are direct offshoots of his theoretical work, that is to say, the formal study of cognitive structure. Lakoff's work on contemporary American politics in his own words is based on his "routine research . . . on the details of our moral conceptual system, especially our system of metaphors for morality."[94] He and his team use their knowledge of American English and U.S. culture to generate examples for their theoretical studies. But Lakoff presumes that a self-generated list of metaphoric expressions is an appropriate basis for studies of political spheres of society. This move assumes that the ideology guiding the construction of American social order can be primarily ascertained through the exploration of the intuitions of a native speaker of American English.

This is often called empirical research, but more appropriately is termed rationalist research, because it is pursued via intuition and deduction. It capitalizes on the rich internalized linguistic competence that (linguists as) native speakers of a language have, and typically involves producing lists of critical sentences. The sentences are then examined for their structural patterning, with the goal of establishing a classification of the pertinent structures and categories, as well as the rules needed to generate all and only the grammatically sound sentences. Thus in researching the scope of adverbial expression, the following set of sentences was produced by a linguist:

a1. He clumsily trod on the snail.
a2. Clumsily he trod on the snail.
b1. He trod clumsily on the snail.
b2. He trod on the snail clumsily.

These sentences were generated by the noted linguist and philosopher of language John Austin. He comments: "Care must be taken too to observe the precise position of an adverbial expression in the sentence. This should of course indicate what verb it is being used to modify: but more than that, the position can also affect the *sense* of the expression, i.e., the way in which it modifies that verb. Here, in a1 and a2 we describe his treading on the creature at all as a piece of clumsiness, incidental, we imply, to his performance of some other action: but with b1 and b2 to tread on it is, very likely, his aim or policy, what we criticize is his execution of the feat. Many adverbs, though far from all (not, for example, 'purposely'), are used in these two typically different ways."[95] Accordingly, to investigate metaphor structure, the rationalist linguist would generate a set of critical sentences that illuminate the semantic structures of the topic at hand.

Exploring intuitions has been an exceptionally productive method in formal linguistics. The greatest portion of contemporary linguistic research employs the rationalist method. Its strength lies in the development of classes of categories that constitute the phenomenon under study. But the method harbors significant research liabilities when the social order of human communities is the object of study.[96]

The objective of this book is to investigate the social values underlying the linguistic expressions concerning a selected set of topics about U.S. Latinos by bringing to light the metaphoric representations of Latinos in contemporary public discourse. Data drawn from principally intuitional, rather than actual, language use would be subject to bias on a number of factors. For one, self-elicited materials of an individual cannot be assumed to be representative of the discourse practices of a community. Without methodical empirical safeguards, intuitionally gathered materials can be taken to be only an imperfect estimation of the language use of one member of any community. Second, because intuitionally retrieved materials are a suspect source of naturally occurring language data of an actual community of speakers, such a database will be problematic for interpretations of social order.[97] As Gertrude Himmelfarb notes, Lakoff asserts that his method is "neutral" and "free of political and moral assumptions," while in fact his data gathering, based primarily on personal intuition rather than an independently occurring data source, misleads the analysis.[98]

To investigate the representations of Latinos in contemporary public discourse, these empirical considerations will be addressed with two distinct data-gathering procedures. The first is a diachronic method that gathers and analyzes a set of materials that has been determined to be representative of the period by some criteria. Paul Chilton exemplifies this method in an excellent study which applies Lakoff's theory to the constellation of metaphors that guided international relations during the forty-year-long Cold War.[99] Crucially, his data source is made up of the prominent policy papers generated by governmental analysts and great public speeches of policymakers that have been separately cited as the key documents in the formulation of international relations during that period.

The use of such texts places one crucial demand on the researcher: the criterion for representativeness must be warranted. In the case of a study of the international relations between governments, the texts should be recognized as centrally influential in the shaping of policy. For this reason, Chilton includes George Kennan's famous "Long Telegraph" and President Harry Truman's 1947 speech to Congress on international relations, among many others. His analysis of the twentieth-century texts crucially led him back in time to other important documents. To justify his analysis of the implications of the Western European conceptualization of the nation-state, for example, Chilton draws on Thomas Hobbes's classic seventeenth-century work, *Leviathan,* to demonstrate the lasting influence of this seminal work on current productive metaphors for the United States, NATION AS BODY and NATION AS HOUSE. Chilton's analysis matches the high quality of his data selection. In later chapters, the continued use of these medieval metaphors in contemporary U.S. texts will be confirmed.

In Chapter 4, where competing public discourses on racism and affirmative action will be compared, selected samples of texts are also analyzed. To highlight the differences in the discourses on affirmative action, an assortment of texts is drawn from two decades, the Sixties and the Nineties, and from two opposing political viewpoints. This is a ready option in longitudinal studies, but as stated above, it may not be available in synchronic studies.

The second synchronic method uses a set of materials which were not individually selected by the researcher. Rather, an independently compiled set of materials is analyzed. In the bulk of this book, metaphor analyses will be done on all the articles that were published during a given period of time by one mass media source, the *Los Angeles Times,* on the key referenda affecting Latinos in the 1990s. Cognitive metaphor theory will be applied to a public data source that is massive but finite. Such a data source is much more impervious to the political preferences of the researcher. With these materials, a late-twentieth-century portrait of Latinos, as colored in terms of public discourse metaphors, can be painted.

## Section 6: Mass Media

In this book the texts of a major mainstream newspaper were chosen to be sampled because the single most influential source of the public's daily comprehension of the changing social climate is the mass media. The role played by the mass media in social transformation has been discussed for years. The position of earlier media scholars was that the news media have minimal consequences on what the public believes. While a full theory about the forces shaping public opinion remains to be developed, public opinion is no longer seen to be independent of mass media sway. Now the pendulum of considered opinion has swung to the other pole. While the mass media lack total autonomy to construct public opinion, their power is tremendous. Robert Entman offers a judicious evaluation: "The media's selection of data makes a significant contribution to the outcome of each person's thinking. . . . [T]he media do not control what people prefer, they influence public opinion by providing much of the information people think about and by shaping how they think about it."[100] Thus, a careful study of the texts produced by a mainstream mass source of news can provide insight into the portrait of Latinos being constructed in the public sphere.

The news media are undeniably powerful, as defined in terms of access. They have unique access to the public ear, and nearly full control over the form of the message that they disseminate. Van Dijk illustrates this power by comparing different groups' ability to express an opinion or to describe an event in the public arena.[101] There are individuals who have what he calls preferential access to the media, for example, the political leaders who are able to command media attention. These leaders are sought out by the media reporters for their opinions of the day's events and characterizations of pressing social issues. Their office provides them with ready access to the media. The media in turn regularly report on these officeholders to the public. Yet these very politicians often grouse that their message is misrepresented in these media presentations.

In contrast to those with preferential access, other persons have much less access to effect any change in public perceptions. Consider the citizen who writes a letter to the editor of a newspaper. It is entirely up to the discretion of the editor whether or not the letter is published, and what form (length, force of expression, and so forth) the letter will take. Then there are people who have no access to the public ear. The homeless, the incarcerated, and the children of this country are just three groups who are most often without a public voice,[102] and who are dependent on others to express their views and opinions to the public at large.

In comparison to people who have modest access to the public's attention, the media enjoy unlimited access. They are the designated reporters to the U.S. public of all subject matter, daily events, and social issues. They have an institutionalized right of narration to the public, access far more extensive than even the highest-ranking officeholder, with incomparable preferential access to the public. Thus mass media have tremendous power. Even the U.S. president must negotiate with the media for prime-time broadcasts.

On occasion each of the last three presidents has been denied free access to televise messages he wanted to during his presidency. In recent years, without doubt, media power is increasing. This institutional power has taken a particularly worrisome direction in the 1990s because of corporate concentration and conglomeration in the United States[103] and the increased globalization of media control.[104] Robert McChesney describes the increasing dangers of the mass media oligopoly, a market dominated by eight incredibly powerful corporations that have seized both control of classic horizontal market share and control of the "vertical" processes, from the production of media content to distribution of the multiple forms of media. McChesney provides a shocking synopsis of the growing power wielded by the corporate mass media oligopoly by inventorying the factors affecting media content, including the pursuit of profit, the immensity of the firms, declining levels of competition, increasing horizontal and vertical integration, growing influence of advertising dollars in all aspects of media, the personal interests of four media moguls who have control over their firms and the media cartel, and the lessening effect of the personal interests of media employees. He also decries the media giants' hypercommercialization of U.S. culture and social life with corporate values and logic, which "carpetbombs" everyone, in particular children and youth.[105]

The second element of power is controlling the shape of the message, which is enacted by the mass media in terms of manipulation of social consensus. Media power is constituted in the ability to characterize the events of the day and the social structure of society in a particular way. Because of institutional conventions (not requisites) governing the construction of mass media newstexts, U.S. news sources tend to exclude heterogeneous views, as McChesney notes:

> Professional journalism is arguably at its worst when the U.S. upper class—the wealthiest one or two percent of the population, the owners, executives and government officials—is in agreement on an issue. In such cases (for example, the innate right of the United States to invade another nation or the equation of private property and the pursuit of profit with democracy), media will tend to accept the elite position as revealed truth and never subject the notion to questioning. . . . Professional journalism is arguably at its best, then, when elites disagree on an issue—such as whether a specific U.S. invasion was tactically sound or not—or when the issue does not affect upper-class interests directly.[106]

Mass media rarely, if ever, offer truly oppositional characterizations of the same events. Herman and Chomsky argue that news media marginalize dissent and allow the government and dominant private interests to get their messages across to the public. Robert Entman does not dispute the power of the media product and has been quoted as saying that media discourses "reflect quite precisely the boundaries and contours of elites' public discourse." However, he qualifies Herman and Chomsky's view by characterizing the power of the producers of the media content as fragmented and not having full autonomy to control its content or political importance. Thus Entman sees these media as having much less capability to create public opinion. To advance the view of Herman and Chomsky, in a stinging marketplace irony, the corporate media cartel in the past decade has seized control of most so-called "alternative" newspapers.[107] The combination of control of the form and content of the daily message, with unmatched access, provides the media with a significant capacity to shape and reinforce an arguably singular way of looking at the day's events.

Media owners attempt to bend the characterization of the world that their employees shape to their advantage at the expense of other social groups, so reinforcing a particular view of the structure of U.S. society is conscious, to a degree. Reinforcing a singular view is also unconscious, particularly on the part of salaried newswriters rushing to make deadlines, inasmuch as they, too, are members of the society in which they practice their social position, and since for these writers the "natural" social order is accepted, as will be detailed below.

In opposition to the foregoing, from a Latin American perspective, Jesús Martín-Barbero argues that the alarmist rhetoric of mass media imperialist colonization of popular culture fails to explain the everyday, heterogeneous actions of the people on the ground. For Martín-Barbero, the transnationalization of culture does not lead to homogeneity, and popular culture is not controlled by corporate mass media cartels distributing hegemonic messages. Rather than mass media dominating popular culture, the people mediate among myriad contradictory media messages, resisting some, taking up a bit of some, and transforming the rest.[108] While I grant Martín-Barbero's view about the limits of mass media, his focus on the independence of popular culture expression may be beside the point. Furthermore, notwithstanding Robert Entman's important caveat about the limits of corporate media power to change a person's opinion, as Entman himself has said, no media scholars maintain the old view that the news media have little effect on what the public believes.

As the institutionally legitimated view of a social issue is repeated over time with minimal variation, the media portrayals become the accepted view. A cognitive science description of this consensus-building is that one metaphor becomes the dominant means by which the public and policy-makers comprehend the issue. When alternative metaphors are rarely used to understand a social issue, then a single dominant metaphor becomes naturalized, that is, it is taken to be the one way to think about the issue. In spite of the fact that all metaphors are contingent, and none is wholly accurate, in the public's view, only one comes to make sense, and no other will be admitted. The dominant way becomes the one and only, hence "natural," way to think about the issue. Throughout this naturalization process, the media's privileged "take" on the issue promotes and reinforces the consensus through its untrammeled and legitimated access to the public, and its control of the message. Thus a news medium is an appropriate source of textual materials to study the public discourse on Latino political issues in the 1990s. While television news has a growing advantage over print media to influence, not control, public opinion, the present analysis relies on the relative accessibility and ease of cataloguing of print media data as its source of public discourse material.

*Public Discourse*

Discourses are quite often referred to as ways of speaking about a topic from a certain point of view.[109] Thus one refers to a capitalist discourse on global warming, or border culture discourse on banda music. In the following chapters the discourses on immigrants and immigration, on affirmative action, and on public education will be evaluated. However, it will become clear in the course of this book that these separate discourses do not stand in isolation, but are consistent with and form part of a congruent, encompassing discourse. That is, related discursive practices are component parts of the U.S. social order. The terminology of discourse and social order invokes multiply embedded communities of people, although they are not usually spoken about in such concrete terms. But it is easy to refer to more encompassing discourses/orders, such as "the West," and smaller ones, such as that of the "illegal immigrants." The range of meanings that are involved in the term "discourse" has already been touched upon. There are two difficulties with the term "social order." One is that it is frequently used to refer exclusively to the top of the social hierarchy and its attendant prerogatives. Nevertheless, a total system of social organization is involved. Second, the notion is used to talk abstractly about social structure. In the present material case, however, a body of people is implicated. Since the representation of Latinos is the object of the present investigation, the widest circle of community that has a direct impact on them is the U.S. public. Thus the present work is designed to consider public discourse, namely, the discourse generally shared by a large portion of the U.S. public.

## *The* Los Angeles Times

To facilitate a discussion on empirically rigorous grounds about what constituted California's public discourse on Latinos during the 1990s, my research team catalogued the metaphoric representations promulgated by the *Los Angeles Times* during California's three statewide referenda with greatest reference to, and greatest impact on, the Latino community: Proposition 187, Proposition 209, and Proposition 227.

The *Los Angeles Times* was selected because it is the newspaper of greatest distribution in California. It is the local newspaper of California's most populous city and home to the nation's largest Latino population. The *Times* is a highly regarded newspaper that has taken relatively moderate positions in recent California politics. It should be noted that the *Times* maintained a professional journalistic standard as it reported on political events. In the content of its coverage, the reporters maintained a decidedly careful balance of professional detachment (as conventionally defined) and civic concern in the face of a set of referenda that polarized California politics.

Making a profit is the goal of the *Los Angeles Times*. Its product is basically a service, namely, to advertise the products and services of its business clients, and to inform its readers about the daily events of note. However, integral to the news is to present the events of the day in a particular way. As Roger Fowler describes it, this involves presenting the events in terms that are familiar and conceptually accessible to the reader.[110] In other words, to present an ideology.

In discursive practice terms, the presentation of news by any media organization is an ideological discourse. But print media institutional discourse is not presented as plainspoken expressions of power or naked designations of unjust social relations. Rather, to be successful, the ideological discourse is disguised, both to the reader and to the newswriters. The institutional processes which create the texts of a newspaper insist that the news be presented in terms of entertainment, rather than bureaucratic text. There are sound capitalistic reasons for this. The reader will not buy a newspaper if it reads like a brochure that comes with the monthly electric bill, which describes its arcane pricing structure. Such bureaucratic brochures are written to be ignored by utility consumers, and we most often oblige.

Consequently the shaping of the message is as important as selecting its content. According to Fowler, the key to understanding how this ideology is promulgated is to note that the ideology is presented in a manner as close as possible to personal discourse. The discursive style that becomes the norm of a successful newspaper finds expression in lively, stylistically diverse, and individually voiced articles. Fowler points out that there is a clear tendency to express the events of the day in terms of oral modes, rather than in abstract, bureaucratic, or intellectual modes. A major part of news media success, then, is to express the events of the day both in terms that are consistent with the ideological presuppositions of the news institution and in terms that are expressed in the personal voice of an individual newswriter. This is what Fowler calls the news reports' "disguise."

However, the disguise can be maintained day after day only because there is reciprocity between the discursive practices of newspaper writing and newspaper reading. The news reporter must have a personal yet newsroom-consistent composition to best achieve the objective of reaching a target audience. The reader, however, performs a complementary practice, unlike an adding machine, which calculates a list of numbers without understanding. The reader generally does not attend to the news with the critical style of *Dragnet*'s Joe Friday, saying: "Just the facts, Ma'am." Rather, the reader constructs meaning, actively "reading in" the ideology which shapes the newspaper's representations.[111] This discursive practice of newspaper reading has reached an optimal level when the reader feels comfortable about the text. This means that the newswriters must have the freedom to exercise a broad range of stylistic techniques to pique interest, entertain, and hold the reader's attention. Yet the newstext must have a certain stylistic familiarity—an achieved normalcy—to best impart the terms and definitions that signal the newspaper's ideological viewpoint.

This all means that the each newspaper develops what Stuart Hall calls its own "public idiom." As quoted by Fowler, Hall states that the modes and style of language employed by the particular newspaper will be "the newspaper's own version of the language of the public to whom it is principally addressed."[112] The ideology of the newspaper comes by way of this idiom, which is a particular version of the range of rhetoric that is comfortable, a set of recurring imagery that is expected and acceptable, and a shared stock of knowledge. It is ironic, then, that newspapers consider themselves the nation's public forum for political and social debate, since the actual range of debate rarely crosses over ideological thresholds to present truly oppositional views and opinions. Reciprocity of discursive practice dictates that the readership would become discomforted and put the paper down, and the newspaper would readjust the language of its message to recapture its readership.

Thus the *Los Angeles Times*, with solid reporting of the highest journalistic caliber, a strong sense of its readership, and a substantial investment in its national and international offices, actively works at being a newspaper of record. It has the fourth-largest circulation among U.S. newspapers (1999 figures), behind the *Wall Street Journal, USA Today,* and the *New York Times.* In comparison, the *San Francisco Chronicle* stands in eleventh place. During the period of study, the *Times* launched a national edition, which was designed "to increase circulation and provide more timely news for readers in Northern California, New York and Washington."[113] Thus it aspires to a national audience, and speaks to its readership with the discourse of the American public, which will be sampled in this analysis.

Students of mass media may consider it improper to generalize the findings from this one newspaper to all U.S. mass media. However, this is not primarily a study of U.S. mass media. The objective is to reveal the metaphoric portrait of Latinos in public discourse during the 1990s. Mass media are the single most influential source of public influence, public dispute, discussion, and dialogue, to wit, discourse. The text media outlet with greatest influence on the California public during this period was the *Times.* It is an empirical question whether other regional newspapers, and other news media, articulate the same kinds of metaphors. I would predict that the dominant representations in other media will be identical.

## Section 7: Methods

*Synchronic Study: Comprehensive Corpus Method*

The text expressions of metaphor will be investigated on a set of topics about U.S. Latinos, as published in blocks of articles appearing in the *Los Angeles Times* over a period of about ninety months, from 1992 to 1998. The first step is gathering the texts.[114] My team sought an independently created and comprehensive data set for public discourse in the texts of the *Los Angeles Times*. We used the *Times* texts on CD-ROM, which permitted computer-aided selection and extraction of the complete texts. In the commercial CD-ROM format, an index of the newspaper articles is included. This indexing allowed us to retrieve every published article on any topic during a given time frame, specifically during the Proposition 187, 209, and 227 campaign periods. Each and every article tagged in the independently created index was designated for study, forestalling criticism that the selection of materials was biased.

The articles were downloaded onto computer diskettes and printed out in full. These printouts of the *Times* articles became the primary material for study. Each instance of a nonfoundational[115] linguistic expression of a metaphor was isolated and inputted for analysis, copying from computer file and pasting into computer database with a minimum of typing, with particular attention to how Latinos, and attended topics concerning Latinos, were characterized.

A database table of rows and columns over 20 columns wide and approximately 4,500 rows long was compiled. Each row was devoted to detailed information on a single text expression of a metaphor, what we call a metaphor token. Journalistic, linguistic, and metaphor information was compiled for each token.[116] Each metaphor token was intersubjectively analyzed, which means that more than one person made free judgments about the source and target domains, as well as other interpretive classifications. A large amount of text associated with each token was provided so each reader/coder was able to interpret the characteristics of the token on the basis of ample context.

Pains were taken to develop a classification procedure that did not prejudice or predetermine the source and target semantic domains of each token. The goal was to conduct a text-directed metaphor analysis that could be replicated. The major instruction given to newstext readers was to read the complete newspaper texts for nonliteral expressions, and to label these tokens. These readers had been guided in basic metaphor theory and trained using unrelated examples of metaphors, so they could assign a mapping of the conceptual structure of a source domain onto a target domain.[117] When these readers assigned a source and target domain to *Los Angeles Times* tokens, they did so knowing that other readers would separately review the same texts for figurative expressions, and label/code these tokens. There was a great deal of variation in the individual interpretation of the tokens. Different readers of the same material brought together their findings and these ad hoc teams of readers worked to reach a consensus on the classification of the tokens. The lineup of reading/coding teams changed, to provide variety and forestall routine, as new data were gathered.

The variation of token labeling was pared down in a cycle of editing the database, beginning with the source domain. Alphabetic sorting placed all tokens with similar source domains together. A standard label was chosen when it became clear that it was warranted, so that with the next alphabetic sorting similar tokens would fall together. In the sort/edit cycles we were careful to clarify the source labels as we could read them, one token at a time in context, rather than forcing a particular conclusion. The cyclical procedure of sorting/editing was repeated six times, until all the tokens were arranged systematically. Through this procedure the research team became familiar with the database, and the major typological dimensions of the source conceptual domains became clear.

The same cyclic procedure was followed for the target domain column, as well as other interpretive classifications, in order to organize and come to understand the full conceptual dimensions of the metaphor database on the representation of Latinos in the *Los Angeles Times*. The cycle was repeated only four times for targets; there was less initial variety in the labels of semantic target domains since they were real-world referents.

These procedures were remarkably enlightening. As for the actual specimens of printed text, metaphors that appear in print in the *Times* are quite varied, but it became clear that prose metaphors in newstexts are relatively underdeveloped stylistic devices, especially if compared to fiction writing about similar political topics.[118] To put it another way, the lexical diversity of token metaphors is extensive, but most tokens of a target domain are drawn from a limited set of source domains. Since the pattern of ontological associations (classification of metaphors) is severely restricted, the representation of a political issue or concept in public discourse is for the most part limited and conventional. As a case in point, only a dozen metaphoric mappings exist for the United States, of which the two most prominent are NATION AS HOUSE and NATION AS BODY. In Chapter 7 the implications of this finding will be developed. Kindred expressions of a single metaphoric mapping are repeated regularly, as Fowler would predict, but it is quite clear that the use of metaphors is not limited to summarizing an article, or to showcasing a personal writing style. Instead, this discourse material is blended into the body of the articles. That is, while metaphors are at times consciously used

for stylistic purposes, these oratorical functions are eclipsed by their conceptualizing and signaling functions.

## Diachronic Study: Selected Materials Method

The 1994–1996 coverage in the *Los Angeles Times* of Proposition 209, in contrast with its coverage of Propositions 187 and 227, rarely addressed the
substantive concept at issue in the initiative, in this case, affirmative action.
This was surprising, since the so-called California Civil Rights Initiative, as
Proposition 209 was termed, was all about affirmative action. Nevertheless,
the *Times* coverage is local and decontextualized, in comparison to its coverage of Propositions 187 and 227. The *Times* does not discuss the origins of
affirmative action, the historical development of its programs, or the contention over concepts which underlie the formulation of affirmative action
and its implementation in terms of merit, fairness, or racism. The coverage
is limited, by and large, to day-to-day political events. The absence of news
report backgrounders may have been due in part to the distraction of the
concurrent presidential campaigns. Both the Democratic and Republican
campaign managers attempted to steer public debate away from the issue
of affirmative action. The major party candidates were unwilling to take a
strong stand on affirmative action during their national campaigns, for fear
of alienating undecided voters. After the fractious Proposition 187 campaign
in California, the 209 initiative was seen by both parties to be a racial wedge
issue to be avoided at all costs, and the news media source complied.

The absence of extended or in-depth discussion of the history and nature
of affirmative action in the *Times* led the research team away from the synchronic corpus of texts method as the principal source for public discourse,
as was applied in the study of the discourses on Proposition 187 and Proposition 227. In Chapter 4 the focus is on a diachronic study of political discourse
on race and affirmative action. The discourse on race of the 1960s, as articulated by highly visible spokespeople in the Civil Rights Movement, will be
compared to the political discourse of the mid-1990s, during the Proposition
209 campaign, as exemplified on the political right by twenty short politically conservative essays on affirmative action which appeared in a public
opinion journal in a special issue dedicated to the topic, as well as by a similar amount of text from a frequently cited book extolling affirmative action
and written for general readers.

The same database building and coding procedures used in the *Los Angeles
Times* corpus of text analysis were followed in the preparation of the text ma-

terials for Chapter 4, including intersubjective readings of the texts in teams, followed by cycles of sorting and editing before systematic analysis of the metaphor database.

## Section 8: Summary

A diverse set of constructivist theoretical models are being drawn upon to address discourse materials and discursive processes of public discourse on Latinos. Each contributes to the description and explanation of the portrayals of Latinos and Latino political issues in U.S. public discourse.

We begin with Lakoff's theory of metaphor, and its claim that human cognition is largely metaphorical, that is, thinking involving the wholesale imposition of the structural schema of some source semantic domain, such as MADNESS, onto another unrelated target domain, e.g., LOVE. At the turn of the last century, positivists would have reeled at this view of language, society, and human nature, but at the height of their power, Miguel de Unamuno summarily rejected their view:

> Language is nothing if not metaphor. Among you I recognize those who . . . seem to deprecate metaphor, much as the eunuch may speak ill of woman. . . . But I, who know that ideas stream from words more than the contrary, know that language, and thought as well, is metaphor. We will never succeed in thinking algebraically, and then, only when algebra is filled with metaphor.[119]

Contrary to positivist models, in cognitive models, metaphor is neither a marginal linguistic phenomenon, nor is it derived from corresponding literal propositions. Rather, metaphor is basic to human thinking, and ubiquitous in human discourse. Metaphoric processes are found across the entire range of human thinking, from foundational corporeal recognition of "up" versus "down," through various aspects of the comprehension of everyday actions and entities, to higher-level activities such as scientific modeling, social institutional functioning, and social policy execution. It makes sense, then, to focus on metaphoric representations in powerful practices of public discourse in the United States to comprehend the construction of Latinos and their political issues in American thought.

Second, in Foucault's theory of the social order, discourse practices enact and reinforce dominance relations, by which social position, relations, and identity are constructed. There is considerable compatibility of discursive formation theory, as it is operationalized by Fairclough, with the cognitive metaphor theory. These dissimilar theories, metaphor-centered cognitive studies and Foucault's theory of the practice of discourse, are both grounded in the philosophy of language which has generated the "linguistic turn" in twentieth-century social thought. Its doctrine, at base, is that meaning determines reference. The meaning of certain crucial words molds concepts and defines social relations. In turn, these social relations give form and direction to the function of social institutions, and the people within them who act to create their social positions, relations, and selves. While cognitive metaphor research focuses on isolating the governing type of discourse material, and explains metaphor's unique role in conceptualizing the social order, Foucault's model offers a more comprehensive explanation of the discourse processes by which the social order is established and maintained.

Finally, by way of Fowler's discussion, the selection of the source of public discourse has been justified. As the principal shared public source of daily reports and commentary on everyday public life, the news media possess considerable power to establish and maintain social structure. Reciprocal discourse processes, namely, newsprint writing and newspaper reading, are implicated as a major means to legitimize societal domination.

The methods employed in this study were based on applying principles of studying natural language expression to the analysis of the texts of the *Los Angeles Times,* cataloguing thousands of metaphors which govern public opinion on Latinos, as documented in the *Times* during the California initiatives. The most recent period of anti-Latino sentiment began in 1993, during the successful campaign to "send a message to Washington" and to rid the state of "illegal immigration" and so-called illegal aliens. Proposition 187 was the referendum, and it is the initiative to which we turn in Chapter 3.

# Analyses

## CHAPTER THREE

# Proposition 187
## Misrepresenting Immigrants and Immigration

The textbooks say the United States is a nation of immigrants. However, while schoolchildren are steeped in the pageantry of American history, they seldom learn to appreciate the depth of its reprehensible acts and persistent inequities. A case in point is the history of Mexican Americans. For most, it is news that in 1846, when President James Polk initiated the U.S.-Mexican War, between 75,000 and 100,000 Mexicans were already living in the Southwest,[1] including my father's family.

The virulent racism with which nineteenth-century white Americans elevated themselves above all other people also infected relations with Mexicans, leading to the view that the Southwest was rightfully granted to white America, and that its Mexican residents were a contemptible mongrel breed.[2] Today's Americans generally are not cognizant that the U.S.–Mexican War ended with the Treaty of Guadalupe Hidalgo, which guaranteed language, property, and citizenship rights to the Spanish-speaking residents of this territory.[3] Moreover, from its establishment in 1848 and on through the twentieth century, the new border between Mexico and the United States was an arbitrary and largely vain restraint on the historic and prehistoric free movement of people north and south.[4] Thus it is particularly painful to have witnessed the continuing mistreatment of Mexicans and Mexican Americans in the twentieth century.

In spite of its overwhelmingly immigrant origin and its self-satisfied adulation of the immigrants' contribution to its strength and wealth, the United States maintains a Janus-faced attitude of self-interest toward immigrants. When the country is in the growth part of the economic cycle, cheap labor is at a premium. During these times, U.S. commerce promotes the virtues of America and its "American Dream" of unbounded opportunity for the hardest worker, no matter who and from what circumstances. When native-born

Americans scorn essential labor, workers from other countries are recruited for the lowest-paid and least desirable work. The immigrants come in great numbers, do the work, dream the Dream, and honor their end of the bargain. For example, from 1880 to 1920, with a population much less than 100 million, the United States accepted 24 million immigrants.[5]

However, as the economic cycle wanes, Janus's second face is manifest toward immigrants and their children. Then the immigrant is regaled as a menace. Evidence for this attitude abounds in American history. For example, between 1921 and 1924 Congress set up a restrictive immigration quota system which disfavored immigrants from Eastern and Southern Europe as well as Asia and Latin America.[6] These attitudes have also turned punitive. Between 1929 and 1935 authorities mobilized the U.S. military to force the repatriation of 500,000 Mexican immigrants and their U.S.-born children,[7] including my mother.

A post–World War II economic upswing in California did not waver for forty-five years. During that time immigrants were recruited by business and industry to power an unparalleled period of economic growth. Middle-class families also employed immigrants to do the gardening, to clean their homes, and to tend their children. With immigrant labor, the middle class achieved a higher standard of living than they otherwise could afford. Today it is rare for middle-class women in Los Angeles to do their own nails, or for suburban homeowners to cut their own lawns on Saturday morning.

However, with the end of the Cold War in 1989, the expansion period of California's military-based economy also came to a close. Over 830,000 jobs were lost between 1990 and 1993, primarily in the defense sector. A ripple effect from the defense industry layoffs and cut-downs was felt throughout the economy. The economic recession led as well to reductions in state and local governmental incomes and created budgetary shortfalls.[8]

The demographic profile of California has also changed in the last decades, becoming decidedly less "Teutonic"[9] and more multiethnic. While there was a general increase of the proportion of foreign-born residents in the United States from 5 percent in 1970 to 8 percent in 1990, these figures (the highest since 1930) belie a skewed distribution of immigrant residence. Sikhs, Mexicans, and Armenians are not settling in Idaho. Seventy-five percent of foreign-born residents settle in seven states, with California at the top of the list. Nearly 25 percent of all documented immigrants settled in California during the decade of the 1980s. And overall, California's foreign-born population was about 22 percent of the population in the 1990s; in

Los Angeles County it was 33 percent. Los Angeles Unified School District officially listed more than seventy-five mother tongues spoken in its kindergartens. While a plethora of cultures is represented, 85 percent of documented immigration during the 1980s was from Asia and Latin America. Adding to an already large population of Mexican-origin citizens, the continued browning of California is inevitable. Latinos now make up over 30 percent of the population of the state. They are projected to become a majority by 2040.[10] In Los Angeles the tendency is more pronounced, since Latinos are projected to be the majority by 2007. For Californians brought up with the unspoken belief that American society means a preeminently Anglo-American culture, these demographic changes have been unnerving.

The first nativist reaction to this sense of a changing social order in the 1990s was Proposition 187. This initiative was overwhelmingly passed by the California electorate even though its provisions had been denounced throughout the campaign as unconstitutional. Indeed, it was enjoined by the courts within hours of its enactment. While the laws of the land already dictated sanctions against employers utilizing the labor of undocumented immigrant workers, and the federal government provided for a policing body, the Border Patrol, to apprehend and deport such immigrants, Proposition 187 was designed to supersede and radicalize federal law. It would have denied to undocumented immigrants a range of public benefits, including education and nonemergency health care. It would also have made school administrators, health care workers, social service personnel, police, and other state employees responsible for determining the residence status of any "apparently illegal alien" (to use the controversial phrasing of the referendum) among their clients and for notifying the Immigration and Naturalization Service of suspected undocumented immigrants for deportation.

This chapter presents the findings of an empirical analysis of the public discourse metaphors in California during the Proposition 187 period, as described in the previous chapter. Over one hundred *Los Angeles Times* articles were published on Proposition 187, as indexed by the commercial distributor of a CD-ROM version of the newspaper. All of these were included in this study. Two issues stood out for the voters and general public: immigration, namely, the demographic process; and immigrants themselves. Consequently, the public discourse on these semantic domains was examined in terms of metaphor use, and will be presented as follows.

In Section 1, the metaphors for IMMIGRATION are described. One dominant metaphor will be discussed more fully than, and separately from, other less prevalent metaphors. Its ontology will be specified, namely, the semantic notions that are imposed on the concept IMMIGRATION by means of the dominant semantic source domain. In Section 2, the context for these immigration metaphors will be presented. This pattern of metaphors, when used, invokes a narrative of the relationship of immigration to the nation. A rendition of the narrative will be presented.

The metaphorization of IMMIGRANT in public discourse is presented in Section 3, beginning with a discussion of the dominant metaphor, its ontology, and associated narrative, followed by Section 4, which lays out the patterning of other metaphors for immigrants in public discourse. In order to provide further support for the study, in Section 5 a formidable test is carried out to probe whether or not these metaphors are as demeaning and unique as the findings suggest. Section 6 provides a comparison of the present findings to other studies of the representations of Latinos during the Proposition 187 campaign, while Section 7 discusses the wider implications of these metaphors.

## Section 1: IMMIGRATION AS DANGEROUS WATERS

One of the two key notions debated during the campaigns for and against Proposition 187 was the demographic process of the movement of people, IMMIGRATION. As a concept at the heart of the political contest, this notion was constantly being referred to in the public discourse of the period, and was frequently metaphorized. This metaphorization reveals the worldview that is promulgated in public discourse. In this section the metaphors that construct and reinforce commonly held views of immigration will be displayed. Although there is overlap of the discourse on immigration and on immigrants, discussion of the people themselves will be undertaken in Section 3.

As will be noted in Table 3.1, there are dominant, secondary, and occasional metaphors. These are three informal groupings of semantic source domains found in the data, combining all instances of closely related semantic domains under a single heading. The dominant metaphor class is composed of scores of textual instances of metaphor with a similar semantic source domain that occur relatively frequently and appear in a great variety of forms. In the *Los Angeles Times* data sampled, the dominant metaphor comprises the greatest proportion of all instances of metaphors characterizing immi-

TABLE 3.1
IMMIGRATION Metaphors Published during the Proposition 187
Campaign

| SOURCE DOMAIN | TYPE | TOTALS | PERCENTAGES |
|---|---|---|---|
| DANGEROUS WATERS, e.g., *floods, tide* | dominant | 113 | 58.2 |
| WAR, e.g., *invasion, takeover* | secondary | 45 | 23.2 |
| ANIMAL, e.g., *curbing illegal immigration* | | 17 | 8.8 |
| BODY, e.g., *disease, burden* | | 6 | 3.1 |
| various metaphors, e.g., AIR, WEED, CRIMINAL, MACHINE, FIRE, etc. | occasional | 13 | 6.7 |
| | TOTAL | 194 | 100 |

SOURCE: 116 *Los Angeles Times* articles published June 1992–December 1994. The list accounts for
immigration metaphors, i.e., the demographic process. It excludes metaphors that target immigrants as
people.

gration. The demographic process of immigration to the United States is
conceptualized in terms of dangerous moving water. Before launching into
a full examination of the dominant public discourse metaphor for immigration, DANGEROUS WATERS, secondary metaphors and those which occur
on occasion in our Proposition 187 database will be presented.

*Secondary Metaphors*

For the moment, discussion of the dominant metaphor will be deferred. Instances of secondary source domains appear much less frequently, and with
less variety of expression, than the dominant metaphor used to characterize immigration. One such metaphor for immigrants is IMMIGRATION AS
INVASION. Still, these secondary metaphors appear with appreciable frequency. Over 20 percent of IMMIGRATION metaphors have a martial source
domain:

1. Some believe that Wilson, by filing a lawsuit against the federal government and arguing that illegal immigration is tantamount to a **foreign invasion,** has made a whipping boy of migrants. (September 27,
1994, A3)

2. "People are saying, 'I don't like this **Third World takeover,'**" said Guy Weddington McCreary, a North Hollywood Chamber of Commerce member favoring the initiative. "It is literally an **invasion** and very upsetting." (September 17, 1994, B3)

3. "**invasion**" of illegal immigrants is causing economic hardship and eroding lifestyles of U.S. citizens and authorized immigrants (October 30, 1994, A1)

4. Oft-voiced fears that California was under "**invasion**" spawned a loose network of community-based groups. (November 9, 1994, A1)

5. "I don't want us to look like that country. If we continue this **alien invasion,** we will be like Mexico." (October 11, 1996, A3)

6. "This is a **state of siege** in California," says an observer from Washington, immigration expert Demetrios Papademetriou of the Carnegie Endowment for International Peace. (September 6, 1993, A1)

The features structuring the semantic domain of INVASION are a subset of the domain of WAR. An invasion is an organized attack by armed forces with the objective of taking over a region or country. One paradigmatic invasion is the Japanese Empire's 1937 invasion of China. This invasion included the infamous "Rape of Nanking," the Chinese capital city, in which 300,000 civilians were raped, murdered, or butchered in one year. This was an offensive action to dominate a neighboring country. Another is the key counteroffensive of World War II, the 1948 D-Day invasion of France by the Allied forces under Eisenhower, which had as its objective the liberation of occupied France. These organized actions are rightly considered acts of war. The war metaphor used during the Proposition 187 campaign stresses a violent aggression against America. This metaphor patently ignores the nation's entire immigration experience, which always has been the search for employment and freedom by unarmed and peaceful individuals. The objective of immigrants is not conquest and spoils, but rather industry and enterprise, and the hope of a better life for their children. IMMIGRATION AS INVASION was the least obscure anti-immigrant metaphor in general use, because of its bold disregard of the evidence. Consequently, it was frequently printed in scare quotes and was explicitly rejected at least once in the *Los Angeles Times* database by the advocates for immigrants:

7. "That is not an **armed invasion** coming across." (September 19, 1993, A1)

These metaphors demonstrate the level of anger focused on immigrants by a significant segment of the citizenry; however, much can be made of these blatant anti-immigrant metaphors. Without further discussion we will concentrate on less overt, all the more insidious, metaphors.

Other secondary metaphors in general use indicate other metaphorically structured worldviews or commonplace understandings of immigration, including IMMIGRATION AS DISEASE or AS BURDEN:

8. The report—which . . . linked illegal immigration to a **host of society's ills**—has been branded by Latino and Asian leaders as insensitive and one-sided. (June 29, 1993, B1)[11]

9. Not stopping or controlling the flow of illegal immigrants because it isn't a magical solution to all of our societal **ills** is not a valid reason for allowing it to continue unchecked. (June 17, 1994, B6)

As is the case with all metaphors, some of the presuppositions of this metaphor have been explicitly drawn out and others remain available for reference.[12] For example, the societal affliction, within the medical model, can be made well with societal remedies.

10. Hernandez also suggested that Umberg's motivation isn't so much to **cure** illegal immigration as it is to make a name for himself. (August 31, 1993, B1)

This metaphor was also contested by the advocates for immigrants during the Proposition 187 campaign:

11. If illegal immigration was a **disease,** Prop. 187 was the **wrong medicine.** (October 26, 1994, A3)

## Occasional Metaphors

Occasional metaphors are expressed only once or a few times. They do not seem to be associated with other more commonly used semantic source domains. All the occasional metaphors in the *Los Angeles Times* database are single or rare instances of a source domain.

12. The membership of the Sierra Club is in the midst of an emotional debate about whether to take a public stand on the hot button topic of the day. "It's not as simple as **clean air,** or like pollution, where less is better," said Executive Director Carl Pope. (September 6, 1993, A1)

13. Another confirmation that immigration from Latin America **powered the engine of change** is that 36 percent of North Hollywood households now speak Spanish, up from 19 percent only 10 years earlier. (June 14, 1992, B3)

14. And more than half the respondents said legal immigration, too, should be **pared back.** (September 19, 1993, A1)

15. Most who choose to "ride the snake," however, are **drawn by the same sirens of economic opportunity** that attracted their Cantonese compatriots to California's "Gold Mountain" more than a century ago. (June 13, 1993, Magazine p. 12)

16. "[the task of the] Border Patrol is so great that the addition of even those officers puts them in the position of trying to **fight a forest fire with a squirt gun**," [Governor Pete] Wilson said. (August 12, 1993, A1)

Some of these metaphors may be more difficult to grasp than others. In excerpt 12 the objective of Carl Pope is to move people's views away from a simplistic view of immigration, whereas in excerpt 13 immigration is the fuel for the engine of change.

### Dominant Metaphor

While 7 percent of all metaphors are individual characterizations which resist consolidation into a single semantic domain, the majority of textual instances of metaphors on immigration are based in only one semantic domain. The major metaphor for the process of the movement of substantial numbers of human beings to the United States is characterized as IMMIGRATION AS DANGEROUS WATERS. Perhaps it should be restated that to characterize the movement of people as moving water might seem quite natural, but such a formulation of movement of people is not the only possible image that can be employed, as can be noted among the secondary and occasional metaphors. Moreover, strongly negative connotations associated with immigration in particular had decidedly negative implications for the target population. A few instances are listed below:

17. **awash under a brown tide** (October 2, 1994, A3)

18. Like **waves on a beach,** these **human flows** are literally remaking the face of America. (October 14, 1993, A1)

19. **a sea of brown faces** marching through Downtown would only antagonize many voters (October 17, 1994, A1)

20. In April, Gov. Pete Wilson sued the federal government to recover

costs associated with illegal immigrants, claiming that they are sapping the state budget, taking jobs from legal residents and **swamping** hospital emergency rooms. (June 12, 1994, A3)

21. **the human surge** (July 5, 1992, A3)

22. **the inexorable flow** (September 22, 1993, A1)

The dangerous waters of immigration come in many forms, *rough seas, treacherous tides, surges.*[13] The DANGEROUS WATERS metaphors do not refer to any aspect of the humanity of the immigrants, except to allude to ethnicity and race. In contrast to such nonhuman metaphors for immigrants, U.S. society is often referred to in human terms. This provides an ironic contrast when these metaphors appear in tandem, as in excerpt 18, which likens the United States to a person who is defaced by an ocean of immigrants.

Within IMMIGRATION AS DANGEROUS WATERS there are clear subcategories. The first is volume, which emphasizes the relative numbers of immigrants. Individuals are lost in the mass sense of these volume terms. The negative connotation is highlighted in the excerpts that contain strong adjectives such as *relentless* and *overwhelming.*

23. the foreigners who have **flooded** into the country (November 10, 1992, World Report p. 1, col. 2)

24. "I thought that it was a waste of time, frankly," [California Governor] Wilson said of [U.S. Senator Robert] Byrd's line of questioning. "What we ought to be doing is focusing on the fact that federal failure continues to provide this **massive flow of illegal immigrants** into my state and the other states." (July 23, 1994, A3)

25. **the relentless flow of immigrants** (May 30, 1993, A5)

26. **an overwhelming flood** of asylum-seekers have put the country in an angry funk (October 1, 1992, A1)

Note that immigration waters are seen to be dangerous, as when coupling an exacerbating adjective to a neutral noun, as with *inexorable flow.* The second subcategory of DANGEROUS WATERS is movement, which emphasizes the direction of waters, primarily northward as from Mexico to the United States. With regard to the destination of the migration, the nation is conceived as a basin or some kind of container and the migration taken to be an inward-flowing stream, in terms such as *influx.*

27. Residents of the San Fernando Valley are increasingly outraged about illegal immigration—if not immigration generally—in the face of eco-

nomic hard times, growing congestion, widespread crime and a **dramatic influx of Latinos.** (August 1, 1993, A1)

28. **the tide and flow of illegal immigration** (October 26, 1994, A27)

29. Glenn Spencer . . . says his interest in the subject was sparked about two years ago when he began noticing that an **influx of minorities had flooded the city.** He compiled research and launched a newsletter that he circulated among his neighbors. Ultimately, he formed Valley Citizens Together, but the group changed its name after residents from other parts of Los Angeles wanted to get involved. . . . When asked what motivates him, Spencer points to the photos of his two blond, blue-eyed grandchildren on the mantel in his orderly living room. "What I'd like to achieve is a little better world for my grandchildren," he said. "I don't want my grandchildren to live in chaos. Isn't that enough?" (November 15, 1994, A1)[14]

30. **the flood of legal and illegal immigrants streaming** into the country (September 7, 1993, A3)

The terms used to characterize the immigration do not describe beneficial and enriching flows, but *dramatic influxes* and *floods* that endanger the country. The third subcategory is the control of dangerous waters. Here the intent to reduce the immigration of undocumented workers pursues a correspondence with the dangerous waters metaphor by describing means by which the waters can be held back, or *stemmed,* which means "to make headway against an adverse tide."

31. an attempt to **stem illegal immigration** (December 22, 1994, B1)

32. the opportunistic criminal element that exploits our **porous borders** (November 27, 1992, A3)

33. On the other hand, [Clinton] warned, if the government is unable to "show some more discipline" in its control of illegal immigration, "I'm afraid the genie out of the bottle will be passion to **shut off legal immigration.**" (August 13, 1993, A1)

34. [The] Executive Director of the Federation for American Immigration Reform . . . said Clinton's approach is akin to "**trying to dam the Mississippi with toothpicks.**" (September 7, 1993, A1)

*Ontology of IMMIGRATION AS DANGEROUS WATERS*

The metaphor labeled IMMIGRATION AS DANGEROUS WATERS is a tightly structured semantic relationship. It is a coupling and mapping of the semantic ontology of DANGEROUS WATERS onto the domain of IMMIGRATION. It establishes semantic associations between the two meaning domains, taking the well-developed framework of everyday knowledge of floods and tides and imposing it on an entirely human activity. In schematic form, the mapping, to wit the ontology of immigration to the United States as dangerous waters, is a four-point relationship as follows:

- *Immigration corresponds to moving waters.*
- *America is a landmass or other entity such as a house that is subject to flooding.*
- *Greater immigration corresponds to an increased threat to America.*
- *America's vulnerability to flooding corresponds to its susceptibility to change.*

Some of the pertinent everyday understandings of this source metaphor, moving water, will be explicitly elaborated in order to present the elements of the source domain that are reinforced with each repetition of the metaphor. These semantic associations obscure or pass over some aspects of the target domain as they highlight others. In the absence of alternative metaphoric imagery, such highlighted features of the source domain, DANGEROUS WATERS, are taken as natural features of the target domain, IMMIGRATION.

Moving water is a fluid. Above all other characteristics, fluids are normally understood and measured in terms of volume and mass, not units. They are most often named with mass nouns, such as *water, milk,* or *beer.*[15] Greater amounts of a fluid are registered in terms of volume, not larger numbers of individuals. The everyday use of such noncount words reflects a motile energy. Water moves, and when placed under pressure cannot be compressed, but forces its way or is channeled in some direction. This dynamism implies kinetic and hydraulic power, and control of the movement of water also requires power. There are naturally occurring masses of water, geophysical bodies such as streams, rivers, ponds, lakes, and oceans, as well as formations created by humans such as channels and reservoirs. With most naturally occurring and all human-made formations, human power and control are involved. The control of water varies from total mastery, such as when people shut off a kitchen faucet, to partial control, as in a hydroelectric dam. Greater volume and movement of water imply greater need for safeguards and controls, and more powerful human agency to control the water (which of course is not a human force). Insufficient human control of the kinetic energy pent up in volumes of water can lead to flooding and other ravages.

The main effect of invoking the DANGEROUS WATERS semantic domain to characterize the IMMIGRATION domain is to transform aggregates of individuals into an undifferentiated mass quantity. Immigrants are not merely described in terms of a mass noun; they are transfigured. The demographic process, immigration, is also vested with potential kinetic energy that is released in its movement, just as when water is commonly discussed. This misleading association is established by the metaphor. Further, salient features of the human immigration process are omitted with this metaphor. At its most simplistic yet still acceptable association, the potency of workers is in their labor, which is just one of a number of aspects of immigration entirely passed over by the IMMIGRATION AS DANGEROUS WATERS metaphor.

For investigators working within cognitive metaphor theory, metaphors have an "inherent logic."[16] In the case of IMMIGRATION AS DANGEROUS WATERS, three weighty presuppositions will be pointed out. These associations are inherited from WATER, the semantic source domain, but are entirely inappropriate characterizations of the demographic process of immigration. Since people conventionally talk about immigration using this metaphor, the presuppositions are often taken as given and overlooked. Since the power of metaphor increases with repetition of such implicit, but unnatural, associations, it is important to point them out. First, by way of the IMMIGRATION AS DANGEROUS WATERS metaphor, aggregates of human beings are reduced to or remade into an undifferentiated quantity that is not human. Second, as this mass moves from one contained space to another, some sort of kinetic energy is released. The contained space referred to is California, the United States, Los Angeles, or other polities. Recall that political entities are not inherently a contained finite space. Third, such movements are inherently powerful, and if not controlled, they are dangerous.

In excerpts 17–34, provided above, the vocabulary of dynamic bodies of water and their movement includes: *tide, sea, flood, influx, flow, waves, drowning, dams, porous, stem,* and *shut off,* to which we can add multiple instances of *swell/ing, absorb, funnel, surge/ing, pour/ing, stream/ing, swamp, pool,* and *safety valve,* among other water terms from the *Los Angeles Times* database.

## Implications of the Metaphor

The implications of this metaphor are extensive. Treating immigration as dangerous waters conceals the individuality of the immigrants' lives and their humanity. In their place a frightening scenario of uncontrolled movements of water can be played out with *devastating floods* and *inundating surges* of brown faces.

The impending flood is taken to be washing away something basic to America. What the anti-immigration advocates initially claimed is that immigrants were an economic threat to the United States and California. However, no presuppositions or entailments built into the DANGEROUS WATERS metaphor imply economics. Consequently the impact of the metaphor does not center on commonsense understandings of the U.S. economy. The threat constructed by DANGEROUS WATERS is cultural.

To make this point it may be useful to compare the implied associations of the frequently invoked *flood* metaphor to other metaphors that have unmistakable economic implications. Compare a metaphor that was often found in the database, *immigration as a burden*. Such metaphors clearly refer to the economic state as human body. If the threat felt by the public was principally a matter of economics, as is often taken to be the case by pundits, one would expect that the dominant metaphor in the public discourse on immigration would reinforce a fiscal message. Yet nearly 60 percent of the metaphors in the public discourse on immigration were DANGEROUS WATERS, while less than 5 percent were BURDEN metaphors. By this measure, although the 1990–1993 recession was the catalyst that initiated the xenophobic animus of the decade, the public discourse metaphors of the time did not have a fiscal focus.

Again, immigrants supply the cheap labor to maintain personal living standards that were higher than otherwise attainable for the average Californian, while at the same time sustaining labor-intensive industries, such as garment manufacturing and certain agribusiness concerns, in an increasingly postindustrial state economy. Moreover, there were counterindications to Governor Wilson's warnings. He repeatedly stated during his reelection campaign that California faced economic disaster, based primarily on $3 billion in purported costs incurred yearly by the state due to immigration. As mentioned in the opening chapter, Wilson's claims proved grossly overstated. Five years later, Wilson supervised the largest budgetary surplus in California history, over $4.4 billion.[17] Neither the deficit nor the surplus was due in large part to immigrant labor.

Instead of budgetary issues, the principal signal that DANGEROUS WATERS expresses is cultural alarm. The fear is that the *rising brown tide* will wash away Anglo-American cultural dominance. The panic expressed in DANGEROUS WATERS metaphors reflecting the perceived threat to Anglo-American hegemony is also articulated by the overtly anti-immigrant IMMIGRATION AS INVASION metaphor. Together, DANGEROUS WATERS and INVASION account for over 80 percent of all metaphors expressed in public discourse on immigration. Hence the relative absence of anomaly in the ready references to the American "complexion," as in excerpt 18, *these human flows are remaking the face of America,* and to the Californian economic body in excerpt 35, below:

> 35. Councilwoman Joyce C. Nicholson said illegal immigration is a serious problem and "the state of California is **drowning** in it." (September 17, 1994, B2)

In this excerpt, while the explicit complaint is economic, the metaphor invokes the state as a person drowning in a body of water representing immigration. During the anti-immigrant period, it was considered above-board to critique immigration on economic terms. However, the most frequent metaphors appearing in public discourse did not refer to fiscal arguments. As seen in this excerpt, there is more implied than a metaphorical reference to state finances. Thus in this excerpt the Los Angeles councilwoman openly called for economic relief, while metaphorically warning her constituency about the cultural threat that immigration seemingly posed. It was common to talk explicitly about the economy, all the while invoking the ostensible danger to Anglo-American cultural hegemony by the use of the DANGEROUS WATERS metaphor.[18]

Since only a trickle of water can be enough to signal an impending flood, warnings about *rising brown tides* are apt metaphors to inspire fear. All other considerations aside, the hardworking, family-oriented immigrant who believes in the American Dream was concealed with the DANGEROUS WATERS metaphor. This allowed California voters to remain comfortable in their daily interactions with the individual immigrant worker, part of an important workforce in the economy, while feeling justified in supporting the referendum and voting to end the only-apparent menace to the social order.

*Narrative of* IMMIGRATION AS DANGEROUS WATERS

A narrative of the dominant metaphor can also be constructed in which its principal presuppositions and social context are made explicit.[19] This metaphor narrative of immigration to the United States is based on the preceding ontological mapping, which, in cognitive semantic terms, established associations between the semantic domains of DANGEROUS WATERS and IMMIGRATION, as well as with the NATION AS HOUSE metaphor we will discuss presently.

> *A flood of immigrants is flowing into the land or house of America. In controlled quantities, America can either channel and absorb the influx unchanged. Because of the enormous volume of these floodwaters, America will be inundated with a sea of people unlike Anglo-Americans. Anglo-America will be engulfed and dispossessed.*

The narrative of immigration to the United States is invoked, and its ideological content reinforced, with each repetition of the metaphor. This constitutes the pattern of social inference on—that is to say, the prevalent way to think about—immigration.

## NATION AS HOUSE

Metaphors do not make sense in isolation. This is the case for poetic metaphor.[20] This is also the case with conventional metaphors that give structure to and reinforce the generally held worldview of U.S. society. These immigration metaphors are comprehensible, as are all metaphors, because they are woven layer upon layer in webs of semantic associations, starting with foundational metaphors that give structure to higher-level ones.[21] This web of associations and presuppositions constitutes the basis for a semantically congruent understanding of the world.

Truly original metaphors, such as IMMIGRATION AS TURTLE FOOD or AS RAINFOREST, fail to make sense because few if any conventional semantic associations can be pressed into service to edify the target domain, IMMIGRATION. Moreover, since these novel metaphors are not woven into the total web of customary metaphoric associations, the link between the source and target semantic domains seems abnormal. The technical semantic term is *anomalous*. Its etymological meaning, "abnormal," highlights the contingent (non-natural) and conventionalized (learned and reinforced to the point of being naturalized) character of everyday semantic mappings.

Thus the IMMIGRATION AS DANGEROUS WATERS, AS INVASION, and AS BAD WEATHER metaphors, in order to be comprehensible in public discourse on immigration, must be associated with some compatible metaphor for the nation. We turn now to one of these metaphors, NATION AS HOUSE, one of the two most productive metaphors for the United States, in order to demonstrate its arbitrary and contingent, non-natural associations. NATION AS HOUSE is also used to refer to other political entities, such as the state of California. It is invoked in many of the preceding excerpts that have been provided. A few more of these include:

36. With recent immigration reforms proposed by President Clinton, the governor and other political leaders, the issue has moved to the **nation's front burner** and it looms as an explosive topic for debate in the 1994 elections. (August 22, 1993, A1)

37. The fantasy of Proposition 187 supporters seems to be that once California is **cleansed** of its illegal menace, welfare recipients can be coerced into the fields. (October 2, 1994, A3)

38. "I understand the principles that our country was **built on,** but **our house is pretty raggedy** and we need to take care of our own first." (August 20, 1993, A1)

A full characterization of the semantic topology of the NATION AS HOUSE metaphor will be provided in Chapter 7. In brief, the NATION AS HOUSE metaphor was used or invoked with regularity in the Proposition 187 campaign with respect to the threats posed by IMMIGRATION AS DANGEROUS WATERS. Many linguistic expressions characterize immigrants in terms of chaos, destruction, and other perils to the NATION AS HOUSE.

39. "That's like saying, 'I've got this **great house, but it's on fire, it's built on a fault and the bank is moving in to repossess it.'"** (June 16, 1993, A1)

40. a growing body of evidence that Canada, long a **haven** for the world's oppressed, is banking its lamp unto the nations. (June 18, 1992, A1)

41. When U.S. Atty. Gen. Janet Reno toured Nogales this month to announce a 30 percent increase of Border Patrol forces in Arizona—she described the state as the "**side door**" to California. (January 30, 1995, A1)

42. "[Wilson] **cut a hole in the fence** to allow millions of illegal immi-

grants in, and now he wants **to patch that hole** because that's what the polls tell him to do." (September 16, 1994, A1)

43. "What are you going to do to **close our borders tight** to illegal aliens and drug-runners?" (June 10, 1993, J1)

44. **"Put up a Berlin Wall!"** cried Vines, an African-American who denies that racism has anything to do with his get-tough stand. He says that any fool can see it: Immigration is bringing this country down. (August 30, 1993, A1)

45. "Lots of folks say we have to **shut the door** now. Others disagree pretty strongly. . . . And so maybe we shouldn't be so quick to **shut the door.**" (October 3, 1993, E1)

The frequency and diversity of (metaphoric) threats to the NATION AS HOUSE, as indicated in Table 3.1, demonstrate that this immigration metaphor was customarily used to impugn the motivation and character of immigrants to the United States.

As will be fully discussed in Chapter 7, the metaphor NATION AS HOUSE came into prominent use in the late fifteenth century and was apt to characterize the emerging European nationhood at a time when the majority of the population did not travel and long-distance communication was dependent on animal transportation. The use of a fixed dwelling place as a metaphoric source for the American political entity is increasingly challenged by the early-twenty-first-century system of rapid global transportation, instant worldwide televisual communication, broadening cross-national regional integration, and an increasingly globalized economy.

However, the inadequacy of NATION AS HOUSE as a metaphor for the United States did not distract from or diminish the impact of the rampant use of the IMMIGRATION AS DANGEROUS WATERS metaphor during the Proposition 187 period. DANGEROUS WATERS divests immigrant workers and their families of their humanity, to become at best a natural resource to be controlled and exploited, and at worst to be feared for the potential damage that *floods* and *rising seas* of brown faces can visit on the nation. Geological metaphors invoke certain unwarranted associations about movements of human beings. In the context of a political campaign, the dehumanizing presupposition of the metaphor was fully exploited, transfiguring people into fear-inspiring floods and dangerous tides.

## Section 2: IMMIGRANT AS ANIMAL

We turn now from metaphors about demographics to the metaphors about the immigrants themselves. An empirical study of metaphor use in the public discourse on immigrants will furnish a principled analysis of how immigrants, as a group, were conceptualized in the United States of the 1990s. In the public discourse presented in the *Los Angeles Times,* immigrants were characterized with decided aversion. This antipathy was articulated metaphorically in several different ways, as illustrated below:

46. For some, the reaction of Valley residents is a natural outgrowth of **onerous burdens**—including budget-busting social service, education and criminal-justice costs—**thrust upon** Southern California by the nation's porous immigration laws. (August 1, 1993, A1)

47. An Orange County Grand Jury called for a nationwide, three-year moratorium on all immigration to the United States in an attempt to ease the **drain** on government programs. (June 17, 1993, B1)

48. The problem [of immigrant clients] is significant, because it has **placed added strain** on the state's public hospitals and has cost programs such as Medi-Cal many millions of dollars. (September 1, 1993, A1)

49. "We now have a **runaway situation** of undocumented aliens coming into this country. We have to stop it. . . ." (June 10, 1993, J1)

As mentioned above, one often-commented-upon aspect of the political debate centered on the fiscal costs associated with an apparent increase of immigrants, particularly undocumented immigrants, in Southern California. The cause of anger and outrage, Proposition 187 supporters repeatedly claimed, was the economic expense incurred by American society due to undocumented immigrants. Excessive fiscal costs with minimal returns were cited by California's governor as an abuse borne by the California taxpayer. When the governor's claims were countered with alternative economic analyses, however, the public debate did not focus on the comparative validity of the contending reports.[22] Had the public discussion emphasized economic analysis, then one could argue that economics was the basis for the outrage. In terms of metaphors, there was some focusing of the political debate over immigration costs, as expressed in excerpts 46–48. But as discussed above, in terms of the metaphoric record, California's economic condition was a lesser consideration. The principal characterization of immigrants in public discourse, as a group of people or as individuals, does not primarily

TABLE 3.2
IMMIGRANT Metaphors Published during the Proposition 187 Campaign

| SOURCE DOMAIN | TYPE | TOTALS | PERCENTAGES |
|---|---|---|---|
| ANIMAL, e.g., *hunted* | dominant | 70 | 31.8 |
| WAR, e.g., *invader, soldier* | secondary | 43 | 19.5 |
| WATER, e.g., *wave, tsunami* | | 38 | 17.3 |
| DISREPUTABLE PERSON, e.g., *marauder, felon* | | 15 | 6.8 |
| BODY, e.g., *burden, parasite* | | 12 | 5.5 |
| COMMODITY, e.g., *resource, traffic* | | 10 | 4.5 |
| ALIEN, e.g., *illegal alien* | | 9 | 4.1 |
| OBJECT, e.g., *tonk, menace* | | 7 | 3.2 |
| WEED | | 5 | 2.3 |
| BIBLICAL, e.g., *angel* | | 5 | 2.3 |
| e.g., *instrument, runner* | occasional | 6 | 2.7 |
| | TOTAL | 220 | 100 |

SOURCE: 107 *Los Angeles Times* articles published June 1992–December 1994. The table accounts for the metaphors for immigrants, as people, and excludes tropes metaphorizing immigration, the demographic process. NB: *Tonk* "immigrant," an INS slang term, mimics the sound of an aluminum baton striking.

focus on their net contribution or cost to California and the country (see Table 3.2).

## Dominant Metaphor

The dominant immigrant metaphor used in the *Los Angeles Times* was IMMI-GRANT AS ANIMAL. Immigrants were seen to be animals to be lured, pitted, or baited, whether the instance was intended to promote a pro-immigrant or an anti-immigrant point of view:

50. [Governor] Wilson said he believed public benefits are a **lure** to immigrants and his intent was to discourage illegal immigration by denying them access to health care, education and welfare programs. (August 22, 1993, A1)

51. "We're not going to play into those games of **pitting workers against each other.**" (November 3, 1994, D1)

52. Once the electorate's **appetite** has been **whet** with the **red meat** of

deportation as a viable policy option, the slope toward more aggres-sive ways of implementing that policy is likely to get slippery. (June 4, 1995, M2)

Immigrants were seen as animals that can be attacked, and hunted:

53. Beaten-down agents, given only enough resources to catch a third of their **quarry,** sense the objective in this campaign is something less than total victory. (July 5, 1992, A3)
54. the I-5 [freeway], where the agents now must **quit the chase** (July 5, 1992, A3)

Immigrants were seen as animals to be eaten, by U.S. industry, by the Im-migration and Naturalization Service or its Border Patrol agents, and by the anti-immigrant Proposition 187 supporters:

55. The truth is, employers **hungering** for really cheap labor **hunt out** the foreign workers. (June 9, 1992, D3)
56. "187 backers **devour the weak and helpless**" (September 6, 1994, B4)

This can also be noted in excerpt 52. At times immigrants were considered, as in the following case, rabbits:

57. The rapid increase comes at a time when many state and federal offi-cials are calling for beefed-up border patrols to **ferret out** illegal immi-grants. (November 30, 1993, A1)

As it happens, ferrets prey on rabbits and other small animals. More often, immigrants were characterized as pack animals:

58. the specter . . . has **spurred** an exodus (August 31, 1992, A1)
59. Those who want to sharply **curb** illegal immigration include conser-vatives, liberals and most unions. [*curb* 'a mouthpiece used to control animals'] (June 9, 1992, D3)

The connotations of IMMIGRANT AS ANIMAL should be abundantly clear. In Western European culture a purported natural hierarchy has been articu-lated since the time of Thomas Aquinas to justify social inequity. In its full extension, it subordinates other living creatures to human beings, and ranks the inherent quality of humans from base to noble. In its elaborated form, it has been called the "Great Chain of Being."[23] Lakoff and Turner provided an extended discussion of the pervasiveness of the Great Chain of Being meta-phor in Western European thinking.[24] This "moral ordering"[25] has justified the social inequality in Europe for two millennia and deprecated people of color in the United States for centuries. Stephen Jay Gould quotes Gunnar Myrdal on Americans' complacent use of biological determinism to main-tain social advantage over people of color:

> "Under their long hegemony, there has been a tendency to assume bio-logical causation without question, and to accept social explanations only under the duress of a siege of irresistible evidence." . . . Or as Con-dorcet said more succinctly a long time ago: they "make nature herself an accomplice in the crime of political inequity."[26]

More recently Gould has stated that the notion of "progress" in evolution, human or otherwise, is incongruous. Gould does not equivocate:

> There is no progress in evolution. The fact of evolutionary change through time doesn't represent progress as we know it. Progress is not inevitable. Much of evolution is downward in terms of morpho-logical complexity, rather than upward. We're not marching toward some greater thing. The actual history of life is awfully damn curious in the light of our usual expectation that there's some predictable drive toward a generally increasing complexity in time. If that's so, life cer-tainly took its time about it: five-sixths of the history of life is the story of single-celled creatures only. I would like to propose that the modal complexity of life has never changed and it never will, that right from the beginning of life's history it has been what it is; and that our view of complexity is shaped by our warped decision to focus on only one small aspect of life's history.[27]

Progress has bankrupted its scientific credentials, according to Gould. In good faith, it cannot be used to hierarchize living things, much less to de-mean people via social determinism. Gould's repudiation will undoubtedly surprise many readers. As an evolutionary biologist, he represents a strong current of contemporary thinking about evolution. Still, this view flies in the face of the commonplace understanding of human evolution, in spite of the increasing number of popular accounts that dispute it.[28]

*Ontology of IMMIGRANT AS ANIMAL*

Again, a metaphor is a tightly structured conceptual correspondence map-ping the structure of the semantic source domain, ANIMAL, onto a very different target domain, IMMIGRANT. The formal ontological mapping of the metaphor labeled IMMIGRANT AS ANIMAL follows:

• *Immigrants correspond to citizens as animals correspond to humans.*

The correspondence allows speakers to use the same frame of reference to reason about immigrants that is commonly employed to reason about animals. In this manner speakers and listeners inadvertently apply to immigrants their knowledge base of what animals are. The power of such metaphoric mappings is robust and productive, since the mapping is conceptual and is not limited to a finite set of linguistic phrases. Many metaphoric mappings are more or less conventional and unchanging.[29] As a political metaphor which is debated and negotiated, this mapping is a less fixed part of our conceptual system.[30] However, as frequently and as exclusively as the mapping is used in daily discourse, the dominant ANIMAL metaphor persists as the major productive way to conceptualize immigrants. Its effects are profound.

It is not hard to document contemporary examples of white racism directed at Latinos premised on the tenets of biological evolutionary progress, particularly by people in positions of power. The remarks of a California senator will illustrate. While presiding over a 1993 meeting of the Special Committee on U.S./Mexico Border Issues, W. A. Craven disputed the right to public education of children of undocumented immigrants, even after these children provide proof of residency. On the official record he stated: "It seems rather strange that we go out of our way to take care of the rights of these individuals who are perhaps on the lower scale of our humanity." Offended, Latino professors and staff at California State University San Marcos wrote letters insisting on a retraction, or at least a clarification, of the senator's comments. None was forthcoming. Instead, the local media excoriated the Latino faculty, while ranking CSUSM administrators assumed their benefactor's patronymic by publicly defending the senator. That same year the administration building at CSUSM was fittingly named Craven Hall.[31]

The ontology of evolutionary progress presupposes an inherent preeminence of one species over another and a superiority of one group over others. The Darwinian imperative of survival of the fittest within the human species has long been viewed as self-evident. This stance recapitulated the social relations of the Great Chain of Being. In the nineteenth century a biological decree replaced the divine apology for injustice. Not surprisingly, many of the same prerogatives of the superior were maintained, such as institutional advantages in juridical, educational, financial, and political spheres. And the same vanities persisted, namely, the presumptions of greater strength, beauty, intelligence, sophistication, and benevolence. With the decline in the twentieth century of racism's biological justification, the immigrant's purported cultural deficits and an associated ideology of Anglo-American cultural superiority became the basis for continuing racism.[32] As a premise for bias, Anglo-American cultural nationalism permits prejudice against individuals who, by all human standards, have merit equal to the citizen. Only by the arbitrary ascription of birthplace, the immigrant is deemed less than the citizen.

When characterized as animals, immigrants are portrayed as less than human, which sets up unmistakable divisions of expectations. Actions that are natural for both humans and animals are lexically distinguished:

60. This woman said she was upset about something else: why the offspring of women who "come across the border and **drop their babies**" are granted American citizenship. (June 10, 1993, J1)

Thus in excerpt 60 the different verbs *give birth* and *drop* distinguish identical human and nonhuman actions. Note the terms found in the *Los Angeles Times* texts used to characterize the immigrant, such as *hungered over, preyed upon, hunted out, targeted, herded, devoured; a menace, animal, dog, rat, rabbit, coyote,* and, of course, *scapegoat.*

Further, other irrevocable divisions ensue. Civil rights and human rights only pertain to humans. The value of life is highest for humans. Slavery has been outlawed for humans but still is permitted for animals, although it is not called slavery. Note that animals are owned, and the same terminology is used for animals as was used for slaves. Animals are said to be wild by nature. At times animals can be domesticated, but due to the biological hierarchy based on progress, they can never be human. When animals are wild, which is to say, uncontrolled by humans, they may be appropriately feared by humans, and are justifiable targets for human hunters. Certain animals become valuable to humans only when domesticated, either as beasts of burden or as sources of food for humans.

The inherent logic of the IMMIGRANT AS ANIMAL metaphor thus includes a biological, or at least birthplace-based, hierarchy, on which purported inborn inferiority is based. On the biological hierarchy, an unequal value set is based, with higher forms being more valued and granted by fiat greater rights and privileges than lower orders of life. Superiors, again naturally, rule over their inferiors, as in the biblical edict in Genesis that human-kind has dominion over the animals and the rest of the Earth, and will rule over them. One critical presupposition of the dichotomy assigns moral, ethical, and judicial considerations to and for humans; these considerations are not invoked to constrain human actions over the less-than-human.

The discourse principle that governs commonly used patterns of inference is metaphor, as a part of the conceptual system shared in large part by speakers of the English language and encoded in part in the ways Americans use the English language. Metaphor permits a shared understanding of the semantic domain of immigrants in terms of the semantic domain of animals. Following Lakoff's formula, these patterns of inferences are presented in terms of the following narrative of the immigrant versus the citizen:[33]

> On the hierarchy of living things, immigrants are animals. Citizens, in contrast, are humans. This hierarchy of life subordinates immigrants to citizens. Human beings are vested with birthright privileges, such as "human rights" and "dignity." Animals have no such privileges and are not equal to humans in the estimation of social institutions. Animals can never become humans by legislation or fiat. Their inferiority is inherent. Humans have full control over animals, from ownership to use as a food source. Animals are either domesticated, that is to say, owned by humans, or are wild and consequently are outside of the dominion of human society, and can be hunted.

The Los Angeles Times documents many statements that demonstrate that immigrants were aware of the widespread racist attitude and behavior that they encounter in the United States. Two will be repeated. In the first excerpt, a Guatemalan mother of three expressed shock that state and federal legislators, one of whom will be quoted below, denied assistance to undocumented immigrants following a major California earthquake:

> 61. Illegal and legal immigrants "are both human beings . . . regardless of what papers they carry. . . . We all felt the earthquake the same," added Dora Ramirez, a tent city resident who said she is undocumented. (February 2, 1994, A14)

The second is the description of treatment that a Los Angeles soccer fan said police officers meted out at a Rose Bowl game, including beating him, dragging him down stairs, uttering racist slurs, and knocking him out:

62. "Like an **animal** was the way I was treated," Aguilar said. "It was racist." (May 3, 1996, B5)

The public discourse about immigrants, then, is not an incidental correlation of words, but a lived reality for immigrants and Latinos in this society. Still, for many the metaphor may be a sobering finding. Its implications will be discussed in a later section of this chapter. In the following section the other metaphoric mappings will be described, although not in the detail of the ANIMAL metaphor. This will be followed by a section in which a counterargument to the force of this major finding is tested. A set of alternative framings of the public discourse on Proposition 187 will be considered in the penultimate section of the chapter. After these considerations, commentary on the implications can be made.

## Section 3: Secondary Metaphors

The metaphor labeled IMMIGRANT AS ANIMAL is not the only mapping used in the *Los Angeles Times.* Below are a few nonanimal metaphors for immigrants. A widely varied mapping, which is tentatively labeled IMMI-GRANTS AS DISREPUTABLE PEOPLE, includes all classes of people who do not merit respect:

63. "I recently had some tourists say that the problem with today's immigrants is that they're so **bizarre** and unpredictable," says O'Donnell. (October 3, 1993, E1)
64. A middle-aged woman tells of the "**marauders**" who take over the streets at night. (September 6, 1993, A1)

Another metaphor that is used is IMMIGRANT AS WEED:

65. take children [of immigrants] and their dream hostage in a crude scheme to **uproot** their parents (September 27, 1994, B7)
66. And while 33 percent said they believed **the new crop** of immigrants have inferior job skills and education than did their predecessors (September 19, 1993, A1)
67. **spring up** among us a generation of ignorant and troubled children who, lacking our common language and political and social ideals, will evolve into a huge, parallel underclass (August 1, 1993, A1)
68. "We see it as our responsibility to **weed out** illegal aliens." (May 16, 1992, A30)

In excerpt 66 the term *crop* associates immigrants not with productivity and wealth but with inferior attributes. These and other secondary mappings degrade the immigrant.

## Section 4: Testing IMMIGRANTS AS ANIMALS

It could be argued that animal metaphors are used to discuss all kinds of people in many situations in daily discourse: "You dog!," "I smell a rat," "Don't be so catty," and so forth. Accordingly, the argument of the skeptic would be that animal metaphors are not used to any greater degree to characterize immigrants than, for example, businesspeople or sports figures. Certainly, following the skeptic's line of thinking, businesspeople are often characterized in negative and unflattering terms. "It's a dog-eat-dog world" is a hackneyed portrayal of the business milieu. Likewise, sports figures are no longer revered as they might have been in a nostalgic past. They are now portrayed as selfish and at times brutish athletes. If the use of animal metaphors to characterize businesspeople and sports figures is similar to the patterns used to characterize immigrants, so the skeptic's argument goes, then the abnegation of immigrants with animal metaphors is not special and should not be overemphasized.[34]

In order to test the skeptic's hypothesis, all the metaphors that characterized sports figures in a month of the *Los Angeles Times* sports section were catalogued.[35] An equivalent amount of text was catalogued, in terms of word count, in the business section of the *Los Angeles Times* from the same period. The discourse about these kinds of people was selected since U.S. newspapers commonly have separate sections devoted to sports and business, which permits straightforward comparison. The skeptic would predict that the animal metaphor is commonly used for sports figures and businesspeople. Consequently the skeptic would state that the IMMIGRANT AS ANIMAL mapping is only part of a broader target domain, and does not single out immigrants.

The writing in sports is much more playful, with more creative use of description than the writing on immigration. Remarkably, no metaphors about sports figures in this sample have animal source domains:

69. "Heather is our defensive **catalyst** and Katie is our offensive **catalyst**." (November 30, 1995, C6)
70. Tyson gets his **tune-up** (November 25, 1995, C7)

71. Holmes has been a **godsend** (November 25, 1995, C10)

72. Franson is a **blue-collar big** man (November 24, 1995, C6)

As for the business section, there is a great deal more written on a typical day on business topics than on sports in the *Los Angeles Times*.[36] In contrast to metaphor use on immigration and immigrant topics, a relatively limited use of metaphor in the business section was noted. Newspaper descriptions of businesspeople tend to follow a formula. They usually are limited to a title, or a title with a limiting clause:

73. Blue Cross Chairman Leonard Schaeffer (November 30, 1995, D2)

74. Analyst Harold Vogel with Cowen & Co. (November 30, 1995, D2)

75. Barry Diller, the Home Shopping Network chairman who is trying to build a TV network from scratch (November 30, 1995, D2)

Most of the metaphors about businesspeople did not have an animal source domain:

76. cost-**cutter** Sanford I. Weill (November 30, 1995, D1)

However, in the data sample, two metaphors about businesspeople appeared that had animal source domains:

77. "The market is going crazy, the foreigners are the ones that appear most **bullish**," a trader said. (November 30, 1995, D4)

78. "I'm looking forward to **squishing** Rupert like a **bug**," Turner said. (November 30, 1995, D2)

In the latter excerpts, there are special circumstances to note. Both instances are direct quotes taken from individuals, rather than the business writer's text. In the lead sentence of the article, as written by the newswriter, a second instance of the bug metaphor is rephrased to direct the metaphor away from the businessperson, and toward the business enterprise.

79. Ted Turner said Wednesday he will **squash** "like a **bug**" an all-news TV network media magnate Rupert Murdoch hopes to launch to compete with Turner's 24-hour Cable News Network. (November 30, 1995, D2)

Thus the quote in excerpt 78 which attributes the animal metaphor to a businessperson was clearly reapportioned in excerpt 79, the lead sentence of the *Times* article, namely, the part of the story that would most likely be read.

From this limited sample it might be concluded that businesspeople use animal metaphors in reference to colleagues and competitors. At the same time it would indicate that *Los Angeles Times* business writers may deemphasize ruder business discourse, presumably to uphold the dignity of commerce.

Business-news writers tend not to use metaphor to characterize businesspeople, but contrastingly, they often cast nonhuman elements of the business world in anthropomorphic metaphors:

80. "This market is like **an old soldier** that just doesn't give up." (November 30, 1995, D3)

81. Stocks **sprinted** higher Wednesday. . . . Broad market indexes **broke records** as well. (November 30, 1995, D3)

82. Bank mergers are **vulnerable** to protests filed under the . . . Act. (November 30, 1995, D2)

Note *crazy* in excerpt 77 as well. Since only two expressions of animal metaphor appeared in a substantial sample of articles on businesspeople, the skeptic's hypothesis was not confirmed. However, the idea was further explored.

A second sampling of articles was gathered on two individuals of particular notoriety in sports and business. The distribution of animal metaphors in these newspaper sections was tallied. Again the skeptic would predict that animal metaphors are used to characterize businesspeople and sports figures no more or less than they are used to characterize immigrants. Note, however, that the skeptic's original claim had to be significantly weakened. The skeptic's second hypothesis is much less sweeping. Now notoriety, rather than normalcy, marks the individuals whose metaphors will be studied. In the second test, Mike Tyson was selected as a boxer who has been as praised for ferocity in the ring as he has been rebuked for his criminality outside of the ring. A financier, Charles Keating, was chosen to represent unscrupulous businesspeople. Keating was convicted in 1993 of bilking small investors out of millions of dollars through his institution, Lincoln Savings and Loan. As an infamous white-collar criminal, Keating is much more likely to be characterized with animal metaphors than the average businessperson. A number of articles on each person were drawn from the *Los Angeles Times* archives using the computerized topic selection function to select a set of articles that would provide approximately similar numbers of words.[37]

Animal metaphors were indeed used for Tyson. However, the boxer is portrayed as a particular kind of animal. In this sample he was characterized as a predatory carnivore, as illustrated by:

83. ". . . into the **lion's** den and take the meat out of the **lion's** mouth" (July 21, 1989, C1)
84. a man who keeps the **tiger** at bay with a long, strong left jab (July 21, 1989, C1)

This sports figure is metaphorically characterized as an animal at the top of the proverbial food chain. These "noble" animals are used as emblems for nations. The lion and tiger, for example, respectively symbolize Great Britain and India. The sports writers sampled in 1989 always wrote respectfully about Tyson. His sports prowess was never deprecated, and for these skills he was respected. It was expected that Tyson would be denigrated with animal metaphors, because of his profession, criminality, antipathies, and race. This expectation was not met. Nevertheless, it should not be concluded that the animal metaphors used to describe Tyson are similar to those used to describe the immigrants, since the animals linked to immigrants are not symbolically noble creatures, but beasts of burden or "lower" creatures.

The foregoing metaphor analysis was made using news reports published prior to Tyson's 1997 fight with Evander Holyfield. In that fight Tyson was disqualified for repeatedly biting Holyfield's ear, which was followed by a spate of sports commentaries which capitalized on TYSON AS CARNIVORE metaphors.

As for the other ill-famed news figure, the case of the felonious businessman is unequivocal. In the sample of news reports catalogued, Keating was never characterized as an animal:

85. **Midas-touch** businessman (April 8, 1990, D3)
86. **the villain, the man in the black hat** (April 8, 1990, D3)

No animal metaphors were used in reference to Keating. The metaphors used by the newswriters tend to focus on his successes, rather than his failings. His political and legal enemies, not the *Times* business writers, call him a *crook* and a *scam artist*. Contrary to the representation of immigrants in the same newspaper, there is no denigration of the man as a human being in the texts sampled.

It should be noted that these *Times* texts were published before 1996, when a judge overthrew Keating's conviction. "That means Keating is no longer a criminal in the eyes of the law—but he is a deadbeat. He still faces roughly $5.2 billion in civil judgments against him stemming from Lincoln's collapse. All his identifiable property, including his home, was long ago auctioned off by the government."[38]

Although the samples of articles on Tyson and Keating are limited, these infamous individuals are not characterized in metaphors as inferiors. In the larger samples of articles on sports figures no animal metaphors were located. For businesspeople, two animal metaphors were found. Both of these excerpts were direct quotes attributable to businesspeople, rather than text written by the *Times* writers. These results provide evidence that animal metaphors are not commonly used in newsprint to describe these types of citizens, as the skeptic predicted, although there was some reason to expect such characterizations. Consequently there is stronger support for the original finding, lamentably, that the ANIMAL domain is uniquely associated with immigrants. Animal metaphors are not generally used in the *Los Angeles Times* to characterize other types of people, even infamous individuals.

## Section 5: Other Analyses of Immigrant Representations during the Proposition 187 Campaign

Analysts with diverse disciplinary backgrounds have proposed alternative accounts of what amounts to the metaphoric framing of the political events surrounding Proposition 187. From the present theoretical position, which emphasizes the metaphoric understanding of social events, a comparison of their views is warranted. Hugh Mehan argues that the proponents of Proposition 187 utilized an IMMIGRANT AS ENEMY discourse strategy.[39] By discourse strategy,[40] Mehan refers to generally unconscious linguistic means to frame a particular view of the world. The discourse strategy framework is generally consistent with the framework used in this book. Mehan uses the ENEMY metaphor as the cover term for the anti-immigrant discourse strategy which includes the use of deixis to split American society into the in-group, us, and the Other.[41] The term deixis refers to the use of words such as *that, this, them, those, here,* and *there,* among others, for purposes of "pointing out" things in the world. As illustrated below, deixis reinforces the differences that are entailed in the dominant metaphor IMMIGRANT AS ANIMAL, i.e., the immigrant is an animal and hence not like us:[42]

> 87. "**They** create problems for jobs. . . . If **they** can go to school and get health care **we're** allowing **them** to be here. . . . **We** can't even take care

of **our own** and **we're** letting more in. **They** should be taking care of **themselves** and not draining **our** pocketbooks." (August 22, 1993, A1) 88. "There are so many more of **them,** so many more of **them** in **our** schools. **Their** parents won't speak **our** language, and **they** don't seem to try to improve **their** lifestyles. There are exceptions, but most of **them** don't." (June 26, 1993, B3)

A second part of the discourse strategy first discerned by Mehan is the difference in the rhetorical style of the proponents of Proposition 187, who use compelling anecdotes rather than scientific discourse to articulate their economic arguments to the electorate. Reliance on anecdotes is associated with what Mehan considers a third part of the discourse strategy, the studied disregard of traditional authorities who were opposed to Proposition 187, including several prominent right-wing politicians, a conservative former U.S. cabinet member, the president of the country, an ecumenical set of clergy, and divers public health, law enforcement, and educational officials. According to Mehan, the fourth element of their discourse strategy was a penurious appeal to self-interest, rather than to the greater public good and human rights. The listed discourse strategy features were all noted in abundance in this independent study of the public discourse of the time period. Mehan's cover term is, of course, copiously instantiated in the IMMIGRANT AS SOLDIER metaphor. In the present work, a good deal of confirmation of Mehan's analysis was located, as noted in Table 3.2.

Mehan notes three other studies of Proposition 187 that are complementary to his own. Carola and Marcelo Suárez-Orozco state that Proposition 187 is a "catharsis . . . that does not necessarily cure the underlying pathology." The pathogen in their analysis is not the immigrant, but the California public's anxiety that has arisen with a seemingly unending series of natural disasters, rage at the videotaped police brutality committed against African American Rodney King, as well as the so-called Los Angeles riots that followed the verdict acquitting the police of wrongdoing. This public uneasiness has been channeled into the re-creation of the Other, the immigrant, to "contain overwhelming anxieties and focus their rage," in particular in the void left by the collapsed "Evil Empire" of the communist Soviet Union.[43] Mehan does not accept the psychocultural analysis of Suárez-Orozco and Suárez-Orozco, which for him ignores "the elite's use, indeed cynical manipulation, of the immigrant-as-enemy construct in public discourse."[44] In spite of Mehan's critique, one can also readily locate reflections of the Suárez-

Orozco analysis in the public discourse sampled in the *Los Angeles Times*. Indeed the IMMIGRANT AS DISEASE and IMMIGRANT AS CRIMINAL are quite salient metaphors, as noted in Table 3.2.

The third commentator, Kitty Calavita, asks why the present period is "focused almost single-mindedly on IMMIGRANTS AS A TAX BURDEN, a focus that is unusual, if not unique, in the history of U.S. nativism."[45] Calavita's answer focuses on economics, and her analysis is framed in terms of ideology:

> With the [federal] deficit seemingly out of control, increased economic uncertainty for all but the most affluent, and the safety net shrinking, frustrated and anxious voters are predisposed to place the blame on excessive government spending and the poor, who are seen as the major cause of such spending. Immigrants are one among several targets consistent with this balanced-budget ideology and the scapegoating of the marginalized "other" that it spawns. . . . Those who are not even citizens—indeed, are not legal residents—are the ideal target of blame, more undeserving even than the traditional "undeserving poor."[46]

She cites "balanced-budget conservatism" as the framework of political values underlying California's Proposition 187. This is Plotkin and Scheureman's term for the general ideological response displayed in U.S. politics to the ongoing crisis of Fordism (reduced industrial profitability of U.S. capitalism since the Seventies). At a time when wages have been cut so much that 14 million full-time workers earn less than the official poverty level, when nonpermanent workers now comprise 30 percent of the entire U.S. workforce, and when the social safety net is being cut, Calavita notes that there has been an ideological assault on the public sector, not the economic sector. The public's attention was not drawn to the massive industrial and capital restructuring "designed to make the workers pay,"[47] rather, its outrage was redirected toward the federal deficit and rising taxes. Antigovernment rhetorical attacks and contempt and hostility expressed toward the poor were hallmarks of the budget-balancing conservative ideology of the 1990s. In contrast to Mehan's ENEMY metaphor, Calavita focuses on the IMMIGRANT AS BURDEN. Again there is a great deal of support for Calavita's analysis in the present *Los Angeles Times* public discourse sampling. Her metaphor of choice is linked to the NATION AS BODY metaphor rather than the NATION AS HOUSE metaphor.

George Lakoff, whose theoretical research over the last fifteen years brought metaphor to scholarly prominence, also used metaphor analysis to study the nature of politics in American society.[48] Based on personal observations of American political life and backed by text examples he generated or sampled on occasion from public discourse sources as he conducted cognitive linguistics research on metaphor, Lakoff claims that the major division in U.S. politics between liberals and conservatives is systematically based on dichotomous models of what ideal families should be. He claims both conservatives and liberals base their different political judgments on distinct forms of a NATION AS FAMILY metaphor. Within this analysis he addresses the U.S. politics of immigration. Consequently, evidence of this division should be found in public discourse expressed with differential use of metaphors.

On the one hand, the conservative view of politics is based on what Lakoff calls the Strict Father model of the family. For the conservatives, immigrants are first and foremost lawbreakers who should be punished. That is why they are called "illegal." Lakoff, speaking from the point of view of conservatives, avows:

> They are not citizens, hence they are not children in *our* family. To be expected to provide food, housing, and health care for illegal immigrants is like being expected to feed, house, and care for other children in the neighborhood who are coming into our house without permission. They weren't invited, they have no business being here, and we have no responsibility to take care of them.[49]

Numerous statements can be cited in the *Los Angeles Times* that corroborate the conservative point of view when referring to actual children, including the following statement by California's governor:

> 89. "We cannot educate every child from here to Tierra del Fuego." (September 16, 1994, A1)

On the other hand, the liberal view of politics is based on the Nurturing Family model in Lakoff's analysis. The NATION AS FAMILY metaphor that maps the politics of liberals characterizes immigrants as powerless people with no immoral intent. Consequently within the metaphor they are seen as:

> innocent children needing nurturance. . . . Through the NATION AS FAMILY metaphor, they are seen as children who have been . . . brought into the national household and who contribute in a vital way to that national household. You don't throw such children out onto the street. It would be immoral.[50]

Again there are quite clear statements in the *Los Angeles Times* that corroborate the liberal point of view, particularly when addressing the actual children of immigrants:

90. How dare we deny education to the children of women who clean our home and raise our children? How dare we deny medical care to those who harvest our crops, clip our lawns and golf courses, bus our dishes, wash our cars and every night leave spotless the very office towers whose top executives support the governor behind this mean proposal? (September 27, 1994, B7)

For Lakoff, metaphoric references to children are an entailment, IMMIGRANT AS CHILD, that emerges from within the mapping of family value to political value in NATION AS FAMILY. In the public discourse on immigrants generated during the Proposition 187 period, one would expect to find an empirical reflection of the NATION AS FAMILY and IMMIGRANT AS CHILD. However, only two instances of metaphors in the *Los Angeles Times* sample make reference to immigrants as children. Both were reported at a press conference called by a California legislator to announce the passage of his bill which denied emergency earthquake relief to undocumented immigrants:

91. For Rohrabacher, of Huntington Beach, the legislative victory gave flight to his more visceral kind of rhetoric. "This will have a real impact on federal agencies' ability to put out a flyer, saying (to illegal immigrants), 'Come on in and get the money.' **We're all part of the same family,** of all racial backgrounds. When you're in an emergency situation, **what kind of person takes limited emergency resources from his own family and gives it to a stranger?** We cannot afford to supply benefits for illegals without hurting our citizens and legal residents." (February 3, 1994, A1)

This inhumane legislative action was commented on by an immigrant quoted in excerpt 61 above. Representative Dana Rohrabacher's explicit reference to the nation as family, however, may well be interpreted as sarcastic. (Note his reflexive reference to race.) Few other IMMIGRANT AS CHILD metaphors appeared in the *Los Angeles Times* dataset.

It is understandable why Lakoff would expect Americans to speak about immigrants as children.[51] Such a metaphor is a more benevolent representation of the immigrant.[52] Unfortunately, the dominant ANIMAL metaphor evidenced in the *Los Angeles Times* of the 1990s did not grant human status to immigrants; it debased them. In the hierarchy of living things held by

Americans, as expressed in metaphor, immigrants are not the children of citizens. They metamorphosed into lower-life forms.

The lack of empirical confirmation in the *Times* of family or child metaphors does not repudiate Lakoff's major assertion that morality is embodied in the commonly used metaphors of political discourse. This is a key empirical finding of the present book.

These four analyses of the anti-immigrant sentiment and its political expression in Proposition 187 were each confirmed in the present sample of the metaphors of public discourse. However, each is only a partial analysis of the public discourse sampled in this chapter. Beginning with the cognitive theorist, Lakoff aims to capture the big picture. As the researcher attending most closely to the material discourse, Mehan focuses on the IMMIGRANT AS ENEMY, while Suárez-Orozco and Suárez-Orozco draw a psychoanalytic portrait centering on the IMMIGRANT AS DISEASE and AS CRIMINAL. Calavita brings economics to the forefront with the IMMIGRANT AS BURDEN metaphor.

Their respective interpretations follow from the proclivities of their respective disciplines. Their findings are consequently particularly germane to the disciplines from which the analysts operate, and yet, with the exception of Mehan, each is conspicuously bounded. The range of each of their separate analyses is encompassed in Table 3.2, which catalogues the range of structuring metaphors about immigrants. Still and all, one omission is common to the four analyses. The most frequent and virulent metaphor was not noted by these investigators. Turning now to the implications of the IMMIGRANT AS ANIMAL metaphor, one must ask what it is that makes this metaphor invisible to the scrutiny of social scientists.

## Section 6: Interpretation of the Dominant Metaphor

The conceptual correspondence IMMIGRANT AS ANIMAL is racist. It deprecates immigrants as it separates noncitizens and citizens, since it assigns the former nonhuman standing. This finding confirms previous research that also investigated racism and metaphor. Toine van Teeffelen, in a study of political metaphor in popular literature, states:

> in its metaphoric meaning racism compares and contrasts the domains of the self and the other. . . . When applied skillfully, metaphors can have a strong impact due to their "literary" quality and visual concreteness. This rhetorical thrust allows them to emphasize particular ele-

ments and linkages, and simultaneously to de-emphasize others. Since they organize the understanding of cause and effect, symptom and essence, and especially praise and blame, metaphors can be employed to serve political aims or interests. When thus used as ideological devices, they privilege, and when turning into common sense, naturalize particular accounts of reality.[53]

The charge of racism can be made on the basis of standard definitions. From a political economics perspective, for example, Robert Miles defines racism as actions that postulate natural divisions among people which are in fact not natural. This false assignment of individuals to groups, on the basis of such so-called natural traits, categorizes people into a false hierarchy. In this way of thinking, racism attributes meaning to

> human beings in such a way to create a system of categorization, and [attributes] additional (negatively evaluated) characteristics to the people sorted into those categories. This process of signification is therefore the basis for the creation of a hierarchy of groups, and for establishing criteria by which to include and exclude groups of people in the process of allocating resources and services.[54]

Certain essentialist criticisms can be made about this kind of definition. Nevertheless the reach of the definition should be clear. Note that this definition presumes that the criteria used by racists characterize the Other merely as an inferior human being, and not the equivalent of horses, rabbits, ferrets, and dogs.

Moreover, the metaphoric mapping IMMIGRANT AS ANIMAL is an element of racist discourse. The present finding thus reaffirms the research of van Dijk in which he demonstrated that racist discourse is replete with animal themes.[55] A definition of racist discourse which does not invoke intrinsic properties follows:

> Racist discourse, in our view, should be seen as discourse (of whatever content) which has the effect of establishing, sustaining and reinforcing oppressive power relations. . . . Racist discourse . . . justifies, sustains and legitimates those practices which maintain . . . power and dominance.[56]

Sustaining a discourse practice is the root power of metaphor. As developed in Chapter 2, following Foucault, such discourse practices uphold social practice, as they embody unreflected and naturalized ideological assumptions about their subject space. The entirely contingent background understandings about social spaces, beliefs, relationships, and identities of our lives are established in daily interactions which we only rarely question. The discourse practices are so frequently and casually used that they become automatic and invisible to our everyday view.

Correspondingly, metaphor, arguably the crucial unit of discursive practice, most effectively influences people when it does not draw attention to itself; when, without the slightest mindfulness on the part of the interlocutors, it invokes and rearticulates the cognitive structure of a source semantic domain to its target semantic domain. Notice that when a truly original metaphor is used, the reader/listener of the fresh turn of phrase is prompted by its novelty to evaluate the metaphor for its appropriateness, creativity, and utility. The mindful reader/listener can choose to reject the linkage. However, if the metaphor does not draw attention to itself, then the reader/listener is most likely to remain unaware that a conventional and contingent semantic link has been reinforced. Moreover, the semantic and cultural presuppositions of the conceptual correspondence are also automatically strengthened. IMMIGRANT AS ANIMAL is a metaphoric mapping that reproduces a view, with semantic associations, and most importantly political and social consequences, to denigrate human beings. Its dominant use sustains a covertly racist worldview.

As for explicitly legitimating a racist discourse, "there can be little doubt that of all forms of printed text, those of the mass media are most pervasive, if not most influential, when judged by the power criteria of recipient scope."[57] While the *Los Angeles Times* newswriters are not overtly racist, their continued use of the metaphor, like that of any other American English speaker, contributes to demeaning and dehumanizing the immigrant worker. Given the *Los Angeles Times*'s privileged role as a major vehicle for political discourse in California, IMMIGRATION AS DANGEROUS WATERS and IMMIGRANT AS ANIMAL are continually reinforced when these dominant metaphors are part of the *Times*'s entrenched discourse practice.

On the other hand, in defense of the newspaper, contemporary cognitive theory claims that prosaic metaphor constructs the fundamental worldview of everyday life. Rather than explicitly legitimating racist practices and power relationships, in these political contexts the newspaper merely reflects the basic, embodied values of the dominant social order. This discursive practice transfigures people—into threatening floods or domestic beasts—as it subjugates their humanity. Since "media practices usually remain within the boundaries of a flexible, but dominant consensus, even when there is room for occasional dissent and criticism . . . fundamental norms, values, and power arrangements are seldom explicitly challenged in the dominant news media."[58] Thus the foundational racism of U.S. society is mirrored in the discursive practice of the *Los Angeles Times*.

First, by way of the use of IMMIGRATION AS DANGEROUS WATERS, the individuality and humanity of the immigrants are replaced with a frightening scenario of *inundating surges of brown faces*. While the ostensible point of Pete Wilson's anti-immigrant campaign was to recoup government costs associated with essential services for undocumented workers and their children, the force of the DANGEROUS WATERS metaphor was not directed toward fiscal deficits. Rather, Wilson capitalized on the sense of increasing loss of sociocultural preeminence among his core constituency, as the *rising brown tides* ostensibly reshaped the Anglo-American hegemonic order.

Second, the IMMIGRANT AS ANIMAL metaphor is unquestionably racist. This racism is constructed in public discourse via the use of the metaphor. This is different from the racist language with which the public is familiar. Racist language is commonly understood to be the blatant invectives and slurs that were common in the United States over most of its history, when it was an openly racist society. These expletives are no longer tolerated in most polite settings. They are no longer common currency in political discourse. Hence, as Frank Reeves noted, such discourse has been "sanitized." However, as will be developed in the next chapter, epistemological racism continues to be expressed via the dominant metaphors most commonly used in the public discourse on immigrants and immigration.

Lastly, the public discourse which distinguishes citizen from immigrant repudiates one celebrated principle of American society. The nation's most distinguished claim is the Great Experiment, which was given expression in the Constitution. Sadly, the experiment has always been compromised insofar as all the people in the country are not included. As Frederick Douglass hammered home with ringing eloquence, their exclusion debases the nation's noble design:

> Its language is "We the people"; not we the white people, not even we the citizens, not we the privileged class, not we the high, not we the low, but we the people; not we the horses, sheep and swine, and wheelbarrows, but we the people, we the human inhabitants; and if Negroes are people, they are included in the benefits for which the Constitution of America was ordained and established.[59]

When Douglass wrote, African Americans were not citizens but had the legal status of domesticated animals. Today's immigrants are spoken about as if they were animals, and via these words actions are taken that disregard their humanity. The principles of the country are debased as long as this current dominant metaphor of public discourse is sustained.

The discursive construction of racism may currently be unobtrusive, but once noted, it is far from subtle. Immigrants are not referred to, in a patronizing but humane manner, as children. While there were other metaphoric mappings evident in the database, such as IMMIGRANT AS WEED, all but one of these were pejorative. The absence of productive dominant metaphors for immigrants and immigration supports the thesis that the U.S. public discourse on immigrants is racist. The metaphoric element of discursive racism is particularly insidious, since the metaphors remain invisible. These metaphors are manifestations of deeply held concepts of *what* (not who) immigrants are. Such a worldview precludes the view that they are vested by birth with the same human rights as citizens, and that they should be shown due respect for the difficult and ill-paid work they provide for U.S. society.

## CHAPTER FOUR

# Proposition 209

## Competing Metaphors for RACISM and AFFIRMATIVE ACTION

Following closely on the heels of Proposition 187 was a second anti-Latino measure, Proposition 209. This referendum, called the "California Civil Rights Initiative" by its promoters, was narrowly passed by the electorate. It eliminated affirmative action in all state hiring and promotions and in higher education admissions.

Strikingly, *Los Angeles Times* coverage of Proposition 209 from 1994 to 1996 was limited by and large to day-to-day political events, with the almost total absence of discussion on the concept of affirmative action itself. The nature of affirmative action or its historical trajectory was rarely developed. There was little public discussion about concepts which underlie its implementation, such as merit, fairness, and especially racism. Consequently the prevalent metaphors in the *Times* were of the political campaign, not the issue of affirmative action per se.

Compared to the intense discourse on immigration during the Proposition 187 campaign, California political discourse surrounding the affirmative action debate, as presented in the *Los Angeles Times,* was indistinguishable from other political debates. This was due in part to the distraction of the concurrent 1996 presidential contest as well as the stance taken in these presidential campaigns. Neither major party candidate was willing to take a strong stand on affirmative action during his national campaign, for fear of alienating voters. Lastly, after the fractious Proposition 187 campaign in California, both major parties avoided the 209 initiative at all costs, because it was seen to be a racial wedge issue.

In the absence of an accessible source of sustained public discourse on affirmative action during the 209 campaign, the diachronic sampling method discussed in Chapter 2 was applied. To highlight the differences in the discourses on affirmative action, texts were drawn from two points in time, and in the contemporary setting from the opposing political positions. The political discourse on race and affirmative action, as articulated by highly visible spokespeople in the Civil Rights Movement of the 1960s, is compared to the political discourse surrounding Proposition 209 in the mid-1990s.

In Section 1, the political and administrative origins of affirmative action are described. A characterization of discourse on race and racism in the United States of the 1960s is also offered, as articulated by powerful public speakers and a prominent blue-ribbon commission report on racism in the nation. In contrast to the previous chapter, this background discussion is comparatively extensive, in order to periodize the discourse. Section 2 provides an analysis of the political discourse of the time, focusing on the most prominent metaphor of racism of the 1960s, along with its ontology. Section 3 begins the study of the political discourse of the 1990s, comparing twenty conservative essays which appeared in a special issue dedicated to affirmative action of a public affairs journal, *Commentary,* to a similar amount of text from a frequently cited book in favor of affirmative action written for general readers by a Special Counsel to President Clinton.[1] In this manner the major critical attacks on affirmative action by neoconservatives, and the origin of the referendum to eliminate it, will be presented. Section 4 reviews further discourse strategies of contemporary anti-affirmative-action spokespeople, and their redefinition of racism. An overview section concludes this chapter.

## Section 1: Background to Affirmative Action: The 1960s

Affirmative action evolved in the late 1960s in response to the U.S. government and public's recognition that the 1964 Civil Rights Act was moving too slowly to redress the effects of three hundred years of legalized racism, during which time the United States was a "racial dictatorship"[2] that disenfranchised people of color. After ten generations of nonhuman status and one hundred years of apartheid, African Americans in the 1960s witnessed the bountiful increase of the standard of living of white Americans in the post–World War II boom years, while they were relegated to grim, segregated, and forgotten corners of the urban landscape. They viewed on television the blatant violence and hatred of white Americans unleashed on the nonviolent civil rights marchers, and experienced it unabated in their daily lives after the Civil Rights Act was enacted. These people of color became increasingly aware of the hypocritical stance of the United States, which boasted of equality and fairness for all in pursuit of the American Dream, while maintaining racist institutions such as the police and public school systems. One civil rights leader, Martin Luther King Jr., gave an assessment in 1967, three years after the passage of the Civil Rights Act:

> The daily life of the Negro is still lived in the basement of the Great Society. He is still at the bottom despite the few who have penetrated to slightly higher levels. Even where the door has been forced partially open, mobility for the Negro is still sharply restricted. There is often no bottom at which to start, and when there is, there is almost always no room at the top. . . . In assessing the results of the Negro revolution so far, it can be concluded that Negroes have established a foothold, no more. We have written a declaration of independence, itself an accomplishment, but the effort to transform the words into a life experience still lies ahead. The hard truth is that neither Negro nor White has yet done enough to expect the dawn of a new day. While much has been done, it has been accomplished by too few and on a scale too limited for the breadth of the goal. Freedom is not won by a passive acceptance of suffering. Freedom is won by a struggle *against* suffering. By this measure, Negroes have not yet paid the full price for freedom. And Whites have not yet faced the full cost of justice. The brunt of the Negro's past battles was borne by a very small striking force. Though millions of Negroes were ardent and passionate supporters, only a modest number were actively engaged, and these were relatively too few for a broad war against racism, poverty and discrimination. Negroes fought and won, but our engagements were skirmishes, not climactic battles. No great victories are won in a war for the transformation of a whole people without total participation. Less than this will not create a new society; it will only evoke more sophisticated token amelioration. The Negro has been wrong to toy with the optimistic thought that the breakdown of white resistance could be accomplished at small cost. He will have to do more before his pressure crystallizes new white principles and new responses. The two forces must continue to collide as Negro aspirations burst against the ancient fortresses of the status quo. . . . Negroes hold only one key to the double lock of peaceful change. The other is in the hands of the white community.[3]

King was noted for his nonviolent philosophy. He is often contrasted with black militants who were less concerned with Christian virtues. Nonetheless, the language of war permeates his appraisal. The political struggle toward civil and societal equity in the 1960s took a decidedly martial tone. The Great Society that King refers to is the United States, of course, but more particularly he evokes the catchword of Lyndon Baines Johnson's presidency. Turning now to Johnson, his oft-repeated views on the effects of racism, and on the nation's task to deal with racism, can be compared below:

The Voting Rights Bill will be the latest, and among the most important, in a long series of victories. But this victory—as Winston Churchill said of another triumph for freedom—"is not the end. It is not even the beginning of the end. But it is, perhaps, the end of the beginning." That beginning is freedom. And the barriers to that freedom are tumbling down. Freedom is the right to share fully and equally in American society—to vote, to hold a job, to enter a public place, to go to school. It is the right to be treated in every part of our national life as a person equal in dignity and promise to all others. But freedom is not enough. You do not wipe away the scars of centuries by saying: "Now you are free to go where you want, do as you desire, and choose the leaders you please." You do not take a person who, for years, has been hobbled by chains and liberate him, bring him up to the starting line of a race and then say, "You are free to compete with all the others," and still justly believe that you have been completely fair. It is not enough to just open the gates of opportunity. All our citizens must have the ability to walk through those gates. This is the next and more profound stage of the battle for civil rights. We seek not just freedom but opportunity—not just legal equity but human ability—not just equality as a right and a theory, but equality as a fact and a result. . . . There is also the lacerating hurt of early collision with white hatred or prejudice, distaste, or condescension. Other groups have felt similar intolerance. But success and achievement could wipe it away. They do not change the color of a man's skin. I have seen this uncomprehending pain in the eyes of little Mexican-American school children that I taught many years ago.[4]

There are four major concepts in these passages from King and Johnson which were often used in the discourse of the civil rights era of the 1960s. The first derives from the POLITICS AS WAR metaphor.[5] This metaphor attributes the elements of organized military combat to a political campaign, whether of a candidate or for a legislative item. In the specific text the POLITICS AS WAR metaphor is articulated with words such as *battles, victories,* and *cam-*

*paigns.* In the everyday understanding of war, people marshal all their resources to dominate another group of people by violent means. A series of smaller skirmishes or larger struggles are orchestrated by opposing groups to dominate or defend against the other.

The metaphorical presupposition in these passages and through much of the civil rights period describes a monumental war for the moral character of the nation that is waged between states' rights advocates and civil rights advocates. Civil rights advocates fight the legislative battles to eliminate societal racism and institutional discrimination against Americans of color, and to effect the full inclusion of previously marginalized populations into U.S. society. States' rights advocates basically fight to maintain the status quo, arguing ostensibly for the primacy of individual rights and respect for the society as it was conceived by the so-called founding fathers.

The second concept derives from the path metaphor. SUCCESS AS A RACE is also a common metaphor, as we will have occasion to elaborate at length in Chapter 5's discussion of U.S. education in general. Third is a metaphor for the nation. King's words, such as *door, basement,* and *no room at the top,* articulate the situation of African Americans and other people of color in the United States, in terms much like Johnson's *gates of opportunity,* utilizing the NATION AS HOUSE metaphor. The last is NATION AS BODY, which Johnson uses with the searing terms *hobbled by chains* and *lacerating hurt* to speak not only of the individual citizen's pain, but that of people of color as a community. There is a reading, too, of the United States as a whole. The metaphors of nation will be taken up in Chapter 7.

In 1967, after four summers of African American uprisings, President Johnson created the blue-ribbon Kerner Commission to answer the burning questions about these civil disturbances.[6] The Kerner Report indicated that these uprisings were not the result of a conspiracy, as Johnson originally suspected. The civil unrest across four summers and most major urban metropolitan areas shared certain features. No episode of urban violence was provoked by a single act of police brutality, but each was the result of a series of such actions occurring over an extended time. One might consider it the chronic condition of the nonwhite inner city. The violence was then precipitated by one more routine, exacerbating police action, when social tensions were already perilously taut. Second, the targets of African American rage were not white citizens per se, but rather the symbols of white society, white authority, and white property. African American citizens suffered the overwhelming majority of casualties and deaths.

## White Racism

The Kerner Commission's findings could not be more to the point. It listed the proximate causes of these civil disturbances as segregation of impoverished people in ghettos, the consequent destruction of opportunity and enforced failure of the youth, a pervasive feeling that no effective alternative to violence existed as a means to redress societal grievances, unfulfilled expectations aroused by the legislative victories of the Civil Rights Movement, the development of a social climate that encouraged violence, and the pervasive discrimination in employment, education, and housing. Determining the root source of these effects, "the most fundamental is the racial attitude and behavior of white Americans." This candor was unprecedented in U.S. history. The Kerner Report concluded that "white racism is essentially responsible" for the civil unrest.[7] The Kerner Commission indictment could not be clearer:

> What white Americans have never fully understood—but the Negro can never forget—is that white society is deeply implicated.

in the inequality and segregation that plague African Americans and other people of color.

> White institutions created it, white institutions maintained it, and white society condones it.[8]

In spite of marked change in certain sectors of U.S. life, thirty years after their publication these descriptions unfortunately remain materially accurate for large portions of racialized minorities.

## Classifying Racism

In contemporary American society, to call someone a racist invariably provokes a quick denial. So it may be useful at the outset to specify the notion. Racists make judgments about individuals in terms of a racial hierarchy that ranks groups of people as superior and inferior on the basis of phenotype, attribute positive and negative qualities to groups of people on its basis, and include or exclude groups of people from societal resources on the same basis. Racism, as social phenomenon, has been studied with increasing sophistication in the past two decades.[9] Scheurich and Young distinguish five kinds.[10] The first is individual overt racism, exemplified by people who consciously make racial slurs. Whites in the United States presume this is the main expression of racism, but in contemporary polite society, covert racism is more prevalent. John Dovidio also calls this behavior "aversive racism," in which the offenders may not realize that they are engaged in racist behavior. One example of covert, or aversive, racism occurs when someone is passed over for a job promotion ostensibly on the basis of acceptable criteria, such as inferior qualifications, when in fact the real reason is race. Dovidio speaks about the suspicions sown among (well-meaning) people who must struggle against their social roles:

> The subtlety and unintentionality of aversive racism can contribute to distrust and tension among racial and ethnic groups. Because aversive racists are unaware of their own prejudice and discriminate only when they can justify their own behavior on grounds other than race, they tend to underestimate the continuing impact of race. They certainly dismiss racism as a motive for their own behavior, and they think blacks or members of other minority groups see prejudice where it doesn't really exist. Members of minority groups, in contrast, see aversive racists denying their own bias and yet sometimes acting in a biased fashion. As a result, it is not surprising that members of minority groups suspect that prejudice exists everywhere.[11]

The third and most studied form is institutional racism, where the standard operating procedures of an institution reduce a nonmajority person's access or advancement. We tend to presume that institutional racism is manifest in overt terms, like apartheid either in South Africa before Nelson Mandela's presidency in 1994, or in the United States before the Civil Rights Act in 1964. However, institutional repression can be as subtle as it is effective. In the case of public education, such racism can be built into the standard pedagogical methods so that they are consistent with the societal expectations and behavior of a privileged group, namely, students raised in a white middle-class culture, at the expense of students raised in other cultural milieus. The unreflected expectation built into the institutional settings is that the actions of Whites are simply natural, not culturally contingent.

The fourth is societal racism. This is when the prevailing cultural assumptions, norms, and concepts of a society favor one race over another. Thus Anglo-American conservatives claim their own contingent depiction of family to be the one-and-only true version of family values, while the family orientations of other U.S. cultures, such as extended families or matriarchies, are disparaged as atavistic or inherently dysfunctional. As Richard

Dyer puts it, "Power in contemporary society habitually passes itself off as embodied in the normal as opposed to the superior. This is common to all forms of power, but it works in a peculiarly seductive way with whiteness, because of the way it seems rooted in common-sense thought, in things other than ethnic difference."[12]

Finally there is foundational racism, what Scheurich and Young call civilizational racism, in which so-called Western European assumptions about reality, about ways of knowing, and about the "contours of right and wrong," namely, "what is the real, the true and the good," are presumed to be rational, reasonable, scientifically based, and natural.[13] With such postulates, even scientists are liable to bias their theories of the social world in terms of these cultural contingencies, as has been demonstrated in the history of science. For example, orthodox nineteenth-century scientific views of biological race once "explained" the failure of minority student academic achievement in terms of genetic inferiority. This theory is easily condemned as racist today, yet equivalent views are currently being promulgated. Cultural deficiency theories are currently used to account for grossly unequal rates of educational attainment across racial groupings, "explaining" failure in terms of the cultures of minority students. Over the years Latino scholars have charged educational researchers and teachers with maintaining overt or covert cultural deficiency theories of Latino students.[14] What King stated in 1967 can well describe the educational setting of Latinos at the outset of the twenty-first century:

> In other spheres the figures are equally alarming. In elementary schools Negroes lag one to three years behind Whites, and their . . . schools receive substantially less money per student than do the white schools. One-twentieth as many Negroes as Whites attend college, and half of these are in ill-equipped Southern institutions. . . . [These figures cannot] be explained by the myth of the Negro's innate incapabilities, or by the more sophisticated rationalization of his acquired infirmities. They are a structural part of the economic system in the United States.[15]

As John David Skrentny points out in his excellent history of affirmative action, the official conclusion of the Kerner Report was more significant because it had been authorized by the President of the United States. It depicted white racism as more than the actions and attitudes of individuals, but as a problem integrally instituted in U.S. society. For the first time, white

Americans were officially held culpable.[16] The Kerner Commission Report, which was a publication phenomenon with 1.6 million paperback copies and twenty editions sold in four years, indicates that at the time race and racism were on the U.S. public agenda. The Commission's call for change was admirably succinct:

> It is time now to turn with all the purpose at our command to the major unfinished business of this nation. It is time to adopt strategies for action that will produce quick and visible progress. It is time to make good the promises of American democracy to all citizens— urban and rural, white and black, Spanish-surname, American Indian, and every minority group. Our recommendations embrace three basic principles: To mount programs on a scale equal to the dimension of the problems; To aim these programs for high impact in the immediate future in order to close the gap between the promise and performance; To undertake new initiatives and experiments that can change the system of failure and frustration that now dominates the ghetto and weakens our society. These programs will require unprecedented levels of funding and performance, but they neither probe deeper nor demand more than the problems which called them forth. There can be no higher priority for national action and no higher claim on the nation's conscience.[17]

The type of racism that the Kerner Commission cited as the reason for black rage was not merely the legislated racism which only ended formally in 1964. Rather, the Kerner Commission specified institutional racism as a crucial feature of U.S. society that had to be proactively eliminated. To be sure, the Commission also decried the covert racism as practiced by individual Whites, which was referred to as "benign indifference." Yet the grand part of the persisting oppression, of which many Whites are oblivious, is societal racism.

A Marshall Plan for America's inner city would have been appropriate to meet endemic white racism of the scale and severity recognized by the Kerner Commission. Indeed, in 1961 the Executive Director of the Urban League, Whitney Young, called for such a program before the passage of the major civil rights legislation and the summer uprisings in the inner cities.[18] For the education system alone, a plan to provide high-quality education to all of America's children of color would have brought about a social revolution. Unfortunately, a reordering of the mission of the inner-city school system was not forthcoming. Congress failed to provide governmental agencies with the requisite enforcement power to oversee the 1964 Civil Rights Act. In lieu of fundamental change, affirmative action was developed. It was the federal government's milksop response to the verdict and counsel of the Kerner Commission.

## Bureaucratic Origin of Affirmative Action

The Equal Employment Opportunity Commission (EEOC) was created to enforce Title VII of the 1964 Civil Rights Act, which outlawed discriminatory employment practices. Its job was, and continues to be, daunting. As soon as the EEOC opened its doors in 1967, tens of thousands of discrimination complaints began to roll in. Yet, of the nearly 9,000 complaints that had been logged from across the country within its first two months of operation, only 110 were completed. The turnaround time for cases grew to over two years. Starting out in disarray, at first the EEOC was perceived as a failure. Nonetheless, complaints continued to be lodged. With time, the mission of the agency became clear, and the staggering urgency of its task became evident. At first it was not surprising that the queue of discrimination cases lengthened. By 1976, over 125,000 pending cases were piled up.[19]

The volume of EEOC cases may be considered a rough measure of the racial equity that the United States has achieved since the Civil Rights Act. Certainly, the halls of Congress would ring with speeches if, after the floodgates were opened in 1967, the huge caseload had trickled down to a handful per year. Legislators would rush to proclaim that the EEOC's mandate was fulfilled and its doors should be closed. Then the United States could declare that it had redressed the effects of three hundred years of legalized racism which disenfranchised great numbers of its people. Unfortunately, the number of cases of racial discrimination brought to the EEOC has not declined. During the 1990s the EEOC's caseload increased by 130 percent, according to a conservative business magazine.[20] In 1995, 87,000 charges of discrimination came before the EEOC, or an increase of 40 percent over the figures of 1990.[21] In 1995 U.S. Senator Nancy Kassenbaum, the chair of the Senate committee overseeing the EEOC, registered with dismay that the agency continued to have a backlog of 100,000 discrimination cases.[22] Meanwhile Christopher Edley noted:

> The federal government alone continues to receive more than 90,000 complaints of employment discrimination (race and gender) every

year. . . . In filings and level of enforcement activities nationwide by federal, state, and local civil rights enforcement agencies over the past two decades, there has been no downward trend that would suggest that the underlying problems of racial discrimination are abating.[23]

During the period of the Proposition 209 campaign, the director of the EEOC stated that his greatest concern was critical underfunding at a time when claims of discrimination had tripled, led by race-based cases.[24] One key reason is that the EEOC was never granted real enforcement power to combat institutional racism, namely, cease and desist authority. Thus, it is not a policing arm of Title VII.

In truth, the EEOC is a paper tiger. Affirmative action emerged over time as a bureaucratic stopgap. All it does is require employers and other organizations to submit records of hiring or admission, promotion or graduation, and firing or dropout records in terms of race. With such limited purpose, affirmative action is ultimately only a scorekeeper to tally the progress the United States is making toward a more equitable society. Thus, the steady stream of new complaints, and the total failure to achieve any level of reasonable parity along racial lines in key institutions of society, signal continuing racism in U.S. society.

## Section 2: Political Discourse of the 1960s

As described at the outset of this chapter, Martin Luther King Jr. and Lyndon Johnson's political war in the 1960s for the moral character of the nation pitted liberal and progressive wings of American society against status-quo conservatives. Thus King evoked a *Negro revolution* paralleling the American Revolution, with its *declaration of independence; freedom won by a struggle;* and *broad war against racism, poverty and discrimination.* Johnson also spoke of the Civil Rights Movement as a *long series of victories,* leading to *a triumph for freedom,* as he looked toward *the next more profound battle for civil rights.* But remarkably, they made little explicit reference to racism, which the Kerner Commission and the social sciences declare is the key principle organizing U.S. social relations.

### Reticence about Discussing Racism

It is as if these eloquent public speakers suddenly became tongue-tied when confronted directly with the issue of racism. Yet their reticence is not exceptional. An African American commentator, Glenn Loury, has described this shyness as a "moral queasiness" that all Americans have when speaking about racism:

> Our moral queasiness about the use of race arises for historically spe-
> cific reasons—namely slavery and Jim Crow segregation. Those rea-
> sons centrally involved the caste-like subordination of blacks, a matter
> that, needless to say, was not symmetrical as between the races. There-
> fore to take account of race while trying to mitigate the effects of this
> subordination, though perhaps ill-advised or unworkable in specific
> cases, should not be viewed as morally equivalent to the acts of dis-
> crimination that effected the subjugation of blacks in the first place.[25]

Ordinarily, metaphor and other figurative language can consciously be used to provide alternate means to discuss the otherwise undiscussable, to avoid direct reference to discomforting situations. However, America's queasiness about speaking about race tended to disable this important use of metaphor in public arenas.[26] While the statements about the political battle against racism may be found, nevertheless, direct reference to racism was only rarely found in compilations of their public speeches. It could be asserted that King and Johnson, as mainstream figures, were unwilling or unable to upset the wider white society.

Thus, to further explore how racism was discussed in the political dis-course of this period of American history when the president's blue-ribbon representatives explicitly held white racism culpable for the black uprisings, the speeches of the period's most powerful advocate for African American autonomy, Malcolm X, will be examined. His detractors called him "fierce, and his black nationalist rhetoric inflammatory. It argued violence, it adver-tised intolerance, it mongered racist hatred."[27] On the other hand, it seemed to his admirers that "he spoke with sincerity, he spoke with passion. He had the gift of the griot, and he seems to have spoken with the voice of the prophet."[28] In the America of the 1960s, he left no one unmoved. Malcolm X was the African American spokesperson least willing to abide by the con-ventions of public discourse of the time, to indulge white sensibilities when he addressed the grievances of African Americans.

## Race Relations, Not Racism

It is remarkable that Malcolm X, given this reputation, also only rarely por-trayed racism, per se. Rather, he spoke of the relations between Blacks and Whites, characteristically personifying racism as a conflict between two individuals. When asked, for example, whether African Americans could succeed in the United States through the vote, this is how he responded:

> Well, independence comes only by two ways: by ballots or by bullets. What you read historically—historically you'll find that everybody who gets freedom, they get it through ballots or bullets. Now naturally everyone prefers ballots, and even I prefer ballots, but I don't discount bullets. I'm interested in freedom. . . . The white man has not given us anything. It's not something that is his to give. He is not doing us a favor when he permits us a few liberties. So I don't think we should approach it like that; I don't think we approach our battle like we're battling a friend. We're battling an *enemy*. Anybody who stands in the way of the black man being free is an enemy of the black man, and should be dealt with as an enemy.[29]

By speaking of *the white man* and *the black man*, Malcolm X uses personifying metaphors to concretize race relations. In this excerpt, again, there is another reference to POLITICS AS WAR—but it is not entirely metaphorical as Malcolm X employs it. As for other racialized citizenry of the United States, he has a binary Afrocentric viewpoint:

> the red, the brown and the yellow are indeed all part of the black nation. Which means that black, brown, red, yellow, are all brothers, all are one family. The white one is a stranger. He's the odd fellow.[30]

The far more moderate King also used personification metaphors to talk about the effect of endemic racism, although he tended not to refer directly to *the white man*,[31] but to use descriptors, such as *liberal, segregationist, white brethren, civil rights forces in Congress, jeering and hostile mobs*, or, as in the following, *adversary*:

> For hundreds of years Negroes had fought to stay alive by developing an endurance to hardship and heartbreak. In this decade the Negro stepped into a new role. He no longer would endure; he would resist and win. He still had the age-old capacity to live in hunger and want, but now he banished these as his lifelong companions. He could tolerate humiliation and scorn, but now he armed himself with dignity and resistance and his adversary tasted the gall of defeat.[32]

King's personification strategy continues for several pages in this one passage, and is generally used to great effect. Returning to the relation between

Blacks and Whites in the following excerpt, Malcolm X employs a penal variant of the NATION AS HOUSE metaphor:

> I think that what you should realize is that in America there are twenty million black people, all of whom are in prison. You don't have to go to Sing Sing to be in prison. If you're born in America with a black skin, you're born in prison, and the masses of black people in America today are beginning to regard our plight or predicament in this society as one of a prison inmate. And when they refer to the President, he's just another warden to whom they turn to open the cell door, but it's no different. It's the same thing, and just as the warden in the prison couldn't rehabilitate those men, the President in this country couldn't rehabilitate or change the thinking of the masses of black people.[33]

When asked if it was the case that the social conditions of the African American had improved over the past decades, Malcolm X rejoins with another personifying metaphor, master/servant imagery:

> They've changed in this sense. If you're a butler for a poor white man, you're a butler and you live but so well and you eat but so well. But if your master becomes rich, you begin to eat better and you begin to live better, but you're still a butler. And the only change that has been made in this society—we occupied a menial position twenty years ago. Our position hasn't changed. Our conditions have changed somewhat, but our position hasn't changed. And the change has been brought about, has been only to the extent that this country has changed. The white man got richer, we're living a little better. He got more power, we got a little more power, but we're still at the same level in his system.[34]

## African Americans

Never one to mince words, Malcolm X used many different, often painful, metaphors to describe African Americans in U.S. society:

> No, there is plenty wrong with Negroes. They have no society. They're robots, automatons. No minds of their own. I hate to say that about us, but it's the truth. They are a black body with a white brain. Like the monster Frankenstein. The top part is your bourgeois Negro. He's your integrator. He's not interested in his poor black brothers. He's usually so deep in debt from trying to copy the white man's social habits that he doesn't have time to worry about nothing else. They buy the most expensive clothes and cars and eat the cheapest food. They act

more like the white man than the white man himself. . . . Then there's the middle class of the Negro masses, ones not in the ghetto, who realize that life is a struggle, who are in a constant state of insecurity in which they live. . . . At the bottom of the social heap is the black man in the big-city ghetto.[35]

I am one who doesn't believe in deluding myself. I'm not going to sit at your table and watch you eat, with nothing on my plate, and call myself a diner. Sitting at the table doesn't make you a diner, unless you eat some of what's on that plate. Being here in America doesn't make you an American. Being born here in America doesn't make you an American. Why, if birth made you American, you wouldn't need any legislation, you wouldn't need any amendments to the Constitution, you wouldn't be faced with civil-rights filibustering in Washington, D.C.[36]

White people want to believe that [African Americans are nonviolent] so bad, because they're so guilty. But the danger is, when they . . . fool themselves into thinking that Negroes are really nonviolent, and patient, and long suffering, they've got a powder keg in their house. And instead of them trying to do something to defuse the powder keg, they're putting a blanket over it, trying to make believe that this is no powder keg; that it is a couch that we can lay on and enjoy.[37]

Thus there is a variety of metaphors in Malcolm X's political discourse about the races, as is the case for King and Johnson.

## Racism

With respect to racism, which might be considered a secondary metaphor, a few scattered instances of well-known biblical metaphors were invoked, as in excerpts 1 and 2. Likewise, racism is represented in various occasional metaphors, as in excerpts 3 and 4:

1. There is an Old Testament prophecy of the "sins of the Fathers being visited upon the third and fourth generations." Nothing could be more applicable to our situation. **America is reaping the harvest of hate and shame planted through generations of educational denial, political disfranchisement and economic exploitation of its black population.** Now, almost a century removed from slavery, we find **the heritage of oppression and racism erupting in our cities, with volcanic lava of bit-**

terness and frustration pouring down our avenues. —Martin Luther King Jr.[38]

2. **The seeds that America had sown—in enslavement**, in many of the things that followed since then—all of **these seeds were coming up today; it was harvest time.** —Malcolm X[39]

3. Now as we stand two-thirds into this exciting period of history we know full well that **racism is still that hound of hell which dogs the tracks of our civilization.** —Martin Luther King Jr.[40]

4. However difficult it is to hear, however shocking it is to hear, we've got to face the fact that America is a racist country. We have got to face the fact that **racism still occupies the throne of our nation.** I don't think we will ultimately solve the problem of racial injustice until this is recognized, and until this is worked on. —Martin Luther King Jr.[41]

However, racism, per se, is represented by these sophisticated public speakers for the most part with only one metaphor. A sampling of the more striking examples of metaphors for racism in a selected set of compilations of their speeches follows:[42]

5. For too long the depth of racism in American life has been underestimated. The **surgery to extract it** is necessarily complex and detailed. As a beginning it is important **to X-ray our history and reveal the full extent of the disease.** —Martin Luther King Jr.[43]

6. So we are evolving an action program that will enable us . . . to carry it into practice right now in the so-called Negro community and eliminate some of the **ills,** the **social ills** and **political ills** and the **economic ills,** that keep our people . . . trapped there in the ghetto. —Malcolm X[44]

7. Like a **boil** that can never be **cured** so long as it is covered up but must be opened with all its **pus-flowing ugliness** to the natural **medicines of air and light, injustice** must be exposed, with all of the tension its exposing creates, to the light of human conscience and the air of national opinion before it can be **cured.** —Martin Luther King Jr.[45]

8. While in **many fields the promise may at the moment seem to be blighted,** the greater probability is that the young people will be **blighting** their own lives if, when the 1970s come, they find that decisions they made today will have **blighted** their own opportunities for participation in a new world that will be open to them then. —Lyndon Johnson, 1963[46]

9. The American people are **infected with racism**—that is the peril. . . . White America has allowed itself to be indifferent to race prejudice and economic denial. It has treated them as **superficial blemishes,** but now awakes to **the horrifying reality of a potentially fatal disease.**—Martin Luther King Jr.[47]

10. History has shown that, like a **virulent disease germ,** racism can grow and destroy nations.—Martin Luther King Jr.[48]

Each is an excerpt from the major spokesmen for their different constituencies. In each instance the same metaphor is invoked: RACISM AS DISEASE. Since this is the dominant metaphor for racism in the 1960s, it is appropriate to review its ontology.

## Ontology of RACISM AS DISEASE[49]

As with all metaphors the source semantic domain, in this case DISEASE, provides a semantic structure for interpreting the target semantic domain, RACISM. The everyday frame of understanding starts with an attack on a body which disrupts its normal functioning. Hence a body is entailed. Health is a state of complete physical, mental, and social well-being, the efficient performance of bodily functions in the widest range of environmental conditions. Ill health, then, is an inability on the part of the body to adapt to changing circumstances, and disease is a distinct pattern of abnormal responses, of disturbed functioning, or some sort of malformation of the human body.

Most frequently the public presumes that the cause of a disease is exogenous, namely, an outside agent attacks the body. However, many diseases are endogenous, that is, arising within the body, due to factors such as chromosomes or hormones. In these conditions, the very constitution of the body leads to imbalanced functioning of the various interrelated systems.

Diseases, to simplify a panoply, reveal themselves in two major ways. They can be quick and nasty acute conditions which totally interrupt normal functioning, or they may be slow and nasty chronic conditions that leave the mind/body operating at a diminished level. Sooner or later disease always involves pain, which can be intense and excruciating, or dull and numbing. Further, diseases can be induced by a weak constitution; by an intemperate style of life; by a good, long life; or by chance, without apparent cause, seemingly the result of their choice to attack a body at random. Lastly, diseases wreak various kinds of havoc. They may kill outright, or devastate the body without ending life, or merely make their mark known and annoy the host.

It is generally recognized that the disease cycle has an onset produced by the disease agent, and sundry symptoms related to the various stages of the disease which in turn reveal clues about the condition of the body. If people get involved, medical interventions can occur, depending on the knowledge of the medical consultant, stage of the disease, age and pocketbook of the patient. These interventions involve diagnosis and treatment of the patient. As people intervene to attempt to disrupt the natural destructive progression of the disease, the life cycle of a disease becomes clear as its various stages manifest themselves in the body. Medical consultants provide a prognosis of the patient's chances, ranging from the fortuitous, it will disappear on its own, to the devastating, a death sentence. The available treatments are variously useful. They can save a patient, partially cure the illness, or make no difference at all. These therapies include prophylactics, and invasive or noninvasive treatments. Many are only placebos. This all is taken as given knowledge about diseases.

The metaphor labeled RACISM AS DISEASE maps such everyday understandings of DISEASE ontology onto the domain of RACISM. It entails a body, and as used in this discourse refers to the United States. The metaphor establishes the quick and lasting conceptual links between these two altogether distinct semantic domains.

King effectively employed this metaphor. He refers to the *poison* of racism: "the largest portion of white America is still poisoned by racism, which is as native to our soil as pine trees, sage brush and buffalo grass." King speaks about a *blight*, and elaborates that the South, as a body, was "retarded by a blight that debilitates not only the Negro but also the white man." This makes racism a disease that is specific to an individual, as well as infecting a society. Excerpt 10, which describes racism as a *virulent disease germ*, provides yet another example. King refers to a *malady*, a *disease in the body politic*, and states that the *nation is sick, extremely sick* with disease.[50]

The metaphor establishes certain semantic associations that are not accurate reflections of RACISM. For example, disease is a natural feature of the human physiology, and its effects are biologically based, not premeditated actions on the part of the disease agent. This cannot be said of racism. More generally, human society is not an organism.[51] Anthills and beehives possess far more similarities to the NATION AS BODY metaphor, with no governing leader and with each insect member acting instinctually to fulfill its genetically appointed task. Human society is not based on instinctual behavior, and while it is composed of hierarchies and its members take on distinct roles, these culture-based relations are entirely learned and demonstrate far more complexity and variability than insect colonies.

In contrast, the features of human society that are appropriately represented by the metaphor include the interrelatedness of the social order and the organization of human behaviors, which are consequences of people's learned capacity to interpret them. Moreover, the RACISM AS DISEASE metaphor highlights the notion of a smooth-functioning society which can become incapacitated by an endogeneous disorder. The normal functioning of society can become so overwhelmed as to destroy it. Such a systemic collapse occurred in South Africa in 1994 with the end of apartheid, and in the Soviet Union in 1989 with the end of empire. Racism and imperialism can be considered fatal afflictions to the national body.

The principal effect of the RACISM AS DISEASE metaphor is to characterize racism as a disease agency affecting not just persons, but the entire society. Individual acts are only manifestations of the systemic racism. This is an accurate feature of the metaphor insofar as the social phenomenon of racism is now understood, because while personal acts of violent and blatant racism are the conscious acts of individuals, these can only be comprehended in the whole context of society.

## RACISM AS CANCER

The kinds of disease that have been associated with racism reveal the nature of its observed effect on society. King speaks of racism as a mental affliction, *schizophrenia,* to express the basic contradiction between the democratic promise and the reality of the American racial state. It is a particularly effective metaphor because schizophrenics, like some apologists for the current state of affairs, are often unaware of their misfortune, do not like their medicine, and resist those who would care for them. As for the people who are injured by a schizophrenic's delusions, the disease is still altogether real and dangerous.

Still and all, the most frequent disease invoked in the 1960s is cancer, a physical affliction that often begins without an outside agent, and which is commonly understood to be a terminal disease, if not treated. In its normal growth sequence, the body may create corrupted cells which grow without control and without regard to the normal body functions. Such malignant cells can develop undetected for years, unnoticed by the body, until a crisis occurs and the whole body is infected as the cancer spreads. When the body at length notices the malignancy, the cancer is already very well established, and intervention must be decisive and often drastic—without treatment the prognosis of cancer is either a quick, painful death or a slow, inexorably debilitating condition as the body's own rogue cells kill it. Thus references to cancer indicate the severity of the social problem of racism—without treatment the democracy will not survive.

Cancer is in reality over two hundred different diseases. The most common cancers (cervical, prostate, ovarian, colorectal, breast, and uterine) illustrate the variety of manifestations and also may evoke in the reader the common dread we feel when confronted with this disease. Treatments of such malignancies cannot be mild; the disease is virulent, which is to say, deadly. Cancer victims often panic and despair, their looming death sentence making them vulnerable. They often deny the severity of their malady. Or they succumb to the lure of quackery, of useless treatments. All victims despair at the treatments which they must undergo, since the treatments often seem more invasive than the disease itself. This, too, is understood when the metaphor RACISM AS CANCER is used. Both Malcolm X and Lyndon Johnson employed this metaphor:

11. Before America allows herself to be destroyed by the "**cancer of racism**" she should become better acquainted with the religious philosophy of Islam, a religion that has already molded people of all colors into one vast family. . . . If Islam can place the spirit of true brotherhood in the hearts of "whites" whom I have met here in the Land of the Prophets, then surely it can also remove the "**cancer of racism**" from the heart of the white American.—Malcolm X[52]

12. But the point of our time is not that discrimination has existed—or that vestiges of it remain. But rather, the point is two-fold: first, that we are making an effort in America to eradicate this **cancer** from our national life, and second, that we must proceed with dispatch in these efforts. —Lyndon Johnson, 1963[53]

*Narrative of RACISM AS CANCER*

Once again, King was the most articulate exponent of this metaphor. A narrative of the metaphor can be constructed from his words in which the principal presuppositions and social context of the metaphor are made explicit.

Such a narrative is based on the cognitive mapping which establishes associations between the semantic domains of CANCER and RACISM, as well as the NATION AS BODY. For King, then, America's body politic has a *cancerous disease*. It suffers from a *malignancy* that is *hate-filled* and yet *curable;* an *unchecked cancer.* From this Southern Baptist minister's perspective, this cancer *scars the soul* of both the racist and the victim. The medical treatment must be on a scale equal to the dimension of the illness, requiring unprecedented kinds and levels of intervention and therapy, which, as the Kerner Report concluded, "neither probe deeper nor demand more than the problems which called them forth. There can be no higher priority for national action and no higher claim on the nation's conscience."[54] Treatment must be decisive and even radical, for without treatment the prognosis is a slow, inexorably debilitating condition. Anything less is incommensurate. If the medication selected for this cancer is tokenism, Reverend King warns, this is merely "a *palliative which relieves emotional distress, but leaves the disease and its ravages unaffected.*" Consequently King exhorts: "We must work assiduously and with determined boldness to *remove from the body politic this cancerous disease of discrimination* which is preventing our democratic and Christian *health* from being realized."[55]

In the 1960s this metaphor was a powerful warning that radical treatment must begin at once, since the incubation period of racism had been long and the crisis was real. The metaphor invoked a death sentence for American democracy, if adequate action were not taken. In spite of such discourse, a mild, noninvasive treatment was self-prescribed by Anglo-American legislators. Affirmative action became the principal remedy for a national affliction of white racism. This governmental scorecard, in effect, was a homeopathic treatment of the American cancer. It would prove insufficient to eliminate the national virulence. Nonetheless, even this became the target of attacks from conservatives.

## Section 3: Political Discourse of the 1990s

### Neoconservative Views

Those who oppose affirmative action as a system of "racist double-standards" and "racial preferences" argue that the very wording of the 1964 Civil Rights Act forbids any reference whatsoever to race and other group characteristics for institutional and governmental purposes. Or they refer to the wording of one of its predecessors, such as President Kennedy's 1961 Executive Order 10925, which states that "The contractor will take affirmative action to ensure that applicants are employed, without regard to their race, creed, color, or national origin." The objective at that time was to eliminate the Jim Crow laws that were an explicit repudiation of American values of equal protection under law, and to begin to redress the endemic injustice of a two-tier society of Whites over Americans of color, which remains the principal objective among affirmative action advocates.

In the anti-affirmative-action view, the United States is already the closest thing on Earth to a pure meritocracy. In a meritocracy, each person is able to earn all that he or she can attain purely by dint of personal industry and the luck of native talent, not by any familial or societal preferences. Since affirmative action is structured to link race and gender to hiring and admission procedures, it is seen as a stricture on individual autonomy, an unacceptable governmental constriction on personal initiative. At times the critics of affirmative action, such as former U.S. Education Secretary William Bennett, express outrage:

> Subverting the ideal of "out of many, one" has wrought tremendous social damage. Numerical equality at the expense of moral equality. Balkanization. The erosion of our national self-understanding. The subordination of individual rights to group rights. The disfigurement of the concept of equal justice. Whatever its original intentions, and whatever benefits have accrued to those who have been on the receiving end of racial preferences (and there are surely some), it should be clear for all to see that affirmative action has created far more injustice than it has dispelled. The most blatant forms of injustice are seen in cases like that of Jennifer Gratz, a young white woman who was denied admission to the University of Michigan. . . . Here was a clearly qualified individual who was nevertheless denied admission to a university—that is, to a place of presumably reasoned reflection—on one ground: she was of the wrong skin color. That is exactly what was done to black applicants at the University of Alabama in the 1950's. . . . It seems to me that in our democracy, we should not leave seventeen-year-olds like Miss Gratz alone to face the formidable and intimidating force of a prestigious university. There is a civic obligation to share her burden. We should not ask her to plead for justice by herself. We should join her.[56]

In this passage, Bennett first appeals to justice. Here justice is disfigured, hence justice is metaphorized as human, and traditionally as a woman. Her "fair" face is blemished, as the political conservative sees it, whenever individual prerogative does not trump claims of social equality. From his point of view, affirmative action violates the sovereign rights of the individual, whatever the claim or reason. Bennett does not mention today's structural inequality which three hundred years of racial injustice created, for which affirmative action was developed as a remedy. His only reference to history is the denial of higher education to blacks in the 1950s, as if this was the main consequence of white racism. In the following excerpt, another conservative critic also disregards history, as s/he condemns affirmative action:

> 13. a large, incoherent system of racial and gender spoils—the only remaining example of institutional racism in America—that by now has entirely lost touch with its original justification of compensation for hard times. (C 40)[57]

Bennett's move is cynical, since his second appeal is to the loss of "national self-understanding." The use of affirmative action, in Bennett's view, somehow obscures U.S. history—particularly the national motto, *e pluribus unum* —from its citizens. One certainly could turn the argument around and say that the diminution of racism by means of affirmative action provides greater access to economic and social fruits of citizenship for all the people of the United States—not just the historically privileged. Bennett conveniently ignores the U.S. history of white men in power who designated people of color as inferior. Lastly, Bennett, among other *Commentary* essayists, appeals to the prospect that affirmative action will *balkanize* the United States. Such references are hyperbole. This is evident as soon as comparisons are made to recent events in the Balkans. Vladimir Gligorov describes balkanization as a military response to economic instability which came with the end of the Communist system. Adding to the instability, the loosening of enforced national unity after Tito's death created further social insecurity which was exploited by Slobodan Milosevic, who revived ancient ethnic enmity. The Serb ethnic movement, a by-product of this insecurity, is based on demagogic calls for autarchy, namely, national economic self-sufficiency. Ellis and Wright point out that using the term *balkanization* for California and the relations among U.S. ethnic groups has little geographical merit, and seriously distorts U.S. demographic trends. Keshav Makath argues that the only parallel between the Balkans and California in the 1990s was the exploitation of intergroup tensions by political opportunists during economic recession, and, one might add, on university campuses, in a period when multiculturalism was making inroads on the previously unchallenged assimilationist hegemony.[58]

In its thirty years of operation, affirmative action has not rent the U.S. social fabric. More accurately, the United States is experiencing greater participation and expression of cultures from a wider array of citizenry with a legitimate place in society, with a modest reduction of the intensity of Anglo-American cultural hegemony. Any reference to international ethnic conflicts is an effort to distract the listener/reader from continuing domestic inequity.

In the context of Bennett's reference to the woman denied admission to a university, it is well to recall the numbers of reverse discrimination cases versus discrimination cases currently pending in the EEOC. Bennett, further, dismisses aversive, institutional, and societal racism. The view articulated presumes that white racism and its repercussions for the education, employment, and housing of citizens of color only sporadically occur in contemporary America.

Moreover, Bennett's argument is that any deviation from the American credo of individualism is an attack on personal liberty. Thus, social justice is antithetical to private liberty. Bennett and others conveniently forget that the idealized color-blind and laissez-faire American Creed that they laud, which was formulated in the eighteenth century, bore twin fruit.[59] One is the justly famous American Experiment. However, it simultaneously produced the infamous U.S. legacy of legitimated racism that created two classes of Americans, white citizens and racialized denizens. This regime, which has not been entirely dismantled, allots cumulative preference and power to the privileged, at the expense of the disadvantaged.[60] On this contradiction Martin Luther King Jr. is eloquent, again with the dominant metaphor of the 1960s:

14. Ever since the signing of the Declaration of Independence, America has manifested **a schizophrenic personality** on the question of race. She has been torn between selves—a self in which she has proudly professed democracy and a self in which she has sadly practiced the antithesis of democracy. . . . Indeed, segregation and discrimination are strange paradoxes in a nation founded on the principle that all men are created equal.[61]

White racism is a challenge as large as representative democracy itself. Most importantly, as clearly stated in the findings of the Kerner Commission, white indifference will not sweeten the bitter products of white racism. Unless the cumulative effects of white racism are proactively eliminated, then the Experiment will fail.

The critics of affirmative action dismiss the enduring endowment of what Gunnar Myrdal called the American Dilemma. It was this unwarranted and prevailing double standard that the Civil Rights Act was formulated to invalidate, which has not been entirely rectified, and what affirmative action was supposed to address.

*Genesis of Proposition 209*

The passage of Proposition 209 in 1996 forbade all public employment, education, and contracting programs in the state of California which took gender, race, national origin, ethnicity, or color into account. The referendum was developed to eliminate reverse discrimination against white males, as defined in terms of government programs that distinguish the gender and race of individuals. The referendum was created to end "the regime of race- and sex-based quotas, preferences, and set-asides" which are a twisted inversion of the "noble goal" of the Civil Rights Act of 1964.[62] Since Proposition 209's proponents believed affirmative action sanctioned discrimination against white males by authorizing preferential treatment of racialized minorities, they claimed the measure would restore equity before the law, establish a color-blind California government, and promote national unity.

The 1994 California elections passed the anti-immigrant referendum, Proposition 187, and reelected Pete Wilson as governor. These midterm national elections also brought a Republican majority to Congress. As Lydia Chávez notes in her fascinating history of the Proposition 209 campaign, the time was ripe for a referendum which addressed the fears of the white male voting bloc.[63] Affirmative action became the next target for termination among conservative activists. During this period of President Clinton's Milquetoast quip "Mend it; don't end it," the depth of the policy's political vulnerability was easy to gauge. In the same month the Regents of the University of California voted to abolish affirmative action in their higher education system.

The wording of the first section of Proposition 209, which was called the California Civil Rights Initiative (CCRI) by its supporters, reads as follows: "The State shall not discriminate against, or grant preferential treatment to, any individual or group on the basis of race, sex, color, ethnicity, or national origin in the operation of public employment, public education, or public contracting." There are some items to note about the deceptive wording of the initiative. *Civil rights* was mentioned in the wording of the initiative and in the name of the organization supporting it. Proposition 209's sponsors argued that it was a civil rights initiative. Critics retorted that this initiative would return California to the state of civil rights that existed before the Act of 1964. Second, while eliminating affirmative action was the specific objective of the CCRI, the words *affirmative action* did not appear in the referendum, which amended the California constitution to exclude preferential treatment for women and racialized minorities.

Beyond the slick packaging, the referendum was also carefully worded to preserve older traditions of "granting preferential treatment" that expressly served the interests of the privileged. By way of illustration, California universities and colleges are still able to preferentially enroll children of alumni on the basis of their political influence.

As it turned out, critics of Proposition 209 were correct to worry that many voters would support the measure only because they would falsely believe their vote would bolster affirmative action rather than destroy it. A *Los Angeles Times* exit poll indicated that 54 percent of Angelinos leaving their voting stations supported affirmative action programs that were designed to help women and minorities obtain better jobs and education. This was the same proportion of voters who supported Proposition 209 in Los Angeles.[64]

The campaign for Proposition 209 was entirely overshadowed by the national campaign for the presidency when, in November 1996, it passed. While only 45 percent of voters overall rejected Proposition 209, the vote broke down along racial lines. Sixty-one percent of Asians voted against it. They had been expected to take a conservative position to enhance their current prevalence in higher education, but as racialized minorities, Asian voters were apparently cognizant of the lasting harmful effects of white racism. Likewise, among African Americans, 75 percent rejected the initiative, as did 76 percent of Mexican American voters.[65]

The University Regents' vote to eliminate affirmative action in the University of California system, which was affirmed with the passage of Proposition 209, sent a strong message: the University of California was not interested in minority community participation in professional and leadership roles across the state. The ultimate damage to California cannot be projected. What is clear, however, is that restricting the higher education of racialized minorities maintains the status quo. It also has a cumulative effect. It restricts access to political and economic power for this population, which is now the state's numerical majority. Each year of educational inequity affects the long-term future of the state. It is not clear when minority students will again attend the University of California in the proportions that they did in 1994, much less when Latinos and other minority students will attend colleges and universities with parity. So, the social damage inflicted on the state will indubitably increase as time passes.

## Less Virulence in the Political Discourse of the 1990s

In keeping with the DISEASE metaphor used in the American discourse on racism, the discourse on affirmative action from its inception has employed the term *remedy*. The original metaphoric representation of affirmative action is medical. It remained so in the 1990s. We find multiple references to AFFIRMATIVE ACTION AS REMEDY by both its advocates and its detractors:

> 15. When it was begun in the early 60's, affirmative action was an attempt to **remedy the ill effects** of past discrimination action against blacks. (C 25)
> 16. Affirmative action on grounds [of diversity] is different from the **remedial** variety. (C 25)
> 17. The justification for undertaking affirmative action programs or passing affirmative action laws may be to assure nondiscrimination (i.e., to prevent future discrimination), or to give a **remedy** for current discrimination, to promote diversity, or to do something else. (E 15)[66]
> 18. At one extreme, affirmative action is seen as a legally sanctioned **remedy** for past and present racial discrimination. (C 43)

References to the medical model are frequent in political discourse, and in political philosophy. This metaphor can be traced to Plato, and may be as old as humankind. For example, in the *Republic* the polity is metaphorized as a body: "our State matured," "true and healthy constitution of the State," and "State at fever-pitch." As for contemporary philosophers, Jürgen Habermas explicitly introduces his analysis of late capitalism with the medical metaphor. In *Legitimation Crisis,* he links economic "crisis" to an illness of the body politic, and autonomy to its health:[67]

> To use the expression "late capitalism" is to put forward the hypothesis that, even in state-regulated capitalism, social development involved "contradiction" or crises. I shall therefore begin by elucidating the con-

cept of crisis. Prior to its employment as a social-scientific term, the concept of crisis was familiar to us from its medical usage. In that context it refers to the phase of an illness in which it is decided whether or not the organism's self-healing powers are sufficient for recovery. . . . We therefore associate with crises the idea of an objective force that deprives a subject of some part of his normal sovereignty. To conceive of a process as a crisis is tacitly to give it a normative meaning—the resolution of the crisis effects a liberation of the subject caught up in it.

*Remedy* implies medical treatment for the ailing body, which links DISEASE and BODY to other compatible semantic associations in the cognitive frame. In this case the medical metaphor for affirmative action as the remedy implies both that the United States is a body and that affirmative action is medicine for the disease of white racism. Perhaps not surprisingly, this is almost the entire range of metaphorizations used during the Proposition 209 debate. Only a few other metaphors were employed:

19. Affirmative action as originally conceived was an attempt **to cast a wide net** and create greater opportunity for blacks. (C 19)
20. Moreover, it is not a single **tool** but a family of **tools**. . . . Decision makers have a **large toolbox** to draw from when they design affirmative action programs. (E 17, 22)

Also see *weave* in excerpt 23 below.

## Proponents' Discourse on Racism

In the political discourse of the 1960s, DISEASE was the dominant metaphor for racism. Otherwise, racism was personified or it was cast in political terms of war. It was rarely discussed on its own terms, so the concept was understood in these metaphorical terms. Consequently, citizens without an advanced degree in social psychology or sociology employed their own medical understandings of the phenomenon in 1965. Thirty-five years later, America's discourse on racism has not advanced at all. Instead, it might be argued that the public's understanding has regressed, as the prevalent discourse reverted to pre-civil-rights-era metaphorizations.

This deterioration will be documented in the review of affirmative action essays of the 1990s, beginning with the pro-affirmative-action point of view. Christopher Edley, a political centrist who pointedly favors the continuation of affirmative action, makes reference in his book to POLITICS AS WAR and POLITICS AS WEATHER, as shown below. Ever sensitive to Americans' queasiness about the phenomenon, Edley deftly avoids direct reference to racism whenever possible. When it cannot be sidestepped, the source domain of the metaphor he used continues to be DISEASE, as in *racial healing:*

21. Each day's news, each season's book list, every major political campaign, assaults us with upsetting evidence about **society's pain** and about the gathering storm clouds. (E 4)

22. This selective amnesia is understandable, for the new taboo against expressions of racial animus has been very effective, but it is important to appreciate that this taboo is an invention of the modern civil rights revolution of the 1960s. **Racial conflict may be congenital in the human species, but even if it is not, it is a common enough disease with no recent history of extended remission.** More, the view of racism and prejudice as **moral malady** has rarely been either widely held or deeply rooted in America. We should not flatter ourselves by thinking otherwise. (E 25–26)

23. It has become cliché to note the enduring complexity and **pathology of race-related thinking in America**—complex in its nature and in the tight weave binding it to other threads of our social and economic fabric, **pathological** in its dispiriting and sometimes brutal expression. (E 5–6)

24. I think of **America's attitudes and behaviors about race** as being **akin to a deep, somewhat debilitating neurosis, a mental disorder or illness. What is the state of the patient today?** (E 47)

It is unfair to compare these metaphors of a law professor writing under the aegis of President Clinton to those of Reverend King, one of America's greatest orators; however, Edley's ambivalence about the nature of racism— whether congenital or contingent—is unfortunate. Fear and hate may be part of the biological makeup of Homo sapiens, but racism is not a part of human nature; humans do not by birth recognize so-called race.[68]

Racism is entirely learned and takes on an American culture-specific configuration. Calling racism a national neurosis, even a *somewhat debilitating neurosis,* namely, a vague mental disorder occasioned by mild anxieties and petty phobias, is a far cry from associating white racism with the virulence of cancer. Edley implies cancer in excerpt 22 when he uses the term *remission,* but in general he presents racism either as a far less perilous medical condition or as a phenomenon that cannot be altered by political intervention, such as weather, as in excerpt 21, or human nature. In a society notorious for its reluctance to take strong medicine, the most widely quoted proponents of affirmative action in the 1990s did not invest American racism with much gravity. Consequently, the advocates for affirmative action did not impress a generally indifferent public.

In my own view, contemporary covert racism is habituated ignorance. As ignorance, it cannot be passively eliminated, in the manner of the sugar cube vaccination against polio. Aggressive education and deterrence are in order. It should be explicitly and aggressively challenged to make the public aware of its threat to each member of society. In particular, each schoolchild should be provided the opportunity of discovering the "softmindedness" of racism, to use Dr. King's phrase.[69] A social affliction of another order that is also a legacy of U.S. history, cigarette smoking, has been much more effectively confronted in the same period. Thirty-five years ago, inhaling superheated soot into the soft pink tissue of our lungs was considered a harmless, enjoyable, and even sophisticated pastime; today no one is ignorant of the facts, with a concomitant change of societal attitude and behavior. It is clear that white citizens, on the other hand, do not realize that white racism continues to regulate the U.S. social order to the detriment of all citizens.

## Neoconservative Discourse on Racism

Neoconservative critics of affirmative action also prefer to avoid discussions of racism. But they are less queasy than liberals and have been considerably more creative in its portrayal, all the while promoting a far more restricted definition. In the *Commentary* essays, reference to white racism is rare, in contrast to the clear-cut references made in the Kerner Report. These conservative essayists made use of a generic reference without victim or perpetrator, as in excerpt 25, or, as will be seen, characterized racism principally as a matter of reverse discrimination:

> 25. But if we are ever to heal our **racial wounds,** it will be through a national determination, morally resolute and backed by law where that is appropriate, never again to give preference by race or color or sex. (C 23)

Moreover, institutional, societal, and foundational racism are rarely mentioned. In the entire sample of neoconservative texts drawn from the *Commentary* issue on affirmative action, the following excerpt is the single example which mentioned structural racism, and yet, as will be discussed below, even it discusses the remedy of affirmative action in narrow legal terms of reparation.

26. In other words, reparative justice is the best rationale for affirmative action—offering a benefit to certain people in order to offset the disadvantages they inherited as a consequence of deep-seated **social pathologies such as racism and sexism.** (C 35)

The *Commentary* essayists tend to presume that racism consists mainly of individual acts of overt antipathy, typically violent acts. They pass over Scheurich and Young's four other types of racism, which are its most prevalent modern forms. Much as Edley characterized above in excerpt 22, overt expressions of racism have almost disappeared from public life, as a reflex of a "new taboo against expressions of racial animus." Neoconservatives take this taboo against guileless signaling of racism to be sufficient evidence that U.S. racism is nearly extinct, except for reverse discrimination, so racialized minorities no longer have much to complain about:

27. Even the category for which affirmative action was originally instituted, African-Americans, includes many today from middle-class backgrounds who have not faced any noteworthy discrimination in academia for decades. (C 29)

In excerpt 27, while racialized members of the middle class are said to suffer no racism in public education, notice that no such presumption is made about the vast majority of racialized working-class Americans. In spite of educational statistics reporting little change in the quality or range of opportunities available to racialized minorities in the late 1990s, the U.S. status quo cannot be faulted, from this right-wing point of view. Accordingly, calls for continued attacks against structural bastions of privilege, and for uninterrupted vigilance against white racism that continues to plague society, at times induce peevish reactions on the part of these commentators:

28. Those who do just well enough at school either fall at a later occupational hurdle—or require a succession of preferences to maintain the elite career that they have been told is their birthright. And because they are clever people (rather than absolutely brilliant), they will sense that their success is bogus and is therefore occasionally resented by their colleagues. Unless they are also of superhuman honesty, they will seek refuge from this uncomfortable self-knowledge and join the dropouts in embracing the theory that white racism is pervasive and explains their various plights. In terms of personal achievement and happiness, everyone is worse off. (C 41)

29. Why have blacks in universities introduced their own system of Jim Crow, with separate dining tables, separate classes, and, where they have succeeded in imposing their demands, separate dorms? However militantly they may talk, what they are doing is huddling against failure, and against the exposure of that failure. (C 24)

## Contesting the Common Criticisms of Affirmative Action

Such conservative commentary is indicative of the pessimism that opponents of affirmative action express, most often with little real proof. In fact, during the Proposition 209 debate, neither side had much empirical evidence to bolster its case. This has changed. Ample evidence now exists to support an optimistic view of human nature. William Bowen and Derek Bok, past presidents of Princeton and Harvard Universities, respectively, have co-authored *The Shape of the River: Long-term Consequences of Considering Race in College and University Admissions*. In it, the academic and career records of eighty thousand minority undergraduates from twenty-eight prestigious liberal arts and research universities are reviewed to provide a complete basis for the critical assessment of affirmative action. Bowen and Bok's textured review of affirmative action in higher education, which goes to great lengths to address criticisms of the policy, returns an overwhelmingly favorable judgment of its success and warranted continuation.

There is "abundant evidence that these minority students had strong academic credentials when they entered college, that they graduated in large numbers, and that they have done very well after leaving college."[70] As an essayist in *Commentary* noted, they enter college with "much higher degree attainment goals that those of their white classmates." However, contrary to the gloomy neoconservative view about these students, as in excerpts 28–29, Bowen and Bok found that of the minority students who matriculated in 1989, 79 percent graduated within six years, far above the 59 percent graduation rates of comparable Whites. They were as likely to receive advanced degrees in law, business, or medicine as their white classmates. Once these affirmative action alumni are in the prime of their lives and careers, they display a tremendous return on the country's investment. The 1976 minority matriculants participated at a higher rate in community and civic undertakings than their white classmates, and are much more likely than Whites to hold leadership positions, "especially . . . those involving social service, youth and school-related activities."[71] Thus, to the common claim that race-sensitive admissions harm and demoralize their intended beneficiaries the authors respond, "if the black students admitted to the most academically demanding schools suffer as a result, they certainly don't seem to know it."[72] Nor is their future penalized, as measured by their documented career trajectories. "Black matriculants do better in their careers, both absolutely and relative to Whites, the more competitive the academic environment."[73] "In the eyes of those best positioned to know, any putative costs of race-based policies have been overwhelmed by the benefits gained through enhanced access to excellent educational opportunities."[74]

Another conservative criticism of affirmative action is that Whites are taken to be inherently antiminority:

> 30. To the extent that preferences have been justified as necessary to overcome racial disadvantage, they have created an incentive to insist upon and exaggerate the pervasiveness of white racism and to contend, contrary to fact, that whites are unalterably opposed to black advancement. To the extent that these programs have been justified as providing "diversity," they have created the incentive for blacks to manifest their "differences" by seeing race at the crux of everything and by developing exceptional skill in the perception of slights. Most basically, racial preferences tend to create an expectation of a general black exemption from ordinary obligations and requirements. The thrust is toward a society in which it will be generally understood that blacks are just "too different" to be expected to conform to the rules applicable to others. (C 32)

As to the view articulated in excerpt 30, the problem is not that racialized minorities believe that Whites are unalterably opposed to the advancement of minorities. As Dovidio noted above, Whites do not always discern the structural and societal racism that are at the foundation of economic and educational inequity, and tend not to be self-aware of their privilege or the aversive and societal racism that suffuse American social life.[75] King turns the mirror on the skeptics, asking the hard questions:

> Why is equality so assiduously avoided? Why does white America delude itself, and how does it rationalize the evil it retains? The majority of white Americans consider themselves sincerely committed to justice for the Negro. They believe that American society is essentially hospitable to fair play and to steady growth toward a middle-class utopia embodying racial harmony. But unfortunately this is a fantasy of self-deception and comfortable vanity. Overwhelmingly America is still struggling with irresolution and contradictions. It has been sincere

and even ardent in welcoming some change. But too quickly apathy and disinterest rise to the surface when the next logical steps are to be taken. . . . As the nation passes from opposing extremist behavior to the deeper and more pervasive elements of equality, white America reaffirms its bonds to the status quo. It had contemplated comfortably hugging the shoreline but now fears that the winds of change are blowing it out to sea. . . . The great majority of Americans . . . are uneasy with injustice but unwilling yet to pay a significant price to eradicate it.[76]

King also made the following appraisal: "A good many observers have remarked that if equality could come at once, the Negro would not be ready for it. I submit that the white American is even more unprepared."[77] Likewise, it is not that racialized minorities are too different to follow the long-established rules of competition; rather, these rules have unfairly sustained the privilege of one group at the expense of others.

In the 1990s, racism is readily ascribed in U.S. public discourse only to two categories of individuals: citizens who are flagrant racists, and foreigners. In the first category we have ex–Ku Klux Klan leader David Duke, Black Muslim spokesman Louis Farrakhan, and felonious police officers, such as Justin Volpe and Charles Schwarz.[78]

In the second, we have foreign despots such as Saddam Hussein or Slobodan Milosevic, or despotic governments such as the Taliban. Note that these foreign leaders are deemed enemies of the United States, so a pseudopsychological diagnosis of racism as sociopathology can be comfortably made. Such a determination then can be used to justify, to the complacent American public, punishing actions by the U.S. military against entire populations, not just their leaders.

Institutional racism is rarely admitted. If public or corporate officials are caught red-handed, an out-of-court financial settlement follows as quickly as possible. Organizational racism is disavowed, and plaintiffs are often gagged as part of the terms of the settlement. By way of illustration, two days before the Proposition 209 vote, national newspapers headlined racism within oil giant Texaco, exposing audiotaped meetings in which blatant racist treatment of 1,400 African American employees was revealed. The lawsuits that followed were quietly settled out of court in ten days with, predictably, no admission of guilt. Texaco officials insisted that the incidents were isolated, announced "diversity training" programs, and most importantly reiterated a blanket disclaimer of corporate racism. The matter quickly disappeared from the major daily newspapers, rather than sparking further investigations of institutional racism.[79]

## Section 4: Neoconservative Discourse Stratagems

Neoconservatives in the 1990s changed the terms of the debate on affirmative action in two moves. One was to discredit the predominant view of racism by confronting the 1960s metaphor for affirmative action. The second was to offer an alternative set of metaphors to replace the medical terminology.

In the first move, neoconservatives rejected the traditional representation of affirmative action in two stages, using the very same metaphor used by its advocates. U.S. Senator Robert Dole, once a stalwart supporter of affirmative action, became a critic when trying to save his failed run for the presidency. He stated in mid-1995 that affirmative action could not heal the sickness it was designed to treat:[80]

> 31. Dole called the affirmative action programs he had supported for more than two decades a "**Band-Aid**" that failed to help minorities and women and "a corruption of the principles of individual liberty and equal opportunity upon which our country was founded."

With this metaphor the opponents of affirmative action simply belittled the idea that affirmative action was a good social medication, and did not contest the conceptual frame of the metaphor. More examples are provided below:

> 32. [Affirmative action] is a **prescription for racial consciousness and conflict** inconsistent with the maintenance of a viable multiracial society; it means abandoning hope for an integrated society and accepting the inevitability of separatism. (C 31)
>
> 33. The effect of racial preferences at selective colleges is virtually to guarantee that students [of color] are placed in institutions at least one level above where they would be fully competitive, a **formula** for frustration and resentment and the source of most of the major problems **plaguing** the American campus today. (C 32)
>
> 34. The fact is that both voluntary segregation and political correctness are **powerful side-effects of the social drug called affirmative action, and it may be time to ask if the cure is worth the price—particularly since the drug itself seems thus far to have shown an alarmingly low rate of efficiency.** (C 28)

In the next stage of the attack, which was used with great effect during the California Proposition 209 campaign, the original RACISM AS DISEASE metaphor is subverted. Here the NATION AS BODY metaphor remains in place, with its attendant entailments of diseases and possible remedies. In this stratagem, neoconservatives retain the metaphor's semantic source domain, MEDICINE, and respecify the target domain.[81] So, affirmative action is said to be worse than simply a medication with bad side effects; affirmative action is a disease:

35. Preference ostensibly given to overcome the legacy of racism **takes the form of racism, nurtures racism,** embitters the national community, and **infects every facet of public life** with racial criteria whose counter-productivity is matched only by their immorality. (C 23)

36. I am deeply impressed by the **toxic consequences** of drawing racial distinctions among people in this multiracial society, particularly when the racial line-drawing is done by the government. (C 35)

37. The relevant issue is not [President Clinton's] benign words regarding a "hand up" to "people who have had a hard time," but his policy's **malignant real-world effects.** . . . Three decades [after President Kennedy's Executive Order on nondiscriminatory hiring], our affirmative-action regime is, in all important respects, a **malignant mutation.** (C 19)

38. When [the Rev. Jesse] Jackson arrived [for the University of California Regents' meeting at which affirmative action was eliminated as a factor in UC admissions, hiring, and promotion, Governor] Wilson's greeting was on the front page of the local newspaper. "We must not allow our country to be **infected with the deadly virus of tribalism,**" the governor warned. Support for affirmative action, Wilson implied, would **put the nation's health at peril.** (Chávez, p. 59)

In excerpt 38 Pete Wilson repudiated both affirmative action and Jesse Jackson's public role as an advocate for social justice issues. The terms of this rebuke, uttered moments before the Regents' vote, indicate the profound confidence Wilson had as a voting ex officio board member who had appointed several of the board members who would cast a ballot. The rebuke was brazen, recalling the nineteenth-century slander of non-Caucasians as primitive "tribal" people. Neoconservatives characterized affirmative action as a disease, subverting the metaphor King and Malcolm X had used to depict white racism. For another excerpt summoning AFFIRMATIVE ACTION

AS DISEASE nomenclature, recall William Bennett's reference to Justice's fair face disfigured, which makes affirmative action the scabies of the U.S. body. Since the same cognitive frame is used as in the 1960s pro-affirmative-action metaphor, critics of affirmative action are able to call upon the same semantic associations. The message put forth is, just as the disease of white racism can be remedied with an appropriate legislative nostrum, the disease of affirmative action can be remedied, in this case with its elimination with the passage of Proposition 209.

## Racism as an Individual's Crime

Critics go well beyond the medical metaphor to reframe the public discourse on affirmative action. Armed with the ostensible contradiction of a color-sensitive program evolving from the color-blind Civil Rights Act language, they next target diversity, the second rationale for affirmative action. As presented in the public discourse of the 1990s, this motive for affirmative action programs is to diversify the primary social institutions of the country, to foster the participation of the full range of people in society. The critics reject the diversity criterion as incompatible with reparative justice, again disregarding institutional and societal racism.

39. The result today is a large incoherent system of racial and gender spoils—the only remaining example of institutional racism in America—that has by now entirely lost touch with its original justification of compensation for hard times. Even its advocates—as shameless a bunch of casuists as you will find outside the public-relations department of Hell—concede this by implication when they shift the argument from hardship and past discrimination to the current justification of "diversity." And the last covers a further multitude of lies. (C 40)

40. For most people, it is simply wrong for government to treat people on the basis of race. Powerful arguments should be required to overcome this obstacle, and yet the arguments offered for racial preferences are surprisingly weak. The primary argument—that preferences compensate for past unjust disadvantage—is patently invalid and obviously uncandid. It is not possible to compensate for an injury to A, inflicted in the past by B, by granting today a benefit to C at the expense of D. Moreover, if disadvantage were the concern, evidence of disadvantage should be the criterion for compensatory treatment. Race is not a proxy for disadvantage. (C 31)

41. Affirmative action has never been simply a "hand up" to "people who have had a hard time." It originally meant preferential treatment for people belonging to the racial group that had had a hard time, namely, American blacks under slavery and Jim Crow, or to the sex that feminists falsely claimed to have had a hard time, namely, American women under motherhood. Many of its supposed beneficiaries, however, had not themselves had a hard time, having been born into rich or successful middle-class families. (C 40)[82]

42. It is race preference (by whatever name it is called) that is to be condemned. For the race preferences commonly given today, the retrospective justification grounded in alleged compensation is almost invariably a fraud. (C 22)

The metaphor of the 1960s, RACISM AS DISEASE, is jettisoned. In its place an individualist ethos is given primacy, and with it, social accountability is discarded. Racism is restricted to the actions of individuals. Like slander or robbery, racism is perpetrated by one wretched person on another. The misdeeds of a racist, then, can be dealt with on a case-by-case basis from the everyday understanding of reparative justice, not social justice. Thus the legal relief should only be compensation to victims by perpetrators for a particular offense. As portrayed in excerpts 39–42, groups of people do not suffer societal racism at all in this society.

## Societal Racism Is More than Individual Crimes

Compensation for individual acts of injustice will not make merit-based achievement possible for all Americans, if racism persists. What racialized minorities want is to eliminate the racial hierarchy and to refit the nation's major institutions to make equal opportunity a reality. The racially discriminatory statutes eliminated in 1964 were not the last rivets in the racist framework of the nation. Beyond the statutory barriers, the social and institutional barriers erected over three hundred years of white American racism against other Americans must be razed so that society's opportunities and responsibilities can be distributed more fairly. In the beginning of the affirmative action enterprise, this was the target, even for Ronald Reagan. As California's governor, in 1974 Reagan formalized a statewide affirmative action program to achieve "a state workforce with each ethnic group and women represented by occupation, responsibility and salary level in proportion to its representation in the labor market."[83] Racial parity remains a legitimate objective to ultimately achieve a postracial state. The rub is that a more equitable distribution of proportional benefits and responsibilities cannot be accomplished by fiat. However, greater access is one crucial part in the process to achieve such a society.

> 43. And—not least important—as race, gender, or other characteristics became more crucial for determining who got what, America became a more divided, a more divisive, society. As we made more people winners in the race for success, we managed to diminish the importance of success. As we moved toward racial equality "as a fact," we made racial differences more salient. As we sought to help those who were hobbled by the legacies of discrimination, we created programs that left many of them ill-equipped to compete. (C 37)

In excerpt 43 the conservative essayist succinctly articulates the fears about affirmative action that people of goodwill may harbor, including that the "rules of the game" for American success have been changed and affirmative action *hobbles* its racialized beneficiaries. It must be reiterated that the "race for success" has been rigged against women and racialized minorities from the beginning of the U.S. experience. This topic will be expanded in the next chapter. Even for the transcendentally talented, success requires an opportunity to compete. In the first years of the twenty-first century, the vaunted American meritocracy remains an illusion for minorities. Equal opportunity is still not available to individuals who are members of the groups that were traditionally shut out of the contest on once-legal racist grounds. As Bowen and Bok document, on the other hand, when given a chance, racialized minority students have risen to the challenge and succeeded, to the benefit of the whole society. The rules have changed precisely to provide greater opportunity for all Americans to compete.

The second fear, that race has become more salient in our society, is true for demographic and representational reasons. The proportion of Americans of color is increasing in this country, an increase that will continue as far as can be projected into this new century. Also, in public culture there is the beginning of representations of racialized populations in ways other than the stereotypic or token presentations that reinforce the long-dominant racial hegemony. Angry reactions to the weakening Anglo-American cultural hegemony were often voiced in *Commentary* among the most inflexible essayists, but most citizens have welcomed the increasingly cosmopolitan character of America.[84]

This begins to address the final concern expressed in excerpt 43, that U.S. society has become more divisive. Historical memory is short and selective, and the U.S. public was never taught or has forgotten the stories of systematic and severe Anglo-American aggression. These include, for example, decades of American Indian genocide, Texas Ranger suppressions, Ku Klux Klan lynchings, and Jim Crow laws. When these national crimes against whole populations are lost to public memory, then the result of such brutality, namely, economic and institutional disadvantage, is easily attributed to the "content of our character" and the ostensible inferiority of minority cultures. As educational researcher Daniel Solórzano has found, children of color in substandard public schools continue to suffer daily "microaggressions," namely, the consequences of these institutional and attitudinal inequities.[85] In contrast, affirmative action has not sparked divisiveness. What affirmative action has generated, however, is insecurity among the privileged who were previously oblivious to their decided leverage. Affirmative action gradually peels away cultural privilege that unfairly shielded some from fair competition with all other Americans. All will be enriched and strengthened in the process.

## Further Anti-Affirmative-Action Metaphors

While contesting and subverting the single dominant metaphor used by liberals who wanted to retain affirmative action, neoconservatives used a range of secondary metaphors to redefine the affirmative action discourse in their own terms. For one, affirmative action is portrayed as an oppressive government:

44. A "diversity" **regime** does not curb discrimination; it invites it. It does not expose racism; it recapitulates and, sometimes, reinvents it. (C 51)

45. There is, in fact, every reason to believe that business would be more effective at drawing blacks into the economic mainstream than is the case under the current affirmative-action **regime**. (C 49)

46. And so should we move—without delay or apology, with purpose and conviction—to lift the burden of the current **regime of racial preferences** from the shoulders of every man and woman, young and old. (C 20)

These references to *regime,* an oppressive government, signal the inherent evils of an activist federal government in the discourse of neoconservative politics, namely, unjust impositions on individual liberty. The term *regime* is also used in medical discourse for a course of treatment. Associated with this conservative political philosophy is the view that affirmative action is antidemocratic.

47. No policy [such as affirmative action] that **contradicts the very democratic premise of America** can be expected to last forever, a fact that should be pondered by affirmative action's supporters before they gird themselves for all-out resistance to alternative arrangements. (C 49)

This is ironic in light of the privilege that institutional racism offers one group at the expense of others. Representativeness is illusory when economic and social parity remains only a dream.

In another metaphor, affirmative action is taken to be a mechanism or organism. As a governmental program which is metaphorically characterized as mechanism, entailments such as broken, inoperative, or corroded can be employed by affirmative action's critics.

48. a program that sounded as good in theory as it had in 1965 but that nearly 35 years of experience should have taught us was inevitably subject to **corruption** in practice. **Corruption?** Let us count the ways. (C 47)
49. It follows from what I have said so far that I cannot see how affirmative action could be mended. It is **rotten at the root,** and the only thing to be done is to abolish it outright. (C 42)

The excerpts above can be compared to excerpt 52 and Senator Dole's reference in excerpt 31. Corruption can be of organic materials, which is the decomposition of dead flesh. Further, such matter finds its way into metaphorical descriptions of affirmative action as political payoffs:

50. The political realities are such that most cities and other public bodies now granting these preferences fight to maintain them, even in the face of Supreme Court proscriptions. It has become the current and accepted form of distributing **political pork.** (C 30)
51. lest some readers start grumbling about the **evils of the public trough** and the alleged similarities between its Irish-American **feeders** and its black ones (both groups, some would say, inclined more to political eloquence than to entrepreneurialism) . . . (C 50)

Also see excerpt 13 above, which refers to political *spoils*. Another metaphor characterizes affirmative action as a government entitlement program and a corporate program of legal expediency:

> 52. I argued strenuously against the inclination of blacks to see affirmative action as a **totem**—a policy assumed to lie beyond the bounds of legitimate criticism, symbolizing the nation's commitment to "do the right thing" for black people. In short I sought to expose the fact that the practice of affirmative action had been corrupted, to the detriment of those it was intended to help. (C 38)
>
> 53. Corporate America is now largely in favor of affirmative action as a **talisman** against discrimination lawsuits. (C 42)

Lastly, some affirmative action critics are less apt to be creative in their use of metaphors, and judge it summarily:

> 54. It would be rhetorically shrewd to put on a mantle of reasonableness and . . . concede a few modest benefits to affirmative action. But it would be wrong. There are no good effects that can be traced to it—none, nil, *nada,* zero. (C 40–41, italics in the original)

## Speaking about Race

In line with neoconservative thinking that American racism is primarily manifested as personal failings, not structural ones, a new problem engendered by affirmative action is that race and "race-related concerns" have inappropriately become more legitimate topics of public discourse.

> 55. The practice of affirmative action has been transmogrified to the point that race-based discrimination has become the centerpiece of the liberal civil-rights agenda, so that today a Jesse Jackson can, with a straight face, make the bizarre claim that "to ignore race and sex is racist and sexist." (C 19)
>
> 56. Instead of reducing the American consciousness of race, affirmative action has increased and exacerbated it. (C 47)
>
> 57. The President insists that we need a "national conversation" on race. In fact, one thing we do *not* need is more talk on race. Our problem is racial obsession. It is hard to think of any issue—education, economics, welfare, the criminal-justice system, celebrity trials, you name it—where the conversation is not eventually reduced to race. (C 19, italics in original)

For the privileged, the status quo is better left unnoticed; for the disadvantaged, pointing out injustice opens up the possibility of change. Accordingly, this neoconservative discourse stratagem calling for an indefinite moratorium on discussions of racism maintains the comfort zone of white Americans. Appealing to the new taboo on discussing racism, neoconservatives' argument is that silence will heal wounds, and constantly mentioning racism will not allow the nation's old wounds to heal. However, silence will not balance the scales of justice. Silence about racism's symptoms, prognosis, and remedies will not lead to its alleviation. Silence absolves the discomforted from the queasiness of discussing a taboo, and allows the wicked to go about their day without dispute. As long as there is silence, the guilty will never relinquish any unfair advantage they maintain. It is as if ending discussions about earthquakes, heart disease, or overpopulation can eliminate their very real threat. To talk about racism acknowledges the social issue, points it out, and begins to address its solution.

## On the Stigma of Affirmative Action

Another attack on affirmative action critiques its effect on its participants. The claim is that beneficiaries who were in fact able to demonstrate their promise and energy as they rose through previously impervious institutions are stigmatized by their association with affirmative action. Consequently, the stigma follows affirmative action recipients who have career success. Affirmative action brands its recipients, fairly or not, so that their subsequent success in the broader world may not be seen as entirely due to their drive and talent. Conservative observers mark them with a Scarlet Double Letter, or what Shelby Steele calls the "stigma of questionable competence."

> The cruelest and most damaging burdens are those imposed upon the members of the preferred minority group as a whole, who are inescapably undermined by racial preferences. When persons are appointed, or admitted, or promoted because of their racial group, it is inevitable that the members of that group will, in the institution giving such preference, perform less well than average. Membership in the minority group most certainly does not imply inferiority; that is a canard—but that stereotype is *reinforced* by preferences. Since the standards for the selection of minorities are inevitably lower when diluted by considerations of color, sex, or nationality, it is a certainty that, overall, the average performance of those in the preferred group will be weaker—not because of their ethnicity, of course, but because many among them

were selected on grounds having no bearing on the work or study to be pursued. Preference thus *creates a link* between minority preferred and inferior performance. This burden is borne not only by those individuals preferred, but by *every* member of the minority group, including the many among them who genuinely excel. The general knowledge that persons with black or brown skins are given preference ensures lower expectations from all whose skins are of those colors. Every minority member is made suspect. No one (including the minorities themselves, of course) can know for sure that any given member of a preferred group has not been awarded special favor. Skin color, the most prominent of personal characteristics, is thus transformed by preference into permanent and public onus. If some demon had sought to concoct a scheme aimed at undermining the credentials of minority businessmen, professionals, and students, to stigmatize them permanently and to humiliate them publicly, there could have been no more ingenious plan devised than the preferences now so widely given in the name of affirmative action. (C 22–23, italics in the original)

The stigma derives from an individualist ethos. It does not occur to observers who acknowledge the power of institutional and societal strictures to deny access to groups of people, that is to say, observers who are willing to accept the existence of modern American racism. Yet it is clear, from a progressive point of view, that at times prominent individuals of color indeed feel such a stigma. It is a price that these pioneers making their way into the upper reaches of U.S. institutions unfairly bear as the society rectifies its attitudes about merit and desert. These unvoiced attitudes, remnants of the once-legitimated doctrine that only Whites can deserve the highest places in U.S. society, will not be lifted off the shoulders of high-achieving people of color for a long while. Before the stigma of being an affirmative action recipient, there was the cruel stigma of being a "token" or institutional "window dressing." In the decade after the passage of the Civil Rights Act, it often seemed that just one person of color was employed in any given institution. That person tended to be the most distinctive face on display for public consumption, and became the target of character assassination. Fortunately as the numbers of such persons increased, the stigma of being the token minority person has become less evident in U.S. society.

The stigma of affirmative action is a part of the conservative worldview. Affirmative action is portrayed as the *cruelest burden,* not the long-overdue opportunity for deserving citizens of color to achieve to their capability.

Moreover, in this excerpt the *Commentary* essayist articulates the falsehood that these persons, for example, University of California minority students, were admitted because of their racial group status—"selected on grounds having no bearing on the work or study to be pursued"—and consequently perform more poorly. The fact is these Chicano and African American students were superior academic achievers in high school before being admitted to the University of California. Once admitted, as Bowen and Bok make clear, they perform exceptionally. They fulfill their academic, professional, and social promise.

Berkeley's Vice Chancellor for Undergraduate Affairs, Genaro Padilla, reported that the 1992 entering class of Latinos, who matriculated with a university-wide affirmative action program in place, graduated at a 71 percent rate. These students are not a privileged upper-middle-class crowd. Nor are they a coddled minority. Padilla pointed out that 45 percent of these university graduates reported a family income of less than $30,000. Seventy percent are first-generation university students, that is to say, neither of their parents holds a four-year college degree. In contrast, 65 percent of the same entering class of Whites have parents who hold a four-year college degree. These deserving Latino students earned their success.[86]

The affirmative action stigma is a reflex of Anglo-American hegemony. From the point of view of progressives, a far more painful infamy continues to burn the souls of people of good conscience—the stigma of unrelenting white racism. Contrary to the conservative essayist's viewpoint, the onus is on the greater society, not the deserving recipients of affirmative action, to reflect on the ideological source of their views. As a *Commentary* essayist, Nathan Glazer poses this somber query:

> But would this [imputed decline in the repute of minority competence] have improved in the absence of affirmative action, and in the face of evidence that disproportionately fewer blacks were qualifying for jobs through traditional means? One cannot be sure.[87]

The criticism of affirmative action on the basis of stigma is immaterial. Society can be distracted from or inured to the fact that white racism for three hundred years restricted the key areas of U.S. life to Whites, hence forgetting that the U.S. racial state was outlawed less than forty years ago. Moreover, affirmative action is a modest program designed to gradually rectify this state of affairs over a very long period of time. Attention deficit disorder does not relieve U.S. society of its obligations, and it is telling that the Bowen and Bok study indicates that recipients of the so-called stigma of affirmative action are not calling for its elimination.

During the Proposition 209 debate and in the *Commentary* essays, one prominent African American was mentioned as being disgraced by this stigma when President Clinton called him a symbol of affirmative action's fulfilled promise. As hero of the Persian Gulf War, in 1996 General Colin Powell was more popular than either Dole or Clinton. Yet, stealing a phrase from Clinton to make a point against affirmative action, a *Commentary* essayist tried to feel Powell's pain:

> But may I be permitted the presumption of saying that I can guess his reaction? Deeply insulted and furious would be my best bet, as any high-achieving black must be at the possibility that his standing in the world is being chalked up to his having been given special consideration for the mere color of his skin. And this was *Colin Powell* the President was talking about, for God's sake, someone who has on various occasions, and by people of various political stripes, been publicly urged to run for the presidency of the United States. Well, perhaps Powell has his own source of inner protection from humiliation. But imagine the experience of a distinguished black professor, say, who may with good reason suspect that he is regarded by the liberal racists in charge of virtually all university administrations as nothing more than a statistic to pride themselves on—indistinguishable, from their point of view, from any of the black charlatans trading on race who may have been hired to teach alongside him. (C 24, italics in the original)[88]

Because Powell is a national figure cited as a victim of the so-called stigma of affirmative action, his judgment on affirmative action is particularly important. "Let's not deceive ourselves into thinking the playing field is equal," he retorted. "We should not deceive ourselves that we are a color-blind society."[89] At a university commencement address, Powell articulated his views on Proposition 209:

> We must resist misguided efforts that seek to shut it all down, efforts such as the California Civil Rights Initiative, which poses as an equal opportunity initiative, but . . . puts the brakes on expanding opportunities for people who are in need.[90]

Again, during his nationally televised speech at the 1996 Republican National Convention, he declared:

And where discrimination still exists, or where the scars of past discrimination still contaminate and disfigure the present, we must not close our eyes to it, declare there is a level playing field, and hope that it will go away by itself. . . . I strongly support affirmative action.[91]

Thus Powell, with whom conservative commentators conspicuously commiserated, stood up and resolutely endorsed affirmative action.[92] So much for the disdain that Powell supposedly had for the program. In the end, those people of color who achieve in U.S. society with or without affirmative action are willing to face the unvoiced scorn of those who do not believe—at a visceral level—in their race's ability or worthiness to participate in all the higher areas of American life.

## Conservative Alternatives to Affirmative Action

The alternatives to affirmative action promoted by the conservative essayists are also consistent with their disavowal of white racism and its contemporary effects. Since, in their view, there are no structural reasons and foundational beliefs holding racialized minorities down, the reason why people of color do poorly is a matter of personal drive and agency. As has been thoroughly documented and critiqued in any number of sources, the *Commentary* essayists accept and advocate the hegemonic values unaltered from the times when actions based on these values were the source of the original racial oppression.

58. Overall, the United States has made considerable strides toward "equality of result" since President Johnson issued his call in 1965. But at the same time, those blacks and others (including disadvantaged Whites) who really have had a "hard time"—and now have deep scars to show for it—have fallen further behind. Nor will affirmative action as it has been practiced be of much use to them, since even preferential policies cannot alone hope to overcome the severe lack of skills and multitude of dysfunctional habits they possess. What might make a difference is affirmative action as it was originally intended. Although there is still much we do not know, we have learned a few things in the past 30 years about improving school achievement, reducing welfare dependency, and making inner-city neighborhoods safer. Moreover, the climate of opinion has shifted. Not only can policies be tried that would have once been thought too radical—such as educational vouchers, or using faith-based organizations

to provide social services—but there is greater support for hard work and decent behavior. (C 37)

59. One such old idea [to use in place of affirmative action] used to have Glenn Loury himself as a forceful and eloquent advocate. Hence when, in the private conversation that followed our little debate, he asked me what I would put in place of affirmative action, I was able to answer with the title of a book of his own in which he argued that government intervention had done more harm than good to his fellow blacks, and that the answer lay in moral regeneration from within: "How about 'one by one from the inside out'?" (C 47)

With the conservative African American commentator Glenn Loury thus singled out for his long-standing criticism of affirmative action, he then becomes the most appropriate person to articulate a pro-affirmative-action position, since he was repeatedly cited by those who disavow its utility, much less its ethical validity, to redress the effects of white racism.

> It is important to distinguish here between legal and ethical modes of reasoning. I stipulate that an isolated individual's race, as such, is ethically irrelevant. That is, the weight given to an affected person's welfare when selecting a course of public action should not depend on race. Nevertheless, there are circumstances where the ability of a public policy to advance the general interest of all persons is enhanced by taking cognizance of the racial identities of particular persons. Under these circumstances, the steadfast refusal, in the name of legal consistency, to take into account the impact that a policy might have on the members of different racial groups can turn out to be an act of moral obtuseness. To illustrate, consider the case I have made elsewhere for "developmental affirmative action." I argue that the public goal of raising the competitive abilities of disadvantaged blacks can be appropriate, even though it is formulated in racial terms. This is because the effects of past racial oppression and, critically, of ongoing social segregation along race lines have been to leave many black families and communities relatively less well-endowed with the cultural and financial resources on which young people depend to acquire their skills.[93]

## Section 5: Conclusion

The nation's public discourse on racism has not advanced in the last thirty-five years. Americans are no more capable of talking about the full range and kinds of contemporary racism. This discourse failing left its one institutional remedy, affirmative action, vulnerable to neoconservative attack in 1995. Frank talk on racism was avoided for years since it would irritate the complacent electorate. Neoconservatives exploited this political aversion to addressing the continuing effects of American racism.

In the 1960s, the Civil Rights movement was characterized by Martin Luther King Jr. and Lyndon Johnson as a moral war against the status quo. It was further dramatized by violent clashes witnessed on television. The moral war for which King and Johnson had rallied their political constituencies was not won. Only major beachheads were secured by passing civil rights legislation, and establishing the new American taboo against blatantly racist behavior, as Edley noted. The war was not won. From the vantage point of today's society, the 1960s proved to be a mixed legacy. Clearly, legally sanctioned public racism was finally outlawed. However, the nation's traditional queasiness about discussing racism was allowed to degenerate into a discursive interdiction. The nation's taboo about talking about race has impaired the society's capacity to reform the persevering principle of U.S. social relations, covert and other modern forms of racism.

During the 1960s King and Johnson characterized racism by means of POLITICS AS WAR metaphors, and by way of personification metaphors. Malcolm X's vivid images of the black man confronting the white man resonated with his primary constituency, for whom the daily confrontation with "the Man" was concrete and painful. As King noted in 1967: "Ten years before, a Mississippi Negro would have submissively stepped to the gutter to leave the sidewalk for a white man."[94] To the white audience, for whom racialized Americans were invisible only ten years before, the personification metaphors made Blacks visible as human beings. They had to be regarded eye-to-eye, for the first time. But personification also allowed white Americans who were not in daily contact with Blacks to believe that their own daily behavior, their own standard of living, and their own way of living in America were not implicated in the continuing racialization of minorities.

The personification of racism allowed white apathy to appear benign. The personification metaphor foregrounds individual overt racism, as it backgrounds societal and foundational racism. Only violent and repugnant actions of insolent Whites such as George Lincoln Rockwell and George Wallace were the focus of the American social agenda.[95] Thirty years since, the hateful actions of these bigots continue to sear America's memory.[96]

Consequently, the nonviolent violence of aversive, societal, and foundational racism in American life was not discussed. In the thirty years after King's death, white Americans have not internalized the reality of modern racism. Normal middle-class white Americans believe that the only white racists are people like Bull Conner,[97] and that racism in no way is reflected in their own lives, beliefs, and actions.

In the 1960s RACISM AS CANCER had captured the public's attention. This metaphor effectively described a chronic condition which had been built into the original constitution of the United States, an affliction of the body politic which precipitated two crises, one in the 1860s and one in the 1960s. The societal cancer was understood to continue to be manifest in everyday life throughout the United States. As a framework to refer to both individual actions and institutional racism, the cancer metaphor of the 1960s was very effective.

However, the major manifestation of white racism changed in the ensuing decades, as Lawrence Bobo and his co-authors demonstrate in their excellent empirical studies.[98] They make clear that the dominant form of white racism was no longer violent white rage at Blacks who were not willing to accept daily personal humiliation. Instead it is more often manifest as covert nonviolent avoidance at the personal level, and indifference to inequity at the societal level.

During this time frame, unfortunately, the nation's discourse on racism did not experience a corresponding shift. Once the civil rights era was over, and its major spokesmen silenced, no further development of the American discourse on race took place. Moreover, with the expanded prohibition against polite discussion about racism, whether overt or covert, the attribution of the CANCER metaphor to the actions of white Americans weakened in public discourse. While the 1960s discourse centered on societal racism, by the 1990s, the discourse was restricted to individuals. Racism came to be characterized as the violent actions of individuals, not societal, institutional, or epistemological expressions and behavior. Currently the public understands racism primarily to be overt personal invective, in spite of the clear evidence that tacit racism sustains social inequity in U.S. life. For example, the unequal prospects of groups of people in institutions are offhandedly justified in terms of cultural values, not societal racism.

During the debate on Proposition 209, neoconservatives capitalized on the constricted public discourse on racism by appropriating the discourse of the Civil Rights Movement, subverting the RACISM AS DISEASE metaphor, and asserting that affirmative action was a dangerous vestige of America's racist past. By employing a narrow definition of racism to reject any claims of institutional racism out of hand, neoconservatives claim that the beneficiaries of affirmative action misappropriate the rewards of head-to-head competition in education and employment.

More recently, conservatives decried President Clinton's 1999 national forums on race. Held in different cities across the country, they were designed to address issues of racism. With their sponsors ever mindful of the taboo against using the R-word, these forums were publicized as opening a dialogue on how to better achieve America's lauded Jeffersonian principles. Conservative criticism centered on the effect of such dialogue, which once again would expose (white) citizens to the distasteful topic.

When racism is solely defined in terms of personal enmity, neoconservatives are able to say that compensation for white racism should apply only to victims of explicit acts of racism, and today's affirmative action recipients are obviously not the victims of the 1963 police dog attacks in Alabama. In their view, the better solution is not affirmative action but greater emphasis on personal sacrifice and initiative on the part of racial minorities: Work hard enough and you'll get your share. This is why the purported stigma of affirmative action weighs on good-hearted neoconservatives, since they feel the pain of self-made minority group members. Colin Powell really succeeded by way of his own initiative, not with the help of the affirmative action program he lauds—otherwise he could not be an American hero.

The 1967 Kerner Commission viewed indifference and ignorance as benign. This was the single flaw in an otherwise cogent analysis of the cause and relief of racial inequity. Unfortunately, in the ensuing years white indifference has reverted to private conceit. As long as one is polite to racialized minorities in public, then one has done enough to rectify the effects of three hundred years of the U.S. racist regime.

During the Proposition 209 debate, affirmative action supporters were significantly hampered by the absence of discourse on the entire range of racism in America. They could not talk about nonviolent racism, and as Lydia Chávez noted, failed to bring the issue of 100,000 pending EEOC cases of racism, or increasing educational inequity between Whites and other Americans, to the debate.

Without awareness of the full effects of American racism, "the mass of smug, somnolent citizens, who are neither evil nor good"[99] voted in 1996 to rid itself of racial discrimination—in the form of affirmative action. The electorate did not comprehend that structural racism continues to figure in U.S. institutions—particularly education. We now turn to the discourse on U.S. public education, as did the public's attention in 1998, with the advent of the third anti-Latino referendum, Proposition 227.

## CHAPTER FIVE

# Student as Means, Not End

## Contemporary American Discourse on Education

Over 1,300,000 children were legally eligible for bilingual education in California in 1998. Eighty percent were Latinos. Children who should be taught in their home language currently constitute one-fourth of California's public-school children.[1] The public has become aware that these and all other Latinos, as well as other students of color, have been receiving an increasingly inadequate education over the last twenty years. The current state of this inadequacy can be illustrated with three sets of figures: While 91 percent of white students received a high school diploma by age twenty-one, only 67 percent of all Latinos were receiving theirs. On average, Latino (and black) high school seniors are able to read and to do math only at the level of white eighth graders. Such disparities are due in large part to unequal instructional quality. Nearly 50 percent of teachers of Latino students are not certifiably proficient in the subject area that they teach, much less holders of bachelor's degrees, while white students contended with uncertified teachers only 14 percent of the time.[2] In 1998, after a great deal of debate, voters made their views on these schoolchildren known when they cast their ballot on Proposition 227, the third major referendum of the 1990s centered on California Latinos.

However abysmal the state of Latino public education, structural inequities were not at issue during the Proposition 227 campaign. Nor was institutional racism under inquiry. Moreover, there was little candid deliberation about what public schools should emulate, or what public education really should be doing. There was even less explicit talk about what learning really is—how children make a concept their own. Instead, all these tangled issues were boiled down to a single up/down vote. In the wording of the referendum passed by the California electorate in 1998, the issue was "that all children in California public schools shall be taught English as rapidly and effectively as possible." As will be shown in the course of this chapter and the next, Proposition 227 was a fallacious diversion from the real structural problems facing Latinos in public schools.

Still and all, because metaphors were used profusely during the Proposition 227 debate to refer to learning and education, a portrait of the U.S. public's understanding of public education can be discerned. In these two chapters, the public discourse on Proposition 227 is scrutinized. The *Los Angeles Times* coverage of the campaign was extensive enough to use the synchronic method of a comprehensive sampling and systematic cataloguing of this public discourse source.

The referendum centered on the utility of bilingual education for Latinos and other immigrant students. The questions about LANGUAGES, ENGLISH, SPANISH, BILINGUALISM, and their relationship to the nation will be developed in Chapter 6.


In the present chapter, the four key metaphors that construct American public education will be depicted. Section 1 takes up the competing conceptualizations of how a child learns—whether mechanically or creatively. Although it might be surprising, it turns out that the contemporary public view of learning is no different than that of Thomas Gradgrind, a character created by Charles Dickens 150 years ago:

> "Now, what I want is Facts. Teach these boys and girls nothing but Facts. Facts alone are wanted in life. Plant nothing else, and root out everything else. You can only form the minds of reasoning animals upon Facts: nothing else will ever be of any service to them. . . . In this life, we want nothing but Facts, Sir: nothing but Facts!" The speaker, and schoolmaster, and the third grown person present, all backed a little, and swept with their eyes the inclined plane of little vessels then and there arranged in order, ready to have imperial gallons of facts poured into them until they were filled to the brim.[3]

Gradgrind, patron of a "model" urban school in 1850, demanded that his school be based on principles of efficiency and industry. Although the reader might be unaware of the implications of these principles, he expounds a thoroughly antiquated view of learning. Still, because a productive metaphor is at its base, this view continues to have a profound impact on the experiences of U.S. schoolchildren today. The second dominant metaphor, for SCHOOL, is presented in Section 2, along with its ontology. This metaphor for schools is also over one hundred years old, and so it can be contrasted in Section 3 with two new-sprung metaphors for the CLASSROOM that have become common only in the last decade. Next, the metaphors of the individual learner are taken up. Two complementary processes make up EDUCATION per se. One is the process of education for the individual. This is to be distinguished from the process of learning something. This metaphor is the third productive metaphor for today's education. The metaphor and its ontology are developed in Section 4. The second process of education (and fourth constitutive metaphor for education) is exemplified with the word *mainstream*. This RIVER metaphor is presented in Section 5. With an interpretation of these productive metaphors, we can begin to understand how U.S. society conceptualizes public education at the outset of the twenty-first century.

## Section 1: Metaphors for Learning

Richard Colvin, a fine education writer for the *Los Angeles Times,* explains to his readership the intricacies of educational policy, theory, and politics, as well as the personalities in the news. While most Americans know something about education from firsthand experience, they are still dependent on writers such as Colvin. The complexities of the educational debates often turn on contending views of what public education is meant to be, and Colvin's knowledge and writing skill carry the reader through the thickets of theories and politics handily. Take, for instance, Colvin's description, and analysis, of a 1997 debate over math curriculum. Since the piece is news analysis, his writing is not merely a description of events, but involves conscious interpretation of the debate. In the following passage he casts the debate in terms of competing theories about the nature of learning:

> Such is the raging debate over math in America that when California dares to ask students to memorize multiplication tables and to "know" rather than simply "identify" a formula, it is lauded—or condemned— as a sharp swing back to the basics. . . . But the shouting must be seen as part of a broader debate over educational philosophy these days. It lurks behind fights over how to teach science (how much like play should it be?), reading (through stories or phonics?) or even spelling (will correcting mistakes hurt the youngster's creativity?). And at issue

are two views of children and how they learn best. Are they like flowers that will bloom naturally if exposed to the sunlight of experiences—in the form of compelling literature or fun math games? Or, are they more like puzzles that, to become whole, need to be assembled piece by piece—through teacher-directed lessons in essential skills such as learning the sounds of letters or those multiplication tables? To be sure, common sense—and research—suggest there should be a blend. No one really believes that phonics alone is enough. Students also need to read good stories and do lots of writing. But when is it not enough that they simply show enthusiasm for, say, geometric shapes? When do we stop calling it success merely because they worked well with others grappling with the Pythagorean theorem?[4]

Interest in the philosophy behind a topic such as education is not commonly expressed in a newswriter's articles. Colvin's use of metaphor to present the competing models of learning is a reference to an old debate that is not aired enough in the national discourse on public education. With contrasting organic and mechanistic metaphors, FLOWER versus PUZZLE, Colvin characterizes the debate between progressive and traditional educators, not only over math curriculum, but over the basic nature of human learning. Still, Colvin's metaphors pose some problems of their own. While he demonstrates a definite tilt to the conservative side of the issue, his metaphors fit neither the conservative nor the progressive model of how students learn, as conceived by educational theorists.[5]

From the point of view of educational traditionalists, machine-learner metaphors are entirely appropriate. These might include the STUDENT AS EMPTY VESSEL to be filled with knowledge, AS COMPUTER to be programmed, or AS MACHINE to be built and tuned by educators. The century-old theory of learning of Edward Thorndike, which is the basis of such metaphors, still makes common sense to the public and many educators. In his theory, published in 1913, learning is a fixed association between a situation and a response that is achieved with rehearsal. Better learning is a demonstrably quicker response to the same situation. With enough repetition, the correct response gets "stamped" into the student's mental template, and errors are "stamped out." The teacher's role is to regulate the students' activities in the classroom to develop the desired repertoire of responses. Thorndike's theory of learning was later superseded by B. F. Skinner's stimulus-and-response behaviorism. Stimulus and response, in its turn, has also been replaced in favor of more adequate models by educational researchers.[6]

In these archaic mechanical models of learning, knowledge is taken to be external modular units, as epitomized by the value of $\pi$. The traditionalist view also holds that mathematical knowledge is qualitatively distinct from other kinds of knowledge. Math is absolute, eternal, and prior, while literary knowledge is subjective rather than absolute, and consequently is a lower-order knowledge. While traditionalists no doubt applaud Colvin's teacher-affirming stance, namely, that a well-trained dispenser of knowledge is essential to make an educated student, they would prefer that he also distinguish the "pure" mathematical facts and skills from subjective literary learning and the associated writing arts. With these metaphors the teacher is taken to be, in some sense, the manufacturer of educated students.

The world's premier critical educator, Paulo Freire, depicted with stunning clarity the societal consequences of this mechanistic model, which guides the conventional experience in most of the world's classrooms, as teachers toil to forge a standardized view of the world in the impressionable minds of children:

> The teacher's task is to "fill" the students with the contents of his narration—contents which are detached from reality, disconnected from the totality that engendered them and could give them significance. . . . The student records, memorizes, and repeats these phrases without perceiving what four times four really means, or realizing the true significance of "capital" in the affirmation "the capital of Pará is Belém." . . . Narration (with the teacher as narrator) leads the student to memorize mechanically the narrated content. Worse yet, it turns them . . . into "receptacles" to be "filled" by the teacher. The more completely he fills the receptacles, the better a teacher he is. The more meekly the receptacles permit themselves to be filled, the better students they are. Education thus becomes an act of depositing, in which the students are the depositories and the teacher is the depositor. . . . This is the "banking" concept of education, in which the scope of the action allowed to the student extends only as far as receiving, filing, and storing deposits. They do, it is true, have the opportunity to become collectors or cataloguers of the things they store. But in the last analysis, it is [people] themselves who are filed away through the lack of creativity, transformation, and knowledge in this (at best) misguided system. For apart from inquiry, apart from praxis, [people] cannot be truly human. Knowledge emerges only through invention and re-invention, through the restless, impatient, continuing, hopeful inquiry [people]

pursue in the world, with the world, and with each other. In the banking concept of education, knowledge is a gift bestowed by those who consider themselves knowledgeable upon those whom they consider to know nothing.[7]

The consequences of the EMPTY VESSEL or BANKING metaphors may now be clear. In his quoted passage, Colvin's PUZZLE metaphor does not capture the crucial associations that traditionalists want to express.

On the other side, progressive educational theorists would also be dissatisfied with Colvin's STUDENT AS FLOWER metaphor. Such an image is unsatisfactory because the plant metaphor implies that the child passively absorbs knowledge. On the contrary, progressive theorists hold that the student does not receive prepackaged units of knowledge from learning brokers, namely, their teachers. Most importantly, these theorists hold the view that each student constructs his/her own knowledge.[8] Thus in the progressive model the teacher has a secondary role as a facilitator, only assisting students as they build knowledge. Knowledge is a construct created by each learner; it is not absolute and external to the child. Even "$1 + 1 = 2$" must be constructed by each child in order for it to become his or her own knowledge. The complete reinterpretation of scientific knowledge, as witnessed in periodic transformation of the paradigms in physics and other sciences, which replace one "law" with another,[9] is compelling evidence for the constructivist viewpoint as discussed in Chapter 2.

Consequently, the STUDENT AS CREATOR metaphor is incompatible with the quiescent FLOWER metaphor that Colvin suggests to capture constructivist theories of learning. Progressives hold that the child is far more dynamic, arguing within the KNOWLEDGE AS CONSTRUCT metaphor rather than within the traditional viewpoint that knowledge consists of external facts. This progressive educational model is consistent with a constructivist epistemology, which stands in opposition to scientific positivism. Recall that positivists maintain the view that knowledge corresponds in some manner to a measurable outside reality. In contrast to the positivists, constructivists hold that the social world is constantly being constructed through interaction.

Colvin created novel metaphors to contrast opposing theories of how students learn. In spite of their drawbacks, it is unfortunate that these metaphors were not taken up in subsequent *Times* articles. The FLOWER metaphor occurred once in other newspaper texts:

1. "It's such a demanding profession," [teacher Rich] Miyagawa said. "And yet, kids are great. They surprise you. And when they **blossom?** Wow. It's awesome, it really is." (September 18, 1995, A1)

Yet the *blossom* in this excerpt refers as much to inherent maturing processes as to the cognitive operations of learning. There are also STUDENT AS PLANT metaphors sprinkled throughout texts, which refer to the yearly cohort of children.[10]

2. The test of their work, Alegre said, will be in the coming years, when the current **crop of youngsters** either opts to join gangs or pursue college degrees. (November 27, 1995, B1)

Newswriter Colvin's creativity should be applauded. He presented both sides of the debate in a manner that can be swiftly grasped by his readers. His metaphors provide vivid images of the competing views of a debate that general society would be wise to join. Colvin presents to the public an important conceptual debate in education—how a child learns—by contrasting metaphors.

This debate was engaged in professional circles decades ago. It deserves much greater public exposure, because of its important implications. When Colvin contrasts images of the student, as recipient or creator of knowledge, he focuses on fundamentals. It becomes possible for the public to judge, from a principled basis, how to best educate America's children. It is noteworthy that the public is apparently unaware, as measured by the metaphoric imagery sampled in the *Los Angeles Times* corpus, that the debate took place in the educational researcher arena, and was lost long ago by traditionalists. Consequently, contemporary public discourse on education is not illuminated by the best new research on how a child learns a concept. Rather, the public discourse on education is framed in exceptionally narrow terms. The EMPTY VESSEL metaphor goes uncontested, as it guides the operationalization of public schooling today. Its near exclusivity in public discussions of education affirms Schön's claims about the power of a generative metaphor.

In the next section, the metaphorization of the school as an institution is reviewed. There it will be clear that Americans continue to unreflectingly accept yet another decrepit metaphor, with all its limitations.

## Section 2: School as Factory

The predominant conceptual metaphor of learning reflects the traditional mechanistic view. This orthodoxy is so deeply embedded in everyday thinking that it is taken as given in public discourse. On the other hand constructivist imagery appears only rarely, and then is presented as a contrasting "theory," which is to say, a junior rival to the orthodoxy. In U.S. educational discourse, as sampled in the *Los Angeles Times* corpus, most metaphors reflect views that children are passively taught by knowledge holders, or that they learn mechanistically. This view is reinforced by metaphors that represent schools as the manufacturing centers of an educated citizenry and can be summarized under the SCHOOL AS FACTORY metaphor. Thorndike's forge theory of learning—"stamping" knowledge into the mental template—corresponds closely to the ontology of the FACTORY metaphor for school, as will be presented below. As determined by this ontology, the components of a factory are imposed on the constituents of the school—the students, the teaching process, the teachers, and the precepts and standards for running the school, as illustrated in the following excerpts:

> 3. Official results of the program won't begin to trickle in until spring 1998, when the first **batch** of students is tested and Newbury Park graduates its first seniors with IB diplomas. (February 28, 1997, B1)
>
> 4. Over the past year and a half, three school districts based in Westminster and Anaheim have won state approval for programs that **drill** more English **into** nonfluent students in the earliest grades. (April 14, 1997, A3)
>
> 5. "I am telling [the educational community], 'You know in my heart that I am your friend, but, collectively, we simply have to **produce a better product**,'" [gubernatorial candidate Gray Davis] said in an interview. (March 13, 1998, A1, A24)
>
> 6. Trustee Robert H. Viviano, who said he is concerned that students taught in their native languages will lack crucial English skills, requested a two-year study to measure the **effectiveness** of these programs. (March 29, 1995, B3)

*Ontology of* SCHOOL AS FACTORY

The ontology of the semantic domain of FACTORY is well known. The evidence of the factory is found everywhere in today's world, and people take its products for granted. The everyday frame of understanding of the FACTORY domain includes the idea that they are set up to produce all kinds of objects, from vitamin pills and light bulbs to cell phones and cars. All such products share at least one property: they are standardized, so that one yellow no. 2 pencil, or one Boeing 747, is indistinguishable from another.

Likewise it is understood that in factories, the production process of such commodities has been broken down into its components and systematized. Each product is manufactured by machines strung together so that the raw material entering the factory is carried along on conveyer belts from one machine to another, each performing one task in the fabrication of the finished product. Factory workers dot the assembly line, each performing a narrowly defined activity. The workers often execute their bit of the manufacturing process over and over in elementary routines. Repetition and boredom, rather than creativity and ingenuity, are characteristic of factory jobs. The raison d'être of factories is the bottom line, that is to say, economics. Although the average person may not know the term "economies of scale," it is common knowledge that assembly-line manufacturing produces carpentry nails more cheaply per unit than a lone blacksmith can.

When the SCHOOL AS FACTORY metaphor is employed, all the major components of the factory are represented in the elements of schools. As described in Dickens's *Hard Times* over 150 years ago, children were "little pitchers who were to be filled so full of facts." In today's SCHOOL AS FACTORY, students are metaphorized as the raw material for the factory, as "economic utility units."[11] Like blocks of plastic, pieces of sheet metal, or bolts of fabric, they are not particularly valuable in and of themselves. While all parents believe that their child is a unique treasure and the most precious end of family life, in the factory metaphor the raw material does not have much inherent value. In this metaphor, the student's innate value is less important than its product potential, since the factory creates valuable items from inexpensive, unfinished stuff. Indeed, the factory is not very capable of dealing with a diversity of raw material. Rather it is built to process standard input; distinctiveness in its raw material is an industrial liability. The manufacturing science of quality control has evolved in response. In order to optimize the manufacturing process, the factory readily rejects supposed nonstandard material (namely, its minority students) at the outset, or at any point in the fabrication process.

The teacher on the SCHOOLHOUSE AS FACTORY FLOOR works within a narrowly defined job description. The skills that the factory worker possesses are restricted; the training is circumscribed; the profession is not highly esteemed. Much has been written about the effects of industrialization on the relationship of people to their occupation. Charles Dickens employed the factory metaphor to characterize the decline of education due to teachers' own fabricated training. In *Hard Times,* Dickens's unfit schoolmaster,

Mr. M'Choakunchild, had "been lately turned at the same time, in the same factory, on the same principles, like so many pianoforte legs."[12] The wide-ranging and cumulative knowledge of a master craftsperson needed to construct a unique finished product has been reduced to its components, and the production workers repeat only a single step in the manufacturing of a standardized version of that same product. Thus the very well-read educators, who once discharged their venerable profession edifying and cultivating their elite clientele over a long period of time, have been replaced by factory-trained instructors who perform a limited set of tasks mechanically. They consequently take less pride in their trade, in their human product, and in themselves. Dickens provides a caricature of the knowledge possessed by a factory-trained teacher:

> Bradley Headstone . . . had acquired mechanically a great store of teacher's knowledge. He could do mental arithmetic mechanically, sing at sight mechanically, blow various instruments mechanically, even play the great church organ mechanically. From his early childhood up, his mind had been a place of mechanical storage. The arrangement of his wholesale warehouse, so that it might be always ready to meet the demands of retail dealers—history here, geography there, astronomy to the right, political economy to the left—natural history, the physical sciences, figures, music, the lower mathematics, and what not, all in their several places—this care had imparted to his countenance a look of care; while the habit of questioning and being questioned had given him a suspicious manner, or a manner that would be better described as one lying in wait. There was a kind of unsettled trouble in the face. . . . He always seemed to be uneasy lest anything should be missing from his mental warehouse, and taking stock to assure himself.[13]

Modern-day Headstones control an even narrower knowledge base, with no compensating reduction of professional defensiveness.

Teachers should not be blamed for their place in the schoolhouse factory; they have resisted their debased position in society throughout the past century. On the floor of the 1901 National Education Association convention, an early educational labor activist, Margaret Haley, warned against the "factoryizing" of education, which made "teachers into automatons 'whose duty it is to carry out mechanically and unquestioningly the ideas and orders of those clothed with the authority of position.'"[14]

One interesting gap in the metaphoric record of the *Los Angeles Times* is a paucity of metaphors for the teacher. Across the sample of over two hundred *Times* articles, while references to teachers appeared steadily, few metaphors characterize teachers. Most are relatively immaterial metaphors, such as the *overburdened teacher*. This absence of metaphors of any kind for teachers or their role may be a matter of euphemism and myth management, to mask their disparaged semiskilled worker status. But evidence abounds that teachers comprise a less professional labor force. The major teachers' organizations are not modeled on professional guilds, but rather on industrial labor unions. Thus the National Education Association and American Federation of Teachers organize their rank and file (90 percent of U.S. teachers), negotiate bread-and-butter issues, sign collective-bargaining contracts, and conduct work stoppages. Although these unions sponsor conferences which focus on professional development, peer-quality monitoring, and other professional society interests, their salient purpose is to obtain fair compensation for educational labor performed, namely, salaries, benefits, grievance procedures, and so forth. They do not operate like the American Medical Association or the American Bar Association.[15] In effect, they are United Mind Workers.[16]

As for the manufacturing process, the SCHOOL AS FACTORY metaphor is entirely consistent with traditional metaphors that conceptualize quiescent pupils who are mechanistically taught extrinsic facts, rather than learning by constructing knowledge for themselves. Moreover, one important implication of both the FACTORY and EMPTY VESSEL metaphors is that no important learning occurs outside of the SCHOOL AS FACTORY walls. It is as if the child enters the school without a thought, inert, mute, with no understanding of the world.[17]

While the child is a passive object, the factory is portrayed as the active agent in the educational process. In many instances, including a preceding excerpt, the term *drill into* signals this metaphor. Consequently children are seen as being furnished with educational skills or as otherwise shaped or regulated by the educational institution and teachers:

> 7. The school has unique needs, with 87% of its 600 students coming from poor homes with limited English. Classes will be **geared** toward fostering literacy and learning **skills,** it says. (April 19, 1997, B2)
>
> 8. But he was also taking classes in English as a second language—the start of a program that would slowly **meld** his fledgling English into his high school course work. (October 29, 1995, B1)

9. Standard English was **drummed into my head** until I decided to speak it exclusively around white people, bougie Negroes and the elders in my family. (January 5, 1997, M6)

The preceding excerpts are entirely consistent with school as active agent operating on a passive pupil. The only text instances which employ the alternative constructivist metaphors that stress active students learning are references to the skills that students develop. From this perspective, as a child constructs more complex understandings and knowledge of the work, she or he develops and masters specific academic skills. In recent years certain school districts have made clear efforts toward recognizing evidence of individual student knowledge. Educational measures such as student portfolios are consistent with the KNOWLEDGE AS CONSTRUCT metaphor. However, these innovations were not reflected at all in the public discourse sampled.

10. Sanchez Sadek believes the organization's best entree is the federal government's own Goals 2000—an education reform framework signed into law in April that calls for every adult American to have the math and language "**skills** necessary **to compete in a global economy.** It's crucial to this country's economic survival," she said. (February 6, 1995, A3)

11. "I'm not against the bilingual program," [school trustee Robert] Viviano said. "I'm for English fluency because it is **an essential tool to function in the marketplace**. . . . If you teach in a foreign language, you can not expect the outcome to be English." (February 14, 1997, B4)

12. **Limited English skills** can also handicap an immigrant in times of emergency because many law enforcement and medical personnel do not speak Spanish. (May 11, 1992, A1)

Yet in the dominant metaphor of the discourse on education, even particular skills are imparted to passive children; children are shaped by the school, by teachers doing their job. In the following excerpts, note the verbs associated with the skills that children achieve:

13. The insurgent [Orange County school districts] say they are reforming a system they contend fails to **give** students the language **skills** needed to advance in society. (April 13, 1997, A1)

14. The program seeks to wean them from the streets and **provide tools** to help them integrate into society. (June 18, 1997, A1)

## Origin and Standard of the FACTORY Metaphor

Historian Ellen Fitzpatrick summarizes why this dominant metaphor, SCHOOL AS FACTORY, was originally adopted:

> No force played a greater role in shaping the substance and character of late nineteenth- and early twentieth-century American intellectual life than did the rise of industrialism. The rapid growth of large-scale industry in the United States during the post–Civil War period posed fundamental challenges to institutions, values and modes of government that had taken form in a rural agrarian society.[18]

Public education first developed in the nineteenth century to train an industrial workforce, and to relieve nativist pressures which were developing during this same period. An uneducated and often foreign-born populace was seen as unprepared either to play their part in the industrialization of the United States or to participate in a democracy in which the franchise was being expanded beyond the traditional oligarchy. Thus this populace had to be shaped and molded into an orderly corps of production workers and a procapitalist electorate.

Nineteenth-century schools were "cultural factories" where immigrants and other workers were molded with so-called American values.[19] Ricardo Stanton-Salazar points out that the objective was to establish industrial behaviors, habits, and values among workers, particularly those from rural backgrounds, to optimize factory work productivity, to develop worker compliance to industrial authority, as well as to dilute the class consciousness so inimical to a nationalist ideology extolling capitalism and the representative democratic state.[20]

Last are the principles (not principals) for running schools. In the nineteenth-century United States, the most salient institutional model was the industrial one, rather than, for example, a church model or legislative model. Industrialists use efficiency as the measure to judge which factories are good or bad. The efficiency metric of industry is its cost-per-good-unit-produced. Correspondingly, as in Gradgrind's pontification in the first quote from *Hard Times,* factory-site productivity and efficiency continue to be the measures of success in public education.

15. Supt. Al Mijares said he will appoint a special task force to study the overall **effectiveness** of bilingual education here. (July 28, 1995, B3)

16. I came to see gangs not as an invading army but as our own offspring—the byproduct of a polarized economy, **ineffective schools,** broken families, exploitative politicians and a history of racial hatred that remains unhealed. (February 19, 1995, Magazine p. 16)

17. "Bilingual programs are only as good and **effective** as the principal, the teachers and the parents at that school," she said. (October 17, 1995, B1)

Effectiveness or efficiency, a high ratio of output to input, is not a necessary or "natural" way to think about institutional success. If another metaphorical model had been chosen, then another metric, or standard, would have applied. For example, a personal quality, such as intellectualism or doctrinalism, might have been the standard for schools based on a church model. Seminaries are set up on this model. Likewise, the public school standard might have been regimentarianism, if public education had been based on a military model, as is the case for military academies. Note once again that the effectiveness metric in the public school as FACTORY is entirely compatible with the EMPTY VESSEL metaphors that constitute commonplace learning theory. The semantic congruence of these metaphors contributes to their persistence.

Immanuel Kant first argued that neither utility nor effectiveness are standards for moral quality, since they can be used to justify immorality. He made this argument to reject Niccolò Machiavelli's belief that the ends justify the means. This evaluation can aptly be extended from a subject's moral quality to the nation's major public institution for human development. Efficiency as a gauge of quality does not recognize the dignity and worth of each person; it does not treat each student as an end. Instead, it relegates the child to the status of a mere object, a product made by the educational factory.

Kant's views notwithstanding, school quality continues to be measured by way of such a metric. By way of illustration, standardized tests take customary units of knowledge, namely, exam items to plot individuals, not against a real population, but against a normalized one. A far better measure of educational success, the student's creative construction of knowledge, is not used. The aggregate of scores is taken to be the appropriate measure of institutional, not individual, quality. The aggregated score of the institution, which is statistically valid for similarly aggregated groupings, is taken far beyond its technical limit. It becomes the justification for the institutional metric which devalues the individual student. The inherent logic[21] of the SCHOOL AS FACTORY metaphor, combined with the EMPTY VESSEL metaphor, conceptualizes the child as a unit of industrial production. Learning becomes an institutionally controlled process, not a matter of personal growth and lifelong edification. Children are degraded to become means to further institutional ends.

The implications are huge. Within this model, children are not inherently valuable subjects. They are viewed as passive recipients of their education. Worse yet, they are commodities. When they walk into the classroom, they are valuable to the extent that they conform to preset quality-control institutional standards. When they leave school, they are valuable only to the extent that they fit in greater society. Students' failure is presumed to be caused by inferior personal qualities, or cultural background brought to class. The institution cannot be at fault. Public education may not be based on profit, like a factory, but U.S. public school performance in the early twenty-first century is certainly based on Gradgrind's criteria, efficiency and industry.

## EDUCATION AS BUSINESS

While the factory model is the most frequent frame of reference for American public schools, another metaphor has appeared which is extolled as a novel, even revolutionary, metaphor for thinking about public schools. This model is the EDUCATION AS BUSINESS model. In the postindustrial age, this BUSINESS metaphor is more frequently used to evaluate the quality of education in terms of profitability than efficiency.

> 18. Total immersion in English will help students become fluent more quickly and give them a better foundation **for entering the American workplace,** said Trustee Robert H. Viviano, the lead proponent for dropping bilingual education. (May 9, 1997, B5)

This so-called updated way of thinking about schooling is not innovative. In *Hard Times,* the patron of the less-than-model school, Thomas Gradgrind, was a businessman as well as an industrialist. The BUSINESS metaphor shares the major weakness of the industrial model. It is centered on the institution—not on the child. The history of U.S. business does not commend it to be the model for the educational development of children. With the end of Fordism, U.S. business has become more streamlined, aggressive, and competitive. What this has meant is that U.S. business will jettison rather than retrain its workforce, discard rather than update its less profitable product lines, and place even greater attention on short-term profit margins than the long-term quality of its company. Because profit, not pupil, is its success metric, the BUSINESS metaphor will exacerbate the current problems of U.S. public education, particularly when money is short. Teachers will more likely become temporary service workers, rather than more highly skilled professionals. Rigorous quality control measures will be set in place earlier in the production cycle, to more efficiently exclude dividend-draining "non-standard" raw material, namely, working-class and language-minority students. Lastly, standards and postproduction testing will become mandatory to ensure a standard end product for consumers.[22] The educated child will become more explicitly the commodity produced by the public education system.[23]

Before turning to the next constitutive metaphor for education, two alarming features of the recent public discourse on education must be presented.

## Section 3: Classroom as BATTLEGROUND or WAREHOUSE

Twenty years ago state expenditures and high prioritization made California public education the envy of the nation at a time when U.S. education was the undisputed best in the world. Nowadays California is responsible for over five million public-school children and its educational system is in crisis. This predicament, which took no one by surprise, was brought on over a generation by three factors. First, the United States required an expansion of education to a greater proportion of its population. Second, there was increased need for a far more educated citizenry in the increasingly postindustrial, information-based economy. Lastly, this demand for enhanced caliber and democratization of education was not met with adequate funding and strong political support. As a result, all California public-school students presently endure a chronically underfunded system. Consequently, two specific hazards threaten today's school-age children. Wrenching metaphors in the public discourse indicate their plight:

19. a **front-line** look at what teachers mean when they talk about education reform (September 18, 1995, A1)

20. As urban schools go, Blair High is not as **battered** and **crime-plagued** as, say, some schools in the inner city. (September 18, 1995, A1)

21. But it is also a story about **the uphill battle** that is public education today, and the daily **struggle** to turn good intentions into good schools. (September 18, 1995, A1)

The *battering* that these students endure is not the traditional difficulties of education, such as the exertion to absorb the lessons of geometry and the dangling preposition. Nor does this *struggle* have much to do with the strife of adolescent awkwardness and rebellion. Rather, greater social inequality and physical violence have created increasingly dangerous public schools. The use of *battle* in excerpt 21 indicates a serious change of outlook in public education.

Metaphors of WAR are most frequently used in the public record to characterize political contests. Such metaphors may be appropriate for politics. In this society, political adversaries are people who disagree about the direction to be taken by American society.

22. The candidates are playing on a **field strewn** with racial **land mines.** (October 16, 1994, A1)

23. And he won't be facing a **fight** over legislative redistricting, always **the bloodiest battle** of the decade. (November 10, 1994, A1)

Yet in politics, the adversaries are adults who agree to the ground rules of the political contest, and although they talk bombastically, their contest more closely resembles a fourteenth-century squabble among gentry than a twentieth-century war of total annihilation. The same cannot be said for the public school classroom.

The classroom was previously seen to be a safe haven for American children.[24] Today public school students spend their days on a battlefield. Too many U.S. public-school children, through no fault of their own, are now placed in a setting that adults would as soon not enter. This setting is a learning experience, and the lesson schoolchildren draw, at school and hence in society, is that they are not treated as ends, nor are they considered to be a national resource. Instead, they are expendable members of society.

In particular, the inner-city schoolchild is dealt with as a second-rate commodity. These innocent children are treated from the start like the shoddy Christmas toy that is expected to bring easy profits. Following the big event, in their first year at school, they are soon deeply discounted. Not much later, they are written off as damaged merchandise. Again from within the FACTORY metaphor, the children of blue-collar, immigrant, and racialized parents are then consigned to the slowest tracks of the factory. Or they are taken off the conveyor belt and relocated far away from the factory floor. Heaped together, without even the guise of receiving an education for the duration, they are placed in substandard facilities under the surveillance of overworked storeroom staff:

24. the children in America's urban areas who are **warehoused** through broken school systems which rob them and our country of hope and promise. (September 28, 1997, B7)

25. We come to the aid of our children and all children, and give them a decent, challenging and dignified education in the private sector, or the rampage of angry youth who spent their childhood **warehoused** in 2,000-plus **student holding tanks** will continue until we can't ignore them anymore. (April 28, 1996, B16)

26. black and brown kids who have been **warehoused** by an education system (August 23, 1995, B9)

27. Save another generation of schoolchildren from the tragedy of being **warehoused** in the name of education. (August 20, 1995, M4)

For a poor or racialized child to advance along the American educational path in such circumstances requires much more effort to overcome these contemptible circumstances.

28. Steven's creed [is] that teachers don't care about him, that education is a joke and that school is a major bore. (May 7, 1997, A3)

Too often academic success for such a child requires the sheer luck of coming across a caring teacher who is willing to take personal interest. I would venture that readers of this book (particularly persons of color or children of poor parents) can recall a particular teacher who made a significant difference in their educational advancement, to whom their consequent professional success at least is partially attributable.[25] These teachers declared an armistice, or refurbished the storage depot to save a child or a classroom from the ravages of the failed factory system.[26] As has been noted by other commentators, the use of terms of warfare is much more widespread for Latino issues than for similar general societal issues. Indeed, war metaphors are used in immigration issues (e.g., the militarization of the border),[27] youth issues (criminalization of the children), and gang issues far and away more frequently concerning Latinos than for the general population. Yet in the present period, the metaphorization of CLASSROOM AS BATTLEGROUND or AS WAREHOUSE has moved beyond inner-city schools, to suburban and rural schools as well.

*Summary*

We began this chapter with a study of current public discourse on education at the cognitive learning level. At its base is a single dominant way of characterizing how learning takes place, in the EMPTY VESSEL metaphor. One quick step in the expansion of such mechanical metaphors is the use of FACTORY metaphors for institutions of public education. All educational programs, including bilingual education programs, are conceived, implemented, and evaluated on the basis of the efficiency metric, rather than on the basis of individual student capacitation. The student is viewed, in the terms of educational theorist John Goodlad, as a unit of economic utility. Consequently the student is not the ultimate measure of organizational success. It is as if toasters are being manufactured. This metaphor is inapt, inasmuch as people are not merchandise.

The metaphoric basis of public education discourse in America is not limited to the concept of learning and institutional relations. Apart from the EMPTY VESSEL and FACTORY models, two additional constitutive metaphors revealed what the public conceives education to be, as it is experienced by the individual. It is to the metaphors of an individual's learning that we now turn.

## Section 4: EDUCATION AS PATH

When the focus is not on the institution but on the individual, a familiar and yet elucidating metaphor structures public discourse. The child proceeds step-by-step in a sequence of classes and grades toward the end of becoming an educated person. The major metaphor that is revealed by a systematic review of over two hundred articles is the EDUCATION AS PATH metaphor. The path is a common metaphor that is used in many aspects of human life. *The course of human life* is just one example. The elements of the source domain, PATH, that are most often associated with the target domain, EDUCATION, include the unidirectional "movement" of an individual "toward" successive goals. Another element of the metaphor is its association with individual volition, namely, that the person moves along the path by his or her own actions. Note that none of these associations is obligatory. In these ways (among others) the metaphor is used to characterize the ways of education. Recall that although this is presently taken to be self-evident, as a metaphoric basis for student education, the PATH is not necessarily the single way to conceive of the nature of education.[28]

In the EDUCATION AS PATH metaphor, there are many expressions of directional movement of a person's education, as exemplified in the following:

29. Opponents contend the [bilingual education] program is an expensive alternative that will almost certainly hurt the **academic progress** of limited-English students. (February 9, 1996, A3)

30. Still, for many of these impressionable foreign-born teens, the **passage** through the bilingual program is about far more than just learning English. (October 29, 1995, B1)

31. Teacher Celso Rodriguez said bilingual teaching allows Spanish-speaking students **to keep pace** with their English-speaking peers as they learn their new language. He also pointedly asked the trustees why they were not targeting other tailored education programs, such as the **advanced** classes for gifted children or special education for children with learning disabilities. (February 14, 1997, B4)

32. "There's not a lot out there for college graduates," says UC Santa Barbara economist Mark Schniepp, who tracks Ventura County's economy. "They're not going to get a lot of **mileage** for their degrees." (June 22, 1997, B1)

33. The **track record** for English acquisition among non-fluent speakers in the Los Angeles Unified School District improved markedly during the last year, even as the number of such students continued to climb. (October 17, 1995, B1)

34. Last year, 1,150 schools around the state with non-English-speaking students failed to **advance** a single student into English fluency. A third of schools failing to **advance** any students to English fluency were teaching only in English; many of the rest taught primarily in English. (May 18, 1998, R1)

Also note other instances of the ubiquitous EDUCATION AS PATH metaphor elsewhere in this chapter, such as *compete* in excerpt 10 and *advance* in excerpt 13. These terms all imply significant effort on the part of the individual student. Apart from the student's progression in stages toward some goal, another central feature is a prescribed series of impediments along the educational path. These impediments are an expected part of the process toward the goal of becoming an educated person:

35. John Perez, vice president of the Los Angeles teachers union, said establishing higher standards [for bilingual education] without a corre-

sponding increase in funds is a recipe for failure of schools, teachers and students. "**If we set the bar of standards so high that a student must pole-vault over it,**" he said, "**we must also give the student a pole.**" (November 21, 1996, A3)

36. Students like Guillen must pass a final **battery of exams** before graduating from the program. (October 29, 1995, B1)

37. Some "latchkey kids" come home and dutifully **plow through** their homework, he said. (May 14, 1995, B1)

A further feature of the EDUCATION AS PATH metaphor is that the progress toward that goal of being educated takes place at a certain *pace,* and that *progress* is an attribute of the child's success.

38. That goes against the recommendations of many language experts who believe that children **fall behind** when they are taught academic subjects in a language they are still learning. However, opponents of bilingual education can also cite research that shows the opposite—that children immersed in all-English classes gain fluency faster. (March 10, 1995, A3)

39. "Right now what we need to do is get our young people **back on track,**" said Ortiz. (March 12, 1995, City Times Section p. 12)

40. Roberta Andrade, who speaks Spanish with her four children, said they would have been **set back** if they had been thrust into English-based classes in the primary grades. Now, she said, all four are bilingual. One has graduated and three are in junior and senior high schools. (April 13, 1997, A1)

41. Extensive research by Oakes into the **progress** of Latino students in public schools has shown that they are consistently **routed into the least academic courses** of study, beginning in elementary school. That so-called "**tracking**" is worse for bilingual-program students, she said, because they are pigeonholed as low-achieving early on. (June 1, 1995, A1)

It is thus appropriate to review the ontology of PATH, the third of the four dominant metaphors in contemporary public discourse on education.

## *Ontology of EDUCATION AS PATH*

The ontology of PATH is an embodied experience of walking along a trail or track to some destination. The everyday frame of understanding of this semantic domain entails a starting point, an endpoint, a route to be traversed, possibly with some impediments, and a sense of directedness on the part of the walker to follow the path toward the endpoint.

The path semantic domain seems to be shared by all people and cultures, and it guides the conceptualization of various aspects of human life. Philosopher Mark Johnson has noted how people employ the PATH metaphor to furnish moral coherence to their life:

> We are basically beings in process, synthesizing creatures. . . . We are situated within a tradition and culture that [supply] a stock of roles, scripts, frames, models and metaphors that are our way of having a world, understanding it, and reasoning about it. Moral judgments . . . make use of these imaginative tools. . . . As the most comprehensive synthesizing process, narrative plays a role in organizing our long-term identity and in testing our scenarios in making moral choices.[29]

At a much more concrete level, anthropologist Naomi Quinn has studied how people employ the PATH schema, using ethnographic interviews to map Americans' use of the PATH domain in metaphors of marriage.[30]

The mapping of the ontology of PATH onto the domain of EDUCATION imposes a well-developed framework of everyday embodied knowledge of walking a path onto a crucial aspect of human life, as well as a central institution. The mapping includes the following correspondences: Education corresponds to a walking pathway. It has a beginning corresponding to a state of being uneducated, a route to traverse corresponding to an established set of *courses* (= routes), and a succession of *grades* (= slopes or gradients of increasing difficulty). There are expected impediments to overcome corresponding to formal batteries of evaluation that require demonstrated mastery of the content of the educational material for each grade. Lastly there is a destination corresponding to the completion of the predetermined *curriculum* (< Latin *currere* 'to run') of a school system, leading to the graduation of the student, certifying achievement of the status of an educated person. Curriculum is the established set of courses that a student has to take to obtain an education. The term *curriculum vitae* correspondingly invokes the EDUCATION AS PATH metaphor. Its etymological meaning, "race of life," has shifted to its current meaning, "detailed account of a career." And notice that the term *career* (< M.F. *carrière* 'street' < Latin *carraria* 'road for vehicles') is also deeply metaphorized in terms of PATH.

When PATH is used to conceptualize domains of education, each person (metaphorically) undertakes a journey from the position of an uneducated person toward the place of an educated person. All the topological elements noted above are fully employed in the EDUCATION AS PATH metaphor in contemporary American public discourse on education.

*Atomizing Entailment*

This metaphor contains three associated elements of inherent logic. One, education within this metaphoric configuration is attained one step at a time. Two, a succession of grades must be passed along the way. Three, an education is attained by one's own motivation. These built-in logical assertions of the EDUCATION AS PATH metaphor play a central role in its constitutive function. They foreground the volition of the individual pathtaker, and background all structural factors that make up the social environment of the public school. As a result, an overly schematized image of the actual educational process of American children is projected.

A critical entailment follows: all first-grade classroom experiences are identical. That is to say, the distinguishing context that makes one person's educational experience unlike another's experience is voided or emptied by the entailment. When the path metaphor is used, the myriad structural differences (such as teacher preparation and experience, school facility size and condition, student population and demographics, per student budget allotment, and professional personnel ratios) which disadvantage poor and linguistic minority children in urban schools are normally overlooked and forgotten, because the entailment logically follows the metaphor.

According to this metaphor, the educational path of every U.S. public-school child is, for all practical purposes, exactly alike. Of course, this is not the case. Still, it follows from this entailment that all high school diplomas are also of equal value. Note how this echoes the commonplace understanding that the finished products of a FACTORY are, for all practical purposes, identical. The entailment dissociates institutional strictures and societal obstacles from the disadvantaged student, as well as advantages from the privileged student, as if each walks along unfettered on identical educational paths. This dissolves, or atomizes, the student's structural relationship to the school.

The atomizing entailment is grossly untrue, and yet is reinforced each time the metaphor is invoked. With this metaphor, the implication is that there are only two real differences between one person's educational success and another's failure: aptitude and determination. All structural difficulties that impair the education of language-minority and working-class children are omitted from the story that EDUCATION AS PATH narrates. Instead, only personal factors bring triumph or failure to the individual student. The atomizing entailment has often been repudiated in scientific studies, and disputed in critical social commentary, such as film.[31] However, as an entailment of a dominant PATH metaphor, it will resist rejection so long as it is uncontested in the public discourse on education.

## Educational Tracking

An important issue which is conceptualized in terms of the EDUCATION AS PATH metaphor is indicated in excerpts 39 and 41. Academic *tracking* involves establishing a rigid sequence of courses for children that places them either on an academic set of courses or a remedial course of studies. Tracking, in the best light, expedites the administrative scheduling problems of assigning students to classrooms and teachers.

> 42. "We don't water down the curriculum," said principal Elizabeth Nordyke. "We don't segregate, and we don't put [students] **on special tracks.**" (April 14, 1997, A3)

Note the compatibility of *tracking* with both the EDUCATION AS PATH and SCHOOL AS FACTORY metaphors, in terms of its congruent reference to assembly-line transport of raw materials along a conveyor belt through a set of manufacturing steps. If the public's thinking is limited to the SCHOOL AS FACTORY constituting metaphor, tracking seems like an appropriate procedure to use. From this point of view, tracking optimizes the use of resources when schools provide an education for thousands of children. It is more efficient to place so-called "fast" children on educational "fast tracks" and "slow" children on "slow tracks."

If the child, particularly the socially marginalized child, is granted the central frame of reference, then the dangers of tracking are easier to perceive. It has been demonstrated in a long series of studies that tracking establishes a self-fulfilling prophecy which reduces the long-term educational advancement of the individual child, particularly the child whose familial background does not conform to the mainstream education prerequisites, which are based on middle-class Anglo-American values.[32] Most disturbingly, the tracking decision most often takes place on the basis of minimal interchange between a teacher and a child. If not based on a child's surname or some other arbitrary basis, it is made on the basis of a few interactions, over only a couple of days, at the beginning of a child's school experience. The child who is not a middle-class Anglo-American in appearance, interactional style, or speech is most likely to be viewed as "slow" or "weak," when the only real difference is culture, not potential.

Once such a child is relegated to the slow track, teachers' lower expectations lead to lower achievement levels on his or her part, which confirms the original prediction and most often seals the educational fate of the child. This places the child in an especially difficult situation of fending off the judgment of adults. Extraordinary energy on the part of parents, other teachers, and school administrators is required to reverse such a decision.[33] Since the slower tracks provide little opportunity for demonstrating excellence, the most likely conclusion of undertrained and inured school personnel is that these children most suitably form part of the bottom ranks of the system. Thus, they are unjustly denied equal educational opportunity. Academic development and the highest levels of social advancement are refused to these children when they are relegated to the least valued position on the educational pathway.

Educational historian and critic Jeannie Oakes described tracking as segregation. It takes place within a school, but it is apartheid. It is a post–*Brown v. Board of Education* response to the prohibition of "separate but equal" status among racially segregated schools. The use of tracking began in earnest soon after schools were forced to integrate in 1954. Minority students are far more likely to be misplaced in special education classes, characterized as having linguistic or other disingenuous "deficiencies," or tracked into vocational or the least academically sophisticated courses because of limited native "abilities." As a result, minority students as a group have been denied equal opportunity and full access to the programs and teachers of the educational system.[34]

The tracking issue is not uniquely a problem for Latino children. Other children of color and working-class white children are subject to this kind of misrepresentative designation in public schools. Still, given the well-demonstrated biases against non-English-speaking children, children of color, and working-class children, tracking targets immigrant and Latino students excessively.[35]

## Narrative of EDUCATION AS PATH

Although it may seem patently obvious and "only natural" to some readers, the ontological relationship created by this metaphor will be presented using an informal narrative of the EDUCATION AS PATH metaphor which summarizes only the main elements of the metaphor:

> *Formal education for students is obtained by taking a well-established path on their way toward becoming educated persons. The path that all students traverse is subdivided into a series of "grades" through which each student passes. Each grade is "passed" when students demonstrate a certain level of mastery over a set of prescribed impediments of both social and educational content associated with the grade. Each latter grade is more difficult in terms of its prescribed impediments than the previous grade. In public education in America the goal of becoming an educated person is marked by the completion of twelve grades of education. There are further steps along the path. Each further grade has its prescribed impediments to be mastered. Greater status is accorded to people who have successfully passed more difficult grades along the educational path.*

The narrative of the educational path is shared by everyone in American society, whether modestly or highly educated. While this narrative may be (even painfully) familiar, it is important to reiterate that it is not a necessary, but only a conventionalized, metaphoric association. In the narrative, different levels of school and life achievement for the individual are seen to be based exclusively on personal initiative. Achievement is cast simply as a consequence of how well one moves along the path. Individualism is a key principle of this metaphor. The atomization entailment preserves the fiction that purely by the dint of native abilities and personal efforts, each person makes his or her way along the path. Thus unequal educational opportunities, dissimilar socioeconomic factors, and institutional racism are backgrounded and ignored, especially in elementary school, when the effects of structural inequity most affect these vulnerable children.

Competition among individuals is also enjoined in the narrative. Greater ascribed status, and social and economic success, are presumed in American public discourse to be a result of greater travel along the educational path. All other things being equal, the amount and quality of a student's efforts involved along the path are understood in this narrative to correspond to the level of accomplishment that she or he has attained. Thus to become a heart surgeon requires overcoming many more educational impediments than to become an auto mechanic, and the social status of the former correspondingly outstrips the latter. Indeed, if a person achieves a high degree of financial or professional success without having taken the presumed educational path, this constitutes a surprising fact which will most often be noted and commented on.

There is significant conceptual rigidity associated with the EDUCATION AS PATH metaphor. To mention only the two most prominent aspects of this orthodoxy, the sequence of stages that must be taken and the tests of mastery of areas of educational content (for example, math, science, art) are quite inflexible. If an individual does not follow the compulsory institutional steps, or does poorly on the prescribed tests, this is often sufficient warrant to be excluded from among the ranks of the educated in this society, regardless of the experiences lived, or the areas of mastery, or the contributions that the individual offers society.

It is quite healthy to suspend for the moment the pairing of the SCHOOL AS FACTORY and EDUCATION AS PATH metaphors, which together legitimize and mask a number of unjust institutional aspects of public schooling, particularly for nonmainstream children. The "good reasons" that have been marshaled over the years to justify the efficiency metric may then begin to sound like brittle rationalizations. The factory model perhaps becomes even more chilling and abhorrent if a child dear to the reader is envisioned as the next nickel chunk of raw material to be forged on the schoolhouse floor.

## The CONTEST Metaphor

The PATH metaphor is used to characterize other aspects of American life. One that is intimately associated with education, and which was involved in the 1996 affirmative action debate, as discussed in the previous chapter, is the notion of success. Americans conceptualize success as involving a path, as seen in the following excerpts drawn from the *Commentary* essays referred to in the previous chapter:

> 43. In the 60s and 70s, preferential affirmative action, ordered by the courts in remedial contexts, probably did **break down racist barriers** to employment. (C 26)
> 44. The original supporters of this policy (again, myself included) naively thought that the only thing keeping blacks down was discrimination. Thus, simply removing the artificial **obstacles** that had been **standing in their way** . . . (C 46)
> 45. All this, though more ambitious than some previous federal programs, was well within the American political tradition of providing mi-

norities and the poor with the kinds of resources that would supposedly enable them to **overcome barriers** and help themselves. (C 36)

From the point of view of conservative essayists, affirmative action places a gratuitous governmental obstacle on the path of individuals moving along the pathway to career and life achievement. As noted with some irony in the next excerpt, affirmative action may carry undeserving recipients along the path to success:

> 46. It turned out she [a working-class student of color whose attitude was not sufficiently deferential to the white professor] was originally from Tennessee, but had gone to the same private preparatory school as Jackie Kennedy once attended. In brief, she had been **given an affirmative action ride** for many years. (C 28)

Within this view of the world, head-to-head competition is seen as the "natural" test among individuals to bring out the best efforts as each person strives to break the tape ahead of everyone else. Success is achieved in a contest against rivals. Thus the metaphor of SUCCESS AS A RACE is an expansion of the EDUCATION AS PATH metaphor. Or, conversely, the education metaphor is a special case of the American race-for-success allegory.

## The Dropout

A very common term in the discourse of American education that has its basis in the PATH and CONTEST models is *dropout,* which appears both as a verb and a noun. In the *Los Angeles Times* in 1996, it appeared at least 135 times in 118 articles which were indexed for public education. *Dropout,* of course, refers to individuals who withdraw from public schooling. This Americanism came into general use in the 1920s,[36] and readily communicates an image of a runner in a track competition, once attention is drawn to its metaphor. However, in its everyday usage it may not be so obvious.[37] The term has become so much a part of everyday parlance that it is presumed to be common to all dialects of English, and was even overlooked by a multivolume dictionary of Americanisms.[38]

## Contest versus Sponsored Mobility

As with other topics of social order, some key studies of education have identified the key metaphors of public discourse. Among those is a forty-year-old study by Ralph Turner. Turner studied how upward mobility was facilitated by public school, and how it was depicted.[39] He did not talk about metaphors, but noted two ideal types generated by different ideologies. The first corresponds to what he considered the U.S. view, in which schools are democratic institutions which promote excellence through a meritocracy.

In this view, the EDUCATION AS CONTEST metaphor articulates competition for social mobility. "Contest mobility is like a sporting event in which many compete for a few recognized prizes. The contest is judged to be fair only if all the players compete on an equal footing. Victory must be won solely by one's own efforts. The most satisfactory outcome is not necessarily a victory of the most able, but of the most deserving." It is "a system in which elite status is the prize in an open contest and is taken by the aspirants' own efforts . . . while the 'contest' is governed by some rules of fair play." The prize of superior social status can be achieved by best efforts of each aspirant. Awards are delayed as long as possible. Further, there is a great deal of fantasy aspiration, since few will ever grasp the golden ring.[40] This model, of course, is fully consistent with the metaphors that have been presented so far.

Turner also offered a second model which he thought more closely described the British system, which he called sponsored mobility. "Sponsored mobility, on the other hand, rejects the pattern of the contest and substitutes a controlled selection process. In this process the elite or their agents, who are best qualified to judge merit, call to elite status those individuals who have the appropriate qualities. Individuals do not win or seize elite status, but mobility is rather a process of sponsored induction into the elite following selection."[41] Here recruits are chosen early in their education, on the basis of factors other than achievement and excellence. Thus, this recruitment is not merit-based. Further, the right to grant the professional credentials needed for mobility is limited to a near monopoly. Not everyone who is deserving can aspire to, much less obtain, the documents needed to become upwardly mobile. The disadvantaged must settle for less.

Turner noted that a "practicality narrative" is used to mitigate the protests of those who are not sponsored for success. This narrative argues that all persons indeed find their place in society, according to their social status and personal merit. In the sponsored mobility model, then, the ideological resources of the dominant elements of society are marshaled to reproduce the status quo. The practicality narrative inculcates students of different classes, races, and ethnicities to accept their class-specific and race-specific place in the national division of labor.

As one might imagine, the sponsored mobility metaphors do not appear frequently in the *Los Angeles Times* discourse on education. This data source is rich with contest metaphors. However, sponsored mobility language is often expressed in private among the citizenry who are not able to exercise their share of talent and perseverance to attain higher class standing because of language, race, and class. For them, irrespective of the dominant metaphors in use, American social mobility is not a contest, and is practiced with reference to race and class.

The ontology and inherent logic of SUCCESS AS A RACE are nearly the same as for EDUCATION AS PATH, with only minor differences. While it may be that the reader's own experiences of reality paint another picture, in this ontology, no one is born into the social circumstances that mark him or her as a winner or a loser; each person traverses the same route, and faces equivalent obstacles on the way to success. Within the inherent logic of the metaphor, individual initiative (and maybe just a bit of luck) determine the outcome. The track and field events of the modern Olympics are the closest realization of this metaphor for Americans. In the race for success, the competitor who is both the most talented and the most competitive wins the laurels, and is entirely entitled to the accolades.

## The Educational Contest and Affirmative Action

There is no shortage of excerpts expressing this constitutive metaphor for the U.S. view of just deserts in life. Again, drawing from the *Commentary* expositions on affirmative action:

> 47. This was a program calling for the aggressive seeking out of blacks . . . who were not yet qualified but showed promise of an ability to **catch up** fairly quickly through special tutoring or training. . . . [T]hey were supposed to **compete** as individuals **on an equal footing** with every other applicant. (C 45)
>
> 48. Thus, simply removing the artificial obstacles that had been standing in their way would create a level **playing field,** either all by itself or with a little additional help to overcome the lingering damage of the past. (C 46)
>
> 49. Many would like to see government and business make an even greater effort to **level the field** for black Americans. (C 34)

Even the most fastidious conservative, who perhaps is drawn to an earlier so-called "natural" hierarchy model of privilege, disdainfully acknowledged the current allegory of merit:

50. But the cynicism of young African-Americans must be as nothing compared with the young white males who know that, for the sake of a **"level playing field"** (that charmless and misguided metaphor), they and their intellectual ambitions have been put permanently **on the sidelines.** (C 28)

The atomizing entailment of EDUCATION AS PATH, which seriously distorts how the public views U.S. education, also misleads us about the experience of the advantaged and the disadvantaged in the American race for success. Conservatives want to presume that the playing field was leveled in a pen-stroke with the 1964 Civil Rights Act, and that all Americans now run the same race course with the same rules of fair play. This crucial entailment dismisses the numerous reports, analyses, and narratives that illuminate the structural inequity and compounding obstacles that racialized portions of U.S. society continue to confront.[42]

51. From [President Johnson's 1965 Howard University commencement address] came the widely accepted notion that government should take steps to help blacks overcome the legacies of slavery and racial discrimination, which had left them **"hobbled"** at the **starting line in the race for success** in American life. . . . If[as President Johnson called for] "equality of result" was the goal, the Great Society's strategy seemed like a lengthy and roundabout way of getting there. It offered little for those blacks already in the **race for success** and perhaps not much more for those just coming to **the starting line.** (C 36)

Since the metaphorical race itself is easy to visualize as equal, real inequities and persistent disparities which favored one group of competitors and disfavored other groups are not attributed to the factors that created these contingent groupings of people. The preparation or native abilities of individuals are imputed. In this narrative, underrepresented minorities simply do not have the "right stuff to play with the big boys" in higher education. Likewise, so the story goes, American society also pays a price for checking the previously unconstrained head-to-head competition:

52. Of course, there was a price to be paid for these accomplishments. Dependency on government, especially (but not only) among those receiving public assistance, grew. In an increasing number of areas, entitlement rather than achievement became the critical factor for success. Partly as a result of this, measures for attainment, such as requirements for

degrees or job-performance standards, loosened, the better to accommodate those who might otherwise fall short. And—not least important—as race, gender, or other characteristics became more crucial for determining who got what, America became a more divided, and a more divisive, society. **As we made more people winners in the race for success, we managed to diminish the importance of success.** As we moved toward racial equality "as a fact," we made racial differences more salient. As we sought to help those who were hobbled by the legacies of discrimination, we created programs that left many of them ill-equipped to compete. (C 37)

53. **Inability to compete at the game being played necessarily leads to demands that the game be changed,** and thus are born demands for black and ethnic studies and "multiculturalism." Such courses function to convince blacks that their academic difficulties are a result not of a lack of preparation but of white racism, and to impress upon whites their own moral shortcomings. (C 32)

54. When persons are appointed, or admitted, or promoted because of their racial group, it is inevitable that the members of that group will, in the institution giving such preference, perform less well than average. Membership in the minority group most certainly does not imply inferiority; that is a canard—but that stereotype is *reinforced* by preferences. Since the standards for the selection of minorities are inevitably lower when diluted by considerations of color, sex, or nationality, it is a certainty that, overall, the average performance of those in the preferred group will be weaker—not because of their ethnicity, of course, but because many among them were selected on grounds having no bearing on the work or study to be pursued. Preference thus *creates a link* between the minority preferred and inferior performance. (C 22, emphasis in original)

Consequently, some conservative critics would label minorities as inferior performers when they are associated with affirmative action, as stated in Chapter 4. Again, from this point of view, the everyday American competition for success is not fraudulent; rather, some of the competitors have inferior pregame training.

55. Affirmative action was about facilitating blacks' acculturation to long-closed workplaces, where the tools and skills of social advancement are acquired. (C 50)

56. Blacks and others from disadvantaged groups fared better when they

acquired the skills and commitments that have traditionally made for success: education, steady employment, a family, and the like. (C 37)

Or they are simply inferior:

57. To my mind there is one good argument for maintaining this racial preference, . . . my principal reason is that our colleges, universities, and professional schools are the central gateways to positions of power, wealth, and influence, and **applying strict meritocratic principles would lead to a catastrophic drop in the number of black students** in these crucial institutions. That would deliver a terrible message to blacks, and would be bad for the country. (C 30)

The most cynical conservative commentators completely disregard the continuing and cumulative effects of racism, and emblazon all affirmative action beneficiaries charlatans. Again, the appeal is to the public's concept of an ordinary footrace, and the notion that racialized minorities cannot compete fairly.

58. Racial preferences, like a handicap in golf, attempt to overcome the fact that those being preferred are **not competitive** with others in terms of the benefit being obtained. (C 31)
59. One does not create an entrepreneurial class by granting contracts to **those who cannot otherwise compete;** on the contrary, one invites fraud and corruption. (C 30)

The atomizing entailment of the RACE FOR SUCCESS metaphor reinforces the view that U.S. society is inherently fair, or very nearly so. All competitors presumably run the same race and leap the same hurdles. It further characterizes affirmative action in higher education and elsewhere as an unwarranted obstacle in the path of white male competitors, which mocks the American myth of just deserts accruing to the winner after fair competition.

The hegemonic assertion that such deserts are fairly distributed has often been criticized. The critique is that merit, which allegedly is accorded to the hardest-working and most talented, is not the sole requisite of success. Rather, the meritocracy myth is a verbal stratagem, to wit, Ralph Turner's practicality narrative, to maintain the advantage of those who are most likely to profit from white middle-class values. As often as this criticism has been made, it has been disputed, even when voiced by blue-ribbon panels like the

Kerner Commission.[43] To appraise the conflicting viewpoints of neoconservatives and progressives, one might consider whether the disparities in measures of success are distributed evenly through the citizenry.

60. I know affirmative action chiefly in its academic context, in my case as a member of a university English department. Here it has tended to **skew normal meritocracy** procedures of hiring and job-getting. . . . (white men, it turns out, not only can't jump; they can't teach, either.) What a discouragement of scholarly passion, **what a denial of merit,** what a shuck and a sham, a hustle and a scam, affirmative action must seem to them! (C 27–28)

61. Least obvious, but victims nonetheless, are the beneficiaries themselves. For instance, as Thomas Sowell has noted, **racial preferences in college admission systematically mismatch talent and opportunity.** The top 10 percent of minority students find themselves competing at Ivy League colleges with the top 1 percent of white and Asian students; the top 50 percent compete with the top 10 percent; and so on down the scale. As a result, many beneficiaries of preferences have no hope of excelling against their supposed peers, struggle hard merely to keep up, get discouraged, perform poorly by their own standards, and even drop out of school altogether. The modestly successful middle-class career they would have enjoyed if they had attended a first-rate second-class school [*sic*] is lost to them, perhaps forever. (C 41)

62. Needless to say, opponents of affirmative action did not like the fact that students who score lower on tests or who have less job experience are admitted to college or promoted **at the expense of the more gifted.** (C 56)

If the atomizing entailment of the metaphor is tacitly accepted, then affirmative action is seen as unfair to individual competition. Conservative commentators will claim that affirmative action undermines the fabled American race for success. These critics can then disregard all evidence of continuing racism in U.S. society, which makes a travesty of the allegory. They adhere to the contest metaphor, with its covert atomizing entailment, and claim that with the passage of the Civil Rights Act no systemic obstacles remain to bar truly free competition among individuals of different races. While conservative commentators need no reminder of their personal moral shortcomings, as expressed with reproach in excerpt 53 above, at times they demonstrate astonishing ignorance of their "possessive investment in whiteness," which each of them has procured at the expense of others.[44] It is the rare conservative who makes the following statement:

> "Merit" is not just something people are born with; it is the product of social processes that, because of our history and the ways we choose to associate with one another, have a racial dimension. Social policy should attend to racial inequality if the consequence of historical discrimination against blacks is not to be a permanent economic disparity.[45]

The critics of affirmative action even more rarely call for changes to the social system to more fairly balance economic disparities and educational inequity, so that the spirit of the daily American Olympics for success can be more closely played out. Ironically, immigrants and most racialized Americans more closely embrace the RACE FOR SUCCESS metaphor as a key part of the American ethic than do some of these privileged white critics their own hegemonic allegory.

Turning from the EDUCATION AS PATH and SUCCESS AS RACE metaphors, which certainly have not been as thoroughly described as public discourse would allow, we now begin a relatively brief discussion on the final metaphor for education, EDUCATION AS RIVER.

## Section 5: EDUCATION AS RIVER

The so-called educational mainstream is one of the most frequent education metaphors in the educational discourse corpus. *Mainstream* refers to a number of distinct elements of the educational system. This one term appears scores of times during the Proposition 227 debate on bilingual education.

> 63. Thus, the school district in one of the nation's most diverse and liberal cities has officially endorsed segregating its immigrant students while they try to learn enough English to join the **mainstream.** (June 1, 1995, A1)
>
> 64. For more than 20 years, federal law has ordered schools to take steps to ensure that limited-English students have equal access to school curricula. In that time, California generally has required school districts with high numbers of limited-English students to teach them first in their

home languages and later move them into **mainstream** classes. (April 13, 1997, A1)

65. District statistics released Monday indicate that more than 24,000 students were transferred out of bilingual program classes and into **mainstream** classes in 1994–95—representing 8.4% of those who were not fluent the year before. (October 17, 1995, B1)

*Mainstream* is used as a noun or adjective in the foregoing excerpts, but is also used as a transitive verb, which indicates actions that discharge the linguistic minority child into the wider educational system.

66. In what may signal a growing attack on bilingual education in Orange County, two school districts are considering resolutions that condemn a state-mandated language program designed to **mainstream** non-English-speaking students. (March 9, 1995, B1)

It is important to explicitly present the ontology of the fourth metaphor that structures public discourse on public education in America today.

## Ontology of EDUCATION AS RIVER

During the 1997–1998 Proposition 227 campaign, the principal uses of the term *mainstream* in educational discourse were in contrast and counterpoint to programs of bilingual education. The source semantic domain of this metaphor is RIVER. Since a river is directed toward a goal, several conceptual relationships of the RIVER metaphor are similar to the source domain of the PATH metaphor. The everyday frame of understanding of river also involves a flowing variable stream with a beginning, traversing some distance, with twists and turns and obstructions that may snag the traveler riding the current, which is making its way toward the sea. However, important contrasts inhere. Unlike the PATH metaphor, to float on the metaphorical river does not invoke a sense of personal propulsion. The river conveys any and all voyagers along in its current. From this ontological difference ensues the distinctive aspects of the RIVER narrative.

Unlike the EDUCATION AS PATH metaphor, for which the primary image is a walking path of a single trekker, the EDUCATION AS RIVER metaphor allows for a swelling stream whose course and current may transport its journeyers in different ways. On the one hand, the mainstream conjures a swift and deep channel where the current is strong, the volume of water is greatest, and the direction narrowly defined. Anyone that is carried along in the river's mainstream will arrive at his or her final destination most quickly.

> 67. Top education officials in Orange [School District] say the results of bilingual education over the last 20 years have been disappointing. They say kids with little English aren't moving fast enough into the **mainstream.** (April 13, 1997, A1)

In contrast, in the shallow periphery of the same educational river the current is slow, the water is shallow and fraught with shoals, sandbars, mudflats, and stagnant pools. The progress of anyone carried along in the shallows is much less secure. More is left to chance. Flotsam, deadwood, and other debris gather along the lazy margins of the river.

> 68. "We'll continue to be in the **backwaters** of public education, and, in an information-driven society, we simply can't afford to let that happen." (October 15, 1995, B1)

In contrast to the PATH metaphor, individual volition is not part of the inherent logic of the RIVER metaphor—everyone is just carried along in the river's current. The educational *mainstream* thus does not invoke notions of perseverance, motivation, talent, or ambition, as does the EDUCATION AS PATH metaphor. Individuals are transported and they get to their destination, according to the volume of the river and their position in the river's flow. Narrow and deep channels run faster and surer than wide, slow-moving currents with meandering switchbacks and alluvial shores.

The river ontology incorporates a second important element. A single river empties a whole region. Whether comprising a local region the size of a school district, or a whole nation, each river blends the waters of smaller distinct streams into a single common waterway. Rivers which drain a whole continent, like the Mississippi or Amazon, combine the waters of large tributaries and tiny runnels, uniting their disparate elements into a single flow. In all rivers, different currents commingle until their diverse sources can no longer be distinguished.

### Assimilation to the Mainstream

The public's view of education is focused on one educational process by which students learn instructional content. This content (math, reading, civics, science, etc.) is mastered, so the PATH metaphor goes, as a consequence of the effort each individual puts into striding along the schooling path. Still, the public school student undergoes a second process which does not involve instructional content or personal effort. Through daily school attendance and classroom ritual and routine, these children are inculcated into the social hierarchies and tenets of the nation's principal socializing institution; in short, they are inculcated into the nation's hegemony.

No volition is implied by the RIVER ontology. Students are simply carried along. The key ontological concept of the river is its swift flow in a narrow channel, in which children are carried along in its waters. In time they eventually blend with and are permeated by the mainstream. This is the assimilation of students into U.S. society, by which the "common" values of society are imparted. As they grow out of childhood in the mainstream school, students acquiesce to the American worldview as they absorb its sanctioned canon, hallowed national myths, and conventional history. The RIVER metaphor expresses this socialization process, which transforms "foreign" children into American teenagers who partake of prevailing American practices, values, and conventional views on community, nation, and world. The mainstream school creates a member of U.S. society who is likely to accept his or her lot in life.

The RIVER metaphor also conveys these students, by their placement and progress in school, to their designated place in American society, for better or worse. The overwhelming majority of Latino students are relegated to the rocky margins of U.S. society.[46] Students learn the social practices available to them within social orders that are expressed in school. Students learn to function within subject positions which are defined (in terms of characteristic discourses/practices) within the encompassing social order. These subject positions confine students in terms of their knowledge and beliefs, social relationships and social identity. The discourse practices of mainstream schools embody the naturalized ideological assumptions about student/societal member subject space. When the discourse practices are enacted by the subject/student, these subject positions are reproduced, and their ideological assumptions are reaffirmed. As students mature, and live their lives as subjects, the institutional practice of public schools that sustains and legitimizes existing power relations through the association of discourse and subject position inculcates them to acquiesce to the ideology of the standing social order, including relations which enact the social inequities associated with minority status. These processes are aptly expressed in the EDUCATION AS RIVER metaphor.

69. Ninth Street's principal, Eleanor Vargas Page, considers the dissatis-faction [with the bilingual education programs] voiced by the Las Famil-ias parents ill-informed. The school retooled its bilingual program just last year, Vargas Page said, infusing it with more English sooner than ever before. Those changes were a response, she said, to parent concerns as well as a districtwide push to speed the transfer of bilingual program students into the **educational mainstream.** (January 16, 1996, B1)

The term *mainstream,* among educators with contrasting political views, means somewhat different things. Different concepts are added into the metaphor, which lead to different views of what *mainstreaming* students will accomplish. For those who take a conservative stance, as will be elaborated in the next chapter, mainstream socialization cannot be achieved via bilin-gual education. It can only be accomplished through English-only instruc-tion, and ultimately requires English-dependency on the part of immigrant students.

70. Fluency in English is a "civil rights matter," said Robert Rossier, a lan-guage expert. . . . "We do not have any evidence that primary language instruction is leading to learning English so these children can join the **mainstream.**" (March 29, 1995, B3)

By guaranteeing the English-language dependence of these students, their "foreign" nature will assuredly be lost as they are channeled into the common American culture, and toward consensus with hegemonic viewpoints.

For the pro-bilingual-education position articulated during the Proposi-tion 227 campaign, *mainstreaming* less obviously refers to assimilation. In the *Los Angeles Times* database, bilingual education advocates are less pre-occupied with student conformity to the so-called national culture. Instead they emphasize the better range of academic objectives and college prepa-ration courses. These resources for social advancement, unsurprisingly, are available only in mainstream classes.

In the final analysis, however, no public school educator will deny that *mainstreaming,* as societal indoctrination of immigrant, linguistic minor-ity, and other marginalized children, is part of the mission of the public schools.[47]

## Summary

Four constitutive metaphors conceptualize America's contemporary pub-lic discourse on education. The first, STUDENT AS EMPTY VESSEL, is archaic. It would be called quaint if it did not structure the way education is understood and operationalized. Since its framing of the learning process is patently obsolete, it is harmful to children. Considering children to be quiescent repositories to be filled with learning has little to commend it. Yet this 150-year-old metaphor remains fully productive in the public discourse evaluated in twenty-five months of *Los Angeles Times* materials. It was not seriously contested in public discourse by more adequate metaphors. Constructivist metaphors, such as STUDENT AS KNOWLEDGE BUILDER, were rarely registered during the same period.

American public discourse also employs the antiquated nineteenth-century FACTORY model for schools. America's children thus are seen, so to speak, as raw material fashioned into products which are filled with knowledge content. They have learning forged into them through repetitive, numbing rehearsal. This metaphor is reiterated, for example, in the annual campaigns to center reading instruction strictly on decoding the letter combinations making up words—phonics—rather than reading for meaning. Moreover, the popular "new" metaphor for education, SCHOOL AS BUSINESS, retains the antiquated elements of the factory metaphor and reinforces the unfairness of the current system that rewards and punishes accidents of birth. It promotes conformity since children who fit the mold are promoted for the accident of their white middle-class upbringing. On the other hand, the native capacities and cultural and linguistic richness of racialized minority and working-class children will continue to be demoted. These children's potential is now casually disregarded insofar as the factory efficiency metric is taken into account. When the business bottom line is employed as the measure for educational excellence, these children will be at greater risk. As soon as a weak market brings down profits, it will begin to make business sense to call into question the supposed social contract to educate all children. Business sense dictates that profitable product lines should be augmented, while poorly performing product lines should be reduced to the minimum. Currently, the public takes it for granted that a public education is a citizen's legal right, but Americans do not have any such constitutional right. It is a mere privilege, which can be contested in the courts.[48]

The third generative metaphor, EDUCATION AS PATH, fits congruently into the key American allegory of the race for success. The two reinforce one another. Both share the atomizing entailment, which falsely holds that the conditions and rules of the race are the same for each competitor. This entailment backgrounds unequal social and structural factors that favor some groups at the expense of other groups. Socioeconomic disparities and continuing institutional racism are passed over in these mythical allegories. The American ethic of fair head-to-head competition, which most Americans avow, is mocked by the entailment.

The fourth constitutive metaphor, again found with abundance in the *Los Angeles Times* database, characterizes a final aspect of public schools:

> 71. There are also **perils** in entering the **mainstream waters** of the Southern California high school. (October 29, 1995, B1)

The socialization process as RIVER is part of growing up in a school setting; it is as automatic as aging a year in 365 days. It is not a matter of will or personal initiative. Mainstreamed children naturally mature to become members of the majority society. The best way to make sure that so-called "foreign" Latino children accord with their well-established roles at the lowest tiers of U.S. society is to move them quickly into the socialization mainstream without providing them critical perspective on who they are, teaching their distinctive nonmainstream histories, and all the while cramming morality tales about the exemplary character of this country.[49] This orientation was illustrated by conservative social critic Linda Chavez when she stated: "I know the efforts [to teach U.S. ethnic history] are well-meaning and that people are concerned about trying to raise achievement among Hispanics. But I don't think [that is] the role of the public school. The role of the public school is to teach American history."[50]

The contemporary discourse on U.S. education does not construct American values of the inherent worth of every child. We *drum* and *drill* values into children rather than cultivate those values. We fabricate citizens and manufacture their opinions, rather than edify students so they can critically choose their own values. We treat children as means, mere things to be processed by educational workers in schools that are subject to an efficiency metric. While individual parents make every effort to treat their children as their family's most important end, the nation treats its children as means, mere commodities that are produced in educational factories. America's posterity is not its most important end.

## CHAPTER SIX

# American Discourse
## on NATION and LANGUAGE
## The "English for the Children" Referendum

Twenty-five years ago, California's public education system ranked number one in the world by any number of measures of quality. In 1997 California ranked number one in the nation only in total number of students, five million. During the past two decades, as the need for an ever more educated citizenry accelerated, the voters starved the system and its quality plummeted. Now it is thirty-seventh in the nation in high school graduation rates; forty-first in per-pupil expenditures; forty-seventh in students-per-computer ratio; fiftieth in students-per-teacher and students-per-principal ratios; and fifty-first in students-per-guidance-counselor and students-per-librarian ratios.[1]

It is no accident that Latinos and other children of color became the majority in public schools during this same twenty-five years of systemwide decline. Latinos constituted nearly 40 percent of the state population, but only 12 percent of the state's voters in 1998.[2] And in the political atmosphere that produced Propositions 187 and 209, no one could be surprised that the most important statewide referendum on public education of the 1990s centered on Latinos. From 1996 to 1998, the public focused its attention on Latino public education, but structural inadequacies and social inequities were not at issue. Instead, Proposition 227, the "English for the Children" referendum, was presented to voters. It was designed to eliminate bilingual education in public school classrooms dominated by Latino students.

Moreover, since the referendum did not dispute the current view of public education, Proposition 227 sounded reasonable to the unconcerned person. As seen in the previous chapter, the conventional view of public education was not debated. Its underlying constitutive metaphors were not contested, so by default, they were accepted. Within the perceptual frame of reference established by these metaphors, it goes without saying that bilingual education in any form is improper. This is because bilingual education, contrary to the EMPTY VESSEL metaphor, affirms the home language and life experiences which Latinos and other non-English-speaking children bring to the schoolhouse door. Bilingual education also fails to conform to the efficiency metric of SCHOOL AS FACTORY, by requiring alternative tracks of studies. And contrary to the logic of the RIVER metaphor, bilingual education instructs these children in so-called nonmainstream languages and encourages nonmainstream worldviews. Instead, these dominant metaphors demand, in the wording of Proposition 227, "that all children in California public schools shall be taught English as rapidly and effectively as possible."

The public's attention during the campaign, from May 1996 to June 1998, was focused on whether teaching with English alone, or a combination of their home language and English, constitutes the best practice to educate Latino children. Still, during the campaign, as many appeals were made to nationhood and the English language as were made to one or another kind of pedagogy. This chapter will explore how the notions of language and nation are entwined, as indicated by the metaphors of public discourse during the Proposition 227 campaign. This interweave of language science and language politics is reflected in the chapter. The first section provides a sketch of the referendum, while Section 2 develops a key metaphor undergirding all English-language thinking about language. One metaphor was employed by both the Proposition 227 advocates and their opponents, much to the confusion of voters. With these preliminaries done, Section 3 offers the first of two sets of metaphors found in the public discourse during the referendum campaign. These metaphors for the language of Latinos turn out to be entirely counterfactual. To set the record straight, Section 4 addresses the fallacies articulated by the advocates for Proposition 227. The principal mistake is believing that literacy development and language acquisition are commensurate processes. This fallacy has been embraced by the general public in spite of a generation of critical commentary by linguists and other researchers. From the perspective gained, other far more injurious public discourse metaphors characterizing the language of Latinos will be presented in Section 5. The implications of the metaphors and Latino response to the measure are discussed in Sections 6 and 7.

# Section 1: Proposition 227

During the 1990s, the news regularly reported on the mounting crisis in California public education, noting that Latinos and other language-minority students in particular were suffering as a result. The state had also regularly certified that many school districts with English-only programs perform no better than their bilingual counterparts. Yet, Ron Unz, a businessman with no educational credentials, drew an irrelevant conclusion. He claimed that the bilingual programs were at fault for the poor showing of Latino students. Unz, who personally sponsored Proposition 227, incorrectly deduced that bilingual education kept those children from learning English, which led to their failing in grossly underfunded schools. Unz's ill-founded conclusion appealed to the electorate. Like Proposition 187, the "English for the Children" initiative led in the polls from its first day in the public eye, and ultimately was approved.

The referendum dictated that bilingual-education-eligible children, in lieu of instruction in their home or primary language, undertake a maximum of one school year of English-as-a-second-language (ESL) classes. To replace bilingual education, Unz trumpeted a method called Sheltered English. It did not matter that it was a relatively untried method for which only a very small number of California teachers had been trained. After one school year—specifically 180 days—and with no further support, Spanish-speaking and other non-English-speaking children were expected to have developed sufficient English to complete a curriculum designed for English-speaking monolingual students. With or without adequate English language competence, these students would then attend classes headed by monolingual teachers who do not have any training to contend with their special needs. Unz had crafted a legal figleaf. Proposition 227 provided the barest legal coverage required to meet very modest equal education provisions for language-minority students.

The proposition was carefully written to compel parents to acquiesce to Unz's narrow vision of public education. Parents now have minimal recourse. Before they can petition the school for a bilingual class for their child, their child must first enroll in English-only classes. Only after one-third of the school year has transpired can parents petition to move their child into a bilingual class. This stipulation forces parents to wait until the middle of the school year to remove their child from the English-only regime that Unz devised. Many parents simply comply with the Unz decree to save their youngster the grief of a midyear classroom change. For those parents who petition for a bilingual education waiver, such a class will be set up only if the parents of nineteen other children of the same grade level also successfully petition the school.

Moreover, Proposition 227 was punitive. It made educators personally liable to lawsuits if class activity did not conform to Unz's provisions. This is contrary to standard provisions of public school liability, which hold school districts (not individual teachers and principals) responsible for curricular statutes.[3]

Proposition 227's sponsoring organization, with its perfectly crafted name, "English for the Children," presented its best face to the public. No one (especially Latino parents!) wants to deny the English language to children. But the largely monolingual electorate did not understand the costs and losses that bilingual children would incur. Unz took pride in stating that his program was based on common sense rather than research.[4] The proposition made sense to 61 percent of the California voting public. This largely white electorate once again reacted to resist the changing cultural order. This can be said without qualification, since Latinos unequivocally rejected the measure, as will be discussed later in the chapter.

The gist of Proposition 227's appeal lies in a truism: "The sooner kids are exposed to English, the sooner they will speak it." This platitude is harmful because it establishes the false supposition that a non-English-speaking child's educational opportunities are enhanced by rapid mainstreaming into an English-only curriculum. Individual professionals might not agree on all the specifics of bilingual education, but Proposition 227 was rejected by all prestigious educational or linguistic organizations,[5] on the basis of two counterintuitive facts: One, adults and early adolescents learn second languages more quickly than young children. Two, language acquisition is a process altogether distinct from those involved in educational advancement. In spite of a concerted effort on the part of educational organizations to inform voters, the non-Latino electorate of California voted with their gut to enact the referendum. The public viewpoint can be discerned through the metaphors constituting the concept of language in the public discourse, to which we now turn.

## Section 2: LANGUAGE AS WATER

As mentioned in Chapter 2, Michael Reddy wrote a classic article on how human beings metaphorize talk.[6] He states that people conventionally speak about communicating in terms of two metaphors. One is the CONDUIT. By way of this metaphor, when a speaker says something, it is as if the speaker uses the English language to encode ideas into packages (words and sentences) which are then sent to the listener, who automatically decodes them. In his rich article, based on five years of research, and marked by a great deal of conceptual effort to stand apart from the English-language frame of reference on communication and language, Reddy notes a second metaphor used to talk about language. "Speakers or writers eject their . . . ideas, thoughts, meanings or feelings . . . into an external 'space.'"[7] This can be exemplified with a few sentences from Reddy's own work:

1. Interesting ideas seem to **pour out** of that man.
2. Those precise thoughts began **circulating** shortly after your birth.
3. He **immersed** himself in the fresher ideas of topology.
4. You have to **absorb** Plato's ideas a little at a time.

People speak as if meanings or ideas are injected into language, as into a fluid medium. Thus, the metaphor is LANGUAGE AS WATER.

In the public discourse on education sampled during the Proposition 227 debate, many examples of the LANGUAGE AS WATER metaphor can be found. In discussions of bilingualism, language use, and, in particular, language acquisition, WATER terms are plentiful. The aqueous term *fluency* is commonly used to talk about linguistic proficiency, as in excerpts 4, 11, 18, 34, 38, 65, and 70 from Chapter 5, as well as those shown below:

5. But then he opened his mouth and out came the one weapon he could wield in the face of inexperience and long odds—a **stream of impeccable Spanish,** professional, courtly, erudite. (September 18, 1995, A1)

6. During sessions, presenters slipped **fluidly** back and forth between the two languages and audience members followed with ease. (February 6, 1995, A3)

7. They consider **English fluency** the key to unlock the handcuffs of poverty, a key they themselves will probably never possess. (January 16, 1996, B1)

Thus it bears defining the ontology of the common metaphor LANGUAGE AS WATER.

## Ontology of LANGUAGE AS WATER

The everyday understanding of the source semantic domain, WATER, that is highlighted and reinforced with each repetition of the metaphor includes water's fluid nature, its dynamic character, its ability to form bodies and to carry things. These are the semantic highlightings, with the use of the metaphor, which come to be taken as a natural part of the target domain, LANGUAGE or COMMUNICATION. Water has kinetic power that can be channeled. This is manifest in multiple ways: fast or slow moving, turbulent or calm, just a trickle or a torrent. As a fluid, water is understood to move, to envelop, and to take up space. But its capacity to carry things is among water's most frequently invoked characteristics when associated with language or communication. The foregoing excerpts attest to this.

The WATER metaphor is invoked to make sense of the socially complex notion, language and communication, by way of an everyday substance with an extensive and cohesive set of characteristics. Language is an everyday part of the social world, but its very complex wholeness (its at times obvious and at other times hidden presence in the social exchange, its wide array of genres and modes, and its myriad functions) makes language hard to comprehend without some kind of physical material in the world with sufficient complexity with which to build our everyday categories of understanding. LANGUAGE AS WATER establishes semantic associations between the complex and commonly experienced everyday substance, WATER, and this pivotal feature of human life. With the metaphor, language can now be seen to be a medium to *transport, suffuse, absorb, freeze, dispense* ideas, thoughts, meanings, and feelings.

## LANGUAGE AS WATER *in Public Discourse*

In the preceding excerpts from the *Los Angeles Times* articles sampling the public discourse on language in education, several aspects of the CONDUIT and LANGUAGE AS WATER metaphors are expressed. Language is characterized as a *stream,* shifting between languages is described as occurring *fluidly,* and linguistic competence and communicative competence are *fluency.* The debate on bilingual education makes frequent reference to water vocabulary. Students are also portrayed as saturated in educational settings of a certain type to enhance their natural acquisition of language, as in excerpt 8. Or they are portrayed as imperiled by the immersion in a new language, as in excerpts 9 and 10:

8. A growing number of Orange County school districts are spurning traditional bilingual education in favor of programs that **steep** students in English—setting a statewide precedent in a divisive classroom debate. (April 13, 1997, A1)

9. Board members said children will not be allowed to simply **flounder** in English-only classes. (January 16, 1998, A3)

10. Critics say Unz' approach remains unproven and would lead to classroom chaos. They say that many students not fluent in English would **drown** under a **"sink or swim"** rule and that English-speaking students in **mainstream** classes would suffer too. (April 3, 1998, A3)

In addition, the *emergence* of bilingualism (as if to break the surface of the water) illustrates an important use of the WATER metaphor. Finally, as seen in many excerpts throughout this chapter, educational programs associated with teaching language fluencies are also described in WATER terms.

## Rivals Use the Same Metaphor

The two contending viewpoints in the Proposition 227 debate may be distinguished by the different theories that they maintain on how to best develop English-language and academic competence among non-English-speaking students. Both theories use the term *immersion,* in keeping with the LANGUAGE AS WATER metaphor.[8] To clarify them, a brief description of the archetypes will be presented, in order to better distinguish the contending models.

### English-Only Instruction

On the one hand are English-only methods. These range from simply placing non-English-speaking children in classrooms with an unaltered monolingual curriculum, to classes which focus solely on English-language learning. These all are referred to with the WATER metaphor:

11. scrapping bilingual education was in the best interest of the children. **Total immersion in English** will help students become **fluent** more quickly . . . , said Trustee Robert H. Viviano, the lead proponent for dropping bilingual education. (May 9, 1997, B5)

12. School districts must teach in native languages only if it is necessary to provide all students with an equal education. Orange Unified has argued that its **English immersion** program, which began last year, reaches that goal. (March 12, 1998, B3)

13. The Unz initiative would essentially end bilingual classrooms. It would place students who are not fluent in English in **an immersion language class.** The language instruction would last one year, after which the students would be returned to English-speaking classrooms. (March 28, 1998, A1)

ESL methods were first designed to teach the English language to literate adults who had grown up speaking other languages. The market for English-speaking skills grew significantly in the last thirty years. As this worldwide market expanded, so too did the methods, now covering advanced technical reading, business communication, and other professional needs. Recently, new methods now aim to develop conversation, again for adult learners. These ESL methods have been secondarily adapted for a different clientele, namely, non-English-speaking elementary-school children. Sheltered English, which Proposition 227 prescribes for a maximum of one year to replace bilingual education, is such a technique. Sheltered English is described by one *Times* writer as a method in which "teachers painstakingly pursued lessons using hand motions and charts,"[9] and by another, in the context of speech therapy, as a method "which uses repetition, simplified vocabulary and visual cues. It's a long process. English-only therapy generally moves at a much slower pace than treatment in the native language of the student."[10]

Although Sheltered English is "painstaking" and proceeds "at a much slower pace," the stated aim of Proposition 227 was to complete the job of providing English linguistic proficiency for children as quickly as possible, in terms of months. The premise is that a child can acquire a language in a short time. The sad truth is that there is no royal road to knowledge; language proficiency cannot be procured in short order. All that ESL can do is facilitate the normal second-language development processes of an individual.

ESL methods are often appended to an otherwise English-only educational program that does not take the issues of the non-English-speaking child's needs into full account. Inasmuch as the primary language of children is considered a problem, and treated as inessential to "real" education, it will not provide a superior education for these children. In many cases, ESL methods are only a short step forward from the infamous sink-or-swim education of language-minority children:

14. Others say the movement [to abandon bilingual education] represents grass-roots politics at its best, reflecting the fundamental shift in public perception that has evolved gradually during the 20 years since the U.S.

Supreme Court ruled against **sink-or-swim** approaches to educating immigrant children. (May 22, 1995, A1)

15. Like many of her current students, Hernandez grew up in a Spanish-speaking family. . . . Success in college and career came in spite of the "**sink or swim**" methods of her early schooling, she said. (April 30, 1996, B2)

16. To [bilingual teachers and advocates], a vote to require English-only instruction is a vote to **toss children into the proverbial ocean without a life vest.** They fear that many of California's 1.4 million public school children who are not fluent in English would **sink.** (February 6, 1998, A3)

17. Childhood immigrants to California, they all started school without bilingual programs. They were **set afloat in a sea of English with few linguistic lifeboats,** an experience they now recount with a mix of pain, pride and occasional humor. (April 26, 1998, B1)

As described by the *Times* newswriters, the method prescribed by Proposition 227, Sheltered English, amounts to the sink-or-swim method augmented with pantomime. It may be a valuable addition to the ESL repertoire of methods, but does not constitute a full pedagogy. In the case of non-English-speaking public school students, it is a diversion from real education. Furthermore, the school year spent in Sheltered English, in which language learning is emphasized at the expense of literacy and other educational content, places the child at an unnecessary disadvantage when the child is then placed in English-only classrooms to compete with monolingual English-speaking peers who did not take a similar educational detour. In the hands of Proposition 227 proponents, the Sheltered English method denies the validity of Spanish and other languages in serious education. Most grievous, normal children are treated as if they suffered from an educational liability. Even though they arrive at school possessing a linguistic advantage, bilingual children are viewed as having a limitation which must be corrected. Sheltered English "repairs" an alleged educational deficit with a remedial program.

Bilingual Education

On the other hand, the family of methodologies called bilingual education uses both the child's home language and English in the classroom to teach educational content. It also aims to develop full linguistic proficiency in both languages. Practitioners of bilingual education use an eclectic mix of methods, including ESL techniques. In the sample of *Times* articles, bilingual education was labeled with the water metaphor, e.g., as in excerpts 18 and 19, as *two-way immersion*.

> 18. a program that has failed to provide "**bilingual and bicultural immersion.**" . . . the program's original intention of **bilingual and bicultural immersion.** (May 29, 1997, A3)
>
> 19. Formal **two-way immersion** programs are rare. The more usual pattern is the one that evolved in San Francisco, where English speakers were added to bilingual classes out of necessity, not by design—when there were not enough non-fluent students to fill a classroom. (June 1, 1995, A1)

Bilingual education is not a set of remediation techniques. It is a complete pedagogy based on how learning can best be facilitated. To be sure, in weakly supported California schools there were certain travesties that went under the name of bilingual education, but good bilingual education practices "begin where the child is," namely, taking into consideration that a kindergartner arrives at school with five or more years of cognitive development and social practices in a language other than English. The bilingual program applies all the teaching methods of the ESL repertoire, including Sheltered English, but critically, it allows the child to build on the foundation of home languages and the cognitive skills that the child has in the home languages. While the child becomes a competent student, or, to use constructivist terms, a skilled educational practitioner, in his or her home language, ESL methods are used to introduce English as a spoken and written language as well as to reinforce educational practices in this language.

In bilingual education the pivotal concern is the uninterrupted growth of cognitive and linguistic development of young children. Moreover, the social background of the children is a central issue in bilingual education, an issue which is far less likely to be addressed in English-only instruction. According to the best research available, bilingual education programs enhance language acquisition processes, as well as reinforce language-associated educational practices of bilingual children, over a four- to seven-year time frame.[11]

*Public Confusion between Rival Programs*

In the public discourse on Proposition 227, both bilingual education and English-only instruction were referred to by the term *immersion*. Among education professionals, the difference is clear. Although the premises of a bilingual pedagogy are incompatible with Proposition 227–style ESL techniques designed to remediate so-called verbal deficits among normal children, this distinction was often lost on the public. For each reference to *bilingual, dual,* or *two-way immersion* in the articles sampled in the public discourse, three references were made to *(English) immersion.* This distinction was often lost on the public. *Immersion* was understood to be English-only instruction and required no qualification, while bilingual education was falsely viewed as just another ESL method. They were seen as doing the same thing, one using one language, the other employing two languages. This mistake is crucial, but easy to make, since the terminology is similar. For bilingual education advocates, this metaphoric concession devalued the superiority of its two-language pedagogy.

## Section 3: Language Metaphors for Latinos

It is remarkable that during the Proposition 227 campaign, the public did not consider the educational disparity of language-minority children to be the result of structural factors (such as the inferior school plants or weaker teaching staffs) or the economic straits of their working-class parents. In the 1996–1998 *Times* corpus, no metaphors referred to class or structural impediments, other than bilingual education programs, to explain why Latino children fare poorly in school.

### ENGLISH AS WATER, LANGUAGE AS BARRIER

Still, the public discourse reiterated that there were far greater difficulties involved on the EDUCATIONAL PATH for Latinos, especially immigrant children, than for middle-class Anglo children. This is reflected in the sheer number of impediment metaphors used in the texts. In the public discourse, the obstacle was the language spoken by these children. In contrast to a popularly supposed "normal" (middle-class, monolingual) child, for whom English is a fluid medium that speeds him or her through school, Latino children found their educational path blocked—by their language. Consistent with the EDUCATION AS PATH metaphor, they bring a LANGUAGE BARRIER to school. Their speech is falsely deemed the greatest obstacle that they face on their path toward education:

> 20. California Assn. for Bilingual Education conference participants . . . wanted to send a form letter to their elected representative. "Without help to **bridge the language barrier,** these [bilingual] students cannot

possibly succeed," the letter said in part. "If these children fail, our state faces a deeply troubled future." (February 6, 1995, A3)

21. Trustee Rick Ledesma, himself a Latino who went through Orange schools before the era of bilingual education, has addressed crowds during the past week at six of the elementary schools effected. [*sic*] An accountant, he frequently wiped his brow and tensed his jaw while some parents jeered and accused him of, among other things, being a racist and speaking Spanish badly. He nonetheless persisted in explaining the philosophical view of the board, that bilingual education is bad for the children. The only path to professional success is fluency in English, and **prolonging the transition** from Spanish just **impedes** children, he said. (March 21, 1997, B1)

22. It was **the seemingly insurmountable language barrier:** Pavel mouthed only a few halting English phrases. (October 29, 1995, B1)

23. In a landmark 1974 ruling, the U.S. Supreme Court held that schools are obliged to help students **overcome language barriers** to the mainstream curriculum. (April 18, 1997, B1)

24. Parents of the English-speaking children in bilingual classes maintain that their children's learning is being **impeded** when the teacher or aide switches back and forth between two languages. (June 1, 1995, A1)

What is to be understood by the LANGUAGE AS BARRIER metaphor? How can language be a barrier and problem if it is commonly recognized that all normal children, by their nature as human beings, fully acquire the languages they need to use, without schooling or any particular training at all? In the space of a dozen years the normal inarticulate human infant interacts enough with other people in any of the six thousand human language systems and, in a nearly unstoppable process, generates his or her own system with full productive and creative control for any occasion throughout his or her whole life. Each child can acquire one, or a half dozen, languages by means of this extraordinary and entirely human process. The languages thus acquired become so much a part of the person that it literally takes severe head trauma for someone to lose his or her native languages. Yet this acquisition process creates in each person, for every language thus developed, such a complex and intricate system that no human language has yet been totally described by linguists. Linguistic researchers have been even less successful, in spite of the boost provided by computers, in emulating the rhythm, pacing, and only apparently simple interactional exchanges of the most casual conversation between two friends. Consequently linguists are constantly astonished by the linguistic aptitude that is latent in each child. No linguist would say that some children are intrinsically deprived by the particular language they speak. Researchers and teachers all know individuals for whom two or more languages are native. It is a human capacity available to all children.

But in the U.S. public's view of education, the bounty of a rich and limitless linguistic acquisition is not a genetic endowment of all children. It is a potent tool—only for the English-speaking child. The metaphor might as well be ENGLISH AS WATER. For language-minority children, in contrast, this defining characteristic of human beings is taken to be the biggest barrier to overcome on their educational path. For these children, according to the public discourse on American education today, the metaphor is LANGUAGE AS BARRIER. This incongruity about the nature of language results from certain common misunderstandings, and an ideology.

*Three Misconceptions about Language Acquisition*

The ENGLISH AS WATER metaphor reinforces the widely accepted and terribly oversimplified view that each child in the United States rapidly and easily acquires the English language in a year or so—whether as a burbling infant or a gangling teenager.[12] In the commonly held view of language and education, this presumably automatic process passively carries immigrant students along on its current, in the same way, to academic English fluency.

The ENGLISH AS WATER view belies language development facts: First, language is acquired in real-time interaction with others; it is not passively acquired.[13] If it were otherwise, by passively listening to audiotape recordings in private, individuals could really learn Japanese in ten days, teach themselves Greek, or master French in their car. This just is not the case. Second, the language functions, whether everyday casual conversation or high-level academic language functions, are skills developed and refined over time by active students when they participate in what they believe to be meaningful and useful social practices—whether talking about pop music or writing biography. Nothing is mastered in 180 days, neither playing a guitar nor learning to speak English. Third, language development is multiplex and additive, and the deepest basis for this unfolding development is on the cognitive foundations of a home language.[14]

25. The school board in southern Orange County's Capistrano Unified School District this month voted to scale back native-language instruction after administrators determined that their limited-English students

showed little progress after as many as seven years of bilingual classes. The new program sets an exit goal of one or two years. (March 23, 1998, A1)

26. "I agree completely that they are still going to have to help kids learn English. But, it doesn't have to be that you have to master the primary language first before you move on. . . . It is a failed program in my view." (September 12, 1995, B3)

The ENGLISH AS WATER metaphor is reified in everyday talk, and reinforced by references to *immersion:* "Just drop them into an English-only class and they'll soak it up. They'll be spouting English in no time." This commonplace assumption follows from two misconceptions. These ordinary mistakes lead to the belief that English language proficiency develops nearly instantaneously.

One, adults do not attend to their own redoubled efforts to make sense of their darling child's immature verbal expression. The linguistic endowment of humans requires an entire childhood to develop fully, just as it takes more than a dozen years for the genes of a burbling baby boy to express themselves fully as a strapping six-foot-tall adolescent. In the same way, we are quite likely to make exceptional visual interpretive adjustments to say, of a three-year-old: "Junior's the spitting image of his dad." Analogously, loving parents only weakly recall the length of time apportioned to, and the level of maturity attained at, the various stages of their children's language development. Parents are not impartial witnesses. They would be loath to proclaim the truth: "Junior learned to speak English like an American teenager in thirteen years!"

Two, people tend to forget that linguistic development continues throughout life. The speech of a ten-year-old does not compare to the speech of the same twenty-year-old. Again, it takes years, not months, to acquire and develop a fully matured language. Within the logic of the WATER metaphor, however, the formation of linguistic as well as educational practices is as fast as it is fluid.

These mistakes lead to another. The second-language development of language-minority students is reflexively normed on the illusory speed and effortlessness of a "normal" student, a monolingual, English-speaking, middle-class child. Non-English-speaking students, whose cognitive development and cultural linguistic practices are based in other languages, tend to be misjudged by adults who grew up as middle-class English speakers. It seems that children in bilingual classrooms do not become fluent in English as rapidly as their own kids, and it seems a waste of time to develop bilingual facility when English is mastered in no time by "normal" (English-speaking) kids. And so it seemed to Ron Unz that bilingual education delays their English-speaking fluency, when all that is needed is to plunge them into English-only classrooms.

These misunderstandings begin to spell out why in U.S. public discourse, the acquisition of a language is a human endowment for the English-speaking child alone. For language-minority children, the same acquisition process is seen to create a barrier on their way to educational advancement.

*English versus Other Languages*

To make better sense of the WATER/BARRIER inconsistency requires exploration of public discourse on what "language" is. The scientific definition and the way linguists and other language professionals conceptualize language are not at issue. Rather, the focus is on the ideological presumptions underlying the prevalent American views on the role of education in society. In contemporary U.S. discourse on education, "language" tends to be a cover term for any kind of speech other than English. This includes all other languages of the world. It also encompasses the speech of English-speaking bilinguals. "Language" contrasts with another kind of speech which seems to be transparent, inconspicuous, and "unaccented," the speech of mono-lingual, middle-class, American English speakers. For Americans, the English language is not really a language—it's just English—namely, that way of talking that is naturally a complete, lucid, and fully sufficient medium for all social intercourse in America.

Evidence for this abounds. Long before the period of anti-Latino public sentiment, the English language was viewed as the only proper one. Consider, for example, the city of Los Angeles. The Spanish language was used by its citizenry long before the English-speaking immigrants arrived. Ever since, Spanish has been in use among a large portion of the city. Los Angeles ranks among the ten largest Spanish-speaking cities in the world. In spite of all that, Spanish has been considered a foreign language in Los Angeles since the 1860s.[15] On that account, the LANGUAGE AS FOREIGN metaphor is articulated in numerous places across the corpus:

27. The programs cited as best by two George Mason University professors are also the least common in the nation's public schools: two-way immersion classes, where **English-speaking** and **foreign language–**

**speaking students** sit side by side, learning each others' languages. (June 13, 1996, A1)

28. Under the **English immersion plan** being submitted to the state, the **Spanish-language instruction** now provided to about 1,200 children in kindergarten through third grade would cease. Special classes would be offered before and after school, and during the summer, to help **foreign-speaking students** with their **English.** (May 9, 1997, B5)

29. "If you teach in a **foreign language,** you can not expect the outcome to be **English.**" (February 14, 1997, B4)

See *native languages* in excerpt 12 as well. Non-English languages are spoken of as *foreign, native,* or *indigenous* languages, regardless of where the speakers live. The coarse term *tongue* is only used to refer to languages other than the English language. In this way the counterfeit distinction between those other languages and the English language is reinforced. The English language is almost never referred to as *the English language.*

Two aspects of conventional language usage contribute to the ideological privileging of the English language over other languages in the public discourse of education. One is that the texts sampled are written in the English language, with all the consequences of self-reference. Second, languages are commonly referred to with proper names, *English* and *Japanese,* rather than lower-case print adjectives, such as *the english language* and *the japanese language.* The use of proper names privileges the referent. Compare two sentences: "Pilar, our goddaughter, has curly hair." Here the subject has privilege of reference over the same referent in the following: "Our goddaughter named Pilar has curly hair." If the English language was not privileged in the United States, *Spanish* and *the Spanish language* would appear as alternate terms for the same reference with frequencies similar to *English* and *the English language.* This is not the case in the public discourse, as sampled from the *Los Angeles Times.* The term *English* proportionally outnumbers the corresponding term for the other language, *Spanish.* The latter is more often referred to as *a foreign language, the Spanish language,* or just *language:*

30. their latest weapon and the newest wave in bilingual education: two-way immersion, in which **foreign language and English speakers are schooled together** and all emerge bilingual. (February 6, 1995, A3)

31. [Stanley Diamond, who led the 1986 campaign to make English California's official language and recently joined the anti-bilingual-education fight,] and others have long battled bilingual education as counter to

their **pro-English** crusade. They believe the time may be ripe to scrap the **native-language approach,** following the passage of Proposition 187, the election of a more conservative Legislature and U.S. Congress, and the recent introduction of a national **English-only** bill. (March 10, 1995, A3)

32. Then, in 1961, Miami schools began offering classes in Spanish for Cuban émigré children, paving the way for other districts to introduce **native-language instruction.** (June 1, 1995, A1)

33. From that performance gap, [Professors] Collier and Thomas concluded that **native language** instruction gives students a solid academic foundation on which to build in any language, while **English immersion's** greater focus on **English acquisition** causes those students to lose ground in other subjects. (January 13, 1996, A1)

34. The earlier study of New York City schools found higher test scores among Korean, Chinese and Russian immigrants—who were likely to be enrolled in **English immersion classes**—than for students who spoke either Spanish or Haitian Creole, who were likely to be enrolled in **native language classes** and who come from poorer and less-educated families. Children with those disadvantages need **native language classes** the most, the George Mason researchers contend, because they are unprepared to shoulder the double burden of learning new academic subjects in a new language. (January 13, 1996, A1)

This separates English from all other spoken languages. It signals an artificial normalcy of the English language at the expense of other somehow less-than-normal languages. It was most apparent in sentences that compare two languages, as exemplified above. The newspaper record of hundreds of articles on the topic of education quite frequently refers to the English language in terms distinct from other human languages. To explore just how prevalent is the asymmetrical referencing of languages, a test was devised using the texts of the public discourse source.

## Testing Whether English Is Just Another Language

A typical month of *Los Angeles Times* articles (March 1998) devoted to education during the Proposition 227 campaign was selected to investigate how the terms *English* and *language* were used. In this sample 222 tokens, that is, text examples, of *English* and 85 tokens of *language* were found and classified. In order to evaluate how these two terms are compared, some tokens were excluded which were not relevant. For example, the word *language* is used in this sample about 20 percent of the time to refer to special vocabularies and phrases, for example, in excerpt 35, or to refer to things other than language, such as educational techniques, as in excerpt 36. Furthermore, 26 percent of the references to *English* or to *language* were also excluded when they appeared in isolation or otherwise were not discussed in a way where they were explicitly or tacitly compared, e.g., excerpts 37 and 38:

35. Noble has found similar **language** in UC Berkeley Extension's contract with America Online and the University of Colorado's contract with Real Education, a private firm working with Microsoft. (March 31, 1998, A1)

36. A long-awaited report on how to best teach children to read calls for a mix of early phonics training and lots of reading, the approach now taken in California after its embrace of the controversial "**whole language**" method. (March 19, 1998, A1)

37. based around public-service announcements on local **Spanish-language television** that encourage viewers to learn more about establishing good credit. (March 3, 1998, D1)

38. Since the return to Chinese sovereignty, white-wigged judges still preside over courtrooms in the British manner, but now defendants can face justice in a **language** they understand. (March 9, 1998, A1)

This left 53 percent of the corpus (n = 45), which were references to two or more comparable languages (including the English language), namely, full linguistic systems acquired by children without any special training as part of their human endowment.

The percentages of these remaining tokens were calculated. From the linguistic point of view, no language is intrinsically privileged. This neutral perspective was maintained in a portion of the comparisons. The English language and the other languages were discussed in a nonprivileging manner about 64 percent of the time, as in excerpt 39:

39. In the Oxnard Elementary School District, about 100 parents have launched a Spanish-**language** media campaign telling parents to refuse the Stanford Nine if their children struggle with **English**. (March 22, 1998, A1)

However, a substantial remainder, 36 percent, privileged the English language, such as in the following excerpts, 40–42:

TABLE 6.1
Word Frequency Comparisons of *English* and *Language*
in Public Discourse

| ALL CONTEXTS WHERE *LANGUAGE* IS USED: | NUMBER | PERCENTAGE |
|---|---|---|
| to mean a "kind of phrase," part of a title, etc. | 18 | 21.2 |
| in isolation, not compared to the English language | 22 | 25.9 |
| neutral comparison of English to other languages | 29 | 34.1 |
| non-neutral comparison of English to other languages | 16 | 18.8 |
| **total** | **85** | **100.0** |
| | | |
| COMPARATIVE SETTINGS: | | |
| neutral comparison of English to other languages | 29 | 64.4 |
| non-neutral comparison of English to other languages | 16 | 35.6 |
| **total** | **45** | **100.0** |

SOURCE: 60 *Los Angeles Times* articles indexed for "education" published March 1–31, 1998, namely, one month during the Proposition 227 campaign.

40. The report says there is evidence that children whose first **language** is not **English** may do better if taught to read first in their **native tongue**—because they are likely to best grasp the meaning of words and sentences in that **language**. (March 19, 1998, A1)

41. A spokesman for the Los Angeles Unified School District said the letter, and translations in **every major language** spoken by Los Angeles students, has [*sic*] been distributed to schools and will continue to be sent home with children. (March 20, 1998, B3)

42. The school board in southern Orange County's Capistrano Unified School District this month voted to scale back **native-language instruction** after administrators determined that their **limited-English** students showed little progress after as many as seven years of bilingual classes. The new program sets an exit goal of one or two years. (March 23, 1998, A1)

In these cases, languages other than English are represented as incomparable to the English language. In contexts that permit contrast, the English language is placed on a different scale than the world's other languages, or, it is simply *the* normal way of speaking (see Table 6.1).

As sampled in the *Los Angeles Times,* a U.S. newspaper of record, and consequently in the nation's public discourse, the English language has been naturalized as a unique form of communication that is qualitatively different from other languages.[16] In contrast, anything that strikes the monolingual English speaker as foreign is a "language."

An intuitive reaffirmation of this mistaken view is provided to American English speakers by their monolingual linguistic competence. Each time they hear Spanish, Armenian, or Khmer, these languages are automatically judged to be qualitatively different from "our own" normal and taken-as-natural English. This is because power in contemporary society habitually passes itself off as embodied in the normal, by contrasting itself with Others. Speech is an especially attractive site to articulate power, because it is linked to intellect, thought, and expression. In the political debate over the legitimacy and place of bilingual education in public schools, and more generally in the context of contrasting the English language with other languages spoken in the United States, such differential terminology delegitimizes the home languages of over one million children affected by Proposition 227.

### Consequences of the False Distinction

Elevating the English language over other human languages aggrandizes one's own subgroup, while oppressing other humans. This is the linguistic equivalent of racism. In 1986 Tove Skutnabb-Kangas coined the term *linguicism* for such practices, which are linguistic reflexes of colonialism.[17] By separating the English language from other languages, however, attaining native speaker competence can be attributed only to children speaking the English language, not to language-minority children.

The same developmental processes leading to linguistic competence in "other languages" can then be considered a significant problem. The student who is a second-language learner can thus be perceived within U.S. educational discourse to have a serious additional educational barrier to overcome. In many countries where the national ideology does not set off one language as superior, the acquisition of a second or third language is just another step along the path to becoming educated, on a par with learning to write a good book report or mastering geometry. For European, Asian, and African young people, becoming multilingual is a normal and expected part of a public education. In contrast, as portrayed in educational discourse during the Proposition 227 campaign, the acquisition of another language is characterized as an endless process, which can only detract from the course of a real education.

43. His family had arrived from the Ukraine just three weeks ago and now this awkward-looking 15-year-old was set to begin **the academic and lin-**

**guistic odyssey** of the Los Angeles Unified School District's bilingual education program. (October 29, 1995, B1)

The totally human process of acquiring a language is thus socially constructed in U.S. public discourse to be a difficult problem—for bilingual children alone. This putative difficulty is not based on what linguistic science knows about the innate acquisitional processes of humans. This is particularly unreal in the context of an English-dominant society, since all children in the United States grow up to become native English-speaking adults. The "problem" is fabricated by an ideology of English monolingualism.

The U.S. public discourse on education erects a fictive difference between the English language and other languages in the world. Then the natural endowment of all children to acquire a language natively becomes the property of American English speakers alone. The acquisition and use of a language other than English fallaciously become a "natural" barrier in the educational progress of the non-English-speaking child.

Likewise, another related metaphor on transcending this language predicament is the children's *passage* over their language barrier.

44. For many of these impressionable foreign-born teens, the **passage** through the bilingual program is about far more than just learning English. (October 29, 1995, B1)

45. There, a map of the state marked with names of Assembly and Senate members guided conference participants who wanted to send a form letter to their elected representative. "Without help to **bridge the language barrier,** these students cannot possibly succeed," the letter said in part. "If these children fail, our state faces a deeply troubled future." (February 6, 1995, A3)

46. In a landmark 1974 ruling, the U.S. Supreme Court held that schools are obliged to help students **overcome language barriers** to the mainstream curriculum. (April 18, 1997, B1)

It should be noted that, contrary to the newswriter's misrepresentation in excerpt 46 (same as 23, repeated for convenience), the Supreme Court did not consider language to be an educational barrier in the 1974 ruling, *Lau v. Nichols.* This decree held that school districts violated Title VI of the 1964 Civil Rights Act if students are excluded from a meaningful opportunity to participate in the educational program because of their inability to speak or understand the language of instruction. Rather, the sink-or-swim indifference as practiced prior to that time was determined to constitute a violation of the Equal Protection Clause of the Constitution's Fourteenth Amendment, and as James Crawford quotes:[18]

> There is no equality of treatment merely by providing students with the same facilities, textbooks, teachers, and curriculum; for students who do not understand English are effectively foreclosed from any meaningful education. Basic English skills are at the very core of what these public schools teach. Imposition of a requirement that, before a child can effectively participate in the educational program, he must already have acquired those basic skills is to make a mockery of public education.

The issue that warranted greater exploration in the debate on Proposition 227 was what constitutes "basic skills" for public school students at the cusp of the twenty-first century. One cynical reading of American discourse is that, for Americans, public education begins and ends with English-language fluency. Such a narrow articulation of the role of education was a consequence of the wording of the referendum, which sought an up/down vote on bilingual education. Still, neoconservatives regularly argue for a narrowly defined purpose of U.S. public education.[19]

On the other hand, more generous expectations for the longer-term educational and life success of public school students were repeatedly articulated in the public discourse on education. One *Times* article presented quotes from over two dozen supporters of Proposition 227 who "echoed one another, returning again and again to the same themes. They viewed fluency in English as the key to success and assimilation—and felt that bilingual instruction didn't move immigrant children into fluency quickly enough."[20] Here, a common confusion between language development and literacy development must be pointed out. Achieving a good education means much more than the ability to converse with one's peers in the dominant language of society.

## Section 4: Language Is Not Literacy

The unnecessary liability imposed on language-minority students in public schools is exacerbated by a common fallacy that equates speaking fluency in English and English literacy, as advocates for Proposition 227 insisted. Literacy is more than word/sound formulas that school children memorize. Rather, literacies are sets of social practices.

People generally consider literacy, like fire making and the number zero, to be a great advance in cultural achievement. For the individual, the story goes, once you learn to read, you are a literate person. And for humankind, conventional history separates societies that use the written word from those who transmit culture by oral tradition.[21] Of course, the latter people were then disparaged as less advanced. This view is taken as obvious. But commonplace understandings can be quite retrogressive. Brian Street's critique of this view of literacy is far-reaching and convincing.[22]

Street argued that the commonly held autonomous skill view of literacy ignores the cultural practices that are integral to being literate. Using myself as an example, although I am a native speaker of English, a U.S.-trained linguist, and have read daily for over forty years, I do not make much sense of the stock market pages of my daily newspaper and cannot interpret the eyeglass prescription that my optometrist dashes off. It is not a matter of decoding words and letters. Literacy is far more than decoding the printed page. Just as it is the case that one has to become a chess player to really understand the best writing about the game, so does a child have to become a competent participant in the social practice of literacy to be a proficient reader.[23] Literacy is much more than an autonomous skill. It requires sharing sets of knowledge and participating with networks of people who carry on close interactions and exchanges that are associated with specific lifeways. Some of the social networks are specialized, like the participants in the practice of coin or doll house collecting, and some are larger, such as the readership of the sports pages, but the practices of literacy all have to be learned in the practice of those networks. Thus the various literacies taught in American schools are practices specific to the culture of the American school.

Children do not become literate in English or any other language just because they grow up in the United States. Concerted effort is needed to develop scholastic and professional literacy. Children most often master these social functions only with a specialized introduction to these social practices.

*The Schoolteacher's Dilemma*

However, a pernicious way of misspeaking about language on the one hand, and literacy on the other, has developed in the minds of some educators and the general public since the *Lau v. Nichols* decision was implemented by public schools. At a social occasion, an assistant principal of a large high school asked me if I was a linguist. She asked whether I would be willing to help her students: "They can't speak English. They are not testing out of ESL classes and I don't want to leave them there. At this rate, they will never be able to graduate from high school." Her students turned out to be native speakers of English. However, their test results indicated that they did not have strong literacy skills. The principal's confusion puts her students at risk. As a consequence of the court-ordered decrees, it is now mandatory to test the linguistic skills of all possibly non-English-speaking children as they enter public school. Schools are also required to appraise the linguistic advancement of children in bilingual education classes to determine which children can transition into mainstream English-only ones.

This poses a dilemma. Since the turn of the century linguists have noted that there is an insurmountable problem involved in measuring the linguistic knowledge (technically, linguistic competence) that a person possesses.[24] This is so because such knowledge is inherently tacit. That means an individual's linguistic competence cannot be directly assayed. The best that the linguist can do is to sample the speech of a person. This measures linguistic performance, not linguistic competence. Performance is necessarily an indirect and irregular reflection of the person's obviously functioning, but only deducible, linguistic knowledge. Tacit knowledge simply cannot be directly measured.

School educators, however, do not have the luxury to simply recognize the linguistic competence of their students and then move on to other things. Given their dual role, first as the designated gatekeepers to the next stage of education, and now as the guarantors of equal educational opportunity as minimally defined by the courts, they cannot avoid the competence/performance paradox. As a consequence, they tend to operate under the assumption that the child's linguistic competence can be evaluated by tests. But tests do not measure linguistic competence. Written tests measure the child's school-trained practice to interpret written texts, namely, literacy. The language tests that are used to evaluate children's linguistic competence in English actually assess how well a child can read, or, more precisely, how well the child has mastered some of the socially contextualized and school-based practices called reading—not language. Even thirty years after sociolinguistics was first added to the curriculum of teacher certification programs, many educators continue to equate language acquisition and the mastery of literacy practices.

### State Board of Education Confusion

As a result, when the children do poorly on these exams, it is not a measure of their linguistic competence. The worst of these exams do not even measure literacy. Consider the task of distinguishing a grammatical subject from a grammatical object in a transitive sentence. This kind of knowledge is not a measure of linguistic competence, nor is it a literacy test. Rather, this is a bit of old-fashioned grammar. This is one kind of information sought on the transition exams. Consequently when Ron Unz, calling for the abolition of bilingual education, claimed that 95 percent of limited-English-proficiency (LEP) children in California each year fail these "language tests" to test out of bilingual education classes, this does not mean that these children are failing to acquire English. They were not being tested for their language competence, irrespective of the beliefs of many concerned individuals. They were being evaluated for their adeptness at certain kinds of literacy practices:

> 47. "Our feeling was this is a model program, and I would expect the board to approve it," said Yvonne W. Larsen, chairwoman of the policy committee. *"We want the kids to be literate. The more quickly they can function in English, the better."* Backers of bilingual education argued that the Westminster proposal would only hurt students struggling to keep up with English-speaking peers while also learning a new language. (February 9, 1996, A3, my emphasis)

In the excerpt above, the President of the California State Board of Education, Yvonne Larsen, equates being literate and functioning in English. This is a specious relationship. In fact, if the child tests well in English-based literacy, particularly school-based practices, chances are good in the United States that the child has also a solid command of spoken English.[25] But it is not the case that fluent verbal functioning in English translates to mastery in scholastic literacy practices. Since all children who grow up in the United States will be capable of conversation in English, something else is the problem.

In excerpt 47 the newswriter also misrepresents the objectives of bilingual education. The real educational aim is not simply to "learn English," but to develop all the academic practices needed to advance along the educational path. Bilingual students as well as other students should learn the content areas of math, civics, and sciences. In order to do so they must develop the wide academic skills and practices associated with these various ways of understanding and effectively interacting with the world. By the way, to control a range of ways to understand and effectively interact with the world is a sound definition of a genuine education.

It is not surprising that language acquisition and literacy development are jumbled among everyday people. However, it is reprehensible that Ron Unz, some educators, and certain key public representatives fail to keep the distinction straight.

## Unz Conflated Literacy and Language

Unz obfuscated literacy practice development and language acquisition. This confusion was at the core of his "English for the Children" referendum. With the passage of Proposition 227, the following muddled wording was added to the California State Educational Code:

> Section 1. Chapter 3. ENGLISH LANGUAGE EDUCATION FOR IMMIGRANT CHILDREN
> Article 1. 300. The People of California find and declare as follows:
> (a) WHEREAS English is the national public language of the U.S. and California, is spoken by the vast majority of California residents, and is also the leading world language for science, technology, and international business, thereby being the language of economic opportunity;[26] and
> (b) WHEREAS immigrant parents are eager to have their children acquire a good knowledge of English, thereby allowing them to fully participate in the American Dream of economic and social advancement; and
> (c) WHEREAS the public schools of California have a moral obligation and a constitutional duty to provide all of California's children with the skills necessary to become productive members of our society, and of these skills, literacy in English is among the most important; and
> (d) WHEREAS the public schools of California currently do a poor job of educating immigrant children, wasting financial resources on costly experimental language programs whose failure over the past two decades is demonstrated by the current high drop-out rates and low English literacy levels of many immigrant children; and
> (e) WHEREAS young immigrant children can easily acquire full fluency in a new language, such as English, if they are heavily exposed to that language in the classroom at an early age.
> (f) THEREFORE it is resolved that: all children in California public schools shall be taught English as rapidly and effectively as possible.

Proposition 227's fallaciousness becomes apparent when Unz's references to language and literacy are compared. Two sections refer to language acquisition. Since children *acquire* English in the United States by an entirely natural process, section (b), which states that immigrant parents want their children to acquire a good knowledge of English, and section (e), which states that immigrant children easily acquire full fluency if they are heavily exposed to the new language, are altogether superfluous. Further, all immigrant children who arrive in this country before ten years of age ultimately become fully native English speakers. Consequently it is not clear at all why children growing up in the United States need "heavy" exposure to English, when purposeful daily contact with English speakers in an English-dominant society does the job. To Unz's discredit, he did not and could not point to any group of California children who, having grown up in the United States, could not speak English. Such a child would be diagnosed as suffering from a pathological condition, by strict medical criteria.

Furthermore, if English-language competence were the single factor needed to ensure educational advancement in the United States, two things would follow. One, every native-born American could count on an excellent shot at the American Dream as a birthright. And two, the current educational crisis would be limited to immigrants. However, the crisis is widespread.

When the referendum campaign was at its peak, two news stories broke which undermined this key premise of Proposition 227. The first was a blue-ribbon commission reporting on U.S. public school literacy. A panel of reading experts convened by the National Academy of Sciences found that "40% of American fourth-graders read poorly—a group that is disproportionately poor."[27] The most affected students were racialized minorities, including four and one-half million African American children. These children certainly speak English, yet African Americans are not exempt from disastrous reading scores. This sad finding undermined Unz's rationale, pointing to the real cause of the educational disaster of the United States.

Another report which appeared during the Proposition 227 campaign also undercut Unz's reasoning:

> More than two-thirds of students entering California State University campuses in the Los Angeles area lacked the math or English skills they should have mastered in high school. . . . Cal State officials find it hard to shrug off the fact that so many freshmen who were supposed to be among the top third of California high school graduates—a criterion for admission—could not pass the rather routine tests asking them to explain the meaning of words or paragraphs. . . . The figures offer a dismaying view of the lack of preparation for college work at many of

the system's schools, particularly those in urban areas. Equally striking were other statistics released by the university system showing that, at some high schools, not a single graduate going on to one of Cal State's campuses passed the basic skills tests.[28]

California public education is failing a great number of its students—not just those in bilingual classes.

All advocates for public education will sadly concur with section (d), which states that the public schools have done a poor job educating immigrant children who suffer low English literacy rates. However, eliminating bilingual education will not alleviate the problem of low reading scores, because the scores were not depressed because of bilingual education. To repeat, academic literacy is a range of socially governed practices used in educational and professional pursuits. These literacies require an extended period of training and practice, and are true measures of education. The acquisition of a language is entirely a different matter. One can learn literacies in a language that one does not speak. Conversely, language acquisition is an innate aspect of being human, and occurs independent of schooling. Thus, language acquisition is quite separate from the academic task of English literacy, and occurs as a matter of course as a child grows up. It is not the true measure of educational success.

Ron Unz built his referendum on a bogus link between literacy and language acquisition. He claimed bilingual education was the cause of schools' failure to educate immigrant children. But students other than immigrants suffer these exact consequences of poor public schooling. Blaming bilingual education was a pretext.

## Benefits and Politics of Bilingual Education

California's failure to provide for immigrant and other children is due to chronic underfunding of public education, a devalued teaching profession, society's degradation of nonmainstream students, and the electorate's antiquated conception of public education. Although it ended bilingual education in California, Proposition 227 did not address the root causes of the educational failure of so many students, not only those in bilingual education.

The full potential of real bilingual education was never realized in California. While it played a considerable role in the politics of education of the state, it played an inconsiderable role in terms of student numbers in California public schools. Three years before the referendum was passed, California had fewer than 11,000 fully credentialed bilingual teachers—one for every 112 students who needed them. And while in the decade before Proposition 227 the population of non-English-speaking students had grown by 150 percent, the number of bilingual teachers increased by only 30 percent.[29] Of every ten bilingual-education-eligible language-minority students, five were already taught in English-only classes. Another two received some other kind of nonbilingual education help in their home language. Proposition 227 affected the classroom language of the three remaining children. In spite of the material and ideological limitations imposed on pedagogy in California, it is still important to state that bilingual education is a superior method to achieve high levels of literacy and to provide for advanced education achievement. It offers the best means to achieve the American Dream for the children of immigrants.

The benefit of bilingual education should be made explicit. Bilingual education curriculum exercises and builds on the six to eight or ten years of language competence of the immigrant child, already developed in Spanish, Bengali, or Korean, rather than discarding this cognitive linguistic development. English and high-level language-based academic practices are added to the child's environment and repertoire in school. These are mastered at high academic levels, on the foundation of the child's home-language linguistic and cognitive background. In time, the child will become fully functional in English, with academic skills in English, as well as fully functional and literate in the home language. This is an undeniable advantage in twenty-first-century life, which is increasingly international, and ever more global.

Alternatively, in the English-only programs, the child must forego his or her developing linguistic competencies and start from scratch.

48. James J. Lyons, executive director of the National Association for Bilingual Education in Washington, said: "I'm encountering teachers who say, 'I cannot go back to looking at children and seeing the spark of learning dimmed in their eyes as I speak to them in a language that they don't understand.'" (March 23, 1998, A1)
49. The consequences are more stark: On her first day of teaching, Nancy Soo—a former teacher's aide with an emergency teaching credential and no Spanish knowledge—walked into a Mid-City-area classroom filled with 32 first-graders, 27 of whom spoke only Spanish. "I was pretty much flipping out," she recalled. "I wanted to do the best job possible and I

knew I wasn't the best person to be doing it." Soo did what she could, using body language and picture books. (May 22, 1995, A1)

Many times during the day the non-English-speaking child will not understand the simplest statement that the English-speaking teacher will be saying. This child will later compete with children who have not had to start from scratch at age six or ten. Certainly in English-only classes, the child begins to acquire English fluency, but that was also the case in well-executed bilingual education classes. In contrast to the California State Board of Education President's statement excerpted in 47, the following quote of a bilingual teacher properly captures the relationship between the development of scholastic literacies, other academic practices, and types of knowledge, on the one hand, and English language acquisition, on the other:

> 50. As Nancy Infante paces in her native-language classroom at Eastman Avenue School on Los Angeles' Eastside, where second-graders are writing essays in Spanish about the Aztec god Quetzalcoatl, the teacher suddenly switches to English. "Claudio! You have crayons on the floor!" Without hesitating, the youngster bends to retrieve his crayons. Is this, as bilingual critics would suggest, evidence that Claudio is ready to learn in English years before Eastman's program will let him? Or, is it proof that the native-language approach does not hinder his ability to understand English, while allowing him to tackle complex subjects in his primary language? Like many bilingual teachers, Infante subscribes to the latter: "Socially they do fine [in English], but they are not academically bilingual," she said. "When it's something new that I'm introducing, I'd rather do it in Spanish because then they understand it completely." (May 22, 1995, A1)

The advantage of bilingualism, much less genuine bilingual education, was rarely mentioned in the public discourse on education as sampled in 1996–1998. The belief was reiterated that language is a barrier in the path of bilingual children, converting their personal and social advantage—proficiency in two languages—into a problem. The elite of all countries send their children to bilingual schools. And practically all national educational systems across the world consider bilingual education to be a superior method to achieve world citizenship and the best set of linguistic tools for economic advancement. Proposition 227 replaced it with a remediation program.

In excerpt 51 the description of the California Department of Education Master Plan demonstrates how ingrained the misrepresentative understanding of bilingual education is. The newswriter falsely describes this plan as undermining what occurs by all means in U.S. society, namely, that children who grow up in the country end up speaking English natively. Further indication can be noted in excerpt 52 in the comments of the highest-ranking educational official in California during the Proposition 227 campaign period:

51. California has the most rigorous bilingual education program in the nation. Under a 14-year-old policy, the state requires school districts with large numbers of non-English-speaking students to teach those children primarily in their **native** language, whenever possible. But critics charge that policy—based on a state law that expired eight years ago—has caused bilingual education to fail at its central mission: **teaching children English.** (May 22, 1995, A1)

52. "We have to be honest enough with one another to say, when something isn't working, it's time to re-examine it," [California State Superintendent of Public Instruction Delaine] Eastin said. "There has to be a point at which we bite the bullet and say, *'At least, they have to learn English.'*" Eastin cited a 1993 report by a state watchdog commission that blamed the state's policies for holding back thousands of students who should be learning English. (May 22, 1995, A1, my emphasis)

California Education Superintendent Eastin called for the accelerated development of English-only dependence, rather than a beneficial multiyear transition of these students to academically functional bilingualism. Still, Eastin was on the record as opposed to Proposition 227. On the bright side, in counterpoint to Unz, Larsen, and Eastin, another education official articulated a sophisticated frame of reference for both literacy and language.

53. Riley, noting that he had been greeted Friday by a choir of children who easily switched from English to Spanish, said two languages are an **asset.** He noted that many Europeans speak at least two. "We have been very lazy in this country about foreign language," Riley said. "We need to get busy." (June 14, 1997, B5)

54. The kids at Heninger Elementary School have a leg up, the U.S. Secretary of Education told them Friday: They speak a second language. But, Secretary Richard W. Riley told them, good reading skills will be the key

to their success. "Reading is something you have to do every day," Riley told a gathering of more than 50 students, teachers, parents and school officials. "You don't get a good job without it. It improves your education, but it's also fun." (June 14, 1997, B5)

U.S. Secretary of Education Richard Riley not only characterized multilingualism as an asset, he emphasized the development of literacy skills—not English dependence—among his audience of bilingual children. During the Proposition 227 period, to talk in terms of English-dependence would have been politically expedient. His emphasis on academic and professional literacy practices more accurately reflects the state of knowledge of learning and literacy researchers, in contrast with dominant public discourse assumptions.

## Bilingualism Is Less than English-Only

It follows in the logic of the unwarranted elevation of the English language over other languages that bilingualism is a barrier along the educational path. One might think that bilingualism, which in the U.S. context means to speak English *plus* another language, would be at least one notch better than non-English monolingualism. Yet, in the manner of speaking of contemporary public discourse on education, "speaking a language" in addition to English is effectively taken to be as much an educational barrier as non-English monolingualism.

Children in bilingual programs end up caught in a double bind. In the best situation, bilingual children are appropriately tested, not for language competence, but for their progress in a range of academic literacy practices that they will use in advanced educational and professional pursuits. However, in the short and intermediate term they do not perform as well on these English-based literacy measures as monolingual middle-class children. For this so-called failing, which is a consequence of the time required for literacy development, bilingual education is condemned by its opponents.

On the other hand, bilingual children are often tested for mere conversational English fluency, which is a nonsensical examination, given the ease with which children acquire conversational English. Of course they do well enough to satisfy the minimal expectations of the adversaries of bilingual education. However, casual speech is no measure of academic advancement. If they can chat amiably with monolingual English-speaking peers, so the fallacious reasoning goes, then they do not need primary language instruction anymore. Once again, this false measure provides fodder for the anti-bilingual-education fire.

Bilingualism can be a cognitive advantage.[30] It is an undeniable educational resource, as well as an economic and social benefit for the student, if it is nurtured. On the other hand, most unfortunately, the children who are too quickly transitioned into monolingual classes only superficially seem ready for mainstream classes. After 180 days, they may converse with the teacher and their monolingual English-speaking peers. However, they are at a disadvantage since they are forced to play catch-up with others who are building on the language development of six, eight, or more years that they bring from home, with no detour in their grade-level educational content. See excerpt 34 on the "double burden" these students bear. The majority of these students will remain behind. Of course, a few overcome the language barrier and ultimately achieve at a high level, providing the opponents of bilingual education with illustrative anecdotes. But these individuals have overcome an additional socially constructed barrier which was unnecessary, and detrimental to their educational growth.

## Hidden Message of Proposition 227

In the public discourse on education, one explicit and another implicit message are packed into the statement "learning English." One, in classrooms of immigrant children, their home language must not be used, and children must be taught in English. Two, the children should lose their home languages. This second step is entirely unnecessary, and no one will deny that a person growing up speaking two or more languages will have a distinct career and life advantage. In fact, academic competence in more than one language contributes directly to the total education of the student. Still, if the second step is not taken, in accord with the metaphors constituting the public discourse, the process is incomplete.

For U.S. students, in contrast to those in much of the world, monolingualism is the presumed result of the one-way travel on the path toward becoming an educated person. Consider, for example, the so-called foreign language classes that U.S. children take for a year or two in high school.[31] In the Spanish classes, Latino students (many who were Spanish-speaking preschoolers) enroll along with their Anglo peers. Both sets of students sit mute during the greater part of the class. Across the United States such classes rarely attain real communication in languages other than English. In contrast to those in other countries, U.S. high school language classes by and large are a sterile environment for language development where time is spent completing fill-in-the-blank exercises and reciting contrived skits. Such classes reinforce the implicit ideology that languages other than English are extremely difficult to master, and in any event they are superfluous for school or career.

Note that there has been no call for greater teacher accountability or language proficiency exit exams for these sorts of classes, as there have been for math and English classes in recent years. The demand for authentic language development among high school students would involve purposeful dialogue with native speakers in a multilingual setting, which in many U.S. cities is a readily available and seldom-exploited opportunity. Moreover, it would entail a sea change in the purpose of American public education because it is counterhegemonic.

In keeping with the conventional point of view, when Latino and other language-minority children have pointedly lost their primary language (and much of the home culture which is passed on via language), only then are they certifiably English-dependent monolinguals, with the language obstacle to their education safely crossed. More evidence will be presented in the following section, as the more severe metaphors leveled against bilingualism and bilingual education are discussed.

## Section 5: Other LANGUAGE Metaphors

The bilingual children who do not make a rapid transition to English-dependence, or who are tested for the actual academic English functions that take six or seven years to develop, are portrayed in the public discourse as being in deep trouble. For them the so-called *language barrier* remains. Of course, this does not mean that these bilingual children do not acquire and speak English—in fact, they may prefer to speak the English language and to use it in most settings. Nevertheless, if they are bilingual, not dependent on English alone, then they are seen to be consigned to linguistic bondage. Language remains a PRISON for these children. And since bilingual education programs house these inmates, bilingual programs are jails. In the logic of the two steps to "learning English," their continued bilingualism constitutes a failure of their educational programs.

### LANGUAGE AS PRISON

Although this metaphor may seem melodramatic, the PRISON metaphor was frequently invoked in the education discourse. This productive metaphor was elaborated in the texts that comprise the *Times* article corpus. In excerpt 55 the prominence of the educator cited adds apparent credibility to his misleading representation of bilingual students:

55. The article, [appearing in the California Teachers Association newsletter and] written at the behest of outgoing CTA President Del Weber, blamed [bilingual education] for **marooning "tens of thousands of California students in 'bilingual' programs for six, seven or even nine years."** (June 5, 1995, A3)

56. Roxie Speer, a parent, presented the board with a 400-signature petition from Parents and Teachers for a Successful Future, a group that supports eliminating the district's bilingual program. "We believe **it places a ball and chain around the legs of our Spanish students for the first three years of their schooling,**" Speer said. (January 29, 1997, B4)

57. As debate over bilingual education rages across the state, some educators applaud [San Francisco Unified School District Superintendent] Rojas' action as a noble attempt to **rescue English-speaking students whose academic progress had been sacrificed** in the district's effort to fill empty seats in bilingual classrooms. (June 1, 1995, A1)

58. "We know children are already acquiring English as a second language sooner . . . but anyone who wants to see statistics right now, I can't give them that," [Principal] Vargas Page said. "The reality is, we won't see how well our children gain until five years into the program." Such a promise of future rewards does not mollify the parents at Las Familias. They consider English fluency **the key to unlock the handcuffs of poverty, a key they themselves will probably never possess.** (January 16, 1996, B1)

59. Unknown numbers of children whose first and only language is English spend their elementary school years **trapped** in Spanish-only "bilingual programs." (Ron Unz, October 19, 1997, M5)

60. Graduating from the program is a **liberation** from slow-moving classes shared with newcomers who speak one of 37 foreign languages at Reseda—students with whom they share little other than an inability to speak textbook English. (October 29, 1995, B1)

The term *maroon* effectively invokes the dangers that non-English-speaking students purportedly undertake on their linguistic *odyssey*. Use of the term *survival* indicates the depth of the socially constituted peril that confronts the hapless child in a bilingual education program. Thus when children transition out of a bilingual education program to become part of mainstream classes, they are said to have been *liberated* from the program. This terminology is not merely rhetorical but constitutive. When a non-English-speaking student is judged by school personnel as likely to remain in ESL throughout high school, other PRISON terms are applied: "The term ESL *lifer* may reveal how some mainstream teachers view ESL programs [to be] *holding cells* where students are placed and never released into 'mainstream' education."[32]

Some Latino parents also believe that oral English language fluency will remove the so-called linguistic *shackles* of poverty, as in excerpt 56. For them, conversational fluency, which is an unremarkable consequence of growing up in the United States, is not differentiated from the real key to economic betterment, advanced literacy practices, which only come in time, with structured educational preparation, and with much practice. Their misunderstanding is particularly poignant since research indicates that elementary Spanish-based literacy skills transfer swiftly in good bilingual education programs, much to the educational advantage of the children. These skills are quickly transformed into English-based literacies. On the other hand, it turns out to be a much more demanding task for these same students to develop high-level English literacy without concurrent literacy in their home language. Bilingual education provides a solid foundation for sustained academic advancement. Yet the LANGUAGE AS BARRIER and AS PRISON metaphors are particularly persuasive calls to limit bilingual education and to prematurely transition these children into the mainstream because they are congruent with metaphors constructing education in this society.

The LANGUAGE AS PRISON metaphor has been used in other U.S. discourses involving Latino political issues. Kathryn Woolard analyzed the use of this metaphor in a 1984 public campaign for English-only legislation.[33] At issue was the bilingual ballot, originally a 1975 Voting Rights Act provision designed to ensure greater electoral participation among the eligible citizenry. Opponents of bilingual ballots in San Francisco successfully constructed an image that non-English-speaking communities were politically incarcerated by their home language. At that time, Latino leaders denounced the measure as a civil rights retreat to the days of English-only ballots, which in practice denied non-English-speaking citizens their right to vote. Nevertheless, the LANGUAGE AS PRISON metaphor was effectively used by conservative campaigners to reconstruct bilingual ballots as a hindrance to participation in the electoral process. The voters of San Francisco accepted the arguments of the bilingual ballot opponents. In a singular display of the power of metaphor to construct a worldview, one of the most liberal constituencies in the country accepted a measure specifically designed to restrict voter participation, ostensibly to aid their non-English-speaking fellow citizens to better exercise their political franchise.

The assumptions and allusions that are made in the short phrase from excerpt 57 can now be worked through: *"Rojas' action [was] a noble attempt to rescue English-speaking students whose academic progress had been sacrificed in the district's effort to fill empty seats in bilingual classrooms."* From *English-speaking,* the average reader of the *Times* will not reflexively visualize the child of a Mexican immigrant, although in the context of California schools the phrase certainly characterizes millions of immigrant children and children of immigrants. Moreover, the fallacious implication is that these children's educational advancement has been retarded in bilingual classes. Their delay is portrayed to be exacerbated by treacherous school administrators who are more concerned with the federal dollars associated with designated bilingual students. Third, *bilingual classes* are conceived as excluding English instruction. In fact, bilingual classes include English instruction—by definition and in practice. Furthermore, the need of a *rescue* is urgent since the English language is mistakenly held to be the sole natural medium of communication, and instruction by means of any (other) language is an unnatural and serious impediment to education. What happens if these bilingual children are not rescued from their so-called language prison?

*LANGUAGE AS HANDICAP*

In a milieu that supposes languages other than English to be foreign and inferior, the logic of the metaphor is relentless. If these *imperiled* children are not quickly liberated, then their life chances become increasingly grim. In the commonplace but mistaken discourse on education, bilingual education programs will *cripple* these children. The notion of a bilingual *handicap* is expressed in excerpt 12 of Chapter 5, and further exemplified in the following newspaper extracts:

61. California Teachers Association President Del Weber blamed [the CTA and bilingual education] . . . which "**crippled** the Spanish-speaking child's educational development." (June 5, 1995, A3)
62. It sounds simple, but although California has had bilingual education for 20 years[,] the results have been uneven[,] and in some cases **crippling** to the child's further education. (April 9, 1996, B6)

63. The number of students **unable to learn completely in English** has grown by more than 40% in the past five years. Such students now occupy almost one in every four desks in the state's classrooms, which makes serving them more costly and complicated. "**These kids are not learning English and they are being handicapped,**" said Wayne Johnson, the [California Teachers Association] vice president. (June 5, 1995, A3)

64. "Fluency in Spanish may prove a significant advantage," Unz wrote in an opinion piece for the Times last October, "but lack of literacy in English represents a **crippling, almost fatal disadvantage** in our global economy." (May 25, 1998, A1)

As excerpted in 64, Ron Unz himself used the wording *crippling* and *almost fatal* to refer to bilingual education. Unz's fallacy was that bilingualism leads to educational failure, while English-dependency guarantees success. Such expressions compelled a compassionate public to action, but they confused language acquisition and literacy development. In terms of the dominant metaphors used to construct these texts, bilingual education is never considered to be a viable alternative for real education in America.

It should be noted that the LINGUISTIC HANDICAP metaphor has a long and sordid history in the United States. This blatantly racist excuse was given by school districts as the reason why Spanish-speaking schoolchildren had to be segregated in grossly inferior "Mexican schools" during the past century.[34] Only the organized and sustained efforts of Chicano parents in California, who rejected this pretext for discrimination, led to the 1945 *Méndez v. Westminster School District* decision, which undermined separation of Mexican and Anglo children throughout the Southwest.

The U.S. educational path assumes that all students will attain advanced English fluency. This view is entirely appropriate in English-dominant U.S. society. However, as constructed by the dominant conceptual metaphors, U.S. public education requires that these children take one more unnecessary and detrimental step, to eliminate their home language. Dependence on the English language alone is the unspoken requisite to travel all the way along the U.S. educational path.

## Section 6: The Hegemony of English Monolingualism

Why this insistence on monolingualism? In spite of its superior pedagogic benefits for all children, bilingual education has always been a controversial methodology in U.S. education. The key to understanding why monolingual English-dependence is believed to be a prerequisite to being educated in the United States can be found among the metaphors of the public discourse of the time.

As indicated by their discourse on education, Americans presume that English is the unique medium for education in the United States. Moreover, it is an emblem of being "truly American." Indeed, during the 1995–1996 presidential campaign, the Republican candidate repeatedly made the connection explicit:

> 65. Last week, Senate Majority Leader Bob Dole called for an end to most bilingual education programs in an attack on those he referred to as the **"embarrassed-to-be-American" crowd.** (September 12, 1995, B3)
> 66. Attacking what he called the **"embarrassed-to-be-American,"** the leading candidate for the GOP presidential nomination told the 77th national convention of the American Legion that "if we are to return this country to greatness, we must do more than restore America's defenses." (September 5, 1995, A1)

For Senator Robert Dole and many other citizens, speaking any language other than English is unpatriotic and un-American. This mainstream candidate absurdly claimed that the languages spoken by many immigrants and citizens diminish U.S. ascendancy.[35] American English signals allegiance and full citizenship. To this exclusionary role of language, a Romanian writer named Emile Cioran gave cheerless form: "One does not inhabit a country; one inhabits a language. That is our country, our fatherland—and no other."[36] His life experience darkly reflects the sentiment that Dole proclaims with exuberance, that multilingualism is somehow traitorous, that speaking another language is a sovereign betrayal. Still, Cioran likewise signals the dark side of monolingualism, as a pitfall, as a prison, as vulnerability.

In still one more setting, the indictment of another colonialist legacy has been made by Njabulo Ndebele, a Lesotho educator and writer: "The problem of society will also be the problem of the predominant language of that society. It is the carrier of its perception, its attitudes, and its goals, for through it, speakers absorb entrenched attitudes. The guilt of English then must be recognized and appreciated before its continued use can be advocated."[37] Ndebele explicitly indicts the linguistic weapon of South Africa's imperialists. Nothing material differentiates the socioeducational repercussions of English-only colonialism on one million Sotho (Lesotho) children, and over one million of California's bilingual children, when their public schools on two continents insist on stripping away their home language.

It is reasonable to assert that English be used in many formal and most professional settings in the United States. This is a legitimate public educational objective. However, a profound cultural insecurity is revealed when this goal is yoked to the demand that students publicly eliminate their Spanish and other primary languages. To hold that it is undemocratic for children to enhance their home language, or despotic to teach in languages other than English, is an ugly sign of the hegemony that privileges English as the one and only legitimate language of real Americans.

> 67. Senate Majority Leader Bob Dole called Monday for an end to most bilingual education . . . as he sought to cast his presidential bid as a **defense of the nation's cultural heritage.** (September 5, 1995, A1)

This is an improper measure of patriotism, given the exceptional record of Chicanos and other Latinos in the U.S. armed services[38] and other public service endeavors. It betrays a weak faith in public education, as well as a shallow trust in children, insofar as the presidential candidate expresses fear that children are incapable of judging for themselves the character of the United States by way of educated comparison.

The preeminence of the English language in the United States is not challenged by any of the American children speaking over one hundred other languages, notwithstanding Dole's defensiveness. Nor is there evidence that English will be replaced as the single dominant language of the United States, even in the states where most bilingual speakers reside. English will not be displaced in twenty-first-century California as the language of commerce, government, and popular culture. Indeed, English is the single most powerful language in the world.[39] Yet bilingual education, which is arguably the best kind of educational program for public-school children, was reduced to a get-English-quick remediation procedure, and even in this diminished state is portrayed as a threatening force.

> 68. "People are concerned about **our social fabric,** and they believe **it's unraveling,**" said Fred Steeper, who shares in the polling responsibilities for Wilson's presidential campaign. "One way to bring things together is to stop illegal immigration and also to **insist that those people who come in legally learn English.**" (September 5, 1995, A1)
>
> 69. Dole asked the audience: "**Do we embrace ideas that unite us,** regardless of our sex or color or religion? . . . Or are we just a crowd of competing groups thrown by fate between two oceans?" (September 5, 1995, A1)

Regardless of the chauvinistic bluster, it is to the advantage of the nation that its children be as well educated as possible, rather than minimally and distrustfully. In California in 1998, bilingual education was only a symbolic threat to the social order. Still, its continued existence, as well as other indices of bilingualism in the United States, exposes the counterfeit privilege of English monolinguals. Whenever Spanish or some other language is used in U.S. public education, the language is legitimated. At that point, the nativist fiction that Spanish is foreign is exposed to scrutiny. Such linguistic parochialism limits today's U.S. high school students, who remain functionally incompetent in "foreign" languages, and who are overly dependent on English. If high school language classes actually provided students with serviceable proficiency in another language, then the hegemonic fiction would be thoroughly discredited, as students became more completely educated. By the way, they would be no less patriotic.

Language parochialism is an unnecessary weakness visited on mainstream U.S. schoolchildren. However, for bilingual children who come to school with home languages other than English, insistence on English-language dependency is linguicism. Linguicism is an ideology and a set of institutional operations used to legitimate and reproduce an unequal division of power and resources between groups—on the basis of language. Linguicism operates in the same way as racism. The dominant group promotes its own way of speech (dialect and language) as the only normal one, in this case American English. It actively stigmatizes other, dominated languages and the children who speak them. Then excuses are made about the unequal relationship between the dominant and subordinate languages to rationalize the discrimination.

## The Hegemonic Narrative of Language

A systematic empirical review of the metaphors appearing in the public discourse on education reveals that LANGUAGE is a radial concept, namely, a concept that can be schematized as a wheel with spokes and a hub. In this case the spokes are BARRIER, FOREIGN, PRISON, HANDICAP. They are linked together at the LANGUAGE hub. The attribute shared among the spokes is that "language" is aberrant and negative. In the public discourse on education, then, "language" is not the scientific notion, and it is falsely assumed to be a barrier in the path of the education of children.

Again, it must be stressed that metaphor is more than a matter of rhetorical flourish. It is a part of the conceptual system shared in large part by speakers of the English language and encoded in the ways Americans tend to use terms like *language* and *English*. Metaphors such as LANGUAGE AS PRISON actively reflect a shared understanding of the domain of LANGUAGE in terms of the domain of PRISON. Moreover, their unreflected and dominant use also actively contributes to this view of the nature of language. In keeping with the conventional presentation of such patterning, the chief ontological principle of the U.S. discourse on language is presented in terms of a dichotomy:

- English is more than just a language, it is the normal and natural medium of human communication, while
- Spanish and other languages are foreign and restrictive.

This governing principle of U.S. public discourse is ironic in California, and particularly in Los Angeles, since neither the national capitals of Spain nor Venezuela can boast of a larger Spanish-speaking population than Los Angeles.

This ontological principle delegitimizes languages other than English for any important functions in U.S. society, particularly public education. Again, to follow the conventional format of cognitive science discussions of metaphoric relations, since the EDUCATION AS PATH metaphor interacts with the multiple language metaphors (BARRIER, PRISON, FOREIGN) which comprise a radial concept, the following summarizing narrative, of the place of the English language in the United States, weaves the various strands of the relationship together:

> *In America, communication in English is transparent and automatic. However, foreigners are not so blessed. They speak languages which, in contrast to English, must be learned with much effort, can never be perfected, and are poor substitutes for the natural fluency of English. In contrast to English, languages pose a serious impediment to learning. Children who come from homes where languages are spoken are at a disadvantage in school, since all real learning takes place by way of English. True English speakers are monolingual, by which they acknowledge that English is natural and sufficient for all communication. If students do not become English monolinguals, they are effectively imprisoned by their language. If not released from this linguistic confinement, they develop a language handicap and are consequently educationally and intellectually impaired. Thus the noble goal of American*

*education should be to speed these children toward becoming true American English speakers.*

In spite of the preponderance of scientific and pedagogic evidence that is regularly reported in the *Los Angeles Times* and elsewhere about the poor educational showing of all students, whether monolingual English speakers or not, this counterfactual narrative steadfastly defies repudiation.[40] In 1998 it operated in the public discourse on education to make Proposition 227 seem sensible. It justifies severe restrictions on educators and their students, not only the students who arrive at the schoolhouse door speaking a language other than English, but English-dependent Anglo-American students, who have a legitimate right to be educated in and about the other languages of the world.

In this narrative, the prolonged use of Spanish and other languages to educate children is worse than frivolous, it is dangerous. Its implications cast a wide net. Since English is the only legitimate form of speech, its use is a symbol of U.S. citizenship and dominance. And it follows that English monolingualism, by way of exclusion, is an emblem of fealty to a parochial brand of American values and worldviews.

## Section 7: Latino Responses to Linguistic Parochialism

For those who lived in California in the 1990s, the link between the vitriol against immigrants and opposition to bilingual education was not incidental. The unity underlying these issues is anti-Latino status politics, according to an influential conservative political operative:

> 70. "There's no question that English-as-an-official-language, immigration reform and affirmative action are all converging emotionally in the minds of our people," said Stanley Diamond, who led the 1986 campaign to make English California's official language and recently joined the anti-bilingual-education fight. "We really do expect dramatic changes now." (May 22, 1995, A1)

In excerpt 70, the ideological ties are made explicit among Propositions 187, 209, and 227, as well as Proposition 63, the 1986 "English as Official Language" referendum.[41] Diamond appeals to emotion rather than understanding in this passage. The *Times* database had numerous explicit ideological links between public education and the IMMIGRATION AS DANGEROUS WATERS metaphor:

71. Assistant Supt. Jesse Franco, head of the district's bilingual program, blamed the decline on peripheral factors unrelated to the program's merit, such as the recent **flood of immigrant students** who enter school speaking no English and require more time for a transition. (July 31, 1995, B1)

72. Some see the mounting pressure to abandon bilingual education as yet another wave of immigrant bashing, a reaction to the **virtual tsunami of non-English-speaking students that has crashed over the state** in the past decade. (May 22, 1995, A1)

*Tsunami* is a Japanese term for a tidal wave created by an undersea earthquake, which for Californians conjures untold destruction to the land, again attributed to immigrants. The increase of immigrant children in public schools has indeed contributed to the perception of a change in the complexion of public schools, but terms such as tsunami send a histrionic signal to the U.S. public.

73. The **revolt** here comes as California schools confront an **exploding** population of children with limited English, most of them Spanish speakers. Last year the state counted 1.3 million students from kindergarten through 12th grade who are not fluent in English. . . . The numbers have been growing steadily, in absolute and percentage terms, for more than a decade. (April 13, 1997, A1)

The three waves of status quo politics, Propositions 187, 209, and 227, were generated by the resentment of citizens who fear for the loss of Anglo-American cultural preeminence. They are closely linked to anxiety at the apparent browning of California and the United States. In contrast to the Proposition 187 campaign, which was precipitated in 1993 by the California economic recession, the Proposition 227 campaign took place when the U.S. economy was experiencing its strongest upswing in decades. Thus the economic climate cannot be the origin of nativist anger. Recalling the mood of the Proposition 187 period, the impetus to eliminate bilingual education had nothing to do with money. It was a matter of culture.

### Latino Responses

Latino responses to the calls to dismantle the bilingual education system frequently recognize the hegemonic narrative, which dominated the debate:

74. "People hear the words 'bilingual education' and think Spanish. I don't think they see the whole picture." Hernandez [a bilingual elementary-school teacher in Santa Ana, California] said she expects increasing assaults on bilingual education. Presidential contender Sen. Bob Dole (R-Kansas) has called for an end to most bilingual education classes, and state Assembly Speaker Curt Pringle (R–Garden Grove) has called bilingual education a "**disaster**" for students. (April 30, 1996, B2)

75. Martinez said Proposition 187 and spin-off movements are fueled by an **unhealthy nativism,** which has ebbed and flowed in California since the "American occupation" began centuries ago. Martinez criticized 187 proponents, whom he characterized as "isolationist," for being fearful of cultural and ethnic differences. (February 2, 1995, B1)

76. Reynaldo F. Macías, a professor at UC Santa Barbara and Director of the Linguistic Minority Research Institute, . . . said bilingual education supporters must become even more aggressive. "The attacks are really motivated by the attempt to eliminate non-English languages. . . . the strategy is to criticize the bilingual programs and create **cultural panic,**" he said. (April 8, 1996, A1)

77. "**Promoting intolerance,** particularly at the presidential level, is not what this country is looking for," contended Raul Yzaguirre, president of the National Council of La Raza, an umbrella group for more than 200 Latino civil rights and community development organizations with a total membership of 2.5 million. (September 5, 1995, A1)

However, the nativist challenge to bilingual education put Latino spokespeople on the defensive. Their response was muted by professional political consultants who advised Latino political associations that the voting public would not permit any contestation of the Unz initiative on social justice criteria, and that any defender of immigrant and Latino public-school children would be labeled a supporter of special interest groups, namely, teachers unions and bilingual teachers. Nor could structural reasons for the educational failure in public schools be raised. Therefore, the "English for the Children" campaigners were free to define the terms of the debate. Latinos were left to defend a repudiated educational status quo.

Latino organizations were unable to articulate a sustained counterhegemonic response along the lines of ENGLISH-DEPENDENCE AS PRISON and BILINGUALISM AS TREASURE, as nearly uniquely exemplified in excerpt 78. The absence of recognition of the richness of Spanish, and all languages, can be noted by the nearly complete absence of metaphoric representations in the public discourse. There were the comments of Secretary of Education Riley, cited in excerpt 53. In the period of time under review, only one *Los Angeles Times* article on bilingual education presented a professional linguist's view. She chose to speak about the Spanish language, using several metaphors emphasizing the richness of a language other than English:

> 78. "Bilingualism is a **richness**," says Alma Flor Ada, a linguistics professor at the University of San Francisco and the author of more than 200 children's books. "I believe that languages are **power.** They're one of the most valuable **tools** that people can have." (October 4, 1995, E3)

However, the *Times* newswriter may have diminished Professor Ada's professional stature by citing only her authorship of children's books, and not her academic work.[42] The newswriter may have further discredited her in the eyes of the public:

> 79. "The prime age [for a language] to be acquired naturally and easily for all human beings is when they are acquiring their first language," says Ada, a Cuban by birth who, despite more than 20 years in this country, still speaks English with a noticeable accent. "So I believe that language should be taught in childhood and facilitated in childhood." (October 4, 1995, E3)

By referring to Professor Ada's pronunciation, her professional qualifications were slighted. Part of the linguistic hegemony of the United States grants greater esteem to those who speak with a so-called "accentless" American English. Spanish-accented English tends to be diminished on this score, particularly from a professor asserting counterhegemonic ideas. In the two-year sample of texts, only one other article, on the bilingual educational system of Miami, Florida, presented bilingual education in a positive light.

It was left to individual Latinos to voice their views candidly. To be sure, the Latino communities are heterogeneous, as are their political views. Some Latinos were proponents of English-only classes, as was the speaker excerpted in 21. However, the majority held that bilingual education is a superior pedagogical program for all students, not just bilingual and immigrant students. The majority of Latinos' own statements, as sampled in the *Times* articles, were made by the teachers or parents of bilingual children. These Latinos either were bilingual themselves or spoke about the impending loss of children's linguistic heritage.

80. Many parents like the mixture of Spanish and English. "I consider Spanish to be a **treasure,**" said one parent, Irene Rosas. "It gives us two **possibilities,** two **windows,** two **worlds** . . . and those who are opposed to Spanish are racists who want to keep us down." (April 8, 1996, A1)

81. More than 800 parents in the district signed a petition expressing concern about the changes [to limit bilingual education]. They have complained bitterly about being brushed aside when the decision was made and argue that the new proposal is racist and unfair. Several of them piled into a van at 3 A.M. Thursday morning to make the [seven-hour, 417-mile] drive to Sacramento for the [California State] Board of Education hearing. They came away with the impression that the decision has already been made. "I just don't think they paid enough attention to it, as they should have," said Juan Carlos Ayala, one of the opposition leaders. "It just seemed that all this . . . has happened down here, and it just funneled up there. . . . It seemed like their minds were really set." (June 14, 1997, B5)

82. Trustees on Tuesday named Wallace R. Davis Elementary School to be the Santa Ana Unified School District's first bilingual school, meaning children will be expected to graduate literate in both English and Spanish. Normally, the goal is to teach children in English only by the fifth grade, officials said. But now, 20% of fifth-grade instruction at Davis will be in Spanish. . . . The proposal was floated not by educators but by parents from the surrounding area. Parents had argued at a previous board meeting that they wanted their children both to maintain their Latino roots and to be literate in English. (April 9, 1997, B5)

It should be noted that these commentaries of everyday Latinos confirm the views maintained by most language policy researchers.[43] The commentary of people who happen to be multilingual also contradicted the view preferred by the *Los Angeles Times,* which repeatedly stated that Latinos, like the rest of the electorate, were generally opposed to bilingual education and in favor of Proposition 227.[44] Despite such grassroots commentary, the *Times* promoted a pro-227 stance, with a previously cited article offering more than a dozen statements by people, including Latinos, who favored the proposition. No opposing assessments were offered in the article.[45]

Latinos were not canvassed accurately. Public opinion polls conducted early in the Proposition 227 campaign suggested that Latinos opposed bilingual education. Caution was voiced early about making too much of this assessment, since, as the director of the *Times* opinion polling service noted, early Latino support for Propositions 187 and 209 "eventually changed to opposition as the races heated up."[46] Still, in March 1998, the San Francisco–based Field Poll independently found that 61 percent of Latinos favored the measure.[47] According to a *Times* poll, by mid-April 50 percent of Latinos supported the measure while 32 percent opposed it. By mid-May, with the vote only two weeks away, the *Times* reported that Proposition 227 was "supported by two-thirds of both registered Latino and white voters, a consensus that was absent in the state's past battles over racially-sensitive initiatives on illegal immigration and affirmative action."[48] This change was straightway elaborated on with another *Times* article:

> Latino support for 227 had actually risen, despite the fact that much of the Latino leadership opposes the proposition. . . . A *Times* poll conducted May 16–20 showed that statewide 62% of Latino registered voters favored Proposition 227, roughly the same level of support found among white voters and a marked increase from April poll figures—when 50% of Latino voters said they would vote for the initiative. . . . The growing Latino support is particularly striking because it runs counter to the trend of two initiatives approved by voters.[49]

If this series of polls was accurate, as Latinos became more familiar with Proposition 227, they increasingly disfavored bilingual education.

In contrast, Los Angeles's largest Spanish-language newspaper disputed the findings of the *Times* and Field polls. *La Opinión* conducted a 1996 poll which found that Latino parents favor bilingual education. Of the parents polled by *La Opinión,* 88 percent thought bilingual education was a good thing for their children, while only 10 percent thought it was bad for their children. This directly controverted the *Times* and Field polls. Of the *Opinión* sampling, 81 percent of Latinos favored maintaining or reforming bilingual education, while only 17 percent favored eliminating the programs. Most significantly, those who were most familiar with bilingual education were its strongest supporters. Only 5 percent of Latino parents whose children attended bilingual education classes at the time wanted to do away with the program.[50]

A look at the key *Times* poll question may explain a good deal of the discrepancy:

> Which of these statements comes closer to your point of view about how to educate students who are not fluent in English?

- "Students should be taught only in English because that is the best way for them to learn English," or
- "Students should be assisted in their native language for only a brief period of time, such as a year or two," or
- "Students should be taught in both their native language and English as long as their educators and parents believe it is necessary"?[51]

The three options may depict symmetrical educational scenarios, but they did not portray the preferred scenario of Latinos. The first option grants the premise of Proposition 227, as expected. However, the third option does not articulate the position of advocates of bilingual education. For them, the issue is not whether students should learn English, but whether "learning English" should be the primary goal of schooling. The *Times* pollsters had acceded to the narrow frame of reference defined by Proposition 227 supporters and failed to comprehend or did not bother to register the Latinos' opposing stance. Nor was any question posed about views on what constitutes a superior public school education, or how the state could reinstitute an exemplary school system.

As it turns out, the *La Opinión* poll reflected Latino voter preference toward the June 2nd ballot, not the *Times* or Field polls. The results indicate that today's Latinos do not share the educational values of the preponderance of the electorate.

### The Big Lie

Latino voters unequivocally rejected Proposition 227. Sixty-three percent of Latinos voted against the initiative across the state. In the heartland of Republican conservatism, Orange County, 71 percent of Latinos voted "no." The proposition was rejected in two dozen precincts in Orange County alone where Latinos accounted for at least half of the registered voters.

Still, in the days after the passage of the referendum, the dominant conceptual system that maintains Anglo-American hegemony and its English-only ideology demonstrated its vigor. The news media also demonstrated that they are oblivious to Latino views that run contrary to the mainstream. Many newspapers across the nation misinformed the wider American public about the California Latino vote. In what Michael Genzuk dubbed "the Big Lie,"[52] a stream of news reports in the days following the vote announced that Latinos had supported Proposition 227.

Charlie Ericksen compiled newspaper reports from across the country which inaccurately declared that Latinos favored the abolition of bilingual education.[53] The *Chicago Tribune* falsely stated that "exit polls indicated that the proposed bilingual education measure was approved by a 3–1 ratio of the state's voters, including a majority of California's Hispanic residents who rejected the state's existing system." The *San Diego Union-Tribune* stated that the "initiative . . . appears to have had strong support among all segments of California's voting communities, including Latinos."[54] *The Plain Dealer* (Cleveland) pronounced that "California voters decided to junk the state's nearly 30-year-old experiment in bilingual education. . . . Despite warnings that [the 227] formula is untested, Californians of all racial and ethnic backgrounds gave the proposal strong support."[55] The *Christian Science Monitor* noted that "Experts say the vote is significant because about two-thirds of the state's Latino voters supported the proposition." The *Monitor* editorial of the same day promoted this falsehood, stating that a "majority of California's huge Hispanic electorate voted for the proposition." The Associated Press wrote: "Eighty percent of limited-English children (in California) are Spanish speakers, but polls suggested the measure had wide support among Hispanic voters." Other newspapers spread the mistake.

As this lie spread, so did the commentary that it provoked. The AP expanded on its misrepresentation by providing an unwarranted forum to a U.S. representative who sponsored federal legislation to eliminate bilingual education. He stated: "Perhaps the most important information about this vote is that an overwhelming number of Hispanic voters—60 percent—voted for Proposition 227." The *Washington Post* confirmed his untruth: "The exit polls suggest . . . sizable support from Hispanics—the very group that the state's bilingual education programs are designed to help the most." This fiction was elaborated by the *Dallas Morning News* and others: "The arguments over the bilingual measure were not as racially charged as those that attended the earlier initiatives, Propositions 187 and 209. One reason for this was the heavy support Proposition 227 enjoyed among Latino voters. Some polls showed nearly the same numbers of Hispanic voters favored the proposition as did whites, although there were indications the Latino vote ended up much closer Tuesday." Columnist Roger Hernández (King Features Syndicate) offered an op-ed, on the basis of the Big Lie, that echoed the *Washington Post*'s view: "Tuesday's anti–bilingual education measure won with strong backing from Hispanics. In effect, large numbers of Hispanics turned against a program originally created for the benefit of immigrant children who do not speak English."[56] No retractions amended any of these news reports in the two weeks following their publication.

Newswriters usually want to get a scoop. However, Ericksen's article was not succeeded by other reports, even though Proposition 227 and bilingual education remained on the national agenda. The absence of reporting indicates it is not newsworthy that California Latinos' views are not reflected in the outcomes of referenda on Latino issues, even when they vote in record numbers, or that English-language polling of the largest ethnic group in California was ineffectual. Still, it would be simplistic to state that a conspiracy prompted these false news reports. From a metaphor analysis of public discourse, these blind spots are marks of the dominant ideological/conceptual framework, which holds English monolingualism to be a domestic virtue and bilingualism to be a foreign liability. In the public eye, Latinos become good Americans insofar as they affirm the standing social order and reject the nonmainstream education of their children. On the basis of the Latino voting on the three referenda, little evidence for such a trend can be noted. Instead, a rift exists.

The split between Anglo and Latino voters marks an ideological divide. In the case of Proposition 227, it separates the English-dependent voter from the multilingual voter. English monolinguals sought to ensure their mode of language use among the next generation of Americans. The electoral majority in effect wanted to sustain the dominant conceptual system that it was raised with, and which apportions white privilege. Conversely, for Latinos and others who have experienced the benefits of bilingualism, and for whom the ideology of English monolingualism rings false, bilingual education is viewed as a tool to achieve a better education for their children. As historian George J. Sánchez stated, when they were at the polls deciding the fate of Proposition 227, Latinos asked themselves how best to teach their children English and if bilingual education as it was taught in California public schools was the best option, while Anglo-American voters simply asked themselves whether or not English was to be taught.[57]

The public discourse of this California referendum continues to constitute Spanish-speaking Americans as foreigners. In the final analysis, the issue underlying "English for the Children" was not education. The referendum served to reaffirm an increasingly antiquated view of America. Proposition 227 will not have any effect on how non-English-speaking children acquire the English language, since language development is in large part beyond the reach of legislation. Nor did it address the most important failings of California's public school system. However, it most certainly diminishes public education for these children, and all California children.

## Section 8: Conclusion

The socially naturalized, but deceptive, elevation of the English language over other human languages in the United States has previously been discussed by linguists, educational researchers, social theorists, and critics.[58] This chapter provides further evidence from a metaphor database drawn from a corpus totaling 671 *Los Angeles Times* articles, May 1992–June 1998, which constitutes a thorough sampling of contemporary American discourse on education.

American English speakers tend to tacitly accept the American narrative presuming the superiority (or peerless normalcy) of the English language, in spite of its resultant repudiation of the rest of human communication. The narrative leads Anglo-Americans to presume (not necessarily consciously aver) that the English language is the one true water of the educational mainstream. The narrative is built on the conventional metaphor of the English language AS WATER and is sustained with the archaic, but still productive, metaphors about public education presented in Chapter 5.

In the public discourse during the Proposition 227 debate, the hegemonic view of public education was never challenged. Latino counterhegemonic views on the character of the English language did not pierce its suit of mail. Both educational researchers and linguists find fault in the failure of their professions to change the everyday views of education and language. These dominant views are based on nineteenth-century worldviews. Given that orthodox nineteenth-century scientific notions of biological race held sway as the hegemonic viewpoint for the greater part of the twentieth century, it may take as long to filter new ways of understanding education and language into the public's perspective.[59] Still and all, in order for change to occur, openings in Unz's "iron-clad" armor must be made with steadfastly recounted counternarratives.


In the preceding chapters, we have reviewed the dominant metaphors framing contemporary American discourse on immigrant and citizen, immigration, race and racism, English and language. These conceptual metaphors reinforce a dominant Anglo-American worldview that has increasingly oppressed the Latino community at a time when it has become sizable and more assertive in the late twentieth century. In order to be comprehensible, these constituting metaphors must be conceptually coherent with each other as well as congruent with the higher-order metaphors that constitute the United States. We move to the first of two concluding chapters by examining the metaphorization of the U.S. republic and associated notions such as citizen/alien and domestic/foreign in public discourse across the decade of the 1990s. The NATION is the subject of the next chapter.

# PART III

# Conclusions

CHAPTER SEVEN

DISEASE or INTRUDER

# Metaphors Constructing the Place of Latinos in the United States

In the first of two concluding chapters, the metaphors constituting every-day understandings of CITIZEN, IMMIGRANT, LANGUAGE, RACISM, and ENGLISH are linked together by way of the most prevalent metaphors of the concept NATION. In the course of the book, the cognitive linguistic theories of Lakoff and his collaborators have been subjected to an extended empirical investigation. These investigators theorized that metaphor, above other structures of language, establishes the basis of people's everyday comprehension of life. Metaphors provide a framework to make sense of behavior, relations, objects, and people, even to the point that people forget that the semantic associations created by metaphors are wholly contingent, not natural. By undertaking this analysis of the material content of conceptual metaphors in contemporary public discourse, we gain purchase on the social practice of everyday Americans making sense of the relationship that Latinos are understood to have with the nation.

From an entirely distinct intellectual tradition, Foucault also characterized discursive practice, which reveals how oppressive social relations are constituted in social interaction. Although for Foucault the term *discourse* is extraordinarily encompassing, incorporating the whole Western world, the theorizing is similar. Discourses, within his formulation, are types of social practices within social orders that are expressed by individuals. People function in terms of certain particular discourses/practices. As the discursive practices are enacted, ideological practices are reproduced and reaffirmed. These subject positions define and confine both oppressor and oppressed in terms of knowledge and beliefs, social relationships and social identity. To use Lakoff's term, these discourse practices "embody" unreflected and naturalized ideological assumptions. While Lakoff holds that metaphoric thinking is a fundamental human cognitive process, Foucault believed that metaphor is a recent, even modern, phenomenon in the realm of political power. Foucault stated that modern society "invented, so to speak, a synaptic regime of power, a regime of its exercise *within* the social body, rather than *from above* it."[1] As people live their lives, they enact the discourse practices associated with their subject positions. In doing so they tend to accept the ideology of the standing social order, namely, the institutional practices that sustain and legitimize repressive power relations. When they go about their daily tasks and obligations, they take for granted a good deal about the sources of oppression. For both Lakoff and Foucault, ideology is the articulation of social relations that individuals generally do not discern because they are taken to be normal and natural. The objective of these writers, then, as summarized by Foucault, is "to criticize the working of institutions which appear to be neutral and independent; to criticize them in such a manner that the political violence which has always exercised itself obscurely through them will be unmasked, so that one can fight them."[2]

This summary chapter reviews the two dominant higher-order metaphors that articulate the social relations of Latinos vis-à-vis the nation. The first section provides a sketch of the primeval BODY metaphor and its ontology. Section 2 develops the second overarching metaphor for almost all the rest of English-language thinking about the United States. This medieval NATION AS HOUSE was expressed in several forms during the 1990s, including NATION AS CASTLE and AS SHIP. The use of this metaphor in a particularly persuasive statement of the so-called immigrant threat, Peter Brimelow's best-selling book, *Alien Nation,* is also discussed in this section. Both BODY and HOUSE metaphors for the nation are becoming increasingly inapt in the twenty-first century. The semantic associations that are maintained by their continued use are the topic of Section 3, including the varying definitions of citizen. Since the metaphors that construct the political notions described in the previous chapters are thought up in congruence with NATION metaphors, a tentative evaluation of the descriptive adequacy of this cognitive linguistic analysis of public discourse can be undertaken in Section 4 of this chapter, in semantic terms of (horizontal) coherence and (vertical) congruence. In Section 5 a dramaturgical script for the discursive practice of these metaphors is presented. This discursive script synopsizes the findings of the previous chapters, spelling out how Latinos are perceived, and how Latinos experience political relations, on the national stage.

## Section 1: NATION AS BODY

As has been indicated at various points throughout the book, the major metaphorization of Latinos and Latino political issues in contemporary public discourse is created in response to two very productive higher-order metaphors for the nation and other polities. The first metaphor employed in contemporary public discourse is NATION AS BODY. The primary associations of the BODY metaphor are corporeal, material, and functional, rather than symbolic and formal. It is common to speak about the economic health of the state, while topographically, for example, referring to parts of the country such as the U.S. heartland. U.S. poets have at times memorably invoked the figurative language of U.S. AS BODY, as in Carl Sandberg's "Chicago of the Big Shoulders," to personify its economic vigor in terms of the human body.

The sociopolitical and cultural encounter that Chicanas/os experience with Anglo-America has been captured succinctly with a BODY metaphor by Gloria Anzaldúa:

> 1,950 mile-long open wound
>      dividing a *pueblo,* a culture,
>      running down the length of my body,
>          staking fence rods in my flesh,
>          splits me           splits me
>                *me raja*               *me raja*
>      This is my home
>      this thin edge of
>          barbwire.

Anzaldúa, a Chicana poet and social theorist, continues with the BODY metaphor, asserting that the U.S./Mexican border is an open wound "where the Third World grates against the first and bleeds. And before a scab forms it hemorrhages again, the lifeblood of two worlds merging to form a third country—a border culture."[3] Anzaldúa's is imagery of a body larger than the United States. It refers to Aztlán,[4] what Américo Paredes called "Greater Mexico." Aztlán is the site of the Chicana/o struggle for land, community, identity, and equality, a (mythic) dominion encompassing the U.S. Southwest and northern Mexican republic. Recently, Mexican novelist and intellectual Carlos Fuentes also used the metaphor for this larger-than-U.S. target domain: "This border is the most exciting border in the world. It is crossed by 200 million people a year. . . . I have always said it is a scar, not a border. But we don't want the scar to bleed again. We want the scar to heal."[5]

Public discourse during the 1990s frequently stated that immigrants are a *burden* on the country. As discussed in Chapter 3, this derogatory and inaccurate statement builds, once again, on the body metaphor. Calavita demonstrated the use of body terminology with reference to immigrants during the Proposition 187 campaign period. Suárez-Orozco and Suárez-Orozco's analysis, in which Latino immigrants were cast as a pathogen of the U.S. body, was readily confirmed in the *Los Angeles Times* database. This is a particularly bitter irony for Chicanos/as, the contemporary descendants of the Spanish-speaking population who have continuously inhabited the U.S. Southwest since the earliest days of colonial establishment. Even conservative historians acknowledge this. Oscar Handlin began his acclaimed history *The Uprooted: The Epic Story of the Great Migrations That Made the American People* in the following way:[6]

> Once I thought to write a history of the immigrants in America. Then I discovered that the immigrants *were* American history. For almost fifteen years now, I have searched the surviving records of the masses of men who peopled our country. As I worked, the conviction grew upon me that adequately to describe the course and effects of immigration involved no less a task than to set down the whole history of the United States.

The nation as body can also suffer from disease, as illustrated in Chapter 4. A classic characterization of adversity affecting one part of the country, as in "the Civil War was the burden of the South," employs the body metaphor.[7] In that chapter we noted the potency of the 1960s metaphorization of white racism as a cancer of the U.S. body, coupled with its medical/legal *remedy* in the form of affirmative action. Critics of affirmative action in the 1990s subverted the WHITE RACISM AS CANCER metaphor, while retaining the NATION AS BODY metaphor. Their various animadversions invoked the metaphor, stating that affirmative action "*embitters* the national community" and that by removing it the "*burden* of the current *regime*" will be lifted.

While the NATION AS BODY metaphor easily can be found in daily public discourse, nevertheless the United States operates in manners that do not conform to the physiology or everyday understanding of the human body. Moreover, this metaphor is superannuated, enduring from earlier forms of society in which, according to Foucault: "the King's body wasn't a metaphor, but a political reality. Its physical presence was necessary for the functioning of the monarchy."[8] The sovereign's human form symbolized the continuity of the community: "The King is dead; long live the King!" Continued use of the increasingly far-fetched ontology of NATION AS BODY can offer insight into the naturalization process of metaphoric thinking.

In this chapter, two distinct notions of *naturalization* are employed. The first is a cognitive process. The second is the legal process involving citizenship. In the first sense, *naturalization* is Norman Fairclough's term for the "sense of orderliness" created in people's daily lives from entirely contingent relations established in discourse. While Fairclough does not give metaphor a principal role in the naturalization process, his formulation of the discursive processes of hegemony, which draws on Foucault's theories, is compatible with the one employed in this book. In the present case, the use of the NATION AS BODY metaphor employs a set of features, based on the human body, which gives conceptual order to the unrelated concept of NATION. By way of the everyday and unchallenged use of this dominant metaphor, it remains common to sense that nations are like bodies and that this is how it "should be, i.e., as one would normally expect."[9] These customarily felt impressions, Fairclough underscores, are also the site of tacit ideological expression, including inequitable social relations. Such conceptual relations set up by the metaphor can "contribute to sustaining unequal power relations, directly or indirectly."[10]

Since the body is a feature that humans comprehend without reflection, much of the following might appear self-evident, rather than an arbitrary relationship that is set up by the metaphor. By reviewing the ontology in this section, that is to say, comparing the semantic elements of BODY to those of NATION, the naturalized contingencies that are sustained with the continuous use of the dominant metaphor might be more readily discerned.

## Ontology of NATION AS BODY

The human body is the archetypal source of embodied preconceptual understanding. As a frame of reference, it is an image-schemata, a kinesthetically grounded perception which is understood bodily by every person, upon which other experiences and sensations are based. The BODY is an enclosed space; a complete system of various interdependent organs with distinct functions; a living organism with a birth, a life span, life stages, and an inevitable death; a physique with weight and volume; a person who can see, stand upright, crouch, grasp things, move in space, and feel pressure. When used to conceptualize a nation, all these various aspects of corporality are summoned.

The target semantic domain, NATION, is conceptualized with the appendages and organs of the human body. The nation is provided, by way of the metaphor, with a head, brain, heart, hands, feet, and other parts; to it can be attributed the basic functions of a body: eating, sleeping, defecating, procreating, moving, and so on. The nation can have motives, desires, and appetites. The boundaries of a body correspond to the nation's borders, which define domestic and international relations. Further, as discussed, the associated frames of reference for bodies become part of the inherent logic of the metaphor; disease and health, strength and weakness, burden and relief are all available for conceptual use. In an unreflected everyday worldview, against all better reasoning and evidence to the contrary, such logic conceptualizes the United States as a person with life stages, purposes, and mortality.

The metaphor constitutes a claim with immense social implications: the nation is an individual with a personality, judgments, failings, and aspirations. All the semantic domain of the human body defines a polity, a politically organized population, a territory containing a population of diverse people. Paul Chilton pointed out in his genealogy of the discourse on nation that it is undoubtedly a metaphor with ancient origins. Recall previous references to instances of the NATION AS BODY in Plato's *Republic*. Chilton notes that its current formulation was established in the seventeenth century by Thomas Hobbes. Indeed, the title of Hobbes's classic work, *Leviathan*, reflects this conceptualization. A conservative thinker even for his time, Hobbes was impressed by Galileo and the then-new sciences of mechanics. He began with the mechanists' metaphor, MAN AS MACHINE. Chilton quotes Hobbes: "Life is but a motion of Limbs, the beginning whereof is some principal part within." To this machine Hobbes linked the medieval European religion (with Christ as God's body incarnate in the Pope and the Catholic Church) and the political state, which was a secular sovereign authority (in the person of a monarch). The secular state, or commonwealth, was thus metamorphosed as a man, "that great Leviathan." The state is thus an artificial man, as Chilton notes,

> with an artificial soul (sovereign) giving it motion, artificial joints (magistrates and other officers of judicature and execution), and artificial nerves (rewards and punishment) "by which fastned to the seate

of the Soveraignty, every joynt and member is moved to performe his duty."[11]

As one of two top-level metaphors, and in the absence of well-articulated alternatives, the NATION AS BODY metaphor continues to impose its antiquated logic on twenty-first-century U.S. citizens. In this global age, with increasing pressures of population, dwindling natural resources, and accelerating economic and cultural interdependence, reconsideration of the metaphor is well advised. Chilton and Ilyin list four options to transform political metaphors.[12] One is to retain the semantic source domain and redefine the metaphor's target semantic domain, in this case, to encompass the Earth itself. People still commonly speak about Mother Earth, which allows humans to evade responsibility by an appeal to infancy. A more appropriate metaphor might be James Lovelock's "Gaia: The World as Living Organism."[13] Varieties of such an enlarged target domain for the metaphor are averred among bioconservationists, in spite of derision by Americans with either a parochial worldview or self-interest in prolonging their unsustainable lifestyle.

This organic metaphor was employed by the earliest sociologists such as Émile Durkheim, following Auguste Comte and Herbert Spencer, to characterize society.[14] The metaphor was systematized in various social science disciplines as functionalist models of society, in which the aggregate of social groups operate in harmony as a biotic unit by way of unequal distribution of property. As pointed out by its critics, the metaphor does not fit reality. Human society does not resemble an ant society, but is composed of groups that maintain conflicting interests. In ideological terms, the metaphor justifies and legitimates the unjust power apportionment of the status quo.

Bryan Turner asserts that this ancient metaphor has been replaced by a liberal discourse on individual rights.[15] This is not apparent in public discourse. Since the human body continues to incarnate preconceptual understanding, in the absence of a first-rate alternative, the organic metaphor will continue to structure everyday knowledge of what a society and the nation comprise. Indeed, evidence from contemporary public discourse indicates that the human body still constructs popular understanding of the nation and was readily accepted in the 1990s when used to invoke traditional nativism against the country's enemies, foreign and domestic, which unfortunately seem to include U.S. Latinos.

## Section 2: NATION AS HOUSE

In this section the second dominant metaphor for nation, U.S. AS HOUSE, will be considered. This metaphor appears with frequency, and gives structure to a number of political metaphors that have been studied in this book. In Chapter 3, for example, the metaphors for the individual person who comes to the United States include CRIMINAL breaking into the house, SOLDIER invading the house, undesirable WEED growing around the house, and FOREIGNER to the house. All these are dependent on the NATION AS HOUSE metaphor frame of reference. A number of geology and real estate metaphors are subsumed in the HOUSE metaphor, such as: *islands of poverty; voting groups that are as diverse and fractured as the geology of California; landslide victory of Proposition 187 . . . opening deep new fissures in the political landscape; positions staked out; widening rift between the predominantly white population and the Latino community;* etc. As for the demographic process of immigration, the dominant metaphor, DANGEROUS WATERS, is realized in a whole range of expressions invoking the HOUSE metaphor. These metaphors articulate the dynamism and impact of immigration as it remakes the U.S. AS HOUSE. For those who are distressed at the direction of cultural change in California and the nation, away from an Anglo-American cultural model toward a multicultural and perhaps Latino cultural paradigm, this metaphor was used to call for restricting late-twentieth-century U.S. immigration. It should be recalled that these metaphors less often refer to economic pressures, in contrast to BODY metaphors. DANGEROUS WATERS are described as threatening the Anglo-American cultural house. Other recurrent metaphors also invoke the NATION AS HOUSE metaphor, such as IMMIGRATION AS WAR or MACHINE destroying the house, and AS FIRE burning the house down. These metaphors all express the anxiety at the apparent loss of Anglo-American cultural hegemony.

In order to make explicit the relations among these metaphors, both their semantic cohesion into a mutually sustaining constellation of representations of Latinos in relationship to their larger American society, and their embodiment by way of a societal discourse that marginalizes Latinos, the ontology of the conceptual metaphor NATION AS HOUSE will be presented in the following section.

*Ontology of* NATION AS HOUSE

Paul Chilton, in his monograph on the metaphors that guided international relations between the capitalist allies of the United States and the Communist bloc during the forty-five-year Cold War, extensively discusses the NATION AS HOUSE, the second metaphor which structures the public's understanding of nationhood.[16] America's everyday understanding of HOUSE is culture-specific, but its presumed cross-cultural central concept is a three-dimensional material container for habitation by people. Thus HOUSE, a higher-level metaphor, builds on the more foundational CONTAINER metaphor, with its center/periphery schema, interior/exterior schema, and bounding structures.[17] Again, in the ordinary U.S. frame of thinking, the house is a manufactured structure, which implies a builder, an architect, and design; materials such as bricks; structures such as roofs, doors, and windows. In U.S. society, it also presumes an owner. Some of the cultural elements presumed in this frame of understanding have already been mentioned. The (metaphorical) construction materials used are particular to the historically contingent perspective of the United States, including the existence and prerogatives of a private property owner.

These elements of the semantic source domain are used to conceptualize the NATION domain. Recall that the United States is not a family-sized dwelling, but a politically organized population of 275 million people.[18] By way of the HOUSE metaphor, the topology of the three-dimensional material abode becomes the frame of reference for the political entity called the United States, a habitation at least designed by the "founding fathers." The semantic mapping from HOUSE domain to NATION may be so obvious as to be self-evident and natural, but if so, then what is taken for granted must be made explicit and interrogated.

By way of an illustration of the cultural specificity of this metaphor, in the U.S. frame of reference, we refer to a single-family residence. This is not the case for other cultural settings. Chilton notes that Mikhail Gorbachev, the last Soviet Premier, proposed a new metaphor to replace the long-standing and restrictive Iron Curtain metaphor as he sought to find a mutually acceptable conceptualization for international relations after 1989. Gorbachev spoke of a "Common European House," using the term *dom.*[19] Gorbachev's metaphor was misunderstood by President George Bush. Bush and other Westerners visualized a single-family dwelling. *Dom* is the generic Russian word for house which has come to mean "apartment building." Thus there was a slippage in translation since the U.S. house is taken to be occupied by a single family, not several. To put it graphically, George Bush could not imagine international relations to be so cozy that the Russians, Germans, and French would all live together at Bush's house. In fact, Gorbachev meant international relations should be viewed as distinct occupants living in separate quarters under a single roof, which is quite an advance over Winston Churchill's Iron Curtain metaphor, which dominated Cold War relations for forty-five years.

In the U.S. view, a house is a single-family home.[20] The architectural style of the American house is surprisingly indeterminate, allowing for any number of representations to be visualized. Whether Victorian, Colonial, or a split-level Ranch style, it is a single-family home. Other features include that the United States is a finite space, similar to a three-dimensional physical container. The owner is sovereign in his or her residence rather than one occupant among others and, within this dominion, enjoys paramount rights over others. Social claims are also made by way of this metaphor. One is that the United States constitutes itself, defining legitimate residency, namely citizenship. Consequently Gorbachev's idea of a multifamily *dom* also contravenes American single-owner sovereignty. Unlike residents of the *dom,* the sovereign American owner can dictate who will be a resident, who will be an outsider, how outsiders will be excluded, even under what circumstances unwanted insiders can be ejected. Significant political references across U.S. history have been made using this metaphor. Abraham Lincoln's "a house divided against itself shall not long stand" is only one example.

The use of the NATION AS HOUSE metaphor began in the fifteenth century and came into prominence in the seventeenth century, as the European monarchies gave way to modern nation-states. Before this, in the medieval world, authority had been established in terms of personal covenants; property was constructed in terms of the Commons and usufruct. Medieval sovereignty was a theocracy, based on a God-given vertical hierarchy from the supreme being to king to commoner to animal and earth. As this medieval model disintegrated, its vertical hierarchy was increasingly replaced with sets of horizontal political relationships, and chief among these was the notion of demarcated self-contained and self-owned political properties, namely nations.

For the past five hundred years European nations and their colony states have been metaphorized on the basis of the HOUSE. The NATION AS HOUSE metaphor encapsulated a particular kind of social relations, differentiating for the first time public, religious, and political spheres of life. The metaphor also reconfigured national territory into bounded areas. New or previously unimportant concepts became critical to the new conceptualization of political "reality." When the new view of NATION AS HOUSE took hold, distinctions that had been secondary, such as citizen versus alien, were redefined and became important, as the previously inconsequential internal and domestic versus external and international dichotomy became salient. The earlier medieval European laminations of partially overlapping geographic territories gave way to a new political order based on mutually exclusive dominions, and mutually exclusive citizenship status for individuals. Chilton details the operationalization of new notions of political space, which were reconceptualized in terms of the HOUSE, with its exclusive property rights and a more restrictive concept of political sovereignty. Chilton also notes that as this new conceptual metaphor of HOUSE took hold, a new political discourse was made coherent, and the incipient modern social order, which had been in flux, became conceptually fixed.

The metaphor NATION AS HOUSE, like NATION AS BODY, certainly predates Hobbes, but his legitimating discourse for the concept of nation made two factors commonly accepted parts of nationhood. The first is the nation as an autonomous territory with a specific boundary. Wars are regularly fought over lines drawn on a map. Second, nations as well as other associated notions such as citizenship are defined in mutually exclusive terms.

## NATION AS CITY, NATION AS CASTLE

Another associated metaphor is the extension NATION AS CITY, which has been used by master politicians with affirmative overtones:

> 1. I've spoken of **the shining city** all my political life, but I don't know if I ever quite communicated what I saw when I said it. But in my mind it was **a tall proud city** built on rocks stronger than oceans, wind-swept, God-blessed and teeming with people of all kinds living in harmony and peace . . . and if there had to be **city walls, the walls had doors and the doors were open** to anyone with the will and the heart to get here. That's how I saw it, and see it still. — Ronald Reagan, 1989 (October 7, 1994, B7)

It should be noted that former President Reagan was articulating what amounted to a pro-immigrant stance. In the Proposition 187 campaign, however, time and again immigrants were seen as threats to the NATION AS CITY, such as *floodwaters:*

2. The **influx** of illegal immigrants is also blamed for the country's "failure to win the war on drugs." (June 19, 1993, A3)

3. Unlike the immigration boom at the turn of the century, more than 90% of the latest **immigrant tide** comes from the Third World. (September 6, 1993, A1)

4. the **flood** of legal and illegal immigrants **streaming into** the country. (September 7, 1993, A1)

5. Wilson turned his fire on President Clinton for failing to **stem the flow of illegal immigrants** into California as he has into Florida and Texas. (September 14, 1994, A3)

6. Meanwhile, politicians vow to **seal** U.S. borders and halt the **flood** of newcomers. (October 3, 1993, E1)

The NATION AS HOUSE is quite readily extended to NATION AS CASTLE, with all the entailments of a defensive fortress:

7. There are extremists—those who would build an **alligator-filled moat,** and those who would **swing the door open.** (July 5, 1992, A3)

The advocates of Proposition 187 frequently invoked associations of the metaphor NATION AS CASTLE, in particular, a (metaphoric) threat of war. Thus, the industrious and peaceable immigrants, by extension, are characterized as invading soldiers, as seen in Chapter 3. Here, the immigrant was habitually portrayed as a fighter, an aggressor, an enemy of good people, and a party to the conquest of California:

8. Californians who despair that we've lost control of the border, who regard illegal immigrants as job-taking, tax-wasting **invaders,** can be proud of the latest Border Patrol innovation. (July 5, 1992, A3)

9. immigrants who become **foot soldiers** in these criminal organizations (June 13, 1993, Magazine p. 12)

10. "We have an **invasion** going on and it has to stop," said a Bakersfield man. (August 13, 1993, A3)

11. "I support immigration, but I'm damned, I mean, tired of illegal aliens **overrunning** us." (October 10, 1994, B3)

12. Increasingly many see an **immigration apocalypse** born of neglect. (September 6, 1993, A1)

U.S. public discourse is not unique in this regard. Contrasting metaphors, OPEN DOOR EUROPE versus FORTRESS EUROPE, presently compete there to become the dominant metaphor in the post–Cold War period, as national governments maneuver to gain an advantage in the development of the European Union in the Maastrich Treaty negotiations. These negotiations will affect the lives of nearly two million so-called "third country nationals," that is to say, immigrants and their children.[21] In passing, *apocalypse* in excerpt 12, originally meaning "revelation," is defined as "all-out final war."

## NATION AS SHIP

Another variant of the HOUSE metaphor is the NATION AS SHIP metaphor.[22] Here the house, an immovable habitation, becomes a vessel. NATION AS SHIP has most of the pertinent semantic associations of NATION AS HOUSE, inasmuch as it is a three-dimensional material container for humans. Vehicles, furthermore, entail an additional conceptual metaphor and image-schemata, PATH. The ship transporting its human cargo has embarked on a voyage, with a starting point, direction, and goal. As discussed in Chapter 5, PATH is used to conceptualize many aspects of daily life, including the *passage* of time, the *course* of history, the *direction* of public policy, the *stages* of individual lives, and America's historical *mission*. Again, it deserves recognition that it is not necessary or natural to conceptualize time, or these other aspects of human experience, in terms of a path. Yet humans are quite casual about their near-total dependence on these world-structuring metaphoric associations. In the case of the last instance, mission, it follows that "the abstract concept 'purpose' is metaphorized as the goal element in the path schema."[23] The logic of the path schema characterizes individuals as goal-oriented, and so history, as well, is taken to have some final end. Finally, the SHIP on its voyage is also particularly subject to hazards along its way.

As used to conceptualize the NATION domain, SHIP, like HOUSE, metaphorizes U.S. polities and society. In contrast to HOUSE, the voyage of a SHIP builds into its automatic associations the nation's passage through time, it implies that the nation has a set of passengers, and it emphasizes the nation's vulnerability on its (metaphoric) cruise.[24] NATION AS SHIP entails the nation's population traveling toward a single shared destination and destiny. All ships can sink, which means the United States can become a *Titanic,* particularly if, as occurred with that ill-fated luxury liner, there are not enough lifeboats for its inhabitants/passengers.

In the context of the Proposition 187 campaign in particular, immigration was the ocean through which the nation as ship found itself sailing. The ship in the *Times* texts was always imperiled on rough seas. At times there was an interesting double view, with immigrants as the perilous ocean as well as passengers on the ship. In these examples the safety of lifeboats is lost when they become overloaded with illegal immigrants:

13. The crush of illegal immigrants in Los Angeles is like **overloading the lifeboats of a sinking ship.** (December 14, 1992, B1)

14. The challenge to affluent Ventura County voters and the officials they elect in future years will be to recognize that all residents "are in the same **boat** together." (October 15, 1995, B1)

15. The U.S. has a proud tradition of being a **lifeboat for the poor and dispossessed but if the lifeboat becomes overloaded, it will sink.** Strict enforcement of our immigration laws will prevent that from happening. (May 12, 1998, B6)

16. compared the **United States to a lifeboat that could only accommodate 10 people at one time.** . . . "If you **put 40 people on a lifeboat it will sink and no one will be saved.**" (October 28, 1994, B3)

The rough seas are caused by the immigrant waves and the economic storms that rock the nation. Recall that the IMMIGRATION AS DANGEROUS WATERS metaphor attributes the source of the danger to immigrants and implies that the native-born are threatened by their presence.

During the 1992–1994 campaign, advocates for the anti-immigrant Proposition 187 promoted their cause by making further use of the SHIP metaphor. They named their organization "SOS, Save Our State." SOS is the Morse code signal used as a distress signal for ships at sea. It conventionally is said to signal "Save Our Ship." Morse code of dots and dashes for these two letters are: s = • • • ; o = - - - . This call for help was originally chosen because of the ease of signaling the sequence • • • - - - • • • , and not because of any reference to meaning. With each mention of the referendum, the mass media formulaically identified the sponsoring organization of the proposition, which invoked the SHIP metaphor associations. The SOS acronym was printed at least 425 times in the *Los Angeles Times* alone between June 1992 and the end of 1994, making it one of the most frequent single metaphoric expressions for political entities of the 1990s.

## Ecology and Xenophobia

The entailments of SHIP as a self-contained vessel carrying a population bound together toward some shared destination and destiny are also used by environmentalists to describe ecology, with the ECOSYSTEM AS SHIP metaphor. Perhaps it was inevitable that growing preoccupation with the living planet made contact with the political discourse of immigration. Note the following excerpt:

> 17. To participants in such [anti-immigrant public] sessions, California's growing ethnic and racial diversity—celebrated by many as a source of strength—is more of a call to arms. For FAIR [Federation for American Immigration Reform] strategists, who are enthusiastic proponents of assimilation, diversity is a suspect notion. "I think people are mistaken in taking a rosy view of multiculturalism," said Garrett Hardin, a FAIR board member and noted ecologist. "If they want to know the ultimate result of multiculturalism, look at Yugøslavia. The more we encourage multiculturalism, the more we encourage conflict and social **chaos**. It leads to **loss of freedom**." Hardin, a co-founder of Zero Population Growth, is an advocate of "**lifeboat ethics.**" Fearing that the nation may soon exceed its "**carrying capacity**" (a term borrowed from fish and game management), Hardin calls famine relief counterproductive and backs incentives for sterilization. Some consider him a genius, but others call his views reprehensible. "**In the long haul**," said Hardin, a professor emeritus at UC Santa Barbara, "every nation . . . must take responsibility for taking care of **its own people**." (November 24, 1993, A1)

In this metaphor-rich passage, Hardin makes a dramatic (metaphoric) call to patriotic arms in defense of the imperiled Anglo-American ship of state. His images of increasing social chaos, and the end of civilization, involve the very same life-raft associations that are used in the SHIP OF STATE metaphor, namely, that the United States is a *lifeboat* with a *carrying capacity* which is strained to the limit not only by immigration of non-Whites, but by multiculturalism, which is to say, the purported decline of Anglo-American cultural hegemony. Although Hardin's reference to the cultural paradigm of multiculturalism may well be irrelevant to the overpopulation threat that he warns about as an expert on human ecology, it is congruent with NATION AS HOUSE. His invocation of the metaphor underscores the anxiety he senses as U.S. society becomes more tolerant of its cultural diversity.

The social implications brought out with the NATION AS SHIP metaphor include, unsurprisingly, that immigration is a danger that threatens the whole country, since as passengers bound together on a voyage in the open sea, Americans share the same fate, particularly if their "ship" sinks. An assumption that is part of the common frame of reference within the SHIP domain is that the ship disembarks with a full or complete complement of passengers and does not take on others in midvoyage, except for an occa-sional castaway. This understanding is altogether inappropriate in the con-text of a nation which is, as Handlin observed, composed almost entirely of immigrants and their children.

## Alien Nation

Peter Brimelow, a conservative business writer, in his best-selling 1995 book *Alien Nation: Common Sense about America's Immigration Disaster,* used these metaphors in a powerful manner, characteristically at the expense of those whom Brimelow perceives to be *alien:*

> 18. The 1965 Immigration Act did not open **the immigration flood-gates: it opened the immigration scuttles—the influx is very substan-tial,** but **it spurts lopsidedly** from a remarkably small number of coun-tries, just as when some of the **scuttles** are opened in one side of a ship. Which is why **the United States is now developing an ethnic list—and may eventually capsize.** (B 18)[25]

In excerpt 18 Brimelow crafts an image which entirely passes over the story of the industrial and agribusiness recruitment for economic exploitation, while focusing on the peril of taking on an *ethnic list.*

It is bitingly ironic that Brimelow, an expatriate Englishman who himself is an immigrant to the United States, distinguishes two types of Americans. He separates people of color from "real Americans." For Brimelow, these Americans are invariably white. However, race is not the only requirement. To be American, Whites must also share his political views. Brimelow re-iterates his dual criteria at many points in his book:

> 19. As late as 1950, somewhere up to nine out of ten Americans looked like me. That is, they were of European stock. And in those days, they had another name for this thing dismissed so contemptuously as "the racial hegemony of white Americans." They called it "**America.**" (B 59)
>
> 20. America at the time of the Revolution was biracial, not multiracial, containing both whites and blacks. But the political nation—the collec-tivity that took political decisions—was wholly white. (B 18)
>
> 21. When the immigrants' absolute numbers in these localities pass a cer-tain point, their communities achieve a critical mass. Their alien languages and cultures become, at least for a while, self-sustaining. And the natives start asking themselves: "Are we still living in **America?**" (B 37)

22. Immigration policy is quite literally driving a wedge between the **American nation,** as it had evolved by 1965, and its future. (B 46)

23. Regardless of whether the immigrant wedge being driven into the U.S. will be a boost or a burden—will it be **American**? (B 56)

24. **The American nation of 1965** is going to have to share its future, and its land, with a very large number of people who, as of that year, were complete strangers. Foreigners. Aliens. (B 48)

25. And in the beginning, the American nation was white. That sounds shocking because blacks were almost a fifth (19.3%) of the total population within the borders of the original Thirteen Colonies. But almost all these blacks were slaves. They had no say in public affairs. They were excluded from what I have called the political nation—aka "the racial hegemony of white Americans" . . . "**America**." (B 66–67)

26. [When Brimelow discussed his thesis] on talk radio all round the country . . . it was not at all unusual to get 100 percent supportive calls—from **real Americans.** (B 280)

27. Immigration enthusiasts—a distinct American subspecies—like to say: "We need immigrants to do the dirty work that **Americans** won't do." (B 8)

By his definition, U.S. citizens who may be sympathetic to some of his political views, such as Linda Chavez or Thomas Sowell, cannot be "American" because of their race. However, as a white immigrant who certainly believes what he believes, Brimelow epitomizes the "real American." Furthermore, in light of the discussion about animal metaphors, it may be clear in excerpt 27 that Brimelow scornfully positions individuals sympathetic to the immigrants' plight at a lower point on his scale of humanity, with the term *subspecies.*

Brimelow's brio is insolent and consummate, and his message was effective in winning over commentators from a range of political persuasions to his point of view. As the book jacket of *Alien Nation* advertises, his enthusiasts include former Senator Eugene McCarthy, who has significant liberal credentials. McCarthy echoes Brimelow's own brash allusions as he glowingly compares Brimelow, who "provides us with much common sense on declaring our independence from the mounting migration pressures coming to bear on our nation," to Thomas Paine.[26] McCarthy's linkage of war and hydraulic metaphors, by the way, affirms the hypothesis of Chapter 3.

While Brimelow thinks that the United States should put an end to immigration, except for white people who share his values, he is able to present his reactionary views in powerful ways to a wide audience by means of straightforward prose and productive metaphors of NATION which are congruent with the American worldview. They resonate with common sense, which is to say, the commonly held nativist values of U.S. society.

Birds of a feather. Former member of the American Nazi Party and the Ku Klux Klan, David Duke restated Brimelow's thesis with much less polish at a pro–Proposition 209 campaign rally in Los Angeles: "I don't want California to look like Mexico. I don't want to have their pollution. I don't want the corruption. I don't want their disease. I don't want their superstition. I don't want us to look like that country. If we continue this alien invasion, we will be like Mexico." At that rally Duke shared Brimelow's ethnocentric view of U.S. history: "The founding elements of this country, the Constitution, the Declaration of Independence, the basis of this nation was created primarily by white Europeans. And we should not be second-class citizens in our own country. We should not face discrimination in the nation the fabric of which we created. I will stand up for equal rights for all in America, including white people in our society."[27]

## Aged but Powerful

The effective use of BODY and HOUSE metaphors to arouse nativist feelings in the electorate indicates the strength of these ancient metaphors. The absence of alternatives which construct a congruent worldview makes refuting the views futile. In a study focused on these metaphors for nation, Chilton studied key documents and policy-setting speeches concerning international relations during the Cold War, 1946–1989, in particular documents which defined NATO's intended policy to "contain" the Soviet empire. One of Chilton's key findings is that even when the actions by Allied and Soviet Bloc political and military operatives rendered the HOUSE and BODY notions of nation "increasingly irrelevant," these dominant metaphors continued to be used. This confirms Donald Schön's dictum that conceptual conflicts are "immune to resolution by appeal to the facts. . . . New facts have a way of being either reabsorbed or disregarded by those who see problematic situations under conflicting frames."[28] In the absence of a viable alternative, the inertia of these productive metaphors is very hard to overcome, irrespective of the conceptual misfit or the societal stakes. In the present century, industrial and financial corporations no longer even bother to resemble national entities, international travel is accessible to many more people, and increasing population and economic pressures make it imperative for families to seek work far from home. The principal direction of migration of the last five hundred years, during which time European colonial powers invaded other lands, has reversed itself. Now colonized populations are moving to the colonizer's territories and creating ever more multicultural nations. The hoary metaphors of NATION AS BODY and NATION AS HOUSE, which first conceptualized an autonomous and homogeneous body politic, have become far less capable of representing polities which are less self-contained, more diverse, and far more interdependent. Nevertheless, the NATION AS BODY and NATION AS HOUSE metaphors constitute 98 percent of all nation metaphors in the contemporary public discourse database.

## Summary of BODY and HOUSE Metaphors

The medieval NATION AS BODY came into use to characterize an emerging European nationhood at a time when the population was overwhelmingly a homogeneous rural peasantry and communication was dependent on animal transportation. In the late fifteenth century, traveling twenty-five miles a day for any length of time constituted an adventure. Visiting another land or taking to the open sea for the great majority of Europeans involved a religious or martial quest. The use of the human body as metaphoric sources for U.S. society is increasingly challenged by accelerating global transportation, instant worldwide televisual communication, broadening cross-national regional integration, and a more interdependent global economy. Similarly, public discourse that employs NATION AS HOUSE is steadily becoming more obsolete, since the central concept for the nation—the bounded finite space of a nuclear family—becomes increasingly inadequate in the daily experience of U.S. residents. "Overlapping systems (economic, legal, political, communicational, cultural), regional integration as well as fragmentation of nation states, have produced diverse and multiple experiences of identity and allegiance, which can no longer be captured by means of images whose inherent logic implies unity, homogeneity and exclusiveness."[29]

Nevertheless, the commonly used NATION AS HOUSE frame of reference remains very strong in the United States. Public discourse does not reflect the ideas of intellectuals who describe the recurrent extranational experiences or increasingly transnational lives of today's immigrants. This rift will expand in the coming century since the U.S. electorate is by and large a staid, mortgage-holding middle class who are shielded from the worst of the shrinking world system and who experience the lifestyles of the transnational rich and famous only vicariously, on television. Dogged defense of exclusive rights (not merely privileges) of property, and the prerogative of nations, with dichotomies of citizen/alien and national/foreign, will arise as the concept of national sovereignty is more frequently contested in the public sphere, as it is now interrogated in the academic sphere. Except for idealistic individual claims to global citizenship, there is no alternative public discourse metaphor to contest the enfeebled NATION AS HOUSE.

The predominance of HOUSE and BODY metaphors is nearly categorical. As noted throughout this book, these metaphors serve as overarching "umbrella" metaphors, providing the semantic source domains for a wide range of political metaphorization. By way of illustration, IMMIGRANT AS INVADER and RACISM AS DISEASE are both affiliated with these umbrella metaphors for the nation. In seventy-four months of sampled public discourse, from May 1992 to June 1998, BODY and HOUSE metaphors and their retinue appeared over 1,400 times, or about 98 percent of all nation metaphors. Only POLITICS AS WAR appeared across the entire database with greater frequency than nation metaphors. A single NATION alternate appears with any frequency. That is *social fabric,* which appeared in the database in slightly more than 1 percent of the nation metaphors. It was used to refer to social cohesion more often than to metaphorize NATION per se.

To speak nothing of the sovereignty claims of American Indians, and regardless of Handlin's view, Latinos have experienced the United States in ways quite unlike the European. This difference in viewpoint has still not been registered by educators of U.S. schoolchildren. The European immigrant made a premeditated ocean-crossing break, which broke associations with the home country in all but possibly symbolic ways. In contrast, Chicanas/os have unbroken cultural continuity with Mexico, which has become stronger rather than weaker in the twentieth century. Handlin called the European immigrant *The Uprooted.* Even more appropriately, European immigrants were airborne seeds setting down in a new environment without natural predators. In contrast, the Latino did not exist in Europe. The Latino is a hybrid which took root on this continent with the contact of civilizations. To continue the botanical metaphor, the Chicano's relationship to Mexican culture is a grass species that propagates from rootstock by runners. Again, with due deference to the prerogatives of American Indians, the so-called deserts of the great Southwest have been a Latino grassland for hundreds of years. In the future it will expand and consolidate, since the Mexican/Chicano was never uprooted. This culture flows back and forth across an increasingly obsolete political border. The U.S. notion of citizen, which has changed sporadically since its first configuration in 1776, will have to deal with this distinctive historical experience in the new century, as will be developed in the following section.

For all the problems created with the use of archaic metaphors of nation, these conceptual difficulties would be much less troublesome for Latinos if they had not been coupled to a racial hierarchy which fully incorporates some people into the body politic while it leaves other citizens out. Sanitized expressions of this still-operative hierarchy were noted in the discourse of the political campaigns of Propositions 187, 209, and 227. The dehumanizing semantic associations of racial metaphors continue to transfigure people of color into fear-inspiring floods and dangerous tides, less-than-human beasts, or commodities to exploit. It is to further consequences of racist metaphors for the notion of citizen that we next turn.

## Section 3: Citizen versus Denizen

The ontology of IMMIGRANT AS ANIMAL can be stated concisely: Immigrants correspond to citizens as animals correspond to humans. Some implications of this conceptual metaphor were drawn out in Chapter 3. Latino immigrants continue to be dehumanized in contemporary discourse, as they have been in U.S. public discourse since the 1860s. Latinos, whether recent immigrants born in Meoqui, Chihuahua, or members of families whose ties to the Southwest predate the U.S. republic, have experienced the negative effects of racialization. This racist discourse of Anglo-Americans was already well-developed by the 1830s, and it was increasing in intensity at the time of the conquest of the northern Mexican territories, over 150 years ago.[30] As the oppression developed, so, too, did the struggle Latinos waged against it.[31]

Within the hierarchy created by this oppression, which was reinforced by the metaphor IMMIGRANT AS ANIMAL, all Latinos were debased by the Anglo-American scale of humanity, which justified inequity and discrimination against them. To the complacent, this indictment might seem to be only a historical footnote, but unfortunately the discourse about Latinos of the 1990s makes it clear that the roots of the nineteenth-century discourse of Anglo-American racism have not been extracted. For those who doubt, this history must be retold.

Mexican citizens who lived in what became the U.S. Southwest in 1848 had been pledged continuance of their civil and property rights, under the provisions of the Treaty of Guadalupe Hidalgo at the cessation of the U.S.

War of Aggression against Mexico. These rights were far more progressive, particularly for slaves and native peoples, than the rights of U.S. citizens. Slavery in Mexico had been outlawed, and Indians were considered full citizens under Mexican law. Anglo-Americans rejected these statutes of a defeated foe. To the century's end, Anglo-Americans elaborated the self-serving concept of Manifest Destiny to deny these rights to the long-time residents of the Southwest, dispossessing Indians and Mexicans of their properties and prerogatives as U.S. citizens. In the hierarchizing discourse of the time, Indians were less than human, and Mexicans were a miscegenation—the issue of an inferior Mediterranean race and Indians. Consequently, neither could possess the same rights as white Americans. Horsman quotes one Anglo-American observer: "There are no people on the continent of America, whether civilized or not, . . . more miserable in condition or despicable in morals than the mongrel race inhabiting New Mexico."[32]

Once the land was theirs, Anglo-Americans sought labor to build their society. U.S. industry, mining, and agribusiness spent millions of dollars to recruit highly productive Mexicans from the interior of Mexico to work. This vigorous recruitment established the sources and direction of the stream of people moving to the United States from the south. The patterns of Mexican immigration set down at that time only increased in volume and extent across the century. With Mexican immigration, U.S. capitalism secured an optimal labor reserve; it proved to be more tractable than any other. The full price of this business arrangement, however, would only become apparent toward the end of the twentieth century. The Mexican population would become impossible to dismiss.

At the beginning of the last century another die was cast: Anglo-Americans considered the Mexican to be their inferior. By the 1920s, Manifest Destiny had been upgraded to a scientific concept, biological determinism, with an accompanying reworking of the racializing discourse that now "explained" why Anglo-Americans were elevated above Mexicans and other people of color. Oscar Handlin cites Madison Grant, a highly regarded anthropologist of the 1920s, who stated that the "new immigration contained a large and increasing number of the weak, the broken, and the mentally crippled of all races drawn from the lowest stratum of the Mediterranean basin. . . . The whole tone of American life, social, moral, and political, has been lowered and vulgarized by . . . human flotsam."[33]

At midcentury, the U.S. fought a war against avowed racists, the Nazis, declared itself the home of the free and the last bastion of democracy. However, at that time the nation did not confront its own racial contradictions. At home, America denied equality to all its citizens, most hypocritically to its uniformed citizens of color.[34] Once again, these disreputable actions were based on the conventional public discourse about Mexicans and other people of color, which placed them at the lower end of the human scale. It was only in the 1960s, with the Civil Rights Movement, that the cancer of the American nation, white racism, was finally acknowledged. Although Lyndon Johnson's penstroke outlawed statutory racism, it did not destroy the social affliction, since institutional racism was systemic, and racializing discourse had not been repealed. Nor did the Civil Rights Act alleviate the chronic pain of white racism that minority communities suffered, and continue to suffer. So, the struggle against white racism has had to carry on.

For example, from the mid-1960s to his death in 1993, César Chávez made the dignity of farmworkers, nonwhite and predominantly Mexican workers who were often treated as a subhuman labor pool, the centerpiece of his great cause:

> There have been too many accidents in the fields, on trucks, under machines, in buses. So many accidents involving farm workers. People ask if they are deliberate. They are deliberate in the sense that they are the result of **a farm labor system that treats workers like agricultural implements and not human beings.** These accidents happen because employers and labor contractors treat us as if we were not important human beings.[35]

In addition to farmworkers, garment, domestic, hospital, hotel, office, and other urban service workers, the majority of whom are Latinos and other people of color, can speak from the same perspective today. Consequently, in his declaration of intent, the *Plan de Delano,* Chávez delineated the social cause that he led and the United Farm Workers' approach to syndicalization. The UFW mission continues to emphasize the human dignity inherent in each farmworker in the face of the dehumanizing actions and attitudes of U.S. agribusiness:

> This is the beginning of a social movement in fact and not in pronouncements. **We seek our basic, God-given rights as human beings.** Because we have suffered, and are not afraid to suffer in order to survive, we are ready to give up everything—even our lives—in our struggles for social justice.[36]

The public discourse that dehumanizes immigrants, then, is not merely rhetorical embellishments, but a lived reality for many Latinos, and an ethical challenge for the remainder of Latinos in this society. At base is the supremacy of property rights over human rights in this society, a principle that has been contested across the centuries, as illustrated in quotes from figures ranging from Frederick Douglass (in Chapter 3) to Chávez. Rather than reiterating the ontology of IMMIGRANT AS ANIMAL elaborated in Chapter 3, the following section will take up the commonplace understanding of what characterizes a citizen, in light of the two dominant metaphors for nation.

*Citizenship*

Consider the term *naturalization,* in which a noncitizen becomes a citizen by statutory procedure. This legal concept is a very old NATION AS BODY term. It was adapted from medieval European "natural law," whereby a minion swears allegiance to a sovereign, in a manner which can only "naturally" be secured through birth.

Two indications of the cultural centrality of citizenship in modern nation-states, and the United States in particular, are the bureaucratic complexity and ritualized ceremony required to naturalize someone. Such is the character of this wholly contingent notion, which, with no small irony, is taken to be an "inalienable" element of the character of U.S. citizens. Thus, as a cell of a living organism, each citizen is integral to the political body. Outsiders are not integral to the function of the body and represent either threats to the well-being of the body politic or resources to be consumed. Lastly, in light of the IMMIGRANT AS ANIMAL metaphor, to be a U.S. citizen, in the eyes of those who possess this civic "birthright," is to be fully vested in humanity, while not being a citizen means not being fully human.

While the meaning of, and eligibility requirements for, U.S. citizenship are taken as known, no single definition has persisted across the centuries. U.S. citizenship is as historically contingent as any other social concept. Moreover, while political discussions often address the legal status of workers without proper papers, the U.S. public often fails to appreciate that "real Americans" were a much more circumscribed group in the recent past.[37] In the beginning, U.S. citizenship, a new civic identity, was crafted by the wealthy framers of the North American Revolution in order to attract support for the uprising from less privileged folk. Yet even as citizenship was promoted as a badge that would allow its bearers to participate in the first full-scale test in self-governance among equals, not just anyone could wear it. For one, the covenant was restricted to a chosen people; and second:

> most persons not so designated and equipped by God and nature might not be eligible for full American citizenship. In 1790 Congress proclaimed that only whites could be naturalized. Blacks could legally be ruled as slaves, Indians as conquered subjects. Women were assigned the citizenship of their fathers or husbands. Only white men could exercise political power. Most of the domestic population was ineligible, on grounds of race, ethnicity, or gender, for the full rights and powers American citizenship conferred. That would remain explicitly true until women received the vote 130 years later, and it would remain functionally true until the successes of the civil rights and women's movements in the 1960s. For some Americans, this legal structuring of American citizenship represents efforts to achieve the homogeneity among citizens successful republics allegedly required. But for many, these were arrangements ordained by God, written into human natural capacities, and affirmed both by scientific evidence and historical experience.[38]

While many people hold the first view of citizen, others maintain unconsciously that citizenship really is a celestial consecration bestowed on special individuals. The definition of citizenship has changed over time due to political battles. If a trend can be discerned, the oligarchic restrictions on American citizenship have been eased, to include a larger portion of the actual inhabitants of the country. This direction is certainly reversible. While U.S. citizenship has, over time, become more inclusive of the nation's inhabitants, recently there have been regular calls to restrict it.[39]

This long-term trend toward greater inclusiveness and fewer restrictions is certainly not a tendency limited to the United States. In England, T. H. Marshall's classic history of Anglo-Saxon citizenship describes its expansion from the limited and subordinate legal status of British subjects in the eighteenth century, to political citizenship (franchise and working-class political equity) in the nineteenth century, and still further to social rights (income redistribution in terms of welfare) in the twentieth century.[40] Thus, British citizenship has also become more liberal and inclusive over these three centuries. Nevertheless, the older, countervailing sensibility holds that to be a real citizen is more than just a matter of one's place of birth. In fact, Marshall believed that the British working class were not really citizens. This was not a matter of birthplace or race; Marshall was referring to a predominantly white working class who were born on the British Isles. Rather, he believed that they lacked the education and economic resources to truly partake of the common British culture, and consequently were not truly citizens. Marshall believed that citizenship consisted in "communal possession and heritage," a "shared identity." What would Marshall say about Britain at the turn of the twenty-first century, much less the United States, each with its far less homogenized populace and its millions of undocumented residents and their children? His fellow countryman, Peter Brimelow, would not hesitate: "At the end of the twentieth century, the central issue in American politics is what might be described as 'The National Question.'" He framed his query in binary terms:

> Can the American nation-state, the political expression of that nation, survive? (B 232)

Perhaps it is not a surprise that Brimelow's answer to his own question is "yes." His pithy solution, however, may not be palatable to the majority of citizens.

> The trick the Americans face now is to be an empire in fact, while remaining a democratic republic in spirit. (B 267)

Thus, Brimelow would diminish the scope of citizenship as he explicitly calls for a U.S. empire. Brimelow's repugnant views were answered by Zbigniew Brzezinski, who said a country "can be an empire or a democracy, but it cannot be both."[41] Brzezinski was referring to Russia, but his admonition applies perfectly to this country. The notion of citizenship involves not only the ethical, but the political, integrity of the country.

Other nations are now dealing with the consequences of their colonizing histories. With an eye on the formation of the European Union, Ulrich Preuß provides an illuminating review of the current European thinking on citizenship that suits the U.S. setting very well. Preuß also argues that the inconsistencies present in the early-twenty-first-century view of nation-state citizenship derive from its medieval city-state origins. The original concept of citizenship is based on the classical republic, a polity of two classes, a small group of equals who rule over the larger population. Citizens make up the select first group; in the fourteenth century they were the "men of the city." At this time the citizens were a privileged paternalistic group who governed the populace living in the city-state. The citizen was distinguished from the majority of people who merely lived in the city; the masses were the city's denizens. The word *denizen* incorporates the French preposition *dedans,* which means "in," and can be compared to *citizen,* literally "of the city." This medieval opposition—citizen versus denizen—still fits with the metaphors conceptualizing nation and race in contemporary American public discourse.

With the changes in the nation-state produced by the Enlightenment and by technological advances, the oligarchic aspects of restricted and privileged citizenship have become increasingly outmoded. Modern states are not alliances of a handful of ruling families who dominate a populace of thousands. They are hundreds of millions of individuals with minimal social ties living within immense geopolitical areas. Without tightly maintained cultural control or sociopolitical alliances, the heterogenizing social tendencies, accelerating technological changes, and economic globalization have rendered obsolete the so-called national culture. Even in 1960 Marshall did not believe that British common culture was widely shared, at a time before great numbers of former colonial subjects moved to England. The common culture that Marshall maintained was a critical feature of citizenship is another term for the set of shared social values, that is to say, the cultural hegemony. Greater preoccupation with the integrity of nations' borders and over the so-called threat of multiculturalism are two responses to the weakening utility of the medieval notion of nation. Consequently, immigration is perceived to be the greatest threat to the nation-state. Brimelow, for his part, provides an unsweetened elixir for a return to better times:

> One right that Americans certainly have is the right to insist that immigrants, whatever their race, become Americans. The full force of public policy should be placed behind another "Americanization" campaign, modeled on that during the last Great Wave of Immigration. All diversion of public funds to promote "diversity," "multiculturalism" and foreign-language retention must be struck down as subversive of this American ideal. . . . The English-language requirement for citizenship should be enforced and the various recent exceptions, such as for spouses and the elderly, abolished—they were symbolic gestures anyway, and now the symbols are needed elsewhere. There must be a concerted legislative attack on bilingual manifestations, beginning with the U.S. Department of Education's promotion of "bilingual" education. . . . A Constitutional amendment making English the official language of the United States could be a decisive step. . . .
>
> The ultimate issue is not whether foreigners show up in the United

States but when they are admitted to the national community and obtain full political rights and privileges. In an era of mass movement, the fact that the children of even illegal immigrants are automatically U.S. citizens is plainly outdated. It must be ended, by amending the Constitution if necessary. . . .

Again, discouraging foreign residents' access to the political community might seem rather grim. But actually it could relax the tension. Many foreign residents in the United States are perfectly happy with their half-and-half status. (B 264–267)

Brimelow's prescription, of course, would eliminate the supposed Latino and immigrant threat to the Anglo-American cultural predominance. Brimelow would reinstate the eighteenth-century limited legal status for most, allocating full citizenship to a select subset. The three California referenda of the 1990s can be seen as political expressions of this impulse. A similar view is maintained by John Fonte, visiting scholar at the American Enterprise Institute, who gave the following testimony to the U.S. Senate Subcommittee on Immigration in 1997:

Citizenship means full membership in the American republic. The goal of the naturalization process that grants citizenship to U.S. immigrants should therefore be Americanization, stated clearly without apology or embarrassment. . . . Americanization means adopting American civic values and the American heritage as one's own. It means thinking of American history as "our" history, not "their" history. . . . There's no reason today's new arrivals can't learn then adopt America's heritage, and *patriotic assimilation* demands it.[42]

Fonte, for his part, advocates that immigrants (and all U.S. citizens) not only study, but commit to, a chauvinistic version of U.S. history. For him, real citizenship means political and cultural allegiance to a particular set of values. The place of immigrants, as well as the citizenship of Latinos and other non-European minority populations, would be diminished. As Brimelow stated, Latinos would be "perfectly happy with their half-and-half status" as they remained denizens, rather than citizens fully vested in their own country.

The question arises why the medieval postulates for citizenship must be maintained in the twenty-first century. Iris Marion Young contests the premise of a common culture. In its place, she proposes that citizenship be based on human rights, rather than on property rights. Young seeks a formulation that transcends group differences, because the common culture postulate is fundamentally unjust, as it oppresses groups who do not share it.

> In a society where some groups are privileged while others are oppressed, insisting that as citizens persons should leave behind their particular affiliations and experiences to adopt a general point of view serves only to reinforce the privileged; for the perspective and interests of the privileged will tend to dominate this unified public, marginalizing or silencing those of other groups.[43]

A human-rights-based definition of citizenship concurs with the calls for equity long made by minority spokespeople across the political spectrum from Malcolm X to Martin Luther King Jr. and César Chávez. The criticisms raised against this notion of citizenship include the observation that citizenship will no longer be what it has previously meant. This criticism is granted. This is precisely Young's objective. Second, Nathan Glazer submits that without a common culture, any hope of fraternity in the nation will be lost.[44] In response, the vision of such a national fraternity is dystopian, since it is inherently exclusionary. Rather than demanding shared identity among nearly 300 million individuals, another often-mentioned basis of nationality might be promoted. As Skrentny affirms: "There are some very general *moral* rules to American politics, rules common to all polities of the modern West: Modern politics, ultimately, is about the achievement of justice and progress."[45] Possibly, then, a more realistic source for unity for the pluralistic U.S. nation might be, not an illusory cultural identity, but rather shared social justice objectives concerning common civil practice, for as John Rawls states:

> Although a well-ordered society is divided and pluralistic . . . public agreement on questions of political and social justice supports ties of civic friendship and secures the bonds of association.[46]

## Section 4: Semantic Coherence and Congruence

The criterion for descriptive adequacy of metaphor studies based on analytic philosophic principles is the rigorous and precise mapping of metaphorical meaning. Such studies, in contrast to the present type of study, focus their attention on establishing the most accurate reproduction of logical relations expressed by a single metaphor in a particular sentence, and as discussed in Chapter 2, assume crucially that metaphoric relations are derived from a corresponding literal sentence.

In contrast, the objective of the present study is not the study of logical relations of a single metaphor in a single sentence. I will use two criteria for evaluating the scientific adequacy of studies of metaphor like the present one, which follows the cognitive linguistic analytic research tradition. One, is (horizontal) conceptual coherence across all textual occurrences of a single metaphor, while the second can be described as (vertical) cross-metaphor congruence. Recall, respectively, Figures 2.1 and 2.2.

First, the cognitive study of metaphor looks for an adequate description of a single metaphor (linking two semantic domains) which is expressed in thousands of different instances via hundreds of different collocations. For example, an ontological mapping was proposed to label closely related text expressions of a metaphor for RACISM (exemplified in King's speech, which characterized racism as an *unchecked cancer;* a *hate-filled* and yet *curable malignancy; the ravaging American disease* which *scars the soul* of both racist and victim, and so on). In this example, RACISM AS CANCER is proposed to be the most coherent label for the ontological mapping linking the source semantic domain, described as CANCER (not a more general notion of DISEASE or ILL-HEALTH), to the target semantic domain, RACISM (rather than HATRED or ANTIPATHY). Horizontal semantic coherence of this single metaphoric mapping is one measure of the quality of the present analysis. The coherence criterion alone is insufficient, since it is always possible to propose another linkage which comprises all and only the full range of individual instances of the metaphor.

The second criterion for descriptive adequacy of this metaphor analysis is congruence, namely, a faithful portrayal of the web of semantic relations across vertically related metaphors. As indicated in Chapter 2, a metaphor is uninterpretable in isolation. Since metaphors are links between semantic domains, to make sense of a single text metaphor requires embodied knowledge, and a network of semantic links to other metaphors. Coherence is the horizontal compatibility of different metaphors across one stratum of semantic relations. Congruence is vertical compatibility, with foundational metaphors at lower levels of semantic relations, as well as with higher-order metaphors.

A metaphor, again, is an ontological mapping of one semantic domain to another domain, which convokes entailments, presuppositions, and other semantic associations. For any metaphor to be understood, it has to be semantically congruent both with lower-level image-schema and foundational metaphors, which are fundamentally grounded in experience, and with higher-level, culturally and historically contingent metaphors.

Higher-level metaphors are interlinked; with constant use their semantic associations become habitual. This conventionalization among the web of higher-level metaphors provides stability, constancy, and routine to our understanding of daily experiences, personal interactions, events, institutional relations, and societal perspectives. All productive metaphors weave together, so to speak, in an undiminished entirety which is conceptually plausible. This is the whole cloth of a congruent worldview.

Plausible, however, does not mean necessary or natural. For example, from daily evidence it can plausibly be concluded that the sun revolves around the Earth. Conventional thinking and political convenience lead to naturalization, in Fairclough's sense of the term. The inertia of routine and unthinking recitation of the conventional conceptualization of social relations makes changing a conventional higher-level metaphor quite a challenge. To invoke another image to describe congruence of meaning, the higher-level metaphors constitute a semantic constellation. While there is near universal experiential cohesion at the lowest levels of metaphors, making them exceedingly resistant to reinterpretation, at the higher levels of metaphor there is greater possibility of new construals of the social world. This may be elucidated in terms of our night sky. The panoply of stars is conventionally recognized in timeworn traditional constellations of concepts. However, if we work at it, the sky can be seen in new celestial arrangements.

The noted paleoastronomer Anthony F. Aveni notes the folly of limiting one's perception of constellations. "While some celestial groupings (e.g., Orion's Belt and the Pleiades) might be universal, too often we force our own heavenly dippers and zodiacal signs upon a culture."[47] For example, the Aztec constellations on the Florentine Codex indicate that the authors of the codex, the forebears of the present-day Nahua, looked upon a strikingly different cosmos than Europeans do. In the region of the Gemini configuration, Nahua speakers pointed to Citlaltlachtli, "the Ballcourt." In lieu of the Little Dipper, they saw part of Xonecuilli, "the Serpent's Tail" constellation, while for most of what English speakers call Orion's Belt, the Aztecs referred to Mamalhuaztli, "Fire Drill," namely, the wooden spindle that is whirled with a bow to start a fire by friction. Indeed, the one stellar constellation that was shared by the ancient Aztecs and Europeans demonstrates how contingent the links are between distinct denotative fields, whether the names of constellations to star groupings, or target semantic domains to source domains for social metaphors. The brightest grouping of stars in the northern hemisphere is called the Pleiades, or Seven Sisters, by Europeans. Ancient

Nahua speakers referred to this cluster of stars as Tianquiztli, "the Market-place."[48] Aveni's admonition against a single proper way of seeing holds for any presumption of uniqueness or naturalness of ideas.

## Section 5: The Script for Latino Relations on the National Stage

In this book, Latinos and Latino political issues in contemporary American public discourse have been illustrated. A review of six recent years of metaphors framing the public's ideas about Latinos is semantically congruent, and very discouraging. The dominant metaphors for and about Latinos that have been discussed in this book (immigrant, education, language) are by and large negative. Likewise, the preponderance of metaphors not described here (such as those characterizing Latino youth, the Latino family, and the Latino community) are also derogatory. Moreover, in the dominant imagery noted in the database, Latinos, whether as part of the BODY or HOUSE, are metaphorized as less integral to the nation than Whites. After over 150 years, the nineteenth-century premises of Anglo-American racism continue to reinforce social inequity. To see how this conceptualization is affirmed in public discourse, we first can look at metaphor distribution. For in the public perception of Californians, immigrants, almost entirely Latinos, are metaphorized in a deprecatory way in over 90 percent of the cases: for example, DISEASE, WEEDS, and ANIMALS. In fact, there was only one affirmative metaphor, IMMIGRANT AS ANGEL, in the entire *Times* database. This is a biblical allusion and was used by the clergy; most frequently cited was then-Archbishop Roger Mahony of Los Angeles. The Old Testament verse "Be not forgetful to entertain strangers, for thereby some have entertained angels unaware" (Hebrews 13:1) was proffered by religious leaders to remind their congregations of the immigrants' humanity. The metaphor and its associations were summarily rejected as an unacceptable linkage of Sunday morality to a workday issue.[49]

The metaphors to conceptualize Latinos, as found in contemporary public discourse, weave a congruent web of marginalization and aspersion. I will employ dramaturgy (definitions, stage directions, and roles and identity) to describe the discourse practice that enacts and affirms the social order. In Erving Goffman's dramaturgical model, the social actor or group of actors perform all the time in real time. People as social actors are motivated by the desire to fit in socially and to avoid public stigma and possible embarrassment. To maintain the ritual order of everyday acts, actors hold to well-drawn scripts, in this case, a discursive public script which determines the place of Latinos on the national stage, situating Latinos vis-à-vis other citizens. The script is written in accordance with the conceptual metaphors uncovered through the length of the book, which define, sustain, and legitimate the relationships of Latinos to the nation.

**Metaphoric Definitions** fix the limits of social identities:

1. Immigrants possess less human value than citizens.
2. Citizen is defined, not in legal terms, but culturally, as follows:
   (a) be a monolingual English speaker,
   (b) have an Anglo-American cultural orientation,
   (c) consent tacitly to the U.S. racial hierarchy.
3. Latinos are immigrants.

**Stage Directions** which are maintained in polite society to reinforce hegemonic illusions of U.S. equality:

1. Don't contest the identities defined by metaphors.
2. Avoid mention of the racial hierarchy.
3. Avoid mention of the foreignness of Latinos.
4. Avow the American meritocracy; avoid mention of structural inequity.

**The Cycle** legitimizes the stage directions by sustaining conventional metaphors:

1. Definitions fix the limits of what is real and what actions are appropriate.
2. Acting out stage directions reinforces the definitions.


Lakoff and Johnson recently have stated that morality is established in terms of "probably not more than two dozen basic metaphors . . . grounded in the nature of our bodies and social interaction."[50] The present empirically driven study of public discourse supports their observation. Beginning with definitions, the IMMIGRANT AS ANIMAL metaphor defines the status of immigrants in relation to citizens. As it demotes human rights and asserts civil privilege, it places immigrants below citizens in terms of what Lakoff and Johnson call a tacit moral order. This is deeply ingrained. Recall that

IMMIGRANT AS ANIMAL, the most abundant and antagonistic metaphor, was not registered by several social scientists who had focused their attention on the anti-immigrant political expression during the Proposition 187 period. The metaphor unjustly absolves U.S. citizens of responsibility for attitudes and actions against Latinos and immigrants, with the logic that nonhumans need not be accorded the same respect as human beings. The national morality is based on the NATION AS BODY metaphor. Lakoff and Johnson note that "immoral behavior is often seen as a contagion that can spread out of control."[51] Again, this was demonstrated with reference to immigration as a disease. Further, similar terms expressed the moral judgment on white racism by liberals in the 1960s, as well as by neoconservatives on affirmative action in the 1990s.

In this metaphor-based social definition, the citizen is a normal member of the nation, while Latinos along with immigrants are grouped apart. This might be difficult to believe for people unfamiliar with the California experience, but it was expressed at many points in the public discourse of the 1990s. Without a doubt, Governor Pete Wilson was the most potent agent articulating this view, especially when broadcasting thirty-second television advertisements during his reelection campaign:

28. The governor began airing a new commercial that tends to arouse the dark side of human nature and further polarize an inflammatory issue. . . . **"They keep coming,"** a narrator intones. "The federal government won't stop them at the border. . . . Gov. Pete Wilson sent the National Guard to help. . . ." The governor then says, in part, "I'm working to deny state services. . . . Enough is enough." It's not the text that is especially nasty, but the pictures and the tone. Played in dramatic black and white and accompanied by a rhythmic bass beat suitable for a horror film, the ad shows Latinos racing across the border at San Ysidro, dodging cars. Some might see it as an **invasion of brown hordes.** Campaign consultants use black and white film to evoke emotion and often to subliminally connote good and evil. The Wilson camp says its border footage originally was in color, then was changed into black and white. That's because the color was of poor quality, it says. (May 19, 1994, A3, wide-set ellipses in original, plus my own narrow ellipsis)

29. But the most disappointing and effective of the current political commercials now polluting the California airwaves is the work of Republican Gov. Pete Wilson. . . . He is running for reelection with the aid of scary black-and-white commercials that show **hordes of Mexican immigrants**

running across the border at San Ysidro, dodging cars as they **pour** into the United States. "**They keep coming**," a narrator's voice declares. . . . [The ad criticizes Wilson's opponent] for not doing enough to halt the "**brown tide**."[52]

30. Gov. Pete Wilson . . . declares that California is **awash under a brown tide**. "**Invaders**," he calls them. . . . Wilson seems to have read well the political mood on this issue, an anger that was captured best by an author of Proposition 187: "You are the posse," he told a gleeful rally in Orange County, "and SOS is the rope." (October 2, 1994, A3)

31. Starting in the early 1990s, Maharidge began studying the effects of what he calls the "browning" of California. He started watching how [white, upper-middle-class] communities dealt with the **influx** of different ethnic groups around the state, but particularly in parts of Los Angeles and in Dana Point, which he researched in depth. In fact, the book's jacket is a photograph of an upscale gated community in Dana Point juxtaposed with a latino grocery store whose opening a few years ago upset some residents there who viewed it as a **Third World incursion** into their seaside community. (December 8, 1996, B2)

Anglo-American anger was primarily aimed at brown-skinned Latinos, including those, as in excerpt 31, who can afford the start-up costs and procure the local and state permits to launch a business. Immigrants may have been the catalyst, but the public's ire was focused on Latinos who did not humbly express regret for their culture while hurrying toward the mainstream. The outrage was palpable:

32. Some Latino leaders fear a rise in hate crimes and heightened suspicion of brown-skinned people. "It could create tense social relations," said Luis Ortiz Franco, a Chapman University mathematics professor. (December 31, 1994, A1)

33. As deputy district attorney Ellen Aragon put it, Los Angeles is, by definition, diverse, which means, "We're all potential targets." (September 15, 1995, E1)

34. "But even so, the atmosphere is there. If you assume someone is illegal, you can say or do anything you want to them." As evidence, he cited vandals who painted "wetbacks out" and "illegals out" on the school's Chicano House the day before the election. (November 10, 1994, B1)

35. Contributing to the volatile mix, community leaders say, are high

unemployment, substandard education and the anger generated by the harsh Proposition 187 debate and related movements viewed by many Latinos as specifically targeting people of Latin American ancestry. (August 7, 1995, A1)

Latinos did not merely sympathize with immigrants, they often personally felt the sting of the public's unsheathed hostility toward undocumented workers. They certainly sensed the public's irritation with Latinos who did not offer excuses for their cultural differences. And they were vexed by the double-edged sword they faced in the political arena. Some conservative commentators said that the electorate's outrage of the 1990s was surgically focused on the "illegal" immigrant. However, Latinos who did not hold conservative views were targeted as fraudulent citizens: Latinos calling for greater emphasis on human rights were labeled divisive; those decrying nativism as undemocratic were labeled un-American. If the public had unmistakably sustained a distinction between undocumented immigrants and Latino citizens, little backlash would have occurred as they exercised their right to protest the politics of Propositions 187, 209, and 227. This was not the case. Indeed, Latino opposition provoked such an intense response among the Anglo-American electorate that many seasoned politicians considered Latino protest to be counterproductive. As often noted by *Times* newswriters, political expression by Latinos was stifled on the very issues that mattered most to them:

> 36. [HEADLINE:] Foes of Prop. 187 Toeing a Difficult Line Strategy: In their fight to maintain immigrant rights, some opponents of the ballot initiative have steered away from the high-profile use of Latinos. "We're keeping **the brown faces** in the background," one says. (September 26, 1994, A16)
>
> 37. Many in the anti-187 coalition—including mainstream Latino groups such as the Mexican American Legal Defense and Education Fund—argued that a massive march barely three weeks before the election was a bad tactic, and attempted to scuttle the event. Several Latino activists privately expressed fears that a **sea of brown faces** marching through Downtown Los Angeles would only antagonize many voters. (October 17, 1994, A1)

Inasmuch as Latinos are portrayed in the public discourse texts as immigrants, or nonmainstream, Latinos remain peripheral to U.S. society. U.S.

Latino culture is considered alien, "immigrants in our own land" in Jimmy Santiago Baca's terms,[53] in spite of being native to the United States,[54] while the racializing metaphors of public discourse constitute the notion that Latinos are inferior to white Americans. Latinos are perceived as nonwhite immigrants, particularly in regions of the United States where their numbers constitute a sizable portion of the total population, and are acted upon in these terms.

The Anglo-American narrative defines Latinos as foreign on three criteria. First, Latinos do not speak English. This assumption is counterfactual, inasmuch as all children growing up in the United States become native English speakers. Even twenty years ago 73 percent of Latinos said they spoke English well, and an estimated 23 percent spoke only English.[55] As noted in Chapter 6, the speed at which non-English-speaking children begin to develop English has since accelerated, in response to the strengthening signal in U.S. society that only one language is natural, and any other is not. Furthermore, to prove their loyalty to the hegemony of Anglo-American culture, Latinos cannot retain two public languages. They must appear to be monolingual English speakers.[56]

The second criterion is that Latinos must present themselves as white-identified. This is acculturation, and is signaled by disavowing all "foreign" qualities associated with Mexico.[57] Of course this does not include all characteristics; some minor elements have been accepted by Anglo-American society, such as tacos, salsa, and Salma Hayek. The real effect of this can be noted within the Latino community itself, which registers a division between families who have a longer history in this country and those whose history is shorter. This division is also fostered within families, across generations. One of Latinos' greatest assets is often severed when children become culturally and linguistically separated from their parents and grandparents.

Lastly, in the effort to become American, Latinos attempt to become white in other ways as well. Rejecting the Spanish language and all things perceived in Anglo eyes to be foreign is insufficient, as historian Neil Foley recently reiterated, if the Latino does not become "wedded" to the Anglo-American hierarchy of race, which ranks citizens by color and regards whiteness as superior.[58] Anthropologist Jane Hill puts it bluntly, "To be White is to collude in these [racializing] practices."[59] Latinos who accept the racializing hierarchy are placed in a no-win situation. The hierarchy, by establishing the definition of what it is to be an American, justifies the deprecation of others, including "darker" or more "Indian"-looking Latinos.[60] Even after acceding to this racist practice, these Latinos will not be perceived as fully American, since they always will be seen as inferior to "real" Americans.

It may be in the public school contexts that the social costs are dearest. The bilingual Latino child is not viewed simply as an American child, or an American child with an advantage of two languages and cultures. Rather, such a child is considered a linguistically impaired student at best—at worst, a racialized foreigner. Since the basic image-schemata of BODY is fundamental, the impact of racialization on minority children transforms their sense of themselves. Recall the torment expressed in Anzaldúa's verse. Franz Kafka offers a fitting allegory with *In the Penal Colony*. In it, an explorer witnesses an inconceivable punishment:

> "Our sentence does not sound severe. Whatever commandment the prisoner has disobeyed is written on his body: HONOR THY SUPERI-ORS!" The explorer glanced at the man; he stood, as the officer pointed him out, with bent head, apparently listening with all his ears in an effort to catch what was being said. Yet the movement of his blubber lips, closely pursed together, showed clearly that he could not understand a word. Many questions were troubling the explorer, but at the sight of the prisoner he asked only: "Does he know his sentence?" "No," said the officer, eager to go on with his exposition, but the explorer had interrupted him. "He doesn't know the sentence that has been passed on him?" "No," said the officer again, pausing a moment as if to let the explorer elaborate his question, and then said: "There would be no point in telling him. He'll learn it on his body. . . . He has had no chance of putting up a defense," said the officer, turning his eyes away as if speaking to himself and so sparing the explorer the shame of hearing self-evident matters explained.[61]

This punishment still is commonplace in U.S. society, and of course is not limited to Latinos. When the child's body is inscribed with a degrading emblem such as race, the impact on his or her sense of self is profound. On the other hand, in this racialized society, if one's body is inscribed with the quality of "white," then the child is a normal child. White Americans still are generally shielded from the daily pain of having race inscribed on their bodies, permitting them to dispute their special privilege that is maintained by means of silent racism.

In U.S. public discourse, the conceptual metaphor IMMIGRANT AS ANI-MAL thus constitutes the identity of Latinos as of lesser value than the typical U.S. citizen. As long as white remains the norm of what constitutes an

"American," Latinos will not be seen as full citizens, inasmuch as the metaphors of public discourse constitute the national stage. Latinos will be seen as foreigners in their native land.[62]

On the national stage as constituted by public discourse, four crucial stage directions guide Latinos in their relationship to the nation. One is Brimelow's edict: Be happy with your half-and-half status! Latinos have resisted this hegemonic command over the past 150 years as they struggled for their birthright and treaty rights, not to mention human rights. The need to contest this edict indicates that the social roles of Latinos in the United States continue to be defined as different from those of the typical American.

The second stage direction builds on the definitions of race and racism in America. As Christopher Edley noted, one success of the civil rights struggles of the 1960s was the invention of a taboo against the public expression of blatant racism. Unfortunately, the struggle did not achieve a total ban on white racism. As discussed in Chapter 4, there are serious consequences following from this incomplete revision of the national stage directions in the daily lives of Americans. Currently racism is defined narrowly as blatant individual acts of violence, while institutional and epistemological racisms are disavowed. Hence, the racial hierarchy that is perpetuated by sanitized racism is not recognized in contemporary public discourse. A corollary to this taboo constitutes another stage direction: Do not publicly call nonviolent injustice based on skin color by the term "racism." As many commentators have noted, if white racism is pointed out by a non-White, heated denials will follow. Among the most indignant are those who believe that since legalized racism was outlawed in 1965, this disease of the American body was cured. However, as the principal beneficiaries of the naturalized racial inequity, Whites do not suffer its worst effects, and are rewarded with privilege, which eventually is presumed to be merit. To counter the daily poison of racism, denial is insufficient; Whites must consciously root out the destructive effects of racism on nonwhite Americans.[63]

Inasmuch as Latinos are seen as maintaining a foreign, non-American culture, a similar stage direction pertains: Do not explicitly refer to Standard English–speaking Latinos as foreigners. This saves face in interpersonal encounters. Note that while one should not call these English-speaking individuals foreign, their culture still is viewed to be foreign, even after nearly two hundred years of intermingling with Anglo-American culture. Stage directions which enjoin silence about the imputed foreign character of Latino values and lifeways pose a conflict that operates at the level of the Latino or Latina individual. To contest racialization or foreignization places the Latino or Latina at odds with these hegemonic instructions. Thus, contestation is a source of social tension between people that causes personal distress. On the other hand, to observe the prohibitions masks injustice. Strict observance of the stage directions allows some fair-skinned individuals to conduct their lives as white people. However, these individuals only obtain privilege, and pass as white, at the expense of other Latinos and other racialized minorities.[64]

The daily foreignization of Latinos and these public bans against pointing out structural racism can be exemplified in any number of societal acts of indifference. For one, the savage inequities forced upon Latino children in public education have never set off a massive public outcry. No non-Latino public official has ever been so outraged to sustain demands for change. Nor has the report of a perfunctory blue-ribbon commission on Latino educational failure made the front page of a national paper. The U.S. public does not give this grave daily injustice any attention. Educational nonachievement is permitted to continue as a matter of destiny for Latino children. There is no public exasperation because, unlike "real American" students, these Latino children are seen to be raised with deficits due to their foreign culture. The absence of clamor among non-Latinos for fundamental change in the educational system on behalf of Latino public school students indicates that the general society accedes to the subordinate status of Latinos. Brimelow had it partially correct: Anglo-American society at large still embraces the continuing half-and-half status of Latinos.

A third stage direction provides instructions on how to visualize social advancement with blinders. This discursive practice enacts and affirms the standing social order, as expressed in the public discourse on Latinos in the United States. All citizens venerate the ostensible American meritocracy, which rewards native talent and personal fortitude in education and social interaction in general. Many of the same citizens disavow the existence of significant structural disparities on the playing field for success. The discourse of educational and societal success, as discussed in Chapter 5, presumes that success or failure is entirely a matter of the individual. That is to say, the educational path and footrace metaphors presume that each competitor vies with no advantage or disadvantage, except those of his or her own making. This stage direction allows the individual who benefits inequitably from gender, race, or class to cast off personal responsibility for the continuing economic and social inequities visited upon America's children of color.

Individuals who participate in mainstream politics accept the tenets of this discourse, which speaks in terms of individual merit, in accordance with the creed that "all men [*sic*] are created equal," and which does not acknowledge the operating racial hierarchy. By and large Americans accept the status quo, irrespective of the structural differences that make a sham of the equality-in-competition credo. This fraud is revealed in differentials of achievement, living style, and life expectancy across the races. In the early part of the twentieth century, this differential was supposed to be a natural outgrowth of white superiority; only in the last thirty years have the rules of public discourse enjoined reference to racial superiority. Yet in that time period these differentials have increased, rather than diminished.

These are the elements of the discursive script on Latinos as expressed by the dominant metaphors. To put it graphically, Latinos have never been the heart or hands of the NATION AS BODY—even where they make up near-majority populations. This is also the case where they have been a very visible presence in their native land since the Anglo-Americans arrived as newcomers. Latinos are not customarily seen to be legitimate inhabitants of the U.S. HOUSE, but rather foreign invaders, soldiers, or surging brown tides that threaten to inundate the home of Anglo-America. Nor are Latinos automatically considered to be first-class passengers on the *U.S.S. Stars & Stripes,* but are typically viewed as the lowly steerage-dwellers, the stowaways, or the crew members employed to swab the deck or change the linen on the beds of "real Americans." As long as the dominant stage directions formulate a marginal place for Latinos on the national stage, Latinos will have to struggle and resist the dominant discursive processes of marginalization, racism, and alienation.

As can be read in the *Los Angeles Times* texts, the Latino response to the three anti-Latino referenda of the 1990s attempted to conform to the strictures of the mainstream discourse, in most cases. This, in effect, accepts the premises articulated in the metaphors that place immigrants below citizens on the human hierarchy, dismisses structural differences in competition for the deserts of U.S. life, denies the continued existence of white racism, and maintains the insistent foreignization of Latino culture. These views are tacitly or even consciously held by a subset of Latinos, as a result of socialization. As noted in voting patterns, this is not the case for the great majority of Latinos. Seventy-seven percent of Latinos rejected Proposition 187; 77 percent repudiated Proposition 209; 63 percent voted "no" on Proposition 227 statewide, with even greater numbers in Republican strongholds.[65] Spokespeople for the majority of Latinos recognized that the highly touted American creeds often rang hollow during the decade of the 1990s, but they did not effectively contest the defamatory mainstream narratives. In the final chapter, political metaphor creation will be explored, in order to encourage alternative worldviews of Latinos in the United States.

## CHAPTER EIGHT

# Insurgent Metaphors

## Contesting the Conventional
## Representations of Latinos

Latinos' place on the American political stage, as has been assessed in the public discourse at the end of the twentieth century, remains subordinate and marginal. Moreover, there are few indications of changes in contemporary public discourse to suggest that Latinos will achieve political, educational, and social parity with the now-favored Anglo-American population in the near term or middle term. Although in the last fifty years we can note that the public discourse on Latinos has been "sanitized,"[1] the underlying nineteenth-century worldview and tacit presumptions of Anglo-American predominance continue to operate to maintain social inequity.

However, unlike metaphors that conceptualize foundational aspects of everyday life, political metaphors are not fixed. They are sites of public conduct. In terms of language use, they are negotiated instruments of social and political action. The silver lining of the dark cloud of today's political metaphors about Latinos is that alternative metaphors can be marshaled in the struggle for more encompassing visions of the nation that do not marginalize its nonwhite people. New or reinvigorated metaphors can contest the dominant concepts of the United States' relationship to Latinos. This final chapter will provide a brief guide to the methodical elaboration of insurgent metaphors.

In the first section support for insubordinate discourses will be discussed. This will be followed by Section 2 on respecifying the metaphors for immigration and immigrants, Section 3 with a commentary on the recent history of the metaphor for racism, and Section 4 on two particularly worthy insurgent metaphors for education. Section 5 discusses respecifying conventional national narratives, scripts, and frames of reference, while Section 6 offers the preliminaries for an insurgent metaphor-creation project.

## Section 1: Insurgent Discourse

To contest the dominant and conventional metaphors that restrict Latinos in their pursuit of greater social justice, three steps are needed. In brief, one should create an insurgent metaphor to challenge the conventional one, expressly elaborate its semantic associations to make it work as an alternative conceptualizing tool, and develop its interpretive context so that it creates a distinctive worldview with its own narratives and cultural frames.

First and foremost, oppressive conventional metaphors should not be tacitly accepted. As long as the dominant hegemonic metaphors are not challenged, the conventional worldview will remain undisturbed. Insurgent metaphors can be created by respecifying the semantic target domain of the current conventional metaphor. Using alternate metaphors for Latinos and Latino political issues in public discourse can compel an audience of one, or a complacent national public of millions, to reconsider a concept in political discourse that is taken to be obvious and natural.

Second, to further question the utility of the current dominant metaphor in the public's mind, as well as to demonstrate the conceptualizing value of any rival metaphor, the entailments and presuppositions of both the current and insurgent metaphors should be articulated. Each time the inaccurate and socially restricting semantic associations of the customary metaphor are contested, an opportunity is created for the public to compare the conventional view of the world with another point of view.

The third move introduces into the public's perception the stories, voices, narratives, people, and perspectives that come with the rival affirming metaphors about Latinos. By developing alternative contexts of interpretation, the conventional contexts of interpretation about Latinos are again interrogated. By contexts of interpretation are meant the cultural frames of reference (for example, the rival definitions of family, home, and racism) and their associated scripts (stories, histories, personages, narratives) about the nature of social reality that is taken as given. In order to change the current dramaturgical scripts about Latinos that are reinforced and sustained as they are uttered again and again on the national stage, so-called counterstories,[2] alternative counterhegemonic stories, should be aired. With each opportunity in the course of public discussion to challenge the previously unquestioned cultural frames that generally operate unimpeded in hegemonic dis-course, an opening in conventional patterns of public thinking is made.

This brisk three-step description, of course, belies the huge task of transforming the worldview of the U.S. public. However, the principal re-sponsibility of Latino and other political progressives, with or without awareness of the cognitive agency of metaphor, is to recast the elector-ate's worldview. Careful attention to the metaphoric foundations of Anglo-American xenophobia and racism will allow the progressive opposition to avoid tacit acceptance of the hegemonic worldview that marginalizes and alienates/foreignizes Latinos, as occurred in the period of Propositions 187, 209, and 227. Sensitivity to the potency of metaphor may accelerate the often erratic process of conceptualizing a better future.

## Section 2: Respecifying Domains:
### IMMIGRATION and IMMIGRANT

These three steps toward the creation and promotion of insurgent world-views will be exemplified in this section by way of a review of the hegemonic metaphors dominating today's public discourse on Latinos, and alternative metaphors that can be used to contest and eventually to supplant them.

As elaborated in Chapter 3, the major metaphors characterizing immi-gration and immigrant in contemporary public discourse were, respectively, DANGEROUS WATERS and ANIMALS. The former metaphor invoked the enduring NATION AS HOUSE metaphor that was discussed in Chapter 7. Other secondary metaphors that also were seen with some frequency in-cluded the IMMIGRANT AS SOLDIER (attacking the HOUSE), AS WEED, and AS DISEASE metaphors.

*Immigration*

As regards immigration, FLOWING WATER is a widely used semantic source domain to characterize this demographic process. There is no ready substi-tute. Scientific demography and geography employ metaphors of flowing water in all discussions of immigration. The objectionable part of the meta-phor, DANGEROUS WATERS, is the fear-inducing references to tides rising beyond the norm or brown rivers surging above flood stage. As elaborated in Chapter 3, the fear focuses on the purported loss of Anglo-American cultural hegemony. Rather than discuss the notion of hegemony in public, which would be counterproductive, the objective of alternative conceptual-ization in this case is to repudiate the fear of cultural inundation. One tactic, among many others, is to speak about the benefits of flowing waters of im-migration, to offset the irrational fear of culture change by referencing the economic gain of a hardworking labor "pool."[3]

Rather than washing America away, immigration can be characterized as an essential part of the country's high productivity:

1. In the American Southwest, the **immigrant stream makes the desert bloom.**

References that speak about the wealth generated in America by the labor, energy, and ambition of immigrants are not novel. In the history of U.S. views on immigration there have been periods when immigration was sought after vigorously. In 1885 Andrew Carnegie, for one, provided a strik-ing assessment of the value of immigrant workers in terms of flowing wealth:

2. Were the owners of every gold and silver mine in the world compelled to send to the Treasury at Washington, at their own expense, every ounce of the precious metals produced, the national wealth would not be en-hanced one-half as much as it is from the **golden stream** [of immigrants] which **flows** into the country each year.[4]

Thus affirmative metaphors are readily available to represent immigration as a beneficial stream, even as expressed by a nineteenth-century robber baron. Along this line of thought, the wealth-generating capacity of immigration can be further linked to the unending need for low-cost, high-productivity labor:

3. The cities of the United States **thirst** for a steady **flow** of immigra-tion for their labor needs.

This example summons the NATION AS BODY metaphor (in this case CITY AS BODY), which in turn entails notions of the body's need for sustenance and, again, economic productivity.

There is no question that today's advocates for immigrants can do better than Carnegie. His appraisal of immigrants is monstrous. He continues his commentary excerpted in 2 by designating a dollar value for their worth uti-lizing the price of slaves: "The value to the country of the annual foreign influx, however, is very great indeed. . . . During the ten years between 1870 and 1880 the number of immigrants averaged two hundred and eight thousand per annum. . . . These adults were surely worth $1,500 each—for in former days an efficient slave sold for this sum. . . . The cash value of immigrants upon this basis for the year 1882 exceeded $1,125,000,000."[5]

Returning to insurgent metaphors for today, an intrepid, but not excessive, claim can be formulated from the NATION AS BODY metaphor:

4. Immigration is the **lifeblood** of the California economy.

The economic health of polities of all sizes is metaphorized in terms of the BODY, as seen in the subject of this sentence, as well as: *a rejuvenated economy, robust sectors, fiscal dives, markets that awaken after a mid-summer slumber,* and *sales running above last year's levels.*[6] One might expect that immigration often would be described in similar terms. This is not the case. It is striking that Mexican immigration is not often referred to in U.S. public discourse in similar terms, in spite of its crucial role in the economic development of the United States. For example, the joint U.S.-Mexican government program for contracting Mexican labor which operated from 1947 to 1964, the Bracero Program, used the Spanish term *bracero* 'hired hand or laborer,' which is a derivation from a body term, *brazo* 'arm.' Although the NATION AS BODY is not the source of this term, it can be effectively associated with the economic body. During the heyday of the Bracero Program, however, Mexican immigrant labor was not conceptualized to be integral to the Anglo-American body. Nor did the advocates for immigrants have much success presenting such a perspective during the Proposition 187 campaign period of 1993–1994.

As Patricia Loo noted in an exploratory review of the metaphors in *Los Angeles Times* articles of 1942 and 1943, rather than men and women whose arms, backs, and shoulders actively constructed U.S. wealth and strength, Mexican braceros have long tended to be metaphorized as passive industrial and farm equipment, as TOOLS to be used by Anglo-Americans:

5. Dodge, manager of the Farm Labor Office, said the current **supply** of labor is adequate for the first week of the grape harvest. (August 17, 1943, I13)
6. A field worker **shortage** is seen. Unless growers act to utilize available Mexican nationals, field crops and vegetable harvests in Ventura County will be **short** more than 2000 workers. (August 4, 1943, I8)
7. A large part of the labor **shortage** can be **remedied** by fuller productivity per **worker unit.** (December 2, 1942, I6).

Only one of the eighty-nine metaphors that Loo compiled might be construed as linked to the NATION AS BODY metaphor. However, this example, *farm hands* (November 14, 1943, I31), is metonymic of farm work, and does not directly invoke nation.[7]

### Immigrant

Turning from demographic process, the individual immigrant has been gravely disparaged by conventional metaphors of the 1990s. Each immigrant is linked to fearful movements of people, by which this human being's life, history, and dreams are effaced. To counteract such dehumanizing discursive processes, public discussions should aim to give the immigrant, as a person, his face and her voice.

The individual immigrant is frequently used to speak about the demographic process. This employs many of the same terms used when the U.S. AS BODY metaphors are employed. Thus the following claim can be made to resonate well in any discussion that aims to shine a positive light on immigrants:

8. Immigrants are the strong working **arms** of California's economy.
9. With other Californians, immigrants plant their **feet** and put their **backs** into the concerted **push** to move our state **forward.**

One expression of this metaphor was located in the *Los Angeles Times,* in excerpt 10:

10. "This country was built on the **backs of immigrants.**" (June 3, 1993, B3)

This kind of metaphoric discourse—creating an integrated and indispensable place for today's immigrants in our economy—blends into nonmetaphoric statements, as in excerpt 11, or judgments, as in excerpt 12:

11. Immigrants work for California's industries, they work in our cities, our businesses, our fields, and our homes.
12. Immigrants earn their place in California each day that they work for our country's future.

Such statements were far too infrequent in the public discourse during the Proposition 187 campaign.

Another tack to take to contest the dominant immigrant metaphors employs the NATION AS BODY metaphor to integrate the immigrant into the U.S. polity and society.

13. Immigrants are the **backbone** of American growth; they are the **heart** of American entrepreneurialism. Immigrants **embody** the spirit of the American Dream, willingly sacrificing themselves for a better life for their children.

Abel Valenzuela, Jr., on the basis of his largest-ever survey of Latino day-laborers, argues that one-third of these immigrants display the classic character traits of entrepreneurs.[8] His is a welcome reinterpretation of this vital but little-studied sector of the economy.

Among the most unabashed promoters of the American entrepreneurial spirit are business magazines such as *Forbes, Entrepreneur,* and *Fortune.* Yet their view of entrepreneurship, shared by many economists and much of the general public, centers on upper-echelon industrialists, capitalists, and merchants, and proprietors in general. For these elites, terms such as *start-up motivation, personal initiative, enthusiasm, action-oriented, risk-taker, at ease with change,* and *self-control* are readily bandied about. However, such words are perhaps more apt to describe immigrants, who put aside familiar ways and defy national border guards and bandits to embrace a new culture and society, all to secure better lives for their families.

The potential of a revision should not be a surprise. A 1994 *Economist* article stated that "immigration has plainly brought huge benefits to America in the past: newcomers have injected energy, ambition and fresh ideas. They are still doing so. Joel Kotkin of the Centre for the New West points to California's economic revival. It has been immigrant-driven, he says. Small, flexible firms and the self-employed—areas in which immigrants excel—have led the way."[9]

With evangelic fervor, today's business publications summon the spirit of New England Calvinism as they extol the American entrepreneur as: *hard-working, thrifty, self-sacrificing, moral,* and *straight-dealing.* One might ask what venture capitalists are actually risking, except capital, and whether their stake is proportional to the venture that immigrants willingly undertake. Many immigrants evince those highly valued American virtues of risking all to earn an honest living to provide a better life for their children. Accordingly, this vocabulary certainly can be employed to describe the immigrant as entrepreneur.

## Counterhegemonic Statements

In the articles of the *Los Angeles Times* and other texts, references that directly rejected the marginalizing discourse on immigrants were rare. One shining refutation captured in the *Times* during the Proposition 187 campaign was David Hayes-Bautista's trenchant comment in excerpt 14.[10]

14. "These people are **carrying more than their own weight.**" (November 10, 1992, B1)

Other exhilarating views were expressed in excerpts 15 and 16.

15. "Migration is something natural, like the air we breathe."[11]
16. No human being is illegal! (March 1, 1993, B6; November 24, 1993, A24; May 29, 1994, A1; June 8, 1994, B6; November 2, 1994, B1)

Regarding Proposition 227 for a moment, bilingual education is characterized not as a remedial measure, but as a means to develop a student's intellect, which made its elimination criminal or worse, in excerpt 17.

17. But Janette Perez, a bilingual teacher in Pomona who used to work in Orange Unified, told the trustees she was shocked at the proposal. "I cannot believe the intolerance of this community to people who speak another language. It is almost **criminal,**" she said. "Children do not come to school to learn English—they come to develop their intellect. You're **crucifying** them. If you put them in English only, they will never go to college." (January 24, 1997, B9)
18. "We've got to send a message to the rest of the nation that California will not stand on a platform of bigotry, racism, and scapegoating," declared Joe Hicks. (October 17, 1994, A1)

In excerpt 18, Hicks effectively subverted a catchphrase used by Proposition 187 backers, that passing Proposition 187 would "send a message" to lawmakers to do something about illegal immigration. To "send a message" meant that the anticonstitutional and divisive character of the referendum should be overlooked in order to inform national leaders of the concerns of certain California citizens over immigration. The *Los Angeles Times* database registered over a score of instances of this expression in 1994. Hicks's contrary comment could have been restated many more times with positive effect.

## Immigrants as Rightful Residents in the U.S. House

Turning now to the NATION AS HOUSE metaphor, a potentially productive set of metaphors can be constructed, as exemplified below:

19. Immigrants **built** America, and they continue to **build** America's future.

20. Today's immigrants continue the task begun by your immigrant grandparents to **build** America's future.

These prototype renegade metaphors put light years of conceptual distance between immigrants and the most degrading aspects of the conventional ANIMAL metaphor:

21. Today's immigrants, just like your grandfather or grandmother, **build** for the future, defer their own rewards, and dream the American Dream for their children.

All are references, metaphoric or otherwise, that establish familial similarity between the voter and the present-day immigrant. Since 95 percent of the electorate (other than American Indians) is also progeny of immigrants, a steady reminder may help neutralize the nativist theme present in the dominant public discourse on immigrants.

The most racist metaphor in today's public discourse, IMMIGRANT AS ANIMAL, continues to place immigrants well below citizens on a scale of humanity. This metaphor will remain in public discourse as long as it is not contested. As Brimelow sniped: "America at the time of the Revolution . . . the collectivity that took political decisions—was wholly white" and "the American nation of 1965 is going to have to share its future, and its land, with a very large number of people who, as of that year, were complete strangers. Foreigners. Aliens."[12] Brimelow, the self-proclaimed British arbiter of American authenticity, casually disregards the legitimate claims of Latinos and other non-Whites whose forebears lived in America in 1965, indeed, since before the Anglo-American contact. The vigorous applause across the country for Brimelow's message occurred because he articulates, without compunction, the unsanitized racist narrative that in earlier times silenced people of color in America. All insurgent and insubordinate metaphors for immigration and immigrants are designed to first contest, and then replace, this narrative, since they can constitute more encompassing worldviews that do not employ arbitrary scales of humanity.

## Section 3: Subverting Conventional Metaphors: The Case of RACISM

We now turn to the lessons to be drawn from our study of the public discourse on affirmative action. Over the past thirty years, the trajectory of racism's public conceptualization goes a long way toward explaining the current retreat from the goal of a non-racist nation. It also demonstrates how changing a metaphor can transform the public's understanding of society.

In the 1960s, strong orators such as Martin Luther King Jr. and Malcolm X metaphorized racism as a disease of the national political and social body. The Kerner Report, which was commissioned by the President, affirmed the characterization by these nonwhite spokespeople. It stated that U.S. racism is white: "White institutions created it, white institutions maintained it, and white society condones it." [13] Because this report was an extraordinary publishing event in an extraordinary time, it is safe to say that the finding of this official commission was understood by the American public at large of the time.

By the mid-1990s, however, neoconservative think tanks had redefined American racism for the public, employing the discredited states' rights arguments of the late 1950s. With substantial funding [14] and a concerted twenty-five-year effort, neoconservatives developed an alternative set of congruent and publicly persuasive arguments focused on reverse discrimination. Their success was marked by the passage of Proposition 209 in 1996 and the general retreat from affirmative action policies across the country.

This rebuke of King's hard-fought social victories and Lyndon Johnson's legislative efforts of the 1960s is particularly painful for political progressives and the great majority of nonwhite citizens. More important in the context of this book, King's metaphor for white racism was subverted and used to stall the march of King's multitude toward greater social equity. Applying the disease metaphor with a new target domain, neoconservatives characterized affirmative action as the one remaining vector of the disease of racism. Their America, which had been miraculously cured of chronic racism with a presidential penstroke in 1964, was (metaphorically) being reinfected with racism by affirmative action.

This turn of events is an object lesson for those interested in advancing a social agenda. It indicates the potency with which discourse constructs public perception by way of metaphors. The current neoconservative argument was no doubt perceived by the public as an incredible, even ludicrous, claim when first heard in the late 1960s. Nonetheless, it became increasingly acceptable and even reasonable to the California voting majority by 1996. Affirmative action, that homeopathic remedy for the cancer of three hundred years of white inhumanity, became the only source of American racism that neoconservatives would acknowledge. These well-rehearsed arguments were regularly presented to the public. A stream of ever more polished arguments and arresting imagery led, over time, to the public's reorientation against affirmative action—on the same grounds it had rejected Jim Crow laws. The progressive and liberal political camps, as well as ethnic spokespeople, must be held responsible for failing to find the means to keep the focus on racism in institutions, and to break through the barriers of white indifference. Had engaging statements been reiterated about the continuing oppression of nonwhite American society (for example, contrasting the backlog of 100,000 cases of job discrimination lodged with the EEOC in one year with the sum total over twenty-five years of 12 cases of reverse discrimination), then subversion of WHITE RACISM AS DISEASE would have been far more difficult.

In my judgment, no metaphor is more salient and effective to characterize racism than CANCER. The ontology of malignancy provides entailments to address almost all aspects of the noxious American scale of humanity that places one group above another. It further allows for ready understanding of the continuing need to monitor the patient for chronic manifestations of the long-neglected infirmity of the U.S. body. Raising levels of social awareness about the current brutalizing effects of institutional and epistemic racism against non-Whites to the heights that were reached, at great cost, during the Civil Rights Movement will be a lengthy and difficult task in the first and second decades of the twenty-first century, but it is as worthy an enterprise as it was in the 1960s.

## Section 4: Insurgent Metaphors for EDUCATION

In the review of the public discourse surrounding the Proposition 227 campaign, it became clear that the concepts characterizing public education across the board should be distinguished from those which constitute the education of Latinos. Starting with education in general, Americans sustain a very old conceptualization of learning. Consequently, they maintain archaic notions about teaching and about the institution of teaching. In today's public discourse on education—just as in Charles Dickens's satire 150 years ago—the student is an inert vessel to be filled with knowledge.

Traditional American anxiety about intellectualism, the nineteenth-century factory model on which the public schools were first modeled, and the feminization of the teaching profession in the twentieth century all contribute to a congruent and oppressive view that has not changed significantly since its formulation. The factory is the conceptualizing metaphor for public schools' mission: to efficiently fill, in Dickens's imagery, those "little vessels then and there arranged in order, ready to have imperial gallons of facts poured into them until they [are] filled to the brim."[15]

Two predominant metaphors for an individual's education are EDUCATION AS PATH and EDUCATION AS RIVER. The PATH metaphor is associated with aspects of personal volition and curricular content, grades, and courses of study. The PATH metaphor seems to Americans to be the most natural and innocuous metaphor in the common parlance. This viewpoint is reinforced by the use of the path to metaphorize other parts of human life. The most damaging aspect of the PATH metaphor—the atomizing entailment—operates with each instance of the metaphor to background and quickly drop all structural factors, so that the concrete differences between rich and poor schools seem incidental at best.

The complement of the PATH metaphor is EDUCATION AS RIVER. The river refers to passive aspects of socialization that affect students as children mature into adolescents and adults within a society. Becoming mainstream, or entering the educational mainstream, is taken to be the most desirable process for all public school students, who are otherwise doomed to U.S. educational backwaters. The culture of the home and all diversity, especially linguistic diversity, are associated with educational shoals and stagnant waters. Upon entering the mainstream, following the logic of this metaphor, the minority child is carried to his/her social and economic place in the United States, as if by nature. In this way nonmainstream student failure is deemed to be the fault of no one. The RIVER metaphor thus obscures the daily decisions and financial allotments which maintain institutionalized inferior treatment of Latino and other minority students in U.S. society, most of whom are unjustly relegated to the lowest rungs of U.S. life. Much like the PATH metaphor, the RIVER metaphor conceals hierarchizing by class, race, and linguistic criteria in education, which occurs by way of inequitable distribution of public resources.

Certain well-known or readily recognized cultural narratives with which the education metaphors are interpreted further crush the educational aspirations of Latinos and other minority-language children in the United States. The ethic of the rugged individual, the chimerical meritocracy of education, and the probity of so-called free competition are such cultural narratives. These frames of reference inform public schooling. Consequently, individual competition is expected in American schools, and the PATH of individual advancement within this frame of reference becomes a contest, a FOOTRACE. As the primary place where American mores are instilled, public education inculcates children with this narrative.

This repressive constellation of metaphors for public education—EMPTY VESSEL, FACTORY, PATH, and RIVER—is overdue for replacement. Two preferable ways of conceiving of education are by way of the metaphors to EDIFY and to CULTIVATE. Each foregrounds important elements of education that have been underemphasized with the current conventional metaphors, in particular with regard to language-minority students. Further, each rejects the conventional atomizing entailment which fortifies racial and linguistic hierarchies. These insubordinate metaphors have the potential to remake much of the public's understanding of the nation's major institution for socialization, including its conceptions of educators and schools.

### LEARNING AS BUILDING: *To Edify*

The first metaphor, KNOWLEDGE AS CONSTRUCT, has been a topic among educational theorists, professionals, and researchers for over one hundred years, since its elaboration by John Dewey:

> I believe that the only true education comes through the stimulation of the child's powers by the demands of the social situation in which he finds himself. . . . The child's own instincts and powers furnish the material and give the starting point for all education. Save as the efforts of the educator connect with some activity which the child is carrying on of his initiative independent of the educator, education becomes reduced to a pressure from without. It may, indeed, give certain external results, but cannot truly be called educative. . . . With the advent of democracy and modern industrial conditions, it is impossible to foretell definitely just what civilization will be twenty years from now. Hence it is impossible to prepare the child for any precise set of conditions. To prepare him for the future life means to give him command of himself; it means so to train him that he will have the full and ready use of all his capacities.[16]

With the TO LEARN IS TO BUILD metaphor, knowledge becomes a construct, with the student as active builder of his or her own intellectual edifice. This metaphor is particularly well-suited to capture modern scientific models of language development, which emphasize the individual's own unique creation of a grammar via specific developmental stages and social interaction. The child, as well as the adult, assembles the framework of understanding of language and other types of knowledge in which s/he will mentally dwell. In this metaphor, then, the teacher relinquishes the role of mind worker and takes on a much more creative role of architectural consultant and master knowledge builder. The teacher thus imparts by example these skills to the student as she progresses, from apprentice to journeyman and finally master builder, within the KNOWLEDGE AS ABODE metaphor. This metaphor reflects the actions that the best teachers have always offered their students across human cultures.

Within the edification metaphor, the school is no longer a FACTORY, but rather becomes a building construction site. The student is no longer a chip of raw material to be drilled, threaded, and stamped into shape along the educational assembly line, judged as a standard issue production unit—if nonstandard, to be marked down as defective, and when overstocked to be warehoused. Nor is the teacher an intellectual drone or industrial worker.

One indication of the conceptual distance between the current SCHOOL AS FACTORY metaphor and the proposed CONSTRUCTION SITE metaphor may be noted in a real-world association of housing with assembly plants. So-called "mobile homes" are generally considered to be substandard housing and are attributed with shoddy construction. This is due to the manufacturing process, which mechanically produces standardized products in a factory to meet the bottom-line considerations of impoverished consumers. Site-built houses, in contrast, are more sturdy, longer-lasting, and objects to be proud of, even modestly priced ones. Regarding education, the contrast is apt—children are unique creatures for whom a custom-built education is inherently superior to assembly-line-produced education.

In addition, from the frame of reference of the edification metaphor, the student does not arrive at school bereft of knowledge. She arrives at school already dwelling in her home abode of knowledge.[17] Among the kinds of knowledge she walks into the schoolhouse with, her language is most conspicuous. Thus, the student comes to school to further build on her knowledge foundation, to become a better builder of her own knowledge residence. Further, the home communities, cultures, and languages of the students are the communal or multifamily houses of knowledge. In the process of building greater knowledge, master builders will not raze a child's home knowledge, or force a child to evacuate the only home she has ever known. Rather, master builders will guide the student to build upon her home knowledge.

In lieu of using industrial efficiency as the gauge of success for evaluating schools, as is the case with the SCHOOL AS FACTORY metaphor, other principles of construction and architecture will predominate, such as order, arrangement, eurythmy, and symmetry, or durability, beauty, and convenience.[18] The distinctiveness of each student will be reflected in the edification, much like freestanding, single-family American homes range in style from Dutch Colonial and Georgian Revival to Prairie School.

With this insurgent metaphor, the school districts and the American institution of public education become more clearly responsible for the kinds of building materials that are provided to students to build their homes of knowledge. Some school districts already offer their children the highest-quality materials and engage educational architects and master builders to guide their students' own construction of mansions. These children build veritable palaces of knowledge in which they will prosper all their lives. Other school systems provide next to nothing in terms of educational materials, and employ only inexperienced and undertrained teachers. The state and more affluent citizens offered many working-class, nonwhite, and language-minority communities only discarded, secondhand materials with which their children could build knowledge. At such construction sites, students will produce as children always do, but can only build hovels with the materials and methods provided. It is for these reasons, again within the edification metaphor, that many of the children reject these entirely impoverished school sites for other, often socially destructive, places for knowledge construction. As James Diego Vigil notes, we give them no choice:

> Institutionalized forms of suppression . . . encourage dropouts; "push outs" are created. . . . Thus, in the context of a consistently high dropout rate for inner-city schools, push-out and kick-out practices propel even more children and youth into the streets.[19]

A decided weakness of the PATH metaphor in today's discussions of public education is its use to conceptualize the instructional content of public education. The PATH metaphor foregrounds process, in terms of grades, courses, and obstacles, and backgrounds subject matter. In contrast, the

HOUSE metaphor provides ample semantic structure for instructional content in terms of foundations, rooms, pillars, windows, floors, keystones, stairways, and other architectural design elements. The PATH metaphor is comparatively unequipped. The construction site orientation also deemphasizes the head-to-head competition incumbent in the American EDUCATION AS FOOTRACE, while it retains the possibility of expression of differential individual development. Finally, the LEARNING AS CONSTRUCT, KNOWLEDGE AS HOUSE, and SCHOOL AS CONSTRUCTION SITE constellation for public education in the United States is consonant with the NATION AS HOUSE metaphor. In this postindustrial, increasingly knowledge-based global economy, the continued strength and security of the American people can readily be linked to the quality of American public education as national house.

## EDUCATION AS CULTIVATION

A second alternative is an agricultural metaphor. The objectives of education in this metaphor include the cultivation of language arts, scientific methods, rational inquiry, and creative thinking. In the context of education, the term *cultivation* has been used most often to metaphorize the education of the elite. It is seldom used to characterize the education of the masses, who are typically provided only the so-called basics of reading, writing, and arithmetic. Modern educational research has revealed that all educational skills, from the rudiments to the most elaborate, are developed by way of the same processes and require years to cultivate. If we consider that the child's mind contains the seeds of learning, like acorns, the child's mind must be cultivated over its lifetime to bear its full potential harvest. From within this metaphor, the role of the teacher is sower and tiller. The teacher's role is critical, but just as important, the school's soil must be fertile, and the school's climate for learning temperate, for the seeds of learning embedded in the mind and hands of each child to sprout and yield their bounty. The best seed falling on barren soil will perish. Hence, the structure of the school and the institution of education are foregrounded within this metaphoric constellation.

The classroom and school site become, within this view, an orchard or vineyard to nurture, with a farmer's dedication supported by all the science of a modern horticulturist. STUDENT AS TREE, CLASSROOM AS ORCHARD, EDUCATION AS CULTIVATION—this constellation eliminates the tendency to view learning as a set of mechanical skills to be drilled or facts to be committed to memory. Life-skill cultivation and lifelong creativity are its hallmarks.

Learning as cultivating can summon the presupposition of an orchard of erudition. In each human child are planted the many seeds that grow in us to make us social creatures (namely, different languages and types of learning). A child's mind, then, is not a vacant vessel, or a half-penny's worth of raw material to be hammered into an industrial product. It is an orchard in which sown seeds of knowledge can germinate and flourish richly over time, if tended carefully by skillful tillers of humankind.

In the relatively bankrupt semantics of the current EDUCATION AS PATH metaphor, only one entailment is foregrounded, namely, individual volition. On the other hand, the cultivation metaphor for learning foregrounds developmental maturation as well as evoking the personal potential of the student. In a vineyard, each vine is unique; some fruit may seem richer, but that is a matter of taste. In the educational context, all children produce abundantly with careful tending. In the place of the mechanical efficiency metric of the factory, the axiom of this agricultural metaphor is inspired stewardship to nurture the inborn potential of the human seed. In place of the footrace, which produces many losers for every winner, the guiding principle of the tiller is to realize the full productivity of the whole orchard. The emblem of the successful cultivator, one who patiently tends vines so they can bring forth their yearly yield of fruit, is the rich harvest of the long-lived MIND AS VINE. This metaphoric constellation does not discount individual volition, nor is it incompatible with the goal of a greater meritocracy. It emphasizes elevating human sensibilities and creativity far better than conventional combative or mechanistic metaphors for education.

## Shared Advantages

Present-day conventional metaphors of education do not semantically link up to HOUSE or BODY, the predominant metaphors of nation in today's public discourse. In its favor, EDIFICATION is semantically congruent with the NATION AS HOUSE metaphor. Likewise, CULTIVATION is consonant with NATION AS BODY. These two gentle alternatives can readily associate the fate of the nation with the quality of public education.

Neither the EDIFY nor CULTIVATE metaphor employs the conventional RIVER metaphor. To use the term *mainstream* in educational or other contexts reinforces as it obscures potent power relations.[20] This is particularly relevant in education, but operates in other institutional spheres as well. For example, consider *mainstream media* or *mainstream politics,* which denote nonethnic, Anglo-American institutional control. To become part of the educational mainstream is to become part of the dominant Anglo-American cultural matrix, while to remain marginal or peripheral is to remain subordinate to more powerful groups.[21] In contrast, with the insurgent EDIFICATION and CULTIVATION metaphors, children are either privileged to attend schools rich enough to edify their home knowledge and cultivate their talents, or they are relegated to schools that neither edify nor cultivate. Such a failed public school builds (in edification terms) or grows (in cultivation terms) powerless and disadvantaged children, through no fault of their own.

## Bilingual Education

As borne out in the campaign for Proposition 227, within the conventional constellation of PATH and RIVER metaphors, bilingualism is deemed to be an *obstacle* along the educational path of students. If not *bridged* or otherwise overcome, this obstacle and its associated institutional locus, bilingual education, become *prisons* of students. Over time, from this viewpoint, if children are not mainstreamed (in other words, made monolingual), they become linguistically and educationally *handicapped*. None of these inaccurate and ruinous conceptualizations is incumbent within the edification or cultivation metaphors for education.

The edification metaphor for education resonates with the commonly used term *home language*. The metaphor is also consistent with the best research on linguistic acquisition and cognitive development. In effect, eliminating a home language demolishes the linguistic home of a child's knowledge. The private residence of erudition of the unmistakably educated person, despite the objections of monolingual nativists, is not English-dependence. Authentic bilingual education, which provides the materials and master builders' guidance for children to develop dual or multiple linguistic competencies, constructs new homes of knowledge.[22]

On the other hand, from the point of view of the cultivation metaphor, to eliminate a child's home language is to rip out the six- or seven-year-old sapling in order to plant a stringy seedling. Current psycholinguistic research indicates that each child has abundant linguistic resources for a whole orchard of languages. Why settle for one fruit, when one can enjoy the bounty of olives and peaches, figs and apples from one's own linguistic orchard? From within this metaphor, the rampant growth of language during the child's whole public school period can be articulated with the vocabulary of richness and lifelong yield, rather than the conventional view of OBSTACLE, PRISON, and HANDICAP.[23]

## Section 5: Insurgent Interpretive Schema and Scripts

Moving beyond this preliminary exploration of insurgent education, immigration, and race metaphors, there are certain interpretive schema, frames of reference, and scripts. These are associated with the current conventional metaphor constellations that make up the U.S. public discourse on race, immigration and immigrants, citizen, desert, education, and language. These schema reinforce and legitimate the narrow conventional view of what makes up society. Many of these have been previously discussed. Among the scripts are: citizens are more worthy than immigrants; the school is a level playing field, hence the race for success is joined in the classrooms of America; and English is the national language of Americans. One often-mentioned frame of reference is: White is normal and nonwhite is marked as different, or is inferior. These scripts and frames of reference have been subject to many social critiques and yet retain their vibrancy in public discourse. When the prevailing metaphors of American public discourse are no longer taken to be natural and given, their associated interpretive schema may become easier to discern and contest.

One alternative frame of reference which Americans, even Latinos, do not understand, in spite of thirty years of linguistic, sociolinguistic, and educational research, is the following:

> *The educational failure of language-minority students is not due to language; it is due to structural inequity and an ideology.*

If it were otherwise, the wealthiest and most privileged parents would not strive to provide multicultural and multilingual experiences for their children, and elite schools would not advertise their linguistic resources.

Likewise, to point out only one of the counterscripts which are often lost on Americans in spite of the historical and self-evident facts, English is not the only language of the country:

> *Spanish is an American language.*

In the U.S. Southwest, Spanish has been spoken for many more years than any other European language, has never been eliminated in the region, and counts more native speakers than ever before. Yet with insistent reinforcement, the conventional script designates Spanish as a foreign language and its native speakers as aliens. These are the kinds of interpretive schema that insurgent metaphors open up for consideration.

## Section 6: Prolegomenon to the Creation of Insurgent Metaphors

A review of the Latino responses to the three anti-Latino referenda, Propositions 187, 209, and 227, reveals implicit assent to the worldview promulgated by conservative, at times nativist, political activists. For whenever references to immigrants as commodities, criminals, invaders, or animals are allowed, or whenever claims that affirmative action is the sole cause of U.S. racism are met with silence, or whenever Spanish is allowed to be called a foreign language, then the view of the social world that is antagonistic to Latinos has been tacitly accepted. Advocates who speak to social issues of Latinos should mind their metaphors. Discourse is always harnessed to pull for a social agenda. Since conventional metaphors construct the status quo, certain actions to challenge them may bring about a swifter revision of worldview. This section outlines eight steps for the social activist.

One, silence is egregious assent to anti-Latino discourse, racism, and other injustices articulated and reinforced by way of the metaphors of public discourse. The conventional metaphor should always be contested. In the course of direct discourse and debate, whether in front of a television audience, in the corridors of power, or on a ten-minute coffee break, the object of counterhegemonic discourse is to open up new cognitive "space," to offer an alternative view of the social world at the level of metaphor.

Two, metaphor should not be brought to the conscious attention of the audience in debate, since the object is to propose a viable alternative vision of the world, not to talk about discourse, which will be seen as quibbling over semantics. Regarding persuasiveness, Jeffery S. Mio has conducted experiments on listener response to political metaphors and found that all metaphors are not equal. It seems effective metaphors trigger or resonate with the preexisting underlying symbolic representations of the listener, so that "extending" or verifying and affirming the operative scripts of an audience will garner a stronger response.[24] In other words, the effective insubordinate metaphor is the congruent one.

Three, in my judgment, a couple of reciprocal actions may judiciously contest the conventional metaphoric worldview. Begin by employing a nonmetaphor to point out the failure of the standard vision of society. This will strip the conventional worldview of its presumed self-evident reality by providing a counterexample that forces the taken-for-granted to be questioned. The nonmetaphor can be a statistic, anecdote, or, even better, a face and a story. Then follow with an insurgent metaphor to recast the social world in more just, and more socially encompassing, terms which are demonstrably comprehensible.

Using a new metaphor without exemplification is just pretty words. For example, if bilingual education or bilingualism is characterized as handicap, illustrate the poverty of this view by presenting an adolescent who exhibits superb control of English (as well as excellent Spanish, Cantonese, or Bengali), and who consequently is better equipped to succeed than a similar English-dependent student. Well-spoken speech which retains a nonstandard accent, either due to second-language acquisition or a social dialect, also flouts the linguistic hegemony that a speaker must speak with a standard English accent to be considered well educated or eloquent.

Another illustration might be in order. To the charge that immigrants are welfare-seeking invaders, call up a statistic and point to the immigrant entrepreneur who has built an economic base comparable to the president of the local Chamber of Commerce. For instance, reference a study of census data which demonstrated that 17 percent of Latino immigrants in Los Angeles County received public assistance in 1990, compared to 42 percent of non-Latino whites,[25] or that six of fifteen top chief executives of Orange County's manufacturing sector are foreign-born bilinguals.[26]

Once the stereotype has been confronted on its own terms, then the time is ripe to articulate a new vision. Offer an alternative metaphor that arguably makes better "common sense." This one-two punch may make the complacent nonpartisan voter reconsider the previously unconsidered conventions of the social order. The aim is to create a bit of cognitive dissonance regarding the taken-as-given, in order to open up a bit of cognitive space for a more encompassing alternative view of humanity and nation.

Four, in the intermediate term, calls for the dissolution of nation will not be well received. Rather, seek to construct metaphors that can be linked to the conventional constellations of NATION AS BODY and NATION AS HOUSE. Venerable conceptualizations of national security and national unity can be harnessed to a progressive political agenda, much in the same terms that they have been for a neoconservative agenda. As the continuing skirmishes over the Maastrich Treaty negotiations for the European Union have demonstrated, these medieval notions of NATION will remain viable long into the twenty-first century.

For alternative views of nation, the FABRIC metaphor, such as "the intricate weave of American peoples into the national fabric," may be considered. Textile invokes often complex warps and weaves which can be associated with patterns of relations among social groups as well as individuals. Fabric is also reticulated, which lends this semantic domain to the social network. Cloth likewise evokes wholeness and inclusivity. Different threads and strands are woven together to create a "whole cloth" which is greater than the sum of its parts. Indeed, the frequent neoconservative complaint against multiculturalism, that it rends the American social fabric, presumes a totality. Because of this ontology, NATION AS FABRIC does not presuppose social exclusion, the insider/outsider entailment, which is the basis for a social covenant that counts some people in and counts others out.

Five, to create and promulgate effective insurgent metaphors requires recognizing the current prevailing metaphors that give shape to today's prevalent worldview. These prevailing views certainly will not match the worldview of minority activists who matured in alienating and subordinating places in society. Careful scrutiny of general public discourse will repay study.

Six, a disturbing tack was noted in the discourse of anti–Proposition 187 partisans, who impugned the ethics of referendum supporters. The *Times* published disparagements, such as this insult directed at the authors of the Proposition 187 referendum ("two mothballed bureaucrats"), and riffs on the pro-187 organization, Save Our State (SOS) ("Snake-Oil Salesmen," "Snoop or Snitch," and "Soldiers of Satan"). Ad hominen attacks are puny attempts to deprecate opponents, and are consonant with the use of metaphor to degrade immigrants as less than human. Such assaults are inadvisable, since they do not offer a more encompassing view of humanity. On the other hand, this is quite different from characterizing proposed anti-Latino legislation or actions in deprecatory terms, particularly if associated with notions with a certain symbolic weight. For example, in the *Times* database is found:

22. "[Proposition 187] is like **target practice** against the Constitution." (October 31, 1994, A1).

Regarding Proposition 227, see references to *criminal* and *crucify* in excerpt 17 above as well.

Seven, along these lines, the designer of new metaphors does not ever own the copyrights on these tools of insurgency. In the same way the 1960s RACISM AS DISEASE metaphor was subverted in the 1990s, alternative metaphors can be usurped by a rival. The maker of metaphors must explore their connotations and entailments thoroughly to work them into tools that bring into sharp relief the shortcomings of the conventional metaphoric constructs, all the while cognizant that political rivals will seek to exploit the weaknesses of these same alternative metaphors.

Finally, it is a fatal error to become oblivious to the contingency and naturalizing effect of metaphor. All metaphors, because they are merely links between preexisting semantic domains, are only approximations of far more complex realities. Each metaphor emphasizes some elements of the social world at the expense of others. The metaphor maker, or "strong poet," has two tasks.[27] One is to work the insubordinate metaphor so that the public comes around to a new view. The second task is to keep in mind the contingent nature of all metaphors while continuing to seek better ones.

## *"Language Speaks Man"*[28]

Americans have great faith in progress, in their country's prowess to subdue the elements of nature to build a better world, to save the people from their own excesses, to liberate the weak from poverty, ignorance, and hate. This Enlightenment legacy holds that by way of rationality, the greatest puzzles of the world would be solved. This view of nature has its reflexes in today's faith in assured social progress toward greater justice and equity.

Pragmatism, among other philosophies, deflates this American pipe dream that the right set of physical, chemical, pharmacological, and political formulas will inevitably be found to solve the nation's social ills. Rather, the onus is on us. People do not find solutions *in* the world; there is no intrinsic nature to be found in nature. Rather, people create the world *within* themselves, even mind, matter, community, and self. One repercussion of this radical standpoint is that the world is created out of the discourse that people use. As Richard Rorty quips, the world does not speak; only people do.[29] Discourse speaks society into existence. The second is that discourse antecedes society, a principal theme of Chapter 2, which reviewed how crucial the discourse of science is for its "advances," how discourse constitutes the institutions which define and govern our social roles, and how discourse makes up the very categories that we operate with in everyday life.

In an incisive analogy, Rorty compares the history of language, hence the history of culture, to Charles Darwin's history of the coral reef: "Old metaphors are constantly dying off into literalness, and then serving as a platform and foil for new metaphors."[30] Culture, then, is a mountain built out of tiny accretions and accumulations that we live on and live through. Note that this coral reef analogy does not invoke an upward trajectory called "progress," irrespective of the strongly held American creed that things will continue to get better. The cultural coral reef does not necessarily advance toward a more excellent form; it is blind to our doctrines.

The chief narrative that promotes hegemonic assent among the U.S. public—particularly its racialized and linguistic minorities—is the faith in inevitable social progress. A requirement for social progress, naturally, is social order and placidity among all parties. For the oppressed, this means deference and restraint, and especially endless patience. Nonetheless, crucial American notions such as progress, race, citizen, and nation, as they are currently defined, will not lead inexorably toward greater equality for or inclusion of minorities. In the six years of public discourse sampled in the *Los Angeles Times,* the conventional use of these terms led to greater domination and less freedom for Latinos to live fully realized lives. Thus, to believe in unfailing social progress is to consent to the public discourse that sustains and legitimizes today's systems of domination and inequity.

Friedrich Nietzsche viewed the downtrodden as chattel and the powerful to be the rightful rulers of the weak. He harbored contempt for the masses, whom he considered sheep for the carnivores of the world to feed on. Nevertheless, he recognized that the seat of power is located, not in individuals, but in the discourse that creates the world order:

> What therefore is Truth? A flexible army of metaphors, metonymies, anthropomorphisms; in short, a sum of human relations which have been poetically and rhetorically intensified, transformed, bejeweled, and which after long usage seem to a people to be fixed, canonical, and binding.[31]

And on that seat, metaphor was Nietzsche's key to power. For contrary to the tenets of the Enlightenment, he believed that Truth did not exist, except as metaphor-guided discursive practices that compose society. The society accepts its rulers because it accepts the vocabulary the rulers use to define it, that is, it accepts cultural hegemony.

The master of public discourse is the master of metaphors. Rorty praises the power of the metaphor maker (whether poet, scientist, or artist) with the protean force to fire the imagination of society, to allow it to sustain new thoughts about itself, and thereby over time to create new relations and re-visions of humankind.[32] Thus "strong poets" create new societies by way of metaphor. Among the strong poets and their metaphors that Rorty points to, there are St. Paul's metaphorical extension of the Greek term *agape*, which transformed the modest notion "charity" into transcendent Christian love, and Sir Isaac Newton's *gravitas*, which meant human psychological "seriousness," but came to refer to a property of attraction of celestial bodies. To this list we can add Frederick Douglass's re-vision of the Jeffersonian axiom "all men are created equal" to include all God's children, together with Martin Luther King Jr.'s eloquent and sustained diagnosis of the nation's racial illness as CANCER. Thus Miguel de Unamuno's laughing rejection of logic should give pause:

> For a single metaphor, I would discard all the syllogisms and their corresponding *therefores* on which so much scholastic verbiage is hung. One metaphor teaches me more; it reveals more to me. Above all, I am inflamed beneath a metaphor. Imagination only works where there is fire.[33]

Unamuno's praise of metaphor should be heeded by Latinos and other social activists. The present was not first envisioned by deduction, logic, and argument, but it is made again each day by metaphor. Unamuno delighted in the potency of the poetic to bring about social change, proclaiming that only the renegade metaphor could incite world-making imagination. If history is a succession of metaphors, then they are the principal instruments by which vocabularies are created to speak society into existence. Insurgent metaphors are tools to construct stronger vocabularies to speak this new society. To contest the current regime of discourse requires the creation of insubordinate metaphors to produce more inclusive American values, and more just practices for a new society.

# Appendix

## Tallies of Political Metaphors

The metaphor database is the empirical foundation of this book. It is composed of more than twenty columns of journalistic, linguistic, and metaphor information for each of 4,485 instances of text metaphors. These individual text metaphors, which we call "tokens," are the rows of the database, and the material basis for this book. The tokens were extracted from 671 *Los Angeles Times* articles, dating from May 1992 to July 1998. This figure excludes all tokens which were not published in the *Los Angeles Times,* notably tokens drawn from the *Commentary* essays. Over a thousand tokens were jettisoned for many procedural reasons, including, for example, those tokens about which the coders did not concur. It is not possible to succinctly present most of the information developed in the database. The challenge is to provide adequate summaries of its most important aspects, without numbing the reader. Adequacy, however, is a judgment call. Throughout the book, discussion has been directed by the patterns of semantic source domains assigned to political concepts such as IMMIGRANT, EDUCATION, and LANGUAGE. So, presenting the contingent relationships among source and target semantic domains that construct worldview is the main object of this appendix. Still, even source and target domain information must be abridged, since a list of all confirmed combinations of semantic source domain and political concept (target domain) is over 2,000 lines long.

Another issue is the relationship between lower-order metaphors and higher-order metaphors. Some very important concepts are rarely metaphorized in public discourse, appearing in the database as metaphor tokens in low numbers. However, these political concepts were indirectly referenced or invoked by thousands of other metaphor tokens. The key political concept of the United States, for example, was explicitly metaphorized in the six-year database on public discourse only twenty times. However, NATION (with clear reference to the United States) is a higher-order metaphor. It is the conceptual source for other metaphors, such as WHITE RACISM is a CANCER of the NATION AS BODY and IMMIGRANT is an INVADER of the NATION AS HOUSE. As an overarching "umbrella" metaphor, NATION was invoked in over 1,400 tokens, or one of every three metaphors noted in the database. Accordingly, both higher-order and lower-order metaphors have been compiled. A tally of the higher-order umbrella metaphors is provided in Table A.1. This is followed by tabulations of selected political metaphors, in Tables A.2 through A.17.

The fifty-one most frequent source domains were, in alphabetical order: ALIEN, ANIMAL, ASTRONOMY, BARRIER, BODY, BOTANY, BUSINESS, CHEMISTRY,

CLOTHING, COLD, COMMODITY, COMMUNICATION, CRIME, DANGER, DIS-
EASE, DREAM, ELECTRIC, FAMILY, FIRE/HOT, FOOD, GEOLOGY, HISTORY,
HOUSE, LAND, LANGUAGE, LAW, LIGHT, MACHINE, MONEY, MUSIC, NATURE,
NAUTICAL, NEGATE, NOISE, PATH, PERSON, PRESSURE, RACISM, RELIGION,
SCIENCE, SIGHT, SLAVE, SPORT, THEATER, TOOL, VEHICLE, VIOLENCE, WAR,
WATER, WEATHER, WORK. The labels for these semantic domains are a minor con-
cern; the range of the domains is crucial to making sense of worldview. For a
frequency-ordered list, see Table A.1 below. These are the most productive source
domains for the creation of political concepts, including NATION, POLITICS, and
EDUCATION. The relative frequency of source domains reflects the content of the
articles from which they are excerpted.

Over three hundred target domains appeared in the database, after several cycles
of thorough editing to standardize the label for the tokens. As with source domains,
the labels of these target domains are primarily mnemonic. The ninety-two most frequent targets (with number of instances in parentheses) were: affirmative action (56),
America (20), American Dream (24), assimilation (13), border (53), bureaucracy
(6), California Civil Rights Initiative (2), citizens and citizenship (6), civil rights
(5), community (42), controversy (10), crime (21), democracy (2), demographics
(14), disease (3), drugs (6), Ebonics (3), economic class (7), economy (75), emotions (11), English language (28), family (5), gangs (68), government (48), health care
(16), hegemony (11), history (5), immigrants (284), immigration (149), individuals
(13), industry (5), Immigration and Naturalization Service (25), investigation (6),
jobs/labor (38), language (203), Latino community (26), Latino heritage (6), Latinos
(65), law courts (3), laws (80), legal decision (23), legal justice (6), legislation (49), life
(9), mass media (23), minority groups (24), money (20), nationalism (2), opportunity (11), police (38), policy (22), polity (93), political action/activism (474), political
climate (19), political commission/committee (24), political debate/campaign (236),
political platform (30), political polls (7), political power (26), politicians (39), population (1), poverty (14), governmental or social programs (149), protest (26), public opinion expressed as beliefs (59), public sentiment expressed as emotions (196),
racism (66), referenda (207), responsibility (3), school achievement (45), school bilingual education (54), school curriculum (107), school data (14), school funding
(13), school policy/debate (80), school students (129), schoolteachers (57), schools
(98), schoolwork (13), social benefits (28), society (11), SOS, the Save Our State
Proposition 187 committee (17), Spanish language (6), suburbia (12), success (34),
various trivial, unique, or immaterial targets (159), urban (7), violence (16), vote
(112), welfare (3), whites (7), women (4). The total number of tokens was 4,485.

TABLE A.1
Umbrella Metaphors

| HIGHER-ORDER TARGET DOMAIN | SUM | SOURCE DOMAINS |
|---|---|---|
| NATION | 1,467 | BODY, HOUSE (including LAND, SHIP), FABRIC |
| POLITICS | 1,122 | WAR, SPORT |
| (various domains) | 854 | WATER (e.g., IMMIGRATION, LANGUAGE, EMOTION), MONEY, FIRE, MACHINE/TOOL, FAMILY, CRIME |
| (none) | 442 | (Highly varied or uncommon sources, or source domains that withstand higher-order generalization.) |
| EDUCATION | 354 | PATH, FACTORY, WATER |
| IMMIGRANT | 221 | ANIMAL, COMMODITY |
| (minor domains) | 25 | SIGHT, FOOD, WEATHER, SCIENCE, RELIGION, PLANT, NOISE, COOK, etc. |
| TOTAL | 4,485 | |

## Higher-Order "Umbrella" Domains for Political Metaphors, by Frequency

The sums of Table A.1 were derived in a separate process of intersubjective judgments, apart from the process used to develop the text-level political concepts, as exemplified in the following tables. This separate process was designed to locate the most productive higher-order metaphors in the database, and may not correspond tightly to the tallies of text-based political concepts.

## A Sampling of Political Concept Metaphors, Tallied Semantic Target Domain by Source Domains

A few metaphors were specific to one political campaign, rather than part of the general American public discourse across time. These are put to one side of the tabulation of overall frequencies. A few others which, if included in the tables, would skew the patterning of political concept metaphorization are also placed below the tables, as in Table A.8.

## TABLE A.2
### AFFIRMATIVE ACTION

| SOURCE DOMAIN | TYPE | TOTALS | PERCENTAGES |
|---|---|---|---|
| BODY, DISEASE, CLOTHING, e.g., *mend it, don't end it; strong dose of human rights; program tailored to minorities* | dominant | 29 | 51.8 |
| CRIME, VIOLENCE, WAR, e.g., *victim of quotas, if affirmative action is gutted* | secondary | 10 | 17.9 |
| TOOL, MACHINE, e.g., *roll back* or *dismantle affirmative action, social engineering* | | 7 | 12.5 |
| PATH, SPORT, HISTORY, HOUSE, RELIGION, WORK, et al. | occasional | 10 | 17.9 |
| | TOTAL | 56 | 100.0 |

Note: All examples in the tables throughout the book are drawn from the database.

## TABLE A.3
### BORDER

| SOURCE DOMAIN | TYPE | TOTALS | PERCENTAGES |
|---|---|---|---|
| HOUSE, (LAND), e.g., *just shut the door, seal off the border, build a moat* | dominant | 21 | 39.6 |
| BODY, e.g., *we want the scar to heal* | secondary | 11 | 20.8 |
| WATER, e.g., *porous borders* | | 8 | 15.1 |
| WAR, e.g., *we will not surrender our borders* | | 6 | 11.3 |
| HISTORY, MACHINE, ANIMAL, CHEMISTRY, et al. | occasional | 7 | 13.2 |
| | TOTAL | 53 | 100.0 |

TABLE A.4
COMMUNITY

| SOURCE DOMAIN | TYPE | TOTALS | PERCENTAGES |
|---|---|---|---|
| BODY (including CLOTHING, DISEASE), e.g., *alter the face of suburbia, violent heart of the Latino community* | dominant | 18 | 43.9 |
| HOUSE, LAND, e.g., *gritty urban community* | | 14 | 34.1 |
| ANIMAL, CHEMISTRY, FAMILY, FOOD, MACHINE, SHIP, SPORT | occasional | 9 | 22.0 |
| | TOTAL | 41 | 100.0 |

TABLE A.5
LANGUAGE

| SOURCE DOMAIN | TYPE | TOTALS | PERCENTAGES |
|---|---|---|---|
| WATER, e.g., *immersion, cloud of incomprehension* | dominant | 144 | 72.0 |
| PATH, BARRIER, e.g., *language barrier* | secondary | 18 | 9.0 |
| BODY, DISEASE, e.g., *a crippling, almost fatal disadvantage* | | 13 | 6.5 |
| TOOL, MACHINE, COMMODITY, e.g., *if you have only one tool in your tool box* | | 13 | 6.5 |
| HOUSE, SHIP, ANIMAL, RELIGION, LAW, WAR | occasional | 12 | 6.0 |
| | TOTAL | 200 | 100.0 |

TABLE A.6
LATINA/O

| SOURCE DOMAIN | TYPE | TOTALS | PERCENTAGES |
|---|---|---|---|
| WAR, VIOLENCE, e.g., *racist element aimed at Latinos, assaults on all Latin American people, Open Season on Latinos* | dominant | 22 | 35.5 |
| BODY, DISEASE, e.g., *Latinos hamstrung by bad economic conditions* | secondary | 15 | 24.2 |
| WATER, e.g., *influxes of Latinos* | | 13 | 21.0 |
| ANIMAL, MONEY, COMMODITY, BOTANY, FAMILY, FIRE, PATH, SPORT, TOOL, SIGHT | occasional | 12 | 19.4 |
| | TOTAL | 62 | 100.0 |

TABLE A.7
POLITY

| SOURCE DOMAIN | TYPE | TOTALS | PERCENTAGES |
|---|---|---|---|
| BODY, DISEASE, CLOTHING, e.g., *state's ills, Ventura Co. is not immune* | dominant | 51 | 58.6 |
| HOUSE, LAND, GEOLOGY, e.g., *if the foundation is weak, the house will fall down* | secondary | 14 | 16.1 |
| WAR, CRIME, VIOLENCE, WATER, MACHINE, TOOL, CHEMISTRY, FAMILY | occasional | 22 | 25.3 |
| | TOTAL | 87 | 100.0 |

TABLE A.8
PUBLIC OPINION

| SOURCE DOMAIN | TYPE | TOTALS | PERCENTAGES |
|---|---|---|---|
| WATER, e.g., *waves of criticism, tide of support is rising* | dominant | 17 | 28.8 |
| ANIMAL, BODY, FIRE, HOT, BOTANY, HOUSE, VIOLENCE, COLD, WAR, ASTRONOMY, WEATHER, ALIEN, LIGHT, MACHINE, MUSIC, THEATER | occasional | 31 | 71.2 |
| | TOTAL | 59 | 100.0 |
| plus: *"send a message"* (limited to the Proposition 187 period) | | 11 | |

TABLE A.9
PUBLIC SENTIMENT

| SOURCE DOMAIN | TYPE | TOTALS | PERCENTAGES |
|---|---|---|---|
| WATER, e.g., *torrents of public condemnation, xenophobic waves* | dominant | 61 | 31.8 |
| BODY, CLOTHING, DISEASE, e.g., *ads strike a nerve of prejudice* | secondary | 49 | 25.5 |
| FIRE, e.g., *stoke the fire of people against him* | | 34 | 17.7 |
| HOUSE, WEATHER, e.g., *climate of hostility and violent confrontation* | | 19 | 9.9 |
| WAR, e.g., *the Proposition self-ignited; it just exploded* | | 13 | 6.8 |
| ANIMAL, MONEY, ELECTRIC, MACHINE, NOISE, CHEMISTRY, MUSIC, NATURE, PRESSURE | occasional | 16 | 8.3 |
| | TOTAL | 192 | 100.0 |

TABLE A.10
POLITICS

| SOURCE DOMAIN | TYPE | TOTALS | PERCENTAGES |
|---|---|---|---|
| WAR, e.g., *campaign, battle, warrior, bombardment, launch, barricade* | dominant | 275 | 64.7 |
| BODY, CLOTHING, DISEASE, e.g., *paralysis, embrace an issue, nightmare* | secondary | 57 | 13.4 |
| SPORT, e.g., *tackle* | | 30 | 7.1 |
| ANIMAL, e.g., *unleash* | | 22 | 5.2 |
| VEHICLE, FIRE, HOUSE, et al. | occasional | 41 | 9.6 |
| | TOTAL | 425 | 100.0 |

Note: The total of this table, n = 425, represents a subset of the database. Proportions are representative of the entire database. From Santa Ana and Rivas 1999.

TABLE A.11
RACISM

| SOURCE DOMAIN | TYPE | TOTALS | PERCENTAGES |
|---|---|---|---|
| BODY, DISEASE, e.g., *painful legacy, White Man's burden, heart of the cancer* | dominant | 28 | 50.0 |
| WAR, CRIME, e.g., *ball and chain, to pander* | secondary | 9 | 16.1 |
| BOUNDARY, GEOLOGY, BOTANY, ANIMAL, ELECTRIC, SIGHT, WATER, DREAM, FIRE, LAW, VEHICLE | occasional | 19 | 33.9 |
| | TOTAL | 56 | 100.0 |

TABLE A.12
REFERENDA

| SOURCE DOMAIN | TYPE | TOTALS | PERCENTAGES |
|---|---|---|---|
| WAR, VIOLENCE, CRIME, e.g., *kill the American Dream, rob students of an education, near-apocalyptic changes* | dominant | 70 | 35.2 |
| BODY, DISEASE, CLOTHING, e.g., *187 potential poison, wrong prescription for a serious disease* | secondary | 45 | 22.6 |
| HOUSE, GEOLOGY, LAND, e.g., *sweeping initiative, 187 a ringing bell heard across the nation* | | 19 | 9.5 |
| PATH, SPORT, ELECTRIC, MACHINE, TOOL, FIRE, RELIGION, WATER, ANIMAL, WEATHER, NATURE, COMMUNICATION, MONEY, NOISE, LAW, THEATER, et al. | occasional | 65 | 32.7 |
| | TOTAL | 199 | 100.0 |

TABLE A.13
SCHOOL ACHIEVEMENT

| SOURCE DOMAIN | TYPE | TOTALS | PERCENTAGES |
|---|---|---|---|
| PATH, SPORT, e.g., *children fall behind when taught in language they are still learning* | dominant | 28 | 66.7 |
| BODY, HOUSE, GEOLOGY, WAR, WATER, PRESSURE, RELIGION, VEHICLE | occasional | 14 | 33.3 |
| | TOTAL | 42 | 100.0 |

## TABLE A.14
### BILINGUAL EDUCATION

| SOURCE DOMAIN | TYPE | TOTALS | PERCENTAGES |
|---|---|---|---|
| PATH, SPORT, e.g., *holding foreign-speaking students back, bilingual education is a training-wheel program* | dominant | 17 | 29.8 |
| BODY, DISEASE, CLOTHING, e.g., *loosen the grip on the primary language* | | 13 | 22.8 |
| WAR, CRIME, VIOLENCE, e.g., *bilingual zealot, bilingual education is great misfired good intention* | secondary | 7 | 12.3 |
| MACHINE, ANIMAL, NATURE, WEATHER, RELIGION, SCIENCE, WATER, MONEY | occasional | 20 | 35.1 |
| | TOTAL | 57 | 100.0 |

## TABLE A.15
### CURRICULUM

| SOURCE DOMAIN | TYPE | TOTALS | PERCENTAGES |
|---|---|---|---|
| PATH, SPORT, e.g., *hitting an academic home run, picking up steam* | dominant | 28 | 57.1 |
| BODY, CLOTHING, e.g., *losing weak students, severe impact on academic skills* | secondary | 10 | 20.4 |
| WAR, VIOLENCE, HOUSE, WORK, ANIMAL, FAMILY, PRESSURE | occasional | 11 | 22.4 |
| | TOTAL | 49 | 100.0 |

TABLE A.16
SCHOOL

| SOURCE DOMAIN | TYPE | TOTALS | PERCENTAGES |
|---|---|---|---|
| WAR, CRIME, e.g., *227 robs students, classroom at Ground Zero, a school lockdown* | dominant | 27 | 32.1 |
| BODY, DISEASE, CLOTHING, e.g., *educational malpractice* | | 22 | 26.2 |
| MACHINE, COMMODITY, e.g., *overhaul school* | secondary | 10 | 11.9 |
| HOUSE, LAND, e.g., *a fixture of schools nationwide* | | 10 | 11.9 |
| SPORT, PATH, e.g., *full-time course load, escaping bad schools* | | 10 | 11.9 |
| ANIMAL, HISTORY, LIGHT, RELIGION, SCIENCE, et al. | occasional | 5 | 6.0 |
| | TOTAL | 84 | 100.0 |

TABLE A.17
STUDENT

| SOURCE DOMAIN | TYPE | TOTALS | PERCENTAGES |
|---|---|---|---|
| PATH (excluding *dropout*), VEHICLE, e.g., *derailing students, diverting students to a new program* | dominant | 49 | 41.5 |
| BODY, DISEASE, e.g., *deteriorating behavior, shouldering a full academic load* | secondary | 19 | 16.1 |
| WAR, VIOLENCE, e.g., *attempts to rescue students* | | 23 | 19.5 |
| ANIMAL, COMMODITY, HOUSE, MONEY, ALIEN, FAMILY, LIGHT, MACHINE, MUSIC, RELIGION, et al. | occasional | 27 | 22.9 |
| | TOTAL | 118 | 100.0 |
| plus: RIVER, e.g., *mainstream* | | 57 | |
| plus: *dropout*, another PATH metaphor | | 44 | |

# Notes

## Chapter One

1. Romano-V. 1968, Ríos 1969, Barrera 1974.
2. See Cockcroft 1994 for an accessible overview of Latina/o resistance.
3. Sánchez 1932a, 1932b, discussed in Vaca 1970a.
4. See Galarza's *Merchants of Labor: The Mexican Bracero Story.* For a summary of Galarza's life, see Chabrán 1985.
5. See Acuña 1972 and Jiménez 1994.
6. U.S. Census figures for 1990 stated that Latinos numbered 22.4 million.
7. *Time,* October 16, 1978, pp. 48–61.
8. Rodríguez and Romero, *Los Angeles Times,* December 27, 1989, p. B7.
9. Menchaca 1993, Almaguer 1994, Martínez 1997, Johnson 1997a, 1997b.
10. Omi and Winant 1994.
11. Lipsitz 1995, 1998.
12. *Economist,* July 5, 1997.
13. The August 10, 1993, "Open Letter" appeared as a full-page paid ad in the *New York Times* and *Washington Post,* and the national edition of the *Los Angeles Times.* The excerpt comes from a fact sheet from the office of Governor Wilson entitled "Highlights of Wilson's Actions to Fight Illegal Immigration."
14. "The Order of Discourse," Foucault 1984, pp. 108, 110.

## Chapter Two

1. Several studies of the representation of Mexicans in the Anglo-American imagination have been conducted. Most recent is M. Anderson 1998. Earlier studies focusing on nineteenth-century Mexicans, or, more broadly, Latin Americans, include Robinson 1963, Powell 1971, Pettit 1980, Johannsen 1985, and Britton 1995. Nineteenth-century Latinos were not viewed by Anglo-Americans in terms of cultural relativism, but in terms of a racial hierarchy which placed Anglo-Americans at its apex and judged Latinos to be inferior. Studies of Chicanos, and studies which include twentieth-century imagery, include Martínez 1969, Ríos 1969, Paredes 1973, Woll 1977, Fernández and Pedroza 1982, Ramírez-Berg 1989, and Keller 1994. Of the latter, Ramírez-Berg's work stands out for its energetic interpretation.
2. Wetherell and Potter 1992 employ an oxymoron, *benign racism,* in their other-

wise elucidating discussions of New Zealand racism, while Reeves 1983 used the term *sanitized* for the case of British parliamentary discourse. Other media scholars describe as "modern racism" contemporary media representations of minorities. Entman employs a three-part definition: general emotional hostility toward minorities, resistance to the political claims of minorities on white resources and sympathies, belief that racism in the United States no longer exists and that racial discrimination no longer inhibits minority achievement (1990a, pp. 332–333). For other studies of interest, see note 1 above. Also consult Entman 1992.

3. In social science, the thesis is strongly stated in Romano-V. 1968, 1970, and Vaca 1970a, 1970b. For historical accounts, see Acuña 1972, De León 1983, Sánchez 1993, Almaguer 1994, Gómez-Quiñones 1994, and Menchaca 1995. For an anthropological framework, see Chávez 1998 and Vigil 1998; for a political science viewpoint, read Barrera 1979. In legal studies, excerpts by a range of scholars have been brought together in Delgado and Stefancic 1998. In linguistics it is stated in Peñalosa 1975 and Hernández-Chávez 1989, 1999. In film studies, read Ramírez-Berg 1989. In the analysis of popular culture, see Hernández 1991 and Gaspar de Alba 1998.

4. Critical discourse analysis was selected because its paradigm has been sufficiently developed to provide guidance in the research. For example, critical discourse analysis avowedly incorporates both micro and macro approaches into its research toolbox. For one, van Dijk 1993b conceives discourse to be the interface between the micro and macro. The focus of micro-studies is the interactional enactment of dominance relationships, as marked by elements of language such as the tone of voice used by interlocutors, the form of the interrogative question posed by a wife to her husband, and the situation that makes for a felicitous perlocutionary act. Macro concerns involve the social position or "space" that these discourse practices enact in societal structures. In contrast to critical discourse analysis, many branches of the social sciences engage in often barren debates on the proper focus of social theory. The basis of contention often seems to be no more than personal predilection. When theoretical prejudices are put aside, each partisan position has been found to be insufficient, since both are indispensable (Alexander et al. 1987, Santa Ana and Parodi 1998). Critical discourse analysis focuses neither on the theoretical preeminence of micro or macro theories on human conduct, nor any other theoretical precept, but rather on understanding the reproduction of unjustifiable social hierarchies.

5. For example, Stubbs 1986, Brown and Yule 1983, and van Dijk 1985.

6. See Fairclough 1989. With the rise of scientific linguistic research, a criterion of explanatory adequacy became the chief measure of success. See Chomsky 1965,

pp. 24–27. Explanatory adequacy is also the primary goal of critical discourse analysis.

7. van Dijk 1993b, p. 253.

8. van Dijk 1993a.

9. van Dijk 1993b, p. 28.

10. Keynote address at the culmination of the 1963 March on Washington for Civil Rights. Reprinted in Washington 1991.

11. Fairclough 1989, pp. 22–108.

12. Bourdieu quoted in Fairclough 1989, p. 41. I add "or say" to the quote.

13. Mehan 1979.

14. Chilton 1996, pp. 37–40; Fairclough 1989, p. 13.

15. "History of Systems of Thought, 1970–1971," Foucault 1977.

16. Laclau 1993.

17. The absence of governing principles in discourse is, of course, an intolerable postulate; if nothing else, language is a set of rules. Several well-established arguments support this linguistic dogma. To offer only one, randomness cannot be acquired. Consequently, any discourse practice that is based on language-based materials must be learned in terms of language-based rules. Thus it follows that the weave of natural language discourse and institutionally codified discourse is governed by a system of rules constrained by the nature of the discourse material.

18. van Dijk 1993b.

19. Each excerpt that is part of the *Los Angeles Times* metaphor database is cited with a date and page number. Thus the quote is December 23, 1992, B2.

20. Lakoff 1993.

21. Black 1993.

22. Searle 1993.

23. Ortony 1993, p. 1.

24. Lakoff 1993.

25. Jackendoff 1983 in Casad 1992, p. 312.

26. *Los Angeles Times,* November 10, 1994, A1.

27. Grice 1975.

28. Gibbs 1994, pp. 99–105.

29. The literature on metaphor is immense. It stretches unbroken from the classical and scholastic discipline of rhetoric, through the philosophical era of language, to its burgeoning twentieth-century study, which is expanding to the new social sciences without receding from any of the older disciplines. I am not conversant, much less expert, in all these arenas of thought. This chapter is informed by, and will be constructed in terms of, the linguistic sciences of metaphor. The exposition of theories in this chapter will serve to introduce the

key issue involved in metaphor theory, namely, metaphor's impact on the construction of human society. It should be noted that the linguistic theories of metaphor are not self-contained, since metaphor and figurative language reach across most areas of human activity.

30. Fernandez 1991, p. 4.
31. Adapted liberally from translations by Pompa 1990, p. 223, and by Goddard Bergin and Fisch 1948, pp. 129–130.
32. Purcell 1990, p. 36.
33. Black 1993, p. 20.
34. Purcell 1990, p. 39.
35. See Grady 1999 for an account of common mistakes in cognitive linguistic studies of metaphor.
36. Lakoff 1987.
37. Lakoff and Johnson 1980, p. 49.
38. Lakoff 1993 reiterates a distinction to be made between the labels of metaphoric mappings and the metaphoric mappings themselves. The labels, such as LOVE IS MADNESS, are shorthand ways of talking, that is to say, mnemonic "names for a set of mappings" of conceptual correspondences between a source domain and a target domain (p. 207). In this book such mappings will be presented, that is to say, our best effort to characterize the ontological correspondences between the entities of the source domain which are mapped onto the target domain. The particular instances of metaphors, the linguistic/discourse material of these metaphors, such as those located in the *Los Angeles Times,* are only textual specimens of the mappings between semantic domains. The mnemonic labels of the mappings will be presented in SMALL CAPITALS, following the convention of contemporary metaphor theory. By convention the names of mappings, as well as their particular material instances, are called the metaphor.
39. Lakoff 1993.
40. Ibid.
41. Bronson 1997.
42. Sweetser 1990.
43. Brugman 1983.
44. Gibbs 1994, p. 157.
45. Gibbs 1993.
46. Gibbs 1994, p. 147.
47. In sequence: Lakoff and Johnson 1980, for time and space; Kövecses 1986, for emotions; Lakoff 1987, 1993, for events; as well as Lakoff and Turner 1989, for talk about ideas.
48. Lakoff and Johnson 1980, pp. 267–268, cited in Goatly 1997, p. 41.
49. Lakoff 1993.

50. Ibid.
51. Gibbs 1994, p. 152.
52. Lakoff 1987. This remark, of course, harks back to Vico's quote.
53. Wilson 1997, pp. 219–220.
54. Kuhn 1962.
55. Kuhn 1993, p. 538.
56. Gibbs 1994, p. 172.
57. Van Besien 1989, pp. 11–19.
58. La Mettrie cited in Gardner 1996, p. xviii.
59. Lend an ear to Searle 1998.
60. Reddy 1979.
61. Fairclough 1989, pp. 22–23.
62. Reddy 1979, p. 165.
63. LANGUAGE AS TOOLMAKER, not TOOL, reflects the so-called linguistic turn in the social sciences. A. C. Grayling (1996, pp. 68–76) credits Wittgenstein for the dynamism of the philosophy of language in late-twentieth-century thought. Cristina Lafont points further into the past for its source, to the German tradition of Wilhelm von Humboldt, and the Anglo tradition exemplified by Gottlob Frege. Both contended that meaning determines reference. "That is, linguistic expressions are held to determine, if not what there *is*, at least what there *can be* for a linguistic community—or what such a community *can say* (i.e., *believe*) that there is. In this sense, the key function of language is held to lie in its *world-disclosing* capacity" (Lafont 1999, p. xii, italics in the original). This philosophy constitutes a critique of Kant's philosophy of consciousness, in which language was a mere tool, or medium, for the expression of prelinguistic thoughts. In the current philosophy-of-language view, language assumes the constitutive role that consciousness played for Kant.
64. Brown 1998, p. 379.
65. Chilton 1996, pp. 37–38 with endnotes.
66. Brown 1998, p. 381.
67. Winter 1988, 1989, 1990. I wish to thank my colleague Laura E. Gómez for pointing out Winter's scholarship.
68. Winter 1989, p. 1110.
69. Ibid., p. 1109, footnote 8.
70. Ibid.
71. Schön 1979, p. 199.
72. Ibid., p. 138.
73. Ibid., p. 145.
74. Ibid., p. 143.
75. Schön and Reim 1994.
76. Quoted in Reddy 1979, pp. 165–166.

77. Schön and Reim 1994, pp. 3–5.

78. Winter 1988, p. 1197.

79. Pitha and Sgall 1990.

80. Violi 1990, p. 329.

81. Hampton 1989, p. 135.

82. Jackendoff and Aaron 1991, p. 324.

83. Lakoff 1987, pp. 106–107.

84. Lakoff 1993, p. 207.

85. Jackendoff and Aaron 1991, p. 325.

86. Jackendoff 1976, 1983, 1990.

87. Jackendoff and Aaron 1991, p. 328.

88. Casad 1992.

89. Jackendoff and Aaron 1991, p. 336.

90. Ibid., p. 321.

91. Casad 1992.

92. For instance, Pancake 1993 and van Teeffelen 1994.

93. A case in point is Lakoff 1996 on U.S. politics.

94. Lakoff 1996, p. 11.

95. Austin 1962, p. 198.

96. See Labov 1972, Chapter 8, for his critique of "asocial" linguistic research.

97. Higgins 1998, p. 426.

98. Himmelfarb 1996.

99. Chilton 1996.

100. Entman 1989b, p. 361.

101. van Dijk 1993a.

102. Santa Ana, forthcoming.

103. Bagdikian 1987.

104. Herman and Chomsky 1988; McChesney 1999, Chapter 2.

105. McChesney 1999, Chapter 1.

106. Ibid., pp. 50, 51.

107. Herman and Chomsky 1988; Entman 1990b, p. 125; McChesney 1999, p. 18.

108. Martín-Barbero 1993.

109. Fairclough 1989, p. 41.

110. Fowler 1991, pp. 45–48.

111. Ibid., p. 46.

112. Ibid., p. 40.

113. *Los Angeles Times,* October 6, 1998, A1.

114. Originally my team of students and I located *Times* articles in the microfiche format. In this format finding the actual metaphors and inputting them into a computerized database were tremendously time-consuming, with irregular results. The problem was the page format of newspapers, which filled each

page with advertising, portions of articles, and photos. This newspaper article format, which places portions of the same article on different pages, is perfectly reasonable for the casual reader, and is an important means of presenting the message behind the news (Fowler 1991, p. 225), but for our purposes only complicates methodical review, since it required a good deal of newspaper shuffling. Developing a database from fiche materials also required retyping of text by hand, which is prone to greater error. Based on a preliminary database gathered via microfiche, the initial analysis of the metaphor tokens revealed significant patterns of expression and construction of Latinos and political issues associated with Latinos. However, given the contentious findings, we revised the original, relatively unsystematic sampling procedure.

115. Fundamental metaphors that can be found in all discourses were excluded from the database, including so-called very general metaphors (Lakoff and Turner 1989, p. 52), such as PURPOSES AS DESTINATIONS, STATES AS LOCATIONS, or EVENTS AS ACTIONS, and orientational metaphors. Examples of the latter from the *Times* include: *the chance to **rise** to positions of authority; "racists who want to **keep** us **down**"; establishing **higher** standards; the rate will **soar**; economic **downturns**; driving children **deeper** into poverty; dropouts **short** on job skills; a sharp **decline** in preventive care has **leveled off**.*

116. For each token, the columns include the following data: hard-copy page and file name; article headline; publication date; article page number in the original newspaper format; word count of each article, when supplied; author's name; newswriter affiliation; whether the token was in the lead or the main body of the text; the type of text in which the metaphor token was located, i.e., a news report, an editorial, a regular or special column, an op-ed article, a letter to the editor, etc.; class of token; source semantic domain of the metaphor token; the target semantic domain of the same token; a unique number for each token; whether the author's writing had a notable pro/con slant with regard to Latinos, or, if the author's writing was neutral, whether the text from which the token was taken had a notable pro/con slant toward Latinos, or if it was neutral, among other kinds of information.

117. From Lakoff and Johnson 1980, Pancake 1993, and other sources.

118. van Teeffelen 1994.

119. In 1908 Unamuno was quoted as saying: "El lenguaje no es sino metáfora. Ya sé que hay entre vosotros algunos que . . . aparentan despreciar la metáfora, como puede el eunuco despreciar a la mujer . . . Pero yo, que sé que las ideas salieron de las palabras más que éstas de aquéllas, sé que el lenguaje, y el pensamiento con él, es metáfora. Jamás llegaremos a pensar en álgebra, y eso que hasta el álgebra está llena de metáfora." In González Egido 1983, p. 129. My loose translation. I want to thank my colleagues Carlos Torres and María Cristina Pons for pointing out the prescience of Unamuno.

# Chapter Three

1. Gutiérrez 1995, p. 13.
2. Gutiérrez quotes such nineteenth-century viewpoints as that of South Carolina's well-known Senator John C. Calhoun, who objected to embracing in the United States a large number of Mexicans. For Calhoun, Mexicans consist of "impure races, not as good as the Cherokees or Choctaws" (1995, p. 16).
3. Griswold del Castillo 1990.
4. Vélez-Ibáñez 1997, in Chapter 1, "Without Borders, the Original Vision."
5. Brownstein and Simon 1993.
6. Higham 1955.
7. Hoffman 1974, p. 126.
8. Davis 1995.
9. "Teutonic" was the nineteenth-century term for the preferred "race" of European immigrant, with "Alpine" and "Mediterranean" successively lower on the scale of purity (Higham 1955, p. 155).
10. Brownstein and Simon 1993.
11. Two kinds of ellipsis are used in the excerpts throughout the book: a wide-spaced version signals the abridgement originally found in the *Times* texts; narrow-spaced ellipses mark my own truncation.
12. Presuppositions are semantic associations accompanying a proposition, or semantic domain. The sentence *"Michael's wife is named Martha"* logically presupposes that *"Michael is married."* Likewise, they are consequences of a semantic association, such as between the source and target semantic domains of a metaphor. In semantics, logical presupposition is narrowly defined. In everyday discourse, a wider range of semantic associations is commonly inferred.
13. Each italicized metaphor appearing in the body of this book, like the sequentially numbered excerpts, is drawn from the *Los Angeles Times* database. Any exceptions are expressly described as fabrications.
14. In the excerpts throughout the book, additional metaphors can be noted which will not be discussed in the body of the book, such as in excerpts 1, *whipping boy*, 3, *erode*, 4, *spawn*, 20, *sap*, and 29, *chaos*. Mixing metaphors in nonliterary genres and everyday talk is rarely noticed. There is little sense of confusion of thought, or of anomalous passages. In the excerpts from the *Times,* there is ready mixing of metaphors that are associated with the distinctive NATION AS HOUSE and NATION AS BODY metaphors.
15. The exception to noncount measures occurs with the use of quantifiers followed by *of,* such as *two teaspoons of vinegar,* in which case the intrinsic liquid nature of fluids becomes secondary to the extrinsic calibration.
16. Lakoff 1987, pp. 141–144; Johnson 1987, pp. 113–119.
17. *Los Angeles Times,* July 6, 1998, B4.

18. On another note, the use of the term *literal,* in excerpts 2 and 18, demonstrates tacit recognition on the part of the writer of the force of metaphor. Since *face of the nation* in excerpt 18 is a metaphor, there is nothing literal to be understood by the term *literally.* In such cases the adverb can only function as an intensifier, meaning "very," or "intensely." Its use is intended to heighten the expressed severity of the effect of cultural change caused by non-European immigration.

19. Lakoff 1993.

20. Lakoff and Turner 1989.

21. As discussed by Gibbs 1994 and reviewed in (and schematized in Figure 2 of) Chapter 2.

22. At the time of the political debate, the studies that contended that immigrants were a net loss to the economy included the 1992 Parker and Rea studies, a San Diego County survey, and the 1993 Huddle studies. Those which indicated that the immigrants were a net gain to the economy included the 1992 Los Angeles County study, a 1993 Urban Institute study, and a 1991 Federal Reserve Bank study. See G. Miller 1993; Simon 1993; A. Miller 1993a, 1993b; Lee 1993. Also see Vérnez and McCarthy 1996 for a meta-analysis of these contending reports and Hinojosa and Schey 1995 for a nontechnical critique of those same studies.

23. Lovejoy 1936.

24. Lakoff and Turner 1989, pp. 170–189.

25. Lakoff 1996, p. 81.

26. Gould 1981, p. 21.

27. Gould 1995, p. 52.

28. For a recent example, see McKie's *Dawn of Man. The Story of Human Evolution,* a book written to accompany a BBC television series (2000, p. 38).

29. Lakoff 1993, pp. 208–209; Lakoff and Turner 1989, p. 55.

30. Chilton and Ilyin 1993.

31. González, Ríos, Maldonado, and Clark 1995.

32. Wetherell and Potter 1992; Valencia 1997.

33. Lakoff 1993.

34. I want to thank my colleague Guillermo Hernández for his commentary which led to this section.

35. In the November 1995 sample, eighteen sports articles, totaling 13,000 words, were reviewed.

36. One day (November 30, 1995) yielded thirty-one business articles, totaling 14,500 words.

37. Seven articles on Tyson were sampled (July–November 1989, totaling 5,750 words). Five articles on Keating were sampled (April–May 1990, n = 5,710 words).

38. Zagorin 1997.

39. Mehan 1997.

40. Gumperz 1982.

41. Said 1978.

42. D. Johnson 1994.

43. Suárez-Orozco and Suárez-Orozco 1995, p. 193.

44. Mehan 1997, p. 267.

45. Calavita 1996, p. 285. I emphasize the metaphor with SMALL CAPITALS.

46. Ibid., p. 296.

47. Piven and Cloward 1993, quoted in Calavita 1996, p. 294.

48. Lakoff 1996.

49. Ibid., pp. 187–188, Lakoff's emphasis.

50. Ibid., pp. 188–189.

51. However, FAMILY may not be a serviceable metaphor for the twenty-first-century nation. This metaphor suggests blood links among compatriots which are stronger bonds than those suggested by the NATION AS HOUSE, or even the NATION AS BODY. Although rarely used these days, the metaphor was used in reference to the United States in earlier centuries. One example will illustrate its problematic implications. In his second State of the Union address, Abraham Lincoln invoked a biblical allusion to the permanence of land:

> A nation may be said to consist of its territory, its people and its laws. The territory is the only part which is of certain durability. "One generation passeth away, and another generation cometh, but the earth abideth forever." It is of first importance to duly consider and estimate this everlasting part. That portion of the earth's surface which is owned and inhabited by the people of the United States is well adapted to be **the home of one national family, and it is not adapted for two or more.** . . . Our national strife springs not from our permanent part; not from the land we inhabit; not from our national homestead. . . . Our strife pertains to ourselves. . . . In this view, I recommend the adoption of the following resolution and articles amendatory to the Constitution of the United States. (Basler 1953, pp. 528–530, emphasis added)

Although the nation was in the midst of the Civil War, Lincoln was not referring to Yankee and Rebel. Zarefsky (1999), among others, argues that the families contending for the nation were slaves and Whites. "Slavery . . . endangered the nation; no one doubted that. Lincoln [in this speech] presented his vision for disentangling the nation from its corrosive foe" (Paludan 1994, p. 163). To preserve the Union, Lincoln suggested in this speech a system of "compensated emancipation," coupled with colonization, to preserve the republic for Whites alone. The government would requisition the slaves from their owners, then these African Americans would be cast out of their homeland to foreign colonies.

The shared ancestry notion that is invoked by the NATION AS FAMILY metaphor places greater weight on lineage than can be sustained in a nation of immigrants, unless one line of descent is privileged over all others.

My colleague Richard Anderson (personal communication) contested this account of Lincoln's address and articulated another view about the NATION AS FAMILY metaphor. Anderson's view is acknowledged by Paludan, who states that "recent historians have downplayed Lincoln's proposal," citing James McPherson, who describes compensatory emancipation as "a peace measure to abolish the institution everywhere by constitutional means" (Ibid., p. 165).

On the second count, Anderson's heartening view on the value of the family metaphor deserves mention: "If we can use a term like 'brethren' to describe persons of another race than our own, then family metaphors need not be racially exclusionary metaphors. Because we perceive the United States as divided by race, there is a tendency among all racial groups to describe themselves as families to the exclusion of other races, but if we were to describe the American family, we might well preempt the use of family metaphors by particular racial groups. This might even contribute to changing the way Americans perceive each other."

52. There are other semantic associations of the NATION AS FAMILY metaphor to consider. Anderson 1999, in a comparative study of Soviet Russia and electoral Russia political discourses, demonstrates that Communist Party leaders employed family metaphors to place themselves "above" an infantilized citizenry, while post-empire Russian political leaders employ fewer vertical and hierarchical metaphors to describe their relationship to the electorate.

53. van Teeffelen 1994, pp. 384–386.

54. Miles 1989 quoted in Wetherell and Potter 1992, pp. 15–16.

55. van Dijk 1987, 1991.

56. Wetherell and Potter 1992, p. 70.

57. van Dijk 1989, p. 42.

58. Ibid., p. 43.

59. From "The Constitution of the United States: Is It Pro-Slavery or Anti-Slavery?" in Foner 1950, p. 477.

## Chapter Four

1. The March 1998 issue of *Commentary* dedicated forty pages to captious and trenchant essays on affirmative action. Its contributors included William Bennett, Linda Chavez, Carl Cohen, Midge Decter, Terry Eastland, Joseph Epstein, Nathan Glazer, Lino Graglia, Tamar Jacoby, Randall Kennedy, Leslie Lenkowsky, Glenn Loury, John O'Sullivan, Orlando Patterson, Norman Podhoretz, Arch Puddington, Jim Sleeper, Abigail and Stephan Thernstrom,

James Q. Wilson, and Alan Wolfe. The establishment's pro-affirmative-action position was articulated in a much more deliberate and rambling way by Christopher Edley, Jr., in *Not All Black and White* (1996). The first two chapters of Edley's essay were sampled.

2. Omi and Winant 1994, pp. 64–65.
3. Washington 1991, pp. 567–569, italics in original.
4. Address to Howard University, June 4, 1965.
5. Santa Ana and Rivas 1999. War metaphors are the common stock of most ordinary as well as extraordinary political discourse. Then there is von Bismarck's pithy comment: "War is nothing more than the extension of politics by other means."
6. The National Advisory Commission on Civil Disorders was established in July 1967 and headed by Governor Otto Kerner of Illinois.
7. Kerner 1988, p. 7.
8. Ibid., p. 11.
9. Wetherell and Potter 1992 provide a review of types of racism, including modern racism (McConahey 1986), symbolic racism (Sears 1988), aversive racism (Dovidio 1997, Dovidio and Gaertner 1986, Kovel 1970), and ambivalent racism (Katz et al. 1986). Entman 1990a, 1992, employs another definition. Bobo 1983, 1988, provides a critique of theories of modern racism, which generally had been static theories predicated on emotional states. Bobo has long argued that modern racism is principally structural and epistemological.
10. Scheurich and Young 1997.
11. Dovidio 1997, p. A60.
12. From Dyer's *White,* quoted in hooks 1996, p. 36.
13. See van Dijk 1993a, p. 80. By reality, Scheurich and Young (1997, p. 6) mean ontology; by ways of knowing, epistemology; and by contours of right and wrong, they are referring to axiology.
14. For instance, Sánchez 1940; Vaca 1970b; Valencia and Solórzano 1997.
15. Washington 1991, p. 559.
16. Skrentny 1996, pp. 96–100.
17. Kerner 1988, p. 2.
18. Skrentny 1996, pp. 31–33.
19. Ibid., pp. 123–124.
20. *Fortune* 134 (2): 156.
21. *Black Enterprise* 26 (11): 27.
22. Chávez 1998, p. 116.
23. Edley 1996, p. 47.
24. *National Law Journal* 18 (11): B1.
25. Loury 1998.
26. Chilton and Ilyin 1993, p. 9.

27. Gallen 1992, p. 38.

28. Ibid., p. 5.

29. Ibid., pp. 179–180, italics in the original.

30. Ibid., p. 116.

31. Seemingly only once in Washington 1991, p. 148.

32. Ibid., pp. 146–150, 171, 565.

33. Gallen 1992, p. 137.

34. Ibid., p. 182.

35. Ibid., p. 118.

36. Breitman 1965, p. 26.

37. Gallen 1992, p. 188.

38. Washington 1991, p. 71.

39. Gallen 1992, p. 190.

40. Washington 1991, p. 621.

41. Ibid., p. 676.

42. Breitman's and Gallen's volumes on Malcolm X combine for a total of 426 pages, Washington's volume on King contains 679 pages, and the compilation of Johnson's speeches in *A Time for Action* is 195 pages long.

43. Williams 1991, p. 119.

44. Gallen 1992, p. 161. I have shortened this passage as elsewhere with ellipses.

45. Williams 1991, p. 295.

46. Johnson 1964, p. 108.

47. Williams 1991, p. 71.

48. King 1967, p. 93.

49. I would like to thank David Zamora for clarifying my thinking about this ontology.

50. Washington 1991: *poison* of racism (p. 208), *poisoned* by racism (p. 316), *blight* (p. 59), *retarded by a blight* (pp. 474–475), a *malady* (p. 355), a *disease in the body politic* (p. 575), *nation is sick* (p. 280), *extremely sick* (p. 355).

51. Jenkins 1996, Chapter 13.

52. Stated in May 1964, cited in Breitman 1965, p. 60, scare quotes in original.

53. Johnson 1964, p. 94.

54. Kerner 1988, p. 2.

55. Washington 1991: *cancerous disease* (p. 147), *cancer* that is *hate-filled* and yet *curable* (p. 383), an *unchecked cancer* (p. 596), cancer *scars the soul* (p. 478), tokenism a *palliative* (p. 113), *this cancerous disease* (pp. 150–151).

56. Bennett 1998.

57. From the March 1998 issue of *Commentary;* examples drawn from this journal are marked with the initial of the journal and the page of the reference, e.g., (C 19).

58. Gligorov 1992; Ellis and Wright 1998; Makath 1994. Espousers of the term

"balkanization" in the United States include Frey 1996, and D'Souza as quoted in Matthews 1995.

59. Skrentny 1996, p. 27.

60. See, for example, Omi and Winant 1994, Rodríguez and Cordero-Guzmán 1992, and Lipsitz 1995.

61. Washington 1991, p. 468.

62. López et al. 1996.

63. Chávez 1998.

64. Ibid., p. 237.

65. Ibid., p. 236. My friend James Kyung-Jin Lee pointed out to me that Park 1998, and Park and Park 1999, recently offer theorized analyses of the heterogeneous Asian American voting patterns in Los Angeles.

66. References to Edley's text are marked with the author's initial and the page number, as in (E 15).

67. On the *Republic* see Jowett 1989, pp. 56–57. I added italics for emphasis. Habermas 1976, p. 1.

68. Gates 1986; Hill 1998 and Templeton 1998, among other articles in *American Anthropologist* 100, no. 3.

69. Washington 1991, p. 493.

70. Bowen and Bok 1998, p. 256.

71. Ibid., pp. 257–258.

72. Ibid., p. 261.

73. Ibid., p. 264.

74. Ibid., p. 265.

75. For solid research on the topic, see Wildman 1996 and Lipsitz 1998. White Americans often find it difficult to recognize the benefits that they accrue as Whites in our racial state. Paul Kivel (1996, p. 30) provides a "White Benefits Checklist," from which four statements (out of thirty) are reproduced: 1. My ancestors were legal immigrants to the United States during a period when immigrants from Asia, South and Central America, or Africa were restricted. 2. My ancestors came to this country of their own free will and have never had to relocate unwillingly once here. 3. I live on land that formerly belonged to Native Americans. 4. I lived or live in a neighborhood from which people of color were barred by discrimination.

76. Washington 1991, pp. 557–558, 562.

77. Stated in 1967, cited in ibid., p. 560.

78. Justin Volpe and Charles Schwarz were convicted in 1999 of sodomizing Abner Louima with a broomstick, to the point of ripping his intestines, while he was in their custody. Louima was targeted because he is a Black Haitian. Three other New York City police officers directly involved were found not guilty, although court testimony indicated that Louima was paraded around the police

station with his pants around his ankles, and that other police officers heard his screams and saw him lying in his own blood in his cell but did nothing. There was even an attempted cover-up. The only reason that Volpe and Schwarz were convicted is that Louima survived the attack and was willing to testify against the officers. In this case there was no judicial response to the institutional racism, which was treated as a crime perpetrated by individuals.

79. Robert 1998.

80. Chávez 1998, p. 67.

81. Chilton and Ilyin 1993 describe this kind of move as one of the four possible political discourse strategies involving metaphor.

82. "Compensation for hard times," "hand up," and "hardship" in this series of excerpts are from a set of President Clinton's comments on affirmative action that were provided to the essayists by the editor of *Commentary* for their responses in this special issue. Unlike Johnson or King, Clinton is not easily understood to have made explicit reference to white racism.

83. López et al. 1996.

84. Wolfe 1998.

85. Solórzano 1998.

86. Padilla 1999.

87. Glazer 1998.

88. As a beneficiary of affirmative action who subsequently earned tenure at a top-tier university, I must point out the essayist's marked unfamiliarity with the tenure process. Race cannot be ignored in any institution in this nation. Tenure evaluations are not granted at the whim of individuals or on the basis of statistics—this would be grounds for litigation. In the best situations, tenure judgments are the responsibility of the body of faculty members, who follow predetermined procedures specifically designed to reduce partiality and prejudice. Contrary to the views expressed by the commentator, higher education cannot afford to focus solely on a racial scorecard; this would be a short-sighted goal. The twin objectives of enhancing the academic distinction of the institution while strengthening its diversity are not mutually exclusive. This is not to say that higher education is a true meritocracy—until a reasonable level of parity is approached, no U.S. institution can afford to suspend its affirmative action efforts, for faculty, staff, and students.

89. Chávez 1998, p. 69.

90. Ellipsis in ibid., p. 120.

91. Ibid., p. 131.

92. Ibid., p. 249.

93. Loury 1998, pp. 38–39.

94. Washington 1991, p. 564.

95. As Martin Luther King Jr. quipped, these men's racist credentials were impec-

cable. Rockwell was president of the American Nazi Party. As Alabama governor, Wallace attempted to stop court-ordered integration of the University of Alabama, personally standing at the schoolhouse door to refuse entrance to black students.

96. In contrast, much of Malcolm X's message, particularly after his June 1964 Mecca pilgrimage and disassociation from Elijah Muhammad's dogma, does not reinvoke loathing, but still rings with acumen. See excerpt 11, for example.

97. Eugene "Bull" Conner, Director of Public Safety of Birmingham, Alabama, ordered the aggravated use of fire hoses and police dog attacks on peaceful civil rights marchers in May 1963.

98. Bobo 1998; Bobo and Licari 1989; Sidanius, Pratto, and Bobo 1996; Bobo and Hutchings 1996.

99. Martin Luther King, Jr., in Washington 1991, p. 327.

## Chapter Five

1. *Los Angeles Times,* April 14, 1997, A3.

2. Kati Haycock of the Education Trust compiled these figures in 1999. Of every one hundred kindergarten students, sixty-seven Latinos (vs. ninety-three Whites) earned a high school diploma; thirty-one Latinos (vs. sixty-two Whites) completed some college; and ten Latinos (vs. twenty-nine Whites) obtained a Bachelor's degree. The different graduation rates (for students by age twenty-one) are derived from the 1993 Bureau of Census report *In-School Enrollment—Social and Economic Characteristics.* On the skill levels of eighth grade white students and twelfth grade nonwhite students, refer to Mullis et al. 1996. On the qualifications of teachers, see Oakes 1990.

3. Dickens 1854, p. 1.

4. *Los Angeles Times,* December 5, 1997, A1, A30–31.

5. Meléndez 1995, pp. 11–59.

6. For a synopsis, see Byrne 1996.

7. Friere continues: "Projecting an absolute ignorance upon others, a characteristic of the ideology of oppression, negates education and knowledge as processes of inquiry. The teacher presents himself to his students as their necessary opposite; by considering their ignorance absolute, he justifies his own existence. The students, alienated like the slave in the Hegelian dialectic, accept their ignorance as justifying the teacher's existence—but, unlike the slave, they never discover that they educate the teacher. . . . Banking education maintains and even stimulates the contradiction through the following attitudes and practices, which mirror oppressive society as a whole: (a) the teacher teaches and the students are taught; (b) the teacher knows everything and the students know nothing; (c) the teacher thinks and the students are thought about; (d) the teacher talks and the students listen—meekly; (e) the teacher disciplines

and the students are disciplined; (f) the teacher chooses and enforces his choice, and the students comply; (g) the teacher acts and the students have the illusion of acting through the action of the teacher; (h) the teacher chooses the program content, and the students (who are not consulted) adapt to it; (i) the teacher confuses the authority of knowledge with his own professional authority, which he sets in opposition to the freedom of the students; (j) the teacher is the Subject of the learning process, while the pupils are mere objects. It is not surprising that the banking concept of education regards men as adaptable, manageable beings. The more students work at storing the deposits entrusted to them, the less they develop the critical consciousness which would result from their intervention in the world as transformers of that world. . . . Education must begin with the solution of the teacher/student contradiction, by reconciling the poles of the contradiction so that both are simultaneously teachers *and* students" (*Pedagogy of the Oppressed,* pp. 57–60, emphasis in the original).

8. Within this family of social constructivist theories, the child actively constructs her own knowledge on the basis of prior experience. The child does not simply mimic the teacher. As James Byrne (1996) summarizes, the learning activity of children is not merely passed on pre-formed from adults, but is developed in children through interaction in the child's social environment (among people) and again within the child, as new concepts are formulated and manipulated by the child herself. Learning in a formal environment is replacing what some Vygotskians call the child's spontaneous conceptualization, i.e., socially conventional thinking, with more scientifically based concepts. Adult intervention is crucial within this model of learning to mediate between a child's conventional thinking and more adequate scientific conceptualizing. Intellectual skills are only mastered progressively, not all at once. Thus error is to be expected on the part of students, and the teacher's role is not to provide knowledge but to "lend a hand," to mediate between the knowledge schemas that a child comes to school with and the master-level concepts that can be achieved. The teacher gauges the progress of the child and provides what some Vygotskians call "scaffolding" to facilitate a learner's march toward mastery. Thus the constructivist metaphors for learning place teachers in a support role and make the learner the protagonist on the stage of learning. See Byrne, pp. 7–33.

9. Kuhn 1962.

10. Agriculture provides adroit metaphors for children in education, as can be noted in Michael Olivas's essay "The Education of Latino Lawyers: An Essay on Crop Cultivation." Further, while flower metaphors have an affirmative aesthetic appeal, the plant metaphor is not always associated with cheerful psychological developments:

(a) The Social Democrats seem more concerned with other problems, while within Kohl's center-right governing coalition, fear of losing voter support to the more extreme rightist parties that have begun to **flower** in the present atmosphere has prevented any visible campaign to counter the present xenophobia. (November 10, 1992, World Report p. 1)

The extension of the plant metaphor is also used for other classes of individuals, as witnessed in the earlier chapter on immigration:

(b) "We see it as our responsibility to **weed out** illegal aliens involved in this disturbance," Moschorak said. (May 16, 1992, A30)

11. John Goodlad quoted in Tell 1999, pp. 14–19.

12. Dickens 1854, p. 15.

13. Dickens 1865. Also see Collins 1963.

14. Quoted in Bradley 1999, p. 31.

15. In fairness, teachers' unions would like to place greater emphasis on professional development and the quality of educators in the classroom:

"Our feeling is that [all teachers] should be fully credentialed, just like fully certified doctors, fully certified nurses and fully certified lawyers," said David Lebow, a longtime high school history teacher who tracks the issue for the California Teachers Association. (July 22, 1997, A1).

16. See Kerchner, Koppich, and Weeres 1997 for an optimistic view that teachers unions can move from a "siege mentality to [a] transformational vision" to improve the craft of teaching, upgrade educational standards, and create a new representational role for unions.

17. A recent innovation in pedagogy specifically addressed this metaphor-driven shortcoming. Dubbed "Funds of Knowledge," this constructivist method calls on the teacher to consciously look for the knowledge base that working-class and racialized children bring to schoolrooms. Luis Moll, who credits Carlos Vélez-Ibáñez (1988) for the concept and term, stresses that teachers should take into account the knowledge that students have already generated in their own lives. Once teachers acknowledge their students' own experiences as knowledge, teachers can build on their students' funds of knowledge.

18. Fitzpatrick 1995.

19. Oakes 1985.

20. Stanton-Salazar (personal communication). This analysis continues to be affirmed in recent studies of the educational system elsewhere in the Americas. See Luykx 1999.

21. Lakoff 1987, pp. 141–144; Johnson 1987, pp. 113–119.

22. "Standard & Poors's Corp., the company that for the last 85 years has been providing investors with information about the credit-worthiness of companies

and local governments . . . is providing assessments, available on the Internet, on what sort of 'return on investment' taxpayers get from school districts. . . . Michigan, the first customer, will pay $10 million over four years for the service" (Colvin 2001, p. A11).

23. The most damning aspect of the SCHOOL AS BUSINESS metaphor is its inefficiency. The *Chronicle of Higher Education* reported on teaching foreign languages at universities which presently employ, and stand to benefit the most from, the corporate model: "Colleges' foreign-language programs, particularly German and French departments, have faced large cutbacks in recent years, as U.S. universities increasingly have modeled themselves after corporations, writes Peter Uwe Hohendahl, a professor of German and comparative literature at Cornell University. Enrollments in French and German departments have dropped about 25 percent since the end of the Cold War, and university administrators, adopting a bottom-line approach, have responded by phasing out tenured faculty jobs and hiring more part-time instructors" (*Chronicle,* March 31, 1998).

24. More accurately, as Ricardo Stanton-Salazar pointed out to me in a personal communication, public schools were seen to be adolescent refuges for the white middle class. Consider the television sitcom *Happy Days,* in which Richie Cunningham and his friends at Jefferson High in Milwaukee, Wisconsin, in the 1950s face an endless series of routine dilemmas and amusing predicaments. In contrast, in the 1955 film *Blackboard Jungle,* the rule in an inner-city school included gangs, multiracial turmoil, and physical danger, even attempted rape. The film was so shocking at the time that it was banned in several cities, and it was denied a venue at the Venice Film Festival. Now such disturbing images of public schools no longer surprise the public.

25. My abiding appreciation goes out to Mrs. Mary Timmons and Dr. James S. "Big-Jim" Griffith.

26. Kohl 1988, pp. 33–38.

27. On immigrant imagery, for example, see in particular Acuña 1972 and Johnson 1995, as well as McWilliams 1949, Fernández and Pedroza 1982, García 1995, Bosniak 1996, and Carrasco's chapter in Perea's 1997 edited volume on the issue. Focusing specifically on the militarization of the border, see, for example, Montoya 1996.

28. Alternative metaphors that are more apt for our present-day view of children and learning include agricultural ones, such as crop cultivation or tending an orchard, or more patently constructivist ones such as house building (with staircases and windows, architects and craftspeople, scaffolding, etc.). These will be developed in Chapter 8.

29. Johnson 1993, pp. 165–166.

30. Quinn 1991.

31. Two unforgettable accounts are Guadalupe Valdés's cogent 1998 study and the 1995 documentary *Fear and Learning at Hoover Elementary,* which was directed by Laura Angélica Simón.
32. Philips 1972, Heath 1982b.
33. Mehan 1979.
34. Oakes 1985.
35. To summarize, the power that teachers have to promote or debase minority children's native ability to learn has been discussed by various researchers; I draw on Edwards 1989. The speech of a child tends to be automatically used to evaluate the potential of the child as learner. If the teacher asks the children in a class how many siblings each has, the student who answers *"I don't got none"* will be less highly esteemed than the student who replies *"I don't have any."* This snap judgment is unconscious, but its effects are significant. The features of English called nonstandard on the one hand, and "proper" on the other, are not inherently inferior and superior ways of speaking. The convention that marks one way of speaking as bad and the other as good is strictly a matter of historical contingency. Further, since children come by their way of speaking by no special effort or talent, but simply by being children born to a family in one or another social situation, the teacher's contrasting appraisals of the quality of the students are based on social conventions, not on any factors which indicate native ability. Yet this is what happens, with grave consequences, since it affects the teacher's estimation of each child and has been shown to transform future performance of children.

Edwards reminds us of the famous experiment of Rosenthal and Jacobson, which demonstrated that teachers' estimation of their pupils directly affects their school performance. When teachers were given false information about children, teachers formed different opinions about who was bright and who wasn't. The "brighter" children were found to perform to the level of the teacher's estimation; when these very same children were later deemed "slower" in a subsequent class, the children again came to believe the teacher's errant expectations and performed down to their falsely imputed level. This self-fulfilling prophecy has been demonstrated to affect children by class. Teachers who feel that lower-class children are inherently less able communicate this appraisal to their students. Children are sensitive to this and respond according to what is expected of them. In due course they do less well, which confirms initial expectations. Early tracking institutionalizes this cycle, and once placed in lower tracks, nonmainstream children have difficulties altering the depreciated evaluations of teachers which affirm specious categorization.

Rist also found that children's pronunciation of English was important in the formation of false estimations of their educability. This is quite widespread. It is most obvious when children are told that their speech is "wrong," "bad," "careless," "sloppy," "sloven," "vulgar." Witness the 1997 Ebonics controversy (Baugh 1999, Wolfram 1998, Rickford 1999). Other ethnic minority children are also unfairly judged inferior on the basis of language.

In the case of multilingual children, Gumperz and Hernández-Chávez's classic study of the teacher's attitudes demonstrated biased judgments were frequently inflicted on bilingual students: "regardless of overtly expressed attitudes . . . teachers are quite likely to be influenced by what they perceive as *deviant speech* . . . thus potentially inhibiting the students' desire to learn" (1972, my emphasis). An example of deviant bilingual speech, the mixing of the two languages in a highly structured way is the target of greatest derision. Such mixing is called codeswitching by linguists. Codeswitching in English and Spanish among Chicanos and Latinos, designated *Spanglish* or *Tex-Mex,* is entirely misunderstood and unfairly disparaged by the general public and language elitist commentators as breaking or corruption of pure languages, to the lasting detriment of bilingual children. A case in point is González Echevarría 1997. Codeswitching in fact is strong and affirmative evidence of two language competencies rather than one, competence in English as well as Spanish.

Ignorance about the social and structural nature of language is not only an American inadequacy but is a part of all public educational systems that delegitimize and disparage working-class speech patterns. This unfairly disparages the innocent children that come by these linguistic patterns honestly and who are no less intelligent or educable as a result. Edwards conducted a study of Irish teachers' attitudes toward disadvantaged inner-city Dublin children. With a questionnaire, teachers were asked what were the salient characteristics of their pupils' disadvantage. Twenty-eight percent stated that their students had "language difficulties." Since pathological language difficulty affects only a minuscule sliver of any population, these teachers' inappropriate judgments were made on the basis of the children's nonstandard language. When the teachers were individually interviewed, they ranked "poor language ability" to be their students' second-most-troubling problem, behind poor living conditions. Edwards returned to Dublin and taped twenty working-class and twenty middle-class Dublin boys. All had been independently determined to be average students. The boys read a story and retold it in their own words. The teachers evaluated the boys on "general voice quality" as well as fluency, vocabulary, and intelligence. The working-class students were viewed less favorably on all measures, even general voice quality, which presumably is not a social measure. Edwards argues that middle-class norms are used to judge the students.

Edwards reports on a series of American studies by Williams. In one study 125 white and 50 black teachers were asked to evaluate children on the basis of six videotaped samples of children's speech in answer to two preselected questions. The students were lower- and middle-class Blacks, Whites, and Chicanos. The teachers' ratings of children corresponded closely to children's ethnicity and socioeconomic status: low-status children were scored less favorably. Among low-status children, Whites were seen more positively than black and Chicano children. The same pattern was found among middle-class children, with Chicanos scored lowest. Teachers, whether black or white, displayed the same responses, which is due to the internalization of mainstream values.

Thus teachers, just like other members of our society, tend to hold stereotyped, biased, and unwarranted views of certain language varieties and their speakers. However, since the teachers' views are privileged, their negative valuation of children's educability, falsely based on mistaken views on bilingualism and nonstandard dialects of English, contributes to the lack of success of these children in school. Nonmainstream children thus endure such language evaluation, which contributes to their unmerited tracking in "slower" and nonacademic courses of study.

36. Chapman 1995.
37. Thanks go out to Rubén García and the other UCLA students who took my "Representations of Latinos in Print Media" course in 1998 for their insight on this very point.
38. Lighter 1994.
39. I would like to thank my friend Ricardo Stanton-Salazar for bringing Turner's work to my attention.
40. Turner 1960, pp. 122, 123.
41. Ibid., p. 123.
42. Barrera 1979, Acuña 1972. Recently Conley 1999 attributed the persistent inequalities between non-Whites and Whites to accumulated wealth disparities. As Lipsitz (1995 and 1998) has argued, such differences are the cumulative effects of (inadvertent) regulatory and governmental racism. One of Lipsitz's examples is the regulations of the Fair Housing Act (FHA) regarding federally funded mortgage guarantees, which for over forty years favored home purchases by (predominantly white) suburbanites, and disfavored (predominantly nonwhite) inner-city residents. Thus, wealth-building legislation was provided for one group of citizens and denied to another. This directly leads to unequal distribution of educational resources across local school districts, since districts are supported in large part by property taxes. In this way equal educational opportunity is denied to most deserving children.
43. Skrentny 1996, pp. 90–96.
44. Lipsitz 1995.
45. Loury 1998, p. 39.
46. See, for example, Valdés 1998.
47. The term *mainstream* is also used to characterize both other types of acceptance of marginalized groups into the encompassing fold of ostensibly non-

ethnic Anglo-America and the advocacy of political positions that are consistent with the commonplace views of the public discourse.

(a) **mainstream** press (= English-language press)
(b) Once written off as a xenophobic movement to drive Spanish out of the classroom, peopled by fanatical teachers, parents and politicians, the campaign to reform bilingual education has found its **mainstream** voice in post-187 California. (May 22, 1995, A1)

48. See Morán 1995.
49. For instance, Acuña 1972, Zinn 1980, Takaki 1993, Loewen 1995, González 1999, among others.
50. Chavez is quoted by Kennedy Manzo 1997.

## Chapter Six

1. *Los Angeles Times,* December 30, 1998, B2.
2. *Los Angeles Times,* June 7, 1998, A1.
3. Article 5 of Proposition 227 imposes criminal sanctions: "Any school board member or other elected official or public school teacher or administrator who willfully and repeatedly refuses to implement the terms of this statute . . . may be held personally liable for fees and actual damages by the child's parents or legal guardian."
4. *Los Angeles Times,* April 3, 1998, A3.
5. Including the American Educational Research Association, Linguistic Society of America, American Association of Applied Linguists, the editorial board of the *Harvard Education Review,* as well as California's Superintendent of Public Instruction, the California Parent-Teacher Association, and scores of individual California school districts.
6. Lakoff and Johnson state that Reddy's 1979 article was the inspiration for their own keystone 1980 work, *Metaphors We Live By.*
7. Reddy 1979, pp. 169, 194.
8. The water metaphor has been noted in Hornberger 1999 and Wolfe 1999.
9. *Los Angeles Times,* October 29, 1995, B1.
10. *Los Angeles Times,* May 24, 1998, B2.
11. See Hakuta, Butler, and Witt 2000, Greene 1998, August and Hakuta 1997, Ramírez et al. 1991.
12. At times linguists promoted this imprecise claim in order to pique interest among university students and the reading public in the formal aspects of linguistics.
13. See, for example, Berko Gleason and Ratner 1993.
14. Among the numerous reviews, see Lalleman 1996, Gass and Selinker 1994, and Cook 1993.

15. Although there will be no opportunity to expand on another important topic, it must be stated that both Spanish and English are colonizing languages that were employed in the destruction of American Indian societies. As colonizing languages, they continue to be used to racialize and disparage native peoples.

16. The belief of American English privilege has only been evident since the mid-nineteenth century, although Noah Webster expounded its alleged superiority in the eighteenth century in the service of nationalism. Its hegemonic novelty may contribute to the insecurity of English-only and Official English proponents. The rise of American English illustrates the historical contingency of language prestige. See articles by Heath 1982a and Kahane 1982.

17. As cited by Ricento 2000. Linguicism has been treated at book length by Phillipson 1992. Also see Pennycook 1994, 1998.

18. Crawford 1992a, p. 190.

19. Kohl 2000.

20. *Los Angeles Times,* May 29, 1998, A3.

21. Goody and Watt 1963.

22. Street 1984.

23. Mehan 1980.

24. Linguistic competence is a technical term to designate the capability (a) to create novel and syntactically governed speech as well as (b) to evaluate other people's speech, a capability accruing to humans who acquire a language in a community of such language speakers. Note that education is not required to attain full linguistic competence in any language. Nor is monolingualism needed for linguistic competence in English or any other language. In fact, in the world today, multilingualism is the norm, while monolingualism is limited to a few (post)colonial powers such as the United States, France, and Japan.

25. Note that there are multiple kinds of literacy, many of which are practices developed outside of school, such as sports page statistics, cereal box, and television literacies.

26. In section (a), the long-standing de facto official language status of English has been elevated to de jure status. As a consequence, an English-only referendum has been made law in the realm of public education. All other languages spoken in California by millions of Americans, including American Indian languages, have been erased by the law's silence about their existence.

27. "The report, which was commissioned by the U.S. Department of Education and the National Institute on Child Health and Human Development, notes that scientists working in such diverse fields as neuroscience, linguistics and biology have produced a detailed picture of the complexities of reading. . . . The report says there is evidence that children whose first language is not English may do better if taught to read first in their native tongue—because they

are likely to best grasp the meaning of words and sentences in that language" (March 19, 1998, A1). For the report, see Snow et al. 1998.

28. The report goes on to say: "The largest percentages needing help were at California State University, Dominguez Hills, where eight out of 10 freshmen who enrolled last fall needed remedial instruction in English. It's also not surprising that Cal State Dominguez Hills was on the bottom of the list, said Boice Bowman, the school's vice president for student affairs, given that it draws many students from low-income parts of communities. Compton High School was one of the high schools whose graduates struggled with Cal State's freshmen placement exams. 89% [of its graduates] failed the English test. 'These are capable students, but they didn't get all of the preparation needed,' Bowman said. 'A large part of our mission is to serve inner-city schools and provide these students with opportunity to be successful in their lives. If we don't allow them to come, then we have done a disservice to our community'" (March 27, 1998, A1).

29. *Los Angeles Times,* May 22, 1995, A1.

30. The case for bilingualism's positive cognitive contribution has recently been summarized by Lee 1996.

31. See, for example, Moore 1999.

32. Faltis and Wolfe 1999, pp. 275–276 (my italics). Also see Valdés 1998 for a poignant characterization of the failure of public schools to provide the environment and facilitation for immigrant children to develop academic language and a solid education.

33. Woolard 1989.

34. San Miguel and Valencia 1998, p. 370.

35. See Wiley 1996 and 1998 for historical reviews of the claim.

36. Cioran 1991, p. 12.

37. Ndebele is quoted in Bailey 1990.

38. E.g., Mariscal 1999, Navarro (forthcoming), Morín 1963, Saenz 1933. Also see Olguín 2000 for more references and a literary critique, and Murphy 1987, 1992, for even more references.

39. See Crystal 1997, esp. pp. 117–130, and the journal *World-Wide English.*

40. This analysis has been previously stated, from various theoretical vantage points, in Giroux 1981, Crawford 1989, 1992b, Tollefson 1991, and Darder 1991.

41. California voters approved Proposition 63 by a vote of 71 percent to 27 percent, granting the right to sue if state officials take actions to "diminish or ignore the role of English as the state's common language." Its impact is centered on official state actions, not public behavior.

42. For example, Ada 1986, 1988.

43. By way of illustration, see the theorists cited in note 40.

44. Although the *Los Angeles Times* took a decidedly antagonistic position against bilingual education, the political position of the *Times* regarding Proposition 227 is not particularly at issue in the present analysis. Instead the *Times* is primarily taken to be a widely disseminated source of California political discourse. For a review of the print media's injurious influence against bilingual education, see McQuillan and Tse 1996.

45. *Los Angeles Times,* May 29, 1998, A3.

46. *Los Angeles Times,* April 13, 1998, A1.

47. *Los Angeles Times,* April 10, 1998, B1.

48. *Los Angeles Times,* May 23, 1998, A1.

49. *Los Angeles Times,* May 29, 1998, A3.

50. Ballesteros-Coronel 1998, n = 503, margin of error ±4 percent. Also, see Craig 1996.

51. *Los Angeles Times,* April 13, 1998, A1, n = 1,409, margin of error ±3 percent. The poll results were 32 percent "only English"; 39 percent "native language for a brief time"; 25 percent "both languages if educators and parents think necessary"; and 4 percent "don't know."

52. Genzuk 1998.

53. Charlie Ericksen, "Media Misleading about Hispanic Vote on Proposition 227," *Houston Chronicle,* June 11, 1998, A33.

54. *San Diego Union-Tribune,* June 3, 1998, pp. A-23:7,8, A-24:1.

55. *Plain Dealer,* June 4, 1998, 15A.

56. Ericksen 1998, A33, for the quotes from the *Christian Science Monitor,* Associated Press, *Washington Post, Dallas Morning News,* and Roger Hernández's column. Further evidence of the "Big Lie" can be found in the *Star Tribune* (Minneapolis), June 4, 1998, 9A; among syndicated columnists such as Joan Beck in the *Denver Post,* June 12, 1998, B11; and in the editorials of the *Chicago Sun-Times,* June 4, 1998, p. 29, the *Denver Rocky Mountain News,* June 6, 1998, 6A, and again in the *Washington Post,* June 8, 1998, A22.

57. "Nativist Responses to Education, Society and Language," a January 1999 lecture given at the University of Southern California at a lecture series entitled Education, Society and Language.

58. Among linguists, see Labov 1969 and Hymes 1974; critical discourse analysts, van Dijk 1993a; educational theorists, Bourdieu 1977, Giroux 1981, Edwards 1985, 1989, Tollefson 1991, and Darder 1991; language policy researchers and theorists, Macías 1984, Phillipson 1992, Pennycook 1994, 1998, Schiffman 1996, Ricento 2000; and social commentators, Crawford 1989, 1992b, and hooks 1991.

59. Wetherell and Potter 1992, p. 19.

# Chapter Seven

1. Foucault 1980, p. 39, italics in the original.
2. Foucault in Rabinow 1984, p. 6.
3. Anzaldúa 1987, pp. 2–3. See also Rosaldo 1996, pp. 216–217, for a discussion of the implications of Anzaldúa's metaphor for the Chicana/o border culture.
4. Leal 1981, Anaya and Lomelí 1989, Pérez-Torres 1997.
5. Carlos Fuentes in *Los Angeles Times,* October 28, 1994, B7.
6. Handlin 1951, p. 3, italics in the original.
7. Woodward 1960, whose title also invokes NATION AS BODY.
8. Foucault 1980, p. 53.
9. Fairclough 1995, p. 28.
10. Fairclough 1989, p. 107, cited in Ohara 1999.
11. Chilton 1996, p. 82.
12. Chilton and Ilyin 1993.
13. I want to thank my friend Carlos Nagel for referring me to Lovelock. "Could a planet, almost all rock and that mostly incandescent or molten, be alive? Before you dismiss this notion as absurd, think, as did the physicist Jerome Rothstein, about another large living object: a giant redwood tree. That is alive, yet 99 per cent of it is deadwood. Like the earth it has only a skin of living tissue spread thinly at the surface" (Lovelock, quoted in Goatly 1997, p. 40).
14. Jenkins 1996, p. 126.
15. Turner 1996, p. 175.
16. Chilton 1996. Also see Lakoff and Johnson 1980, pp. 96–105.
17. Chilton 1996, Lakoff 1987.
18. May 2000 estimate of the United States population. U.S. Census Bureau Web site: http://www.census.gov/population/estimates/nation/
19. Chilton 1996, p. 267. Chilton and Ilyin 1993 discuss medieval Russian political discourse that employed derivations of the same root, *dom.*
20. Hence Lakoff's expectation (Lakoff 1996) that politics in the United States is conceptualized in terms of a single metaphor—NATION AS FAMILY—with two competing views of what a family means. Lakoff analyzes U.S. politics to be metaphorized in two versions of family morality. He juxtaposes families dominated by a stern father (conservative politics) to those headed by a nurturing mother (liberal politics). Lakoff's intuitions are more commonly expressed in terms of NATION AS HOUSE.
21. See Preuß 1996 on the public discourse on European nations and immigration.
22. I want to thank Eduardo Rivas, who contributed to the NATION AS SHIP analysis.
23. Chilton 1996, p. 149.
24. Ibid., p. 52.

25. Excerpts drawn from Brimelow's *Alien Nation* are marked with the initial of the author and the page of the reference, e.g., (B 18).

26. In 1776, the British immigrant author Paine published a pamphlet entitled *Common Sense,* in which he advocated that the North American colonies immediately declare their independence.

27. Chávez 1998, pp. 201, 202.

28. Quoted in Reddy 1979, pp. 165–166.

29. Chilton 1996, p. 409. For an exposition of the trends undermining the discourse of sovereignty, see Camilleri and Falk 1992.

30. See, for example, Acuña 1972, De León 1983, and Almaguer 1994. It should be noted that Mexican society also operated with a racial hierarchy based on bloodlines and skin color. This hierarchy is a Spanish colonial legacy. Indigenous Mexican Indians are at the bottom of the hierarchy, while dark-skinned mestizos are lower than "whiter," more European-looking Mexicans. In Greater Mexico it is still common to congratulate the parents of a fair-skinned newborn with reference to the infant's skin color. Compliments to the parents of an infant born with a darker complexion often do not mention pigmentation, particularly for female infants. See Mörner 1967.

31. By way of illustration, see Paredes 1958, Acuña 1972, Cockcroft 1994, Vigil 1998.

32. Horsman 1981, p. 212. Also see Estrada, García, Macías, and Maldonado 1981; De León 1983; Menchaca 1993; and Almaguer 1994, among others.

33. Handlin 1957, pp. 93–94.

34. The men of my family wore U.S. military uniforms during this period. On my father's side, my Tio Alvaro served in the Twenty-Ninth Infantry. He was one of only five of his unit to survive the terrible seventeen-day Battle of the Bulge, earning him an offer of a commission, which he refused. Alvaro later served in Korea. Uncle Hector piloted a B-17 for the Eighth Air Force. He flew 35 combat missions, twice being forced down after taking flack while over German targets. During the Cold War, he flew a remarkable 127 missions as part of the Berlin Airlift. Hector retired a lieutenant colonel. My father served in the Fifth Air Force during the occupation of Japan, in an aircraft control and warning squadron.

My mother's brothers, wrongly deported as Mexican nationals during the Great Repatriation, nonetheless returned to their birthplace and enlisted. My Tio Kiko fought as a machine gunner in the bloody Luzon campaign of the Philippines. Yet another, Vincente Arriola, paid the ultimate price. He died in action and is buried in a French military cemetery. At times I reflect on how he and his generation regarded their country. They willingly served, fought, and at times died for the United States, which in turn denied them their full measure of citizenship, and humanity.

35. Hammerback and Jensen 1998, p. 79, who cited Taylor 1975, p. 7. Boldface my emphasis.
36. Hammerback and Jensen 1998, p. 80. Boldface my emphasis.
37. Skrentny 1996, p. 8; Smith 1998, pp. 121–124.
38. Smith 1998, p. 122.
39. This section draws on the scholarship and theorizing of Preuß 1996, Rocco 1998, Kymlicka and Norman 1994, Turner 1990, and "The Birthright Citizenship Amendment: A Threat to Equality," *Harvard Law Review* 1994.
40. Marshall and Bottomore 1992.
41. Brzezinski 1994. Polish-born Brzezinski (Ph.D. Harvard, 1953) served as National Security Advisor to President Carter.
42. Excerpts were published in Fonte 1997, p. 72, reproduced with Fonte's own italicization.
43. Young 1989, p. 257. Also see Hernández-Truyol 1996.
44. Glazer 1983, cited in Kymlicka and Norman 1994.
45. Skrentny 1996, p. 11, reproduced with original italics.
46. Rawls 1971, p. 540.
47. Aveni 1980, p. 30.
48. Ibid., pp. 30–35. Parenthetically, in Mexican Spanish the present-day word for marketplace, *tianguis,* stems from this Nahua source.
49. Carvajal and Martínez 1994.
50. Lakoff and Johnson 1999, pp. 303–304.
51. Ibid., p. 291.
52. Lou Cannon, "Smeared in California," *Washington Post,* May 31, 1994, A17, my ellipses.
53. Baca 1979.
54. Romano-V. 1968; Saragoza, Juárez, Valenzuela, and González 1992; Perea 1995; Johnson 1997a, 1997b.
55. Santa Ana 1993, on the basis of the 1980 national census.
56. Rodriguez 1982, pp. 9–40.
57. Sosa 1998.
58. Foley 1998. Also see Menchaca 1993.
59. Hill 1998, p. 684.
60. This racial hierarchy was established by Anglo Californians in the early days of the state, as detailed in Almaguer 1994. Foley (p. 54) quotes Toni Morrison: "In race talk the move into mainstream America always means buying into the notion of American blacks as the real aliens." I would like to thank my colleague Eric Ávila for bringing Foley's 1998 article to my attention.
61. Kafka [1948] 1975, pp. 191–199.
62. This claim has been made since 1848. Weber 1973 provides two nearly identical quotes: an 1858 statement by a Tejano, Juan Nepomuceno Seguín; and a speech

in 1856 by a Californio, Pablo de la Guerra. Recently the issue has been reconsidered in light of Latino Critical Race Theory legal scholarship. See Johnson 1997a and Martínez 1998, as well as a number of selections in Delgado and Stefancic 1998.

63. Kivel 1996.
64. There is much literature on the phenomenon of "passing" as white, most of which has been written by African Americans. See Williams 1991, Harris 1993.
65. *Los Angeles Times,* April 13, 1998, A1.

Chapter Eight

1. Reeves's (1983) description of the changes in racial references in British parliamentary discourse.
2. See in Delgado's and Stefancic's reader Olivas, "My Grandfather's Story"; Delgado, "Storytelling"; Montoya, "Masks and Resistance"; and Montoya, "Masks and Acculturation," as well as Said's *Cultural Imperialism.*
3. Present in another set of water metaphors noted in the *Times* public-discourse database are notions of wealth or resources, whether labor or capital:

   (a) while she understands the plight of most undocumented workers, she is concerned that it **erodes** her meager paycheck (August 22, 1993, A1)
   (b) The Orange County Grand Jury on Wednesday called for a nationwide, three-year moratorium on all immigration to the United States in an attempt to ease the **drain on government programs.** (June 17, 1993, A1)
   (c) They're not on welfare, they're not **draining** society, they are here contributing. (February 8, 1993, D4)

   Since this metaphor, like immigration, has a WATER source domain, it can be utilized to refer to the benefits of immigration.
4. Carnegie 1885, p. 27, cited in part in Calavita 1996.
5. Carnegie 1885, p. 27.
6. These come from one page of the *Times* business section, September 22, 1999.
7. Other references were to BRACEROS AS CURE for what was explicitly called the *plague* that was seen as befalling farm owners, as in excerpt 7 above. The most affirming metaphor of the time compared Mexican laborers to soldiers who were fighting for the interests of the Allies in World War II. Loo asserts that this placed the "laborers in the same category as the American soldiers who were risking their lives for the country."

   (a) Consul Gutierrez stated that **"you are soldiers fighting on the production front."** (November 19, 1942, II9)
   (b) A small **army** of farmers [i.e., braceros] . . . (December 1, 1942, II9)
   (c) The Mexicans **marched** to the fairgrounds. (November 19, 1942, II9)

Even excerpt (a) was not representative of Anglo-Americans' views of the braceros. It was quoted at a pep rally at which the Mexican government official spoke to assembled braceros.

8. Valenzuela 2001.

9. *Economist,* May 7, 1994.

10. Hayes-Bautista is informed by the research that he and his collaborators (1994) have conducted, which developed a portrait of today's Latino immigrant that repudiates many nativist myths and stereotypes.

11. Translated from *La Opinión,* December 16, 1994, D1.

12. Brimelow 1995, pp. 17–18, 48.

13. Kerner 1988, p. 11.

14. See Stefancic and Delgado 1996.

15. Dickens 1854, p. 1.

16. Dewey 1897, pp. 20–22.

17. The child's home and community knowledge is also her "funds of knowledge," to use the term coined by Carlos Vélez-Ibáñez 1988 and made current by Luis Moll.

18. Ching 1995, p. 8.

19. Vigil 1999, p. 277. This thesis may have first been drafted by George I. Sánchez, in the *Journal of Applied Psychology,* vol. 18, as noted in Vaca 1970a, p. 15.

20. Terrence Wiley 1996, and *viva voce.*

21. In some spheres, for example, the creative arts, such marginal stances are more or less accepted struggles of cultural insubordination against the high cultural hegemony. However, as my colleagues Judith Baca (personal communication) and Alicia Gaspar de Alba (1998) have argued, there are clear limits to what is acceptable rebellion in the arts.

22. Another construction metaphor, LANGUAGE AS TOOLMAKER, is Reddy's recommendation (1979) to linguists and society to better understand that languages are means to build knowledge and construct communication.

23. The terms used in 1999 by the California State Department of Education to describe various language programs in the post–Proposition 227 period are: (1) Sheltered English immersion classes, (2) mainstream classes, and (3) alternative courses of study. A more explicit description of these programs is: (1) English language teaching programs, (2) English-only programs, and (3) bilingual or language enrichment programs. It does not serve language-minority children to mask English-only pedagogy by other names.

24. Mio 1996, 1997; Mio and Lovrich 1998.

25. Carlson 1994.

26. *Economist* 1994.

27. The following section draws heavily on Rorty 1989, who employs "the strong poet," Harold Bloom's term.

28. The adage is attributed to Heidegger by Rorty 1989, p. 50.
29. Ibid., p. 6.
30. Ibid., p. 16.
31. In "Truth and Knowledge," translated in Schacht 1983, p. 73.
32. Rorty 1989, p. 20.
33. Unamuno said: "Doy por una metáfora todos los silogismos, con sus ergos correspondientes que le puedan garapiñar en la garrafa escolástica; la metáfora: me enseña más, me alumbra más y, sobre todo, encuentro calor debajo de ella, pues la imaginacíon sólo a fuego trabaja." Quoted in Gómez de la Serna 1961, p. 544.

# References

Acuña, Rodolfo F. 1972. *Occupied America: The Chicano Struggle for Liberation*. San Francisco: Canfield Press.

Ada, Ana Flor. 1986. "Creative Education for Bilingual Teachers." *Harvard Education Review* 56 (4): 386–394.

———. 1988. "The Pajaro Valley Experience: Working with Spanish-speaking Parents to Develop Children's Reading and Writing Skills in the Home through the Use of Children's Literature." In *Minority Education: From Shame to Struggle,* ed. Tove Skutnabb-Kangas and James Cummins. Philadelphia: Multilingual Matters.

Ada, Ana Flor, Violet J. Harris, and Lee Bennett Hopkins. 1993. *A Chorus of Cultures: Developing Literacy through Multicultural Poetry*. Carmel, Calif.: Hampton-Brown Books.

Alexander, Jeffrey C., Bernard Giesen, Richard Münch, and Neil J. Smelser, eds. 1987. *The Micro-Macro Link*. Berkeley and Los Angeles: University of California Press.

Almaguer, Tomás. 1994. *Racial Fault Lines: Historical Origins of White Supremacy in California*. Berkeley: University of California Press.

Anaya, Rodolfo A., and Francisco Lomelí, eds. 1989. *Aztlán: Essays on the Chicano Homeland*. Albuquerque, N.Mex.: Academía/El Norte Publications.

Anderson, Mark C. 1998. "What's to Be Done with 'Em? Images of Mexican Cultural Backwardness, Racial Limitations, and Moral Decrepitude in the United States Press, 1913–1915." *Mexican Studies—Estudios Mexicanos* 14 (1): 23–70.

Anderson, Nick. 1997. "Smaller Classes Mean More Novice Teachers." *Los Angeles Times,* June 22, p. A1.

———. 1998. "Study Lays Out Problems State Faces. The Nonpartisan Report, 'How California Compares,' Ranks Public Schools Poorly in Many Categories. It Urges Officials to Examine Examples Set Elsewhere in the Nation." *Los Angeles Times,* December 30, p. B2.

Anderson, Richard D., Jr. 2001. "Metaphors of Dictatorship and Democracy: Change in the Russian Political Lexicon and the Transformation of Russian Politics." *Slavic Review* 60 (2): 312–335.

Anzaldúa, Gloria. 1987. *Borderlands/La Frontera: The New Mestiza*. San Francisco: Spinsters/Aunt Lute.

Árias, M. Beatriz. 1986. "The Context of Education for Hispanic Students: An Overview." *American Journal of Education* 95 (1): 26–57.

August, Diane, and Kenji Hakuta. 1997. "Bilingualism and Second-Language Learning." In *Improving Schooling for Language Minority Children: A Research Agenda,* ed. Diane August and Kenji Hakuta, pp. 29–51. Washington, D.C.: National Academy Press.

Austin, John L. 1962. *Philosophical Papers.* Oxford: Clarendon Press.

Aveni, Anthony F. 1980. *Skywatchers of Ancient Mexico.* Austin: University of Texas Press.

Baca, Jimmy Santiago. 1979. *Immigrants in Our Own Land.* Baton Rouge: Louisiana State University Press.

Bagdikian, Ben H. 1987. *The Media Monopoly,* 2d ed. Boston: Beacon Press.

Bailey, Richard W. 1990. "English at Twilight." In *The State of the Language,* ed. Leonard Michaels and Christopher Ricks. Berkeley and Los Angeles: University of California Press.

Balderrama, Francisco E., and Raymond Rodríguez. 1995. *Decade of Betrayal: Mexican Repatriation in the 1930s.* Albuquerque: University of New Mexico Press.

Baldwin, James. 1979. "If Black English Isn't a Language, Then Tell Me, What Is?" *New York Times.* Reprinted in *The Real Ebonics Debate: Power, Language, and the Education of African-American Children,* ed. Theresa Perry and Lisa Delpit, pp. 67–70. Boston: Beacon Press.

Ballesteros-Coronel, Mary. 1998. "Mayoría respalda educación bilingüe: Sondeo indica que una gran cantidad de quienes envían sus hijos al LAUSD se opone a eliminar este sistema de enseñanza." *La Opinión,* February 9, p. A1. ["Majority Support Bilingual Education: Poll Indicates That the Great Number of Those Who Send Their Children to LAUSD (Los Angeles Unified School District) Oppose the Elimination of That System of Education."]

Barrera, Mario. 1974. "The Study of Politics and the Chicano." *Aztlán: A Journal of the Social Sciences and the Arts* 5 (1–2): 9–26.

———. 1979. *Race and Class in the Southwest: A Theory of Racial Inequality.* Notre Dame, Ind.: University of Notre Dame Press.

Basler, Roy P., ed. 1953. *The Collected Works of Abraham Lincoln,* vol. 5. New Brunswick, N.J.: Rutgers University Press.

Baugh, John. 1986. "Bilingualism and Bidialectalism among American Minorities." In *Problems of Standardization and Linguistic Variation in Present-Day English,* ed. Gerhard Nickel and James C. Stalker. Heidelberg: J. Groos Verlag.

———. 1988. "Communicating Racism: Ethnic Prejudice in Thought and Talk." *American Journal of Sociology* 94 (3): 683–686.

———. 1999. *Out of the Mouths of Slaves: African American Language and Educational Malpractice.* Austin: University of Texas Press.

Bennett, William J. 1998. "Is Affirmative Action on the Way Out? Should It Be? A Symposium." *Commentary* 105 (3): 19–20.

Berko Gleason, Jean, and Nan Bernstein Ratner. 1993. "Language Development in Children." *Psycholinguistics,* ed. Jean Berko Gleason and Nan Bernstein Ratner, pp. 1–40. New York: Harcourt Brace Jovanovich Publishers.

Black, Max. 1993. "More about Metaphor." In *Metaphor and Thought,* 2d ed., ed. Andrew Ortony, pp. 19–41. Cambridge: Cambridge University Press.

Bobo, Lawrence. 1983. "Whites' Opposition to Busing: Symbolic Racism or Realistic Group Conflict?" *Journal of Personality and Social Psychology* 45 (6): 1196–1210.

———. 1988. "Group Conflict, Prejudice and the Paradox of Contemporary Attitudes." In *Eliminating Racism,* ed. Phyllis A. Katz and Dalmas A. Taylor, pp. 85–114. New York: Plenum Press.

———. 1998. "Race, Interests, and Beliefs about Affirmative Action: Unanswered Questions and New Directions." *American Behavioral Scientist* 41 (7): 985–1004.

Bobo, Lawrence, and Vincent L. Hutchings. 1996. "Perceptions of Racial Group Competition: Extending Blumer's Theory of Group Position to a Multiracial Social Context." *American Sociological Review* 61 (6): 951–973.

Bobo, Lawrence, and Frederick C. Licari. 1989. "Education and Political Tolerance: Testing the Effects of Cognitive Sophistication and Target Group Affect." *Public Opinion Quarterly* 53 (3): 285–309.

Bolinger, Dwight. 1980. *Language—the Loaded Weapon: The Use and Abuse of Language Today.* London: Longman.

Bosniak, Linda S. 1996. "Opposing Proposition 187: Undocumented Immigrants and the National Imagination." *Connecticut Law Review* 28 (3): 555–620.

Bourdieu, Pierre. 1977. "Cultural Reproduction and Social Reproduction." *Power and Ideology in Education,* ed. Jerome Karabel and A. H. Halsey, pp. 487–510. New York: Oxford University Press.

Bowen, William G., and Derek Bok. 1998. *The Shape of the River: Long-Term Consequences of Considering Race in College and University Admissions.* Princeton, N.J.: Princeton University Press.

Bradley, Ann. 1999. "The Not-Quite Profession: The Course of Teaching. Lessons of a Century." *Education Week* 19 (2): 31–37.

Breitman, George, ed. 1965. *Malcolm X Speaks: Selected Speeches and Statements.* New York: Grove Weidenfeld.

Brimelow, Peter. 1995. *Alien Nation: Common Sense about America's Immigration Disaster.* New York: Random House.

Britton, John A. 1995. *Revolution and Ideology: Images of the Mexican Revolution in the United States.* Lexington: University of Kentucky Press.

Bronson, Fred. 1997. *The Billboard Book of #1 Hits,* revised and updated 4th ed. New York: Billboard Books.

Brown, Gillian, and George Yule. 1983. *Discourse Analysis.* Cambridge: Cambridge University Press.

Brown, Joanne. 1998. "Language." In *A Companion to American Thought,* ed. Richard Wightman Fox and James T. Kloppenberg, pp. 379–381. Malden, Mass.: Blackwell.

Brownstein, Ronald, and Richard Simon. 1993. "Hospitality Turns to Hostility. California Has a Long History of Welcoming Newcomers for Their Cheap Labor—Until Times Turn Rough." *Los Angeles Times,* November 14, p. A1.

Brugman, Claudia M. 1983. *Story of "Over."* Bloomington: Indiana University Linguistics Club.

Brzezinski, Zbigniew. 1994. "Premature Partnership (U.S. and Russia)." *Foreign Affairs* 73 (2): 67–83.

Byrne, James P. 1996. "Theories of Cognitive Development and Learning." In *Cognitive Development and Learning in Instructional Contexts,* ed. James P. Byrne. Boston: Allyn and Bacon.

Calavita, Kitty. 1996. "The New Politics of Immigration: 'Balanced-Budget Conservatism' and the Symbolism of Proposition 187." *Social Problems* 43 (1): 284–305.

Camilleri, Joseph A., and Jim Falk. 1992. *The End of Sovereignty: Politics of a Shrinking and Fragmenting World.* Brookfield, Vt.: E. Elgar.

Carlson, Margaret. 1994. "Alienable Rights." *Time,* October 31, p. 39.

Carnegie, Andrew. 1885. "The American People." In *Triumphant Democracy or Fifty Years' March of the Republic,* pp. 18–35. New York: Doubleday, Doran & Co.

Carrasco, Gilbert Paul. 1997. "Latinos in the United States: Invitation and Exile." In *Immigrants Out! The New Nativism and the Anti-Immigrant Impulse in the United States,* ed. Juan F. Perea, pp. 190–204. Albany: New York University Press.

Carvajal, Doreen, and Gebe Martínez. 1994. "Clergy Struggles to Address Volatile Issues of Prop. 187." *Los Angeles Times,* October 3, p. A1.

Casad, Eugene H. 1992. Review of George Lakoff's *Women, Fire and Dangerous Things* and Ray Jackendoff's *Semantics and Cognition. Word* 43 (2): 297–317.

Chabrán, Richard. 1985. "Activism and Intellectual Struggle in the Life of Ernesto Galarza (1905–1984) with an Accompanying Bibliography." *Hispanic Journal of Behavioral Sciences* 7 (2): 135–152.

Chapa, Jorge, and Richard R. Valencia. 1993. "Latino Population Growth, Demographic Characteristics, and Educational Stagnation: An Examination of Recent Trends." *Hispanic Journal of Behavioral Sciences* 15 (2): 165–187.

Chapman, Robert L. 1995. *Dictionary of American Slang.* New York: HarperCollins.

Chávez, Leo R. 1992. *Shadowed Lives: Undocumented Immigrants in American Society.* New York: Harcourt Brace Jovanovich College Publications.

Chávez, Lydia. 1998. *The Color Bind: California's Battle to End Affirmative Action.* Berkeley: University of California Press.

Chavira, Ricardo. 1977. "A Case Study: Reporting of Mexican Emigration and Deportation." *Journalism History,* vol. 4, pp. 59–61.

Chilton, Paul A. 1996. *Security Metaphors: Cold War Discourse from Containment to Common House.* New York: Peter Lang.

———, and Mikhail Ilyin. 1993. "Metaphor in Political Discourse: The Case of the 'Common European House.'" *Discourse and Society* 4 (1): 7–31.

Ching, Francis D. K. 1995. *A Visual Dictionary of Architecture.* New York: Van Nostrand Reinhold.

Chomsky, Noam. 1965. *Aspects of the Theory of Syntax.* Cambridge, Mass.: MIT Press.

Cioran, Emile M. 1991. *Anathemas and Admirations,* trans. Richard Howard. New York: Arcade Publishing.

Cockcroft, James D. 1994. *The Hispanic Struggle for Social Justice: The Hispanic Experience in the Americas.* New York: Franklin Watts.

Collins, Philip A. W. 1963. *Dickens and Education.* London: Macmillan.

Colvin, Richard. 1997. "Math Changes Reflect Broader Schools Debate." *Los Angeles Times,* December 5, pp. A1, A30–31.

———. 2001. "Firm That Aids Investors Now Studies Schools. Standard & Poor's Has a Web Site That Evaluates Local Districts." *Los Angeles Times,* May 26, p. A11.

Conley, Dalton. 1999. *Being Black, Living in the Red: Race, Wealth, and Social Policy in America.* Berkeley: University of California Press.

Cook, Vivian. 1993. *Linguistics and Second Language Acquisition.* New York: St. Martin's Press.

Cotter, Colleen. 1999. Personal communication.

Craig, Barbara A. 1996. "Parental Attitudes toward Bilingualism in a Local Two-way Immersion Program." *Bilingual Research Journal* 20 (3–4): 383–411.

Crawford, James. 1989. *Bilingual Education: History, Politics, Theory and Practice.* Trenton, N.J.: Crane Publishing.

———. 1992a. *Hold Your Tongue: Bilingualism and the Politics of "English-Only."* Reading, Mass.: Addison-Wesley.

———. 1992b. *Language Loyalties: A Source Book on the Official English Controversy.* Chicago: University of Chicago Press.

Croft, William. 1993. "The Role of Domains in the Interpretation of Metaphors and Metonymies." *Cognitive Linguistics* 4 (4): 335–370.

Crystal, David, ed. 1997. *English as Global Language.* New York: Cambridge University Press.

Darder, Antonia. 1991. *Culture and Power in the Classroom.* Westport, Conn.: Bergin & Garvey.

Davis, Mike. 1995. "The Social Origins of the Referendum." *NACLA Report on the Americas* 29 (3): 24–28.

De León, Arnoldo. 1983. *They Called Them Greasers: Mexicans in Texas, 1821–1900.* Austin: University of Texas Press.

Delgado, Richard, and Jean Stefancic, eds. 1998. *The Latino/a Condition: A Critical Reader.* New York: New York University Press.

Delpit, Lisa. 1995. *Other People's Children: Culture Conflict in the Classroom.* New York: New Press.

Dewey, John. [1897] 1959. "My Pedagogic Creed." *Dewey on Education,* ed. Martin S. Dworkin, pp. 19–32. New York: Teachers College Press.

Dickens, Charles. [1854] 1995. *Hard Times.* London: Penguin.

———. [1865] 1997. *Our Mutual Friend.* London: Penguin.

Dovidio, John. 1997. "'Aversive' Racism and the Need for Affirmative Action." *Chronicle of Higher Education* 43 (46): A60.

Dovidio, John, and Samuel L. Gaertner. 1986. "Prejudice, Discrimination and Racism: Historical Trends and Contemporary Approaches." In *Prejudice, Discrimination, and Racism,* ed. John F. Dovidio and Samuel L. Gaertner, pp. 1–34. Orlando, Fla.: Academic Press.

Dyer, Richard. 1997. *White.* New York: Routledge.

*Economist.* 1994. "Return of the Huddled Masses." Vol. 331, no. 7862, pp. A25–27.

Edley, Christopher, Jr. 1996. *Not All Black and White: Affirmative Action and American Values.* New York: Farrar, Straus & Giroux.

Edwards, John. 1985. *Language, Society and Identity.* New York: Basil Blackwell.

———. 1989. *Language and Disadvantage.* London: Cole and Whurr Publishers.

Ellis, Mark, and Richard Wright. 1998. "The Balkanization Metaphor in the Analysis of U.S. Immigration." *Annals of the Association of American Geographers* 88 (4): 686.

Engelmann, Siegfried. 1999. "The Benefits of Direct Instruction: Affirmative Action for At-Risk Students." *Educational Leadership* 57 (1): 77, 79.

*English World-Wide.* 1980–present. Heidelberg: Julius Groos Verlag.

Entman, Robert M. 1989a. *Democracy without Citizens: Media and the Decay of American Politics.* New York: Oxford University Press.

———. 1989b. "How the Media Affect What People Think: An Information Processing Approach." *Journal of Politics* 51 (2): 347–370.

———. 1990a. "Modern Racism and the Images of Blacks in Local Television News." *Critical Studies in Mass Communication* 7 (4): 332–345.

———. 1990b. "News as Propaganda." Review of Edward Herman's and Noam Chomsky's *Manufacturing Consent: The Political Economy of the Mass Media. Journal of Communications* 40 (1): 124–127.

———. 1992. "Blacks in the News: Television, Modern Racism and Cultural Change." *Journalism Quarterly* 69 (2): 341–361.

Ericksen, Charlie. 1998. "Media Misleading about Hispanic Vote on Proposition 227." *Houston Chronicle,* June 11, p. A33.

Estrada, Leobardo F., Chris García, Reynaldo Flores Macías, and Lionel Maldonado. 1981. "Chicanos in the United States: A History of Exploitation and Resistance." *Daedalus* 110 (2): 103–132.

Fairclough, Norman. 1989. *Language and Power.* New York: Longman.

———. 1995. *Critical Discourse Analysis: The Critical Study of Language.* New York: Longman.

Faltis, Christian J., and Paula M. Wolfe, eds. 1999. *So Much to Say: Adolescents, Bilingualism, and ESL in the Secondary Schools.* New York: Teachers College Press.

Fauconnier, Gilles. 1985. *Mental Spaces.* Cambridge, Mass.: MIT Press.

Fernández, Celestino, and Lawrence R. Pedroza. 1982. "The Border Patrol and News Media Coverage of Undocumented Mexican Immigration during the 1970s: Quantitative Content Analysis in the Sociology of Knowledge." *California Sociologist* 5 (2): 1–26.

Fernandez, James W. 1991. "Introduction: Confluents of Inquiry." In *Beyond Metaphor: The Theory of Tropes in Anthropology,* ed. James W. Fernandez, pp. 3–13. Stanford, Calif.: Stanford University Press.

Fishman, Joshua A., and Heriberto Casiano. 1969. "Puerto Ricans in the Press." *Modern Language Journal* 53 (3): 157–162.

Fitzpatrick, Ellen. 1995. "Industrialism." In *A Companion to American Thought,* ed. Richard Wightman Fox and James T. Kloppenberg, pp. 340–342. Malden, Mass.: Blackwell Publishers.

Foley, Neil. 1998. "Becoming Hispanic: Mexican Americans and the Faustian Pact with Whiteness." *Reflexiones 1997: New Directions in Mexican American Studies,* issue editor Neil Foley, pp. 53–70.

Foner, Philip S. 1950. *The Life and Writings of Frederick Douglass, Pre–Civil War Decade 1850–1860.* New York: International Publishers.

Fonte, John. 1997. "Taking Citizenship Seriously." *American Enterprise* 8 (2): 72.

Foucault, Michel. [1970–1971] 1977. "History of Systems of Thought, a Summary of a Course Given at Collège de France." In *Language, Countermemory, Practice: Selected Essays and Interviews by Michel Foucault,* ed. Donald F. Bouchard, pp. 199–204. Ithaca, N.Y.: Cornell University Press.

———. 1980. *Power/Knowledge: Selected Interviews and Other Writings 1972–1977,* ed. Colin Gordon. New York: Pantheon Books.

———. 1984. "The Order of Discourse." *Language and Politics,* ed. Michael J. Shapiro, pp. 108–138. New York: New York University Press.

Fowler, Roger. 1991. *Language in the News: Discourse and Ideology in the Press.* London: Routledge.

Freire, Paulo. 1970. *Pedagogy of the Oppressed.* New York: Seabury Press.

Frey, William H. 1996. "Immigration, Domestic Migration, and Demographic Balkanization in America: New Evidence for the 1990s." *Population and Development Review* 22 (4): 741–764.

Galarza, Ernesto. [1964] 1978. *Merchants of Labor: The Mexican Bracero Story: An Account of the Managed Migration of Mexican Farm Workers in California 1942–1960,* 3d ed. Santa Barbara, Calif.: McNally & Loftin, West.

Gallen, David, ed. 1992. *Malcolm X as They Knew Him.* New York: One World Ballantine Books.

Gamio, Mario. [1930] 1969. *Mexican Immigration to the United States.* New York: Arno Press.

García, Rubén J. 1995. "Critical Race Theory and Proposition 187: The Racial Politics of Immigration Law." *Chicano-Latino Law Review,* vol. 17, pp. 118–148.

Gardner, Martin. 1996. *The Night Is Large: Collected Essays, 1938–1995.* New York: St. Martin's Griffin.

Gaspar de Alba, Alicia. 1998. *Chicano Art: Inside/Outside the Master's House. Cultural Politics and the CARA Exhibition.* Austin: University of Texas Press.

Gass, Susan, and Larry Selinker. 1994. *Second Language Acquisition.* Hillsdale, N.J.: Lawrence Erlbaum Associates.

Gates, Henry Louis, Jr. 1986. "Introduction: Writing 'Race' and the Difference It Makes." *"Race," Writing and Difference,* pp. 1–20, 400–409. Chicago: University of Chicago Press.

Gee, John Paul. 1993. "What Is Literacy?" In *Linguistics for Teachers,* ed. Linda Miller Cleary and Michael D. Linn, pp. 257–264. New York: McGraw-Hill.

Genzuk, Michael. 1998. "Bilingual Initiative Fails the Test." *U.S. News & World Report,* June 22, BC-41–42.

Gibbs, Raymond W., Jr. 1993. "Process and Products in Making Sense of Tropes." In *Metaphor and Thought,* 2d ed., ed. Andrew Ortony, pp. 252–276. Cambridge: Cambridge University Press.

———. 1994. *Poetics of the Mind: Figurative Thought, Language and Understanding.* Cambridge: Cambridge University Press.

Giroux, Henry. 1981. *Ideology, Culture, and the Process of Schooling.* Philadelphia: Temple University Press.

Glazer, Nathan. 1998. "Is Affirmative Action on the Way Out? Should It Be? A Symposium." *Commentary* 105 (3): 29–31.

Gligorov, Vladimir. 1992. "Balkanization: A Theory of Constitution Failure." *East European Politics and Societies* 6 (3): 283–303.

Goatly, Andrew. 1997. *The Language of Metaphors.* London: Routledge.

Goddard Bergin, Thomas, and Max Harold Fisch. 1948. *The Third New Science of Vico.* Ithaca, N.Y.: Cornell University Press.

Gómez de la Serna, Ramón. 1961. "Don Miguel de Unamuno." *Retratos Completos,* pp. 542–566. Madrid: Aguilar.

Gómez-Quiñones, Juan. 1994. *Roots of Chicano Politics, 1600–1940.* Albuquerque: University of New Mexico Press.

González, Gerardo M., Francisco A. Ríos, Lionel A. Maldonado, and Stella T. Clark. 1995. "What's in a Name? Conflict at a University for the 21st Century." In *The Leaning Ivory Tower: Latino Professors in American Universities,* ed. Raymond V. Padilla and Rudolfo Chávez Chávez, pp. 165–188. Albany: State University of New York Press.

González, Manuel G. 1999. *Mexicanos: A History of Mexicans in the United States.* Bloomington: Indiana University Press.

González, Norma, Luis C. Moll, Martha Floyd-Tenery, Anna Rivera, Patricia Rendón, Raquel González, and Cathy Amanti. 1993. *Teacher Research on Funds of Knowledge: Learning from Households.* Educational Practice Report number 6, University of Arizona. Web site maintained by the National Center for Research on Cultural Diversity and Second Language Learning, http://www.ncbe.gwu.edu/miscpubs/ncrcdsll/epr6.htm.

González Echevarría, Roberto. 1997. "Is Spanglish a Language? Spanglish, the Composite Language of Spanish and English That Has Crossed Over from the Street to Hispanic Talk Shows and Advertising Campaigns, Poses a Grave Danger to Hispanic Culture and to the Advancement of Hispanics in Mainstream America." *New York Times,* March 28, p. A29.

González Egido, Luciano. 1983. *Salamanca, La gran metáfora de Unamuno.* Salamanca: Ediciones Universitarias de Salamanca.

Goody, Jack, and Ian Watt. 1963. "The Consequences of Literacy." *Comparative Studies of Society and History* 5 (3): 304–345.

Gould, Stephen J. 1981. *The Mismeasure of Man.* New York: W. W. Norton & Co.
———. 1995. "The Pattern of Life's History." In *The Third Culture,* ed. John Brockman, pp. 52–73. New York: Simon & Schuster.

Grady, Joe. 1999. "Typology of Motivation for Conceptual Metaphor." Manuscript. Author's personal collection, UCLA.

Grayling, A. C. 1996. *Wittgenstein.* Oxford: Oxford University Press.

Greenberg, Bradley, Michael Burgoon, Judee K. Burgoon, and Felipe Korzenny. 1983. *Mexican Americans and the Mass Media.* Norwood, N.J.: Ablex.

Greene, Jay P. 1998. *A Meta-Analysis of the Effectiveness of Bilingual Education.* Claremont, Calif.: Tomás Rivera Policy Institute.

Grice, H. Paul. 1975. "Logic and Conversation." In *Syntax and Semantics,* vol. 3, *Speech Acts,* ed. Peter Cole and Jerry L. Morgan, pp. 41–58. New York: Academic Press.

Griswold del Castillo, Richard. 1990. *The Treaty of Guadalupe Hidalgo: A Legacy of Conflict.* Norman: University of Oklahoma Press.

Gumperz, John. 1982. *Discourse Strategies.* Cambridge: Cambridge University Press.

Gumperz, John, and Eduardo Hernández-Chávez. 1972. "Bilingualism, Bidialectalism and Classroom Interaction." In *Functions of Language in the Classroom,* ed. Courtney Cazden et al., pp. 84–110. New York: Teachers College Press.

Gutiérrez, David G. 1995. *Walls and Mirrors: Mexican Americans, Mexican Immigrants, and the Politics of Ethnicity.* Berkeley: University of California Press.

Gutiérrez, Felix. 1977. "Chicanos and the Media: Bibliography of Selected Materials." *Journalism History* 4 (2): 34–41, 65–67.

Habermas, Jürgen. 1976. *Legitimation Crisis.* Boston: Beacon Press.

Hakuta, Kenji, Yuku Goto Butler, and Daria Witt. 2000. *How Long Does It Take English Learners to Attain Proficiency?* University of California Language Minority Research Institute Policy Report 2000–1. Santa Barbara, Calif.: LMRI.

Halliday, M. A. K. 1978. *Language as Social Semiotic.* London: Edward Arnold.

Hammerback, John C., and Richard J. Jensen. 1998. *The Rhetorical Career of César Chávez.* College Station: Texas A&M University Press.

Hampton, James A. 1989. Review of George Lakoff's *Women, Fire, and Dangerous Things: What Categories Reveal about the Mind. Mind and Language* 4 (1–2): 130–137.

Handlin, Oscar. 1951. *The Uprooted: The Epic Story of the Great Migrations That Made the American People.* Boston: Little, Brown & Co.

———. 1957. *Race and Nationality in American Life.* New York: Anchor Books.

Harpham, Wendy Schlessel. 1998. *Diagnosis: Cancer.* New York: W. W. Norton & Co.

Harris, Cheryl I. 1993. "Whiteness as Property." *Harvard Law Review* 106 (8): 1707–1791.

*Harvard Law Review.* 1994. "The Birthright Citizenship Amendment: A Threat to Equality." Vol. 107, no. 5, pp. 1026–1043.

Hayes-Bautista, David E., Werner O. Schink, and Gregory Rodríguez. 1994. *Latino Immigrants in Los Angeles: A Portrait from the 1990 Census.* Los Angeles: Alta California Policy Research Center.

Heath, Shirley Brice. 1982a. "American English: Quest for a Model." In *The Other Tongue: English across Cultures,* ed. Braj B. Kachru, pp. 237–249. Urbana: University of Illinois Press.

———. 1982b. "What No Bedtime Story Means: Narrative Skills at Home and School." *Language in Society,* vol. 11, pp. 49–76.

———. 1984. "Linguistics and Education." *Annual Review of Anthropology,* vol. 13, pp. 251–274.

Herman, Edward S., and Noam Chomsky. 1988. *Manufacturing Consent: The Political Economy of the Mass Media.* New York: Pantheon Books.

Hernández, Guillermo E. 1991. *Chicano Satire: A Study in Literary Culture.* Austin: University of Texas Press.

Hernández-Chávez, Eduardo. 1984. "The Inadequacy of English Immersion Education as an Educational Approach for Language Minority Students in the United States." In *Studies on Immersion Education: A Collection for United States Educators,* pp. 144–183. Sacramento: California State Department of Education.

———. 1989. "The Role of Suppressive Language Policies in Language Shift and Language Loss." *Estudios Fronterizos,* vols. 18–19, pp. 123–125.

———. 1999. "La política lingüística y su papel en el desplazamiento del español en los Estados Unidos." In *La lengua española en los estados unidos,* ed. Javier Wimer, pp. 153–157. México, D.F.: Talleres Gráficos de México.

Hernández-Chávez, Eduardo, Andrew Cohen, and Anthony Beltramo, eds. 1975. *El lenguaje de los chicanos.* Arlington, Va.: Center for Applied Linguistics.

Hernández-Truyol, Berta Esperanza. 1996. "Building Bridges: Bringing International Human Rights Home." *La Raza Law Journal* 9 (1): 69–80.

Higgins, Mark. 1998. Review of George Lakoff's *Moral Politics: What Conservatives Know That Liberals Don't. Language* 74 (2): 425–426.

Higham, John. 1955. *Strangers in the Land: Patterns of American Nativism, 1860–1925.* New Brunswick, N.J.: Rutgers University Press.

Hill, Jane H. 1993. "Hasta La Vista, Baby! Anglo Spanish in the American Southwest." *Critique of Anthropology* 13 (1): 145–176.

———. 1995. *Mock Spanish: A Site for Indexical Reproduction of Racism in American English.* Web site moderated by J. Overton and D. Glick; address: http://www.cs.uchicago.edu/l-c/archives/subs/hill-jane.

———. 1998. "Language, Race, and White Public Space." *American Anthropologist* 100 (3): 680–689.

Himmelfarb, Gertrude. 1996. "Strictly Family." Review of George Lakoff's *Moral Politics: What Conservatives Know That Liberals Don't. TLS: Times Literary Supplement,* no. 4870, August 12, p. 12.

Hinojosa, Raúl, and Peter Schey. 1995. "The Faulty Logic of the Anti-Immigration Rhetoric." *NACLA Report on the Americas* 29 (3): 18–23.

Hoffman, Abraham. 1974. *Unwanted Mexican Americans in the Great Depression: Repatriation Pressures, 1929–1939.* Tucson: University of Arizona Press.

Holland, Dorothy, and Naomi Quinn, eds. 1987. *Cultural Models in Language and Thought.* New York: Cambridge University Press.

hooks, bell. 1990. "Postmodern Blackness." *Postmodern Culture: An Electronic Journal of Interdisciplinary Criticism,* vol. 1, no. 1, 15 paragraphs, September.

———. 1996. *Killing Rage: Ending Racism.* New York: Owl Books.

Hornberger, Nancy H. 1999. Foreword. In *So Much to Say: Adolescents, Bilingualism, and* ESL *in the Secondary Schools,* ed. Christian J. Faltis and Paula M. Wolfe. New York: Teachers College Press.

Horsman, Reginald. 1981. *Race and Manifest Destiny: The Origins of American Racial Anglo-Saxonism.* Cambridge, Mass.: Harvard University Press.

Hymes, Dell. 1974. *Speech and Language: On the Origins and Foundations of Inequality among Speakers.* New York: Norton.

Jackendoff, Ray. 1976. "Toward an Explanatory Semantic Representation." *Linguistic Inquiry,* vol. 7, pp. 89–150.

———. 1983. *Semantics and Cognition.* Cambridge, Mass.: MIT Press.

———. 1990. *Semantic Structures.* Cambridge, Mass.: MIT Press.

Jackendoff, Ray, and David Aaron. 1991. Review of George Lakoff and Mark Turner's *More than Cool Reason: A Field Guide to Poetic Metaphor. Language* 67 (2): 320–338.

Jenkins, Richard. 1996. *Social Identity.* London: Routledge.

Jiménez, Carlos M. 1994. *The Mexican American Heritage.* Berkeley, Calif.: TQS Publications.

Johannsen, Robert W. 1985. *To the Halls of the Montezumas: The Mexican War in the American Imagination.* New York: Oxford University Press.

Johnson, Donna M. 1994. "Who Is We? Constructing Communities in U.S.–Mexico Border Discourse." *Discourse and Society* 5 (2): 207–231.

Johnson, Kevin R. 1995. "An Essay on Immigration Politics, Popular Democracy, and California's Proposition 187: The Political Relevance and Legal Irrelevance of Race." *Washington Law Review* 70 (3): 629–674.

———. 1997a. "Racial Hierarchy, Asian Americans and Latinos as 'Foreigners,' and Social Change: Is Law the Way to Go?" *Oregon Law Review* 76 (2): 347–368.

———. 1997b. "Some Thoughts on the Future of Latino Legal Scholarship." *Harvard Latino Law Review,* vol. 2, pp. 101–144.

———. 1999. *How Did You Get to Be Mexican? A White/Brown Man's Search for Identity.* Philadelphia: Temple University Press.

Johnson, Lyndon Baines. 1964. *A Time for Action: A Selection from the Speeches and Writings of Lyndon B. Johnson, 1953–64.* Introduction by Adlai E. Stevenson. New York: Atheneum Publishers.

Johnson, Mark. 1987. *The Body in the Mind: The Bodily Basis of Meaning, Imagination, and Reason.* Chicago: University of Chicago Press.

———. 1993. *Moral Imagination: Implications of Cognitive Science for Ethics.* Chicago: University of Chicago Press.

Jowett, Benjamin, translator. 1989. *The Republic and Other Works by Plato.* New York: Doubleday.

Kachru, Braj B., ed. 1982. *The Other Tongue: English across Cultures.* Urbana: University of Illinois Press.

Kafka, Franz. [1948] 1975. *In the Penal Colony.* New York: Schocken Books.

Kahane, Henry. 1982. "American English: From a Colonial Substandard to a Prestige Language." In *The Other Tongue: English across Cultures,* ed. Braj B. Kachru, pp. 229–250. Urbana: University of Illinois Press.

Kanellos, Nicolás. 1994. *The Hispanic Almanac.* Detroit: Visible Ink Press.

Katz, Irwin, J. Wackenhut, and G. Hauss. 1986. "Racial Ambivalence, Value Duality, and Behavior." In *Prejudice, Discrimination, and Racism,* ed. John F. Dovidio and Samuel L. Gaertner, pp. 35–60. Orlando, Fla.: Academic Press.

Keller, Gary D. 1994. *Hispanics and United States Film: An Overview and Handbook.* Tempe, Ariz.: Bilingual Review/Press.

Kennedy Manzo, Kathleen. 1997. "Hispanics Want School Courses to Reflect Their History." *Education Week* 14 (33): 1, 24.

Kerchner, Charles T., Julia E. Koppich, and Joseph G. Weeres. 1997. *United Mind Workers: Unions and Teaching in the Knowledge Society.* San Francisco: Jossey-Bass.

Kerner Commission. [1968] 1988. *The Kerner Report: The 1968 Report of the National Advisory Commission on Civil Disorders.* New York: Pantheon.

King, Martin Luther, Jr. 1967. *Where Do We Go from Here: Chaos or Community?* New York: Harper & Row Publishers.

Kivel, Paul. 1996. *Uprooting Racism: How White People Can Work for Racial Justice.* Gabriola Island, B.C.: New Society Publishers.

Kohl, Herbert. 1988. *36 Children.* New York: Plume.

———. 2000. Review of Diane Ravitch's *Left Back: A Century of Failed School Reform. Los Angeles Times Book Review,* October 10, p. 3.

Kövecses, Zoltán. 1986. *Metaphors of Anger, Pride and Love: A Lexical Approach to the Structure of Concepts.* Philadelphia: John Benjamin.

Kovel, Joel. 1970. *White Racism: A Psychohistory.* New York: Pantheon.

Krashen, Stephen D. 1991. *Is There a Case against Bilingual Education?* Washington, D.C.: National Clearinghouse for Bilingual Education.

Krippendorff, Klaus. 1980. *Content Analysis: An Introduction to Its Methodology.* Beverly Hills, Calif.: Sage Publications.

Kuhn, Thomas S. 1962. *The Structure of Scientific Revolutions.* Chicago: University of Chicago Press.

———. 1993. "Metaphor in Science." In *Metaphor and Thought,* 2d ed., ed. Andrew Ortony, pp. 533–542. Cambridge: Cambridge University Press.

Kumar, Krishnan. 1995. Review of *The Balkanization of the West: The Confluence of Postmodernism and Postcommunism. Sociology* 29 (2): 376–379.

Kymlicka, Will, and Wayne Norman. 1994. "Return of the Citizen: A Survey of Recent Work on Citizenship Theory." *Ethics* 104 (2): 352–381.

Labov, William. 1969. "The Logic of Nonstandard English." *Georgetown Monographs on Language and Linguistics,* vol. 22, pp. 1–22, 26–31.

———. 1972. *Sociolinguistic Patterns.* Philadelphia: University of Pennsylvania Press.

———. 1984. "Field Methods of the Project on Linguistic Change and Variation." In *Language in Use,* ed. John Baugh and Joel Sherzer, pp. 29–53. Englewood Cliffs, N.J.: Prentice-Hall.

Laclau, Ernesto. 1993. "Discourse." In *A Companion to Contemporary Political Philosophy,* ed. Robert E. Goodin and Philip Pettit, pp. 431–437. Malden, Mass.: Blackwell Publishers.

Lafont, Cristina. 1999. *The Linguistic Turn in Hermeneutic Philosophy,* trans. by José Medina. Cambridge, Mass.: MIT Press.

Lakoff, George. 1987. *Women, Fire and Dangerous Things: What Categories Reveal about the Mind.* Chicago: University of Chicago Press.

———. 1991. "Metaphor and War: The Metaphor System Used to Justify War in the Gulf." In *Engulfed in War: Just War and the Persian Gulf,* ed. Brian Hallet, pp. 95–111. Honolulu: Spark M. Matsunaga Institute for Peace.

———. 1993. "The Contemporary Theory of Metaphor." In *Metaphor and Thought,* 2d ed., ed. Andrew Ortony, pp. 202–251. Cambridge: Cambridge University Press.

———. 1996. *Moral Politics: What Conservatives Know That Liberals Don't.* Chicago: University of Chicago Press.

Lakoff, George, and Claudia Brugman. 1986. "Argument Forms in Lexical Semantics." In *Proceedings of the Twelfth Annual Meeting of the Berkeley Linguistics Society,* ed. Vassiliki Nikiforidou, Mary Van Clay, and Deborah Feder.

Lakoff, George, and Mark Johnson. 1980. *Metaphors We Live By.* Chicago: University of Chicago Press.

———. 1999. *Philosophy in the Flesh: The Embodied Mind and Its Challenge to Western Thought.* New York: Basic Books.

Lakoff, George, and Mark Turner. 1989. *More than Cool Reason: A Field Guide to Poetic Metaphor.* Chicago: University of Chicago Press.

Lalleman, Josine. 1996. "The State of the Art in Second Language Acquisition Research." In *Investigating Second Language Acquisition,* ed. Peter Jordens and Josine Lalleman, pp. 2–69. Berlin: Mouton de Gruyter.

Langacker, Ronald W. 1987. *Foundations of Cognitive Grammar. Vol. I: Theoretical Prerequisites.* Stanford, Calif.: Stanford University Press.

Leal, Luís. 1981. "In Search of Aztlán." *Denver Quarterly,* vol. 16, pp. 16–22.

Lee, Henry K. 1998. "Rally in San Leandro." *San Francisco Chronicle,* October 2, p. A21.

Lee, Patrick. 1993. "Studies Challenge View That Immigrants Harm Economy." *Los Angeles Times,* August 13, p. A1.

———. 1996. "Cognitive Development in Bilingual Children: A Case for Bilingual

Instruction in Early Childhood Development." *Bilingual Research Journal* 20 (3–4): 499–522.

Lighter, Jonathan E. 1994. *Random House Historical Dictionary of American Slang.* New York: Random House.

Lippi-Green, Rosina. 1997. *English with an Accent: Language, Ideology and Discrimination in the United States.* New York: Routledge.

Lipsitz, George. 1995. "The Possessive Investment in Whiteness: Racialized Social Democracy and the 'White' Problem in American Studies." *American Quarterly* 47 (3): 369–387.

———. 1998. *The Possessive Investment in Whiteness: How White People Profit from Identity Politics.* Philadelphia: Temple University Press.

Loewen, James W. 1995. *Lies My Teacher Told Me. Everything Your American History Textbook Got Wrong.* New York: Touchstone, by arrangement with Simon & Schuster.

Loo, Patricia. 1998. "How Mexican Immigrants Were Portrayed in the Print Media during the Bracero Program." Manuscript. Author's personal collection, UCLA.

López, Gerald P., Enid Colson, and Courtney Schaberg. 1996. *An Affirmative Action Manual: Understanding What It Is, Analyzing the Attacks against It, Articulating the Arguments in Support of It.* Web site: http://www.law.ucla.edu/Classes/Archive/CivAA.

*Los Angeles Times.* June 1992–June 1998. *CD-News.* New Canaan, Conn.: News Bank, Inc.

Loury, Glenn C. 1998. "Is Affirmative Action on the Way Out? Should It Be? A Symposium." *Commentary* 105 (3): 38–40.

Lovejoy, Arthur O. 1936. *The Great Chain of Being: A Study of the History of an Idea.* Cambridge, Mass.: Harvard University Press.

Lovelock, James. 1986. "Gaia: The World as Living Organism." *New Scientist,* March 24, pp. 1–4.

Lucas, Tamara, Rosemary Henze, and Rubén Donato. 1990. "Promoting the Success of Latino Language-Minority Students: An Exploratory Study of Six High Schools." *Harvard Education Review* 60 (3): 315–340.

Luykx, Aurolyn. 1999. *The Citizen Factory: Schooling and Cultural Production in Bolivia.* Ithaca, N.Y.: State University of New York Press.

McChesney, Robert W. 1999. *Rich Media, Poor Democracy: Communication Politics in Dubious Times.* Urbana: University of Illinois Press.

McConahey, J. B. 1986. "Modern Racism, Ambivalence, and the Modern Racism Scale." In *Prejudice, Discrimination and Racism,* ed. John F. Dovidio and Samuel L. Gaertner, pp. 91–126. Orlando, Fla.: Academic Press.

Macías, Reynaldo F. 1984. "Language and Ideology in the United States." *Social Education (Journal of the National Council for Social Sciences)* 49 (2): 97–100.

———. 1993. "Language and Ethnic Classification of Language Minorities: Chicano and Latino Students of the 1990s." *Hispanic Journal of Behavior Sciences* 15 (2): 230–257.

McKie, Robin. 2000. *Dawn of Man. The Story of Human Evolution.* New York: Dorling Kindersley Publishing.

McLaren, Peter. 1999. "A Pedagogy of Possibility: Reflecting upon Paulo Freire's Politics of Education." *Educational Researcher* 28 (2): 49–54.

McQuillan, Jeff, and Lucy Tse. 1996. "Does Research Matter? An Analysis of Media Opinion on Bilingual Education, 1984–1994." *Bilingual Research Journal* 20 (1): 1–27.

McWilliams, Carey. [1949] 1961. *North from Mexico: The Spanish-Speaking People of the United States.* New York: Monthly Review Press.

Makath, Keshav. 1994. "Balkanization of California: Demagogy, Not Just Economy." *Humanist* 54 (2): 4–7.

Mariscal, George, ed. 1999. *Aztlán and Viet Nam: Chicano and Chicana Experiences of the War.* Berkeley: University of California Press.

Marshall, Thomas Humphrey. 1965. *Class, Citizenship, and Social Development: Essays.* Garden City, N.Y.: Anchor Books.

Marshall, Thomas Humphrey, and Tom Bottomore. 1992. *Citizenship and Social Class.* London: Pluto Press.

Martín-Barbero, Jesús. [1987] 1993. *Communication, Culture and Hegemony: From the Media to Mediations,* trans. Elizabeth Fox and Robert A. White. London: Sage Publications.

Martínez, George A. 1997. "The Legal Construction of Race: Mexican Americans and Whiteness." *Harvard Latino Law Review* 2 (1): 321–347.

———. 1998. "African-Americans, Latinos and the Construction of Race: Toward an Epistemic Coalition." *Chicano Latino Law Review,* vol. 19, pp. 213–222.

Martínez, Thomas. 1969. "Advertising and Racism: The Case of the Mexican American." *El Grito: A Journal of Contemporary Mexican American Thought* 2 (4): 3–13.

Matthews, Frank L. 1995. "Interview: Dinesh D'Souza's Disquieting Views of Race, Racism and Culture." *Black Issues in Higher Education* 12 (16): 38–40.

Mehan, Hugh. 1979. *Learning Lessons.* Cambridge, Mass.: Harvard University Press.

———. 1980. "The Competent Student." *Anthropology & Education Quarterly* 11 (3): 131–152.

———. 1983. "The Role of Language and the Language of Role in Institutional Decision Making." *Language in Society,* vol. 12, pp. 187–212.

———. 1997. "The Discourse of the Illegal Immigration Debate: A Case Study on the Politics of Representation." *Discourse and Society* 8 (1): 249–320.

Meléndez, Thelma Esther. 1995. "Rubrics of Knowledge: A Case-Study Examination of Conflicting Mathematics and Literacy Theories of Learning among Practicing Teachers." Ph.D. diss., University of Southern California.

Menchaca, Martha. 1993. "Chicano Indianism: A Historical Account of Racial Repression in the U.S." *American Ethnologist* 20 (3): 583–603.

———. 1995. *The Mexican Outsider: Community History of Marginalization and Discrimination in California.* Austin: University of Texas Press.

Miles, Robert. 1989. *Racism.* New York: Routledge.

Miller, Alan C. 1993a. "Data Sheds Heat, Little Light, on Immigration Debate Studies. The Number of Illegal U.S. Residents Is Elusive. Their Impact on Jobs, Public Services Is at Best Ambiguous." *Los Angeles Times,* November 21, p. A1.

———. 1993b. "Outcry against Immigration Is Loud in Valley." *Los Angeles Times,* August 1, p. A1.

Miller, Greg. 1993. "Immigrant Costs Overstated, Study Finds." *Los Angeles Times,* September 3, p. B1.

Miller, Steven I., and Marcel Fredericks. 1990. "Perceptions of the Crisis in American Public Education: The Relationship of Metaphors to Ideology." *Metaphor and Symbolic Activity* 5 (2): 67–81.

Mio, Jeffery S. 1996. "Metaphor, Politics, and Persuasion." In *Metaphor: Implications and Applications,* ed. Jeffery S. Mio and A. N. Katz, pp. 127–146. Mahwah, N.J.: Lawrence Erlbaum Associates.

———. 1997. "Metaphor and Politics." *Metaphor and Symbol* 12 (2): 113–133.

Mio, Jeffery S., and Nicholas P. Lovrich. 1998. "Men of Zeal: Memory for Metaphor in the Iran-Contra Hearings." *Metaphor and Symbol* 13 (1): 49–68.

Montoya, Margaret E. 1996. "Border Crossings in an Age of Border Patrols: Cruzando Fronteras Metafóricas." *New Mexico Law Review* 26 (1): 1–8.

Moore, Zena. 1999. "Media Depictions of Teaching Foreign Languages: French on Saturday Night Live." Paper presented at the annual conference of the American Educational Research Association, Montréal, Canada.

Morán, Rachel F. 1995. "Demography and Distrust: The Latino Challenge to Civil Rights and Immigration Policy in the 1990s and Beyond." *La Raza Law Journal* 8 (1): 1–24.

Morín, Raúl. 1963. *Among the Valiant: Mexican-Americans in WWII and Korea.* Los Angeles: Borden Publishing.

Mörner, Magnus. 1967. *Race Mixture in the History of Latin America.* Boston: Little, Brown.

Morrison, Toni. 1996. *Lecture and Speech, upon the Award of the Nobel Prize for Literature, Delivered in Stockholm on the Seventh of December, Nineteen Hundred and Ninety-three.* New York: Alfred A. Knopf.

Mullis, Ina V. S., Jay R. Campbell, and Alan E. Farstrup. 1996. *Executive Summary* of the NAEP 1992 *Reading Report Card for the Nation and the States: Data from the National and Trail State Assessments.* Washington, D.C.: U.S. Dept. of Education, Office of Educational Research and Improvement, Educational Resources Information Center.

Murphy, Edward F. 1987. *Vietnam War Heroes.* New York: Ballantine Books.

———. 1992. *Korean War Heroes.* Novato, Calif.: Presidio Press.

Navarro, Salvador D. Forthcoming. *The Valedictorian and Other Stories.* Tempe, Ariz.: The Bilingual Press/Editorial Bilingue.

Noriega, Chon A., ed. 1992. *Chicanos and Film: Representation and Resistance.* Minneapolis: University of Minnesota Press.

Nunberg, Geoffrey. 1987. "The Nonuniqueness of Semantic Solutions: Polysemy." *Linguistics and Philosophy,* vol. 3, pp. 143–184.

Oakes, Jeannie. 1985. *Keeping Track: How Schools Structure Inequality.* New Haven, Conn.: Yale University Press.

———. 1990. *Multiplying Inequities: The Effects of Race, Social Class, and Tracking on Opportunities to Learn Mathematics and Science.* Los Angeles: Rand Corporation.

Ohara, Yumiko. 1999. "Ideology of Language and Gender: A Critical Discourse Analysis of Japanese Prescriptive Texts." In *Language and Ideology: Selected Papers from the 6th (IPrA) International Pragmatics Association Conference,* vol. 1, ed. Jef Verschueren. Antwerp: IPrA.

Olguín, Ben. 2000. "Sangre Mexicana/Corazón Americano: Identity, Ambiguity, and Critique in Mexican American War Narratives." Ford Foundation Fellows Annual Conference, University of California—Irvine, October 14.

Olivas, Michael A. 1994. "The Education of Latino Lawyers: An Essay on Crop Cultivation." *Chicano-Latino Law Review,* vol. 14, pp. 117–138.

Omi, Michael, and Howard Winant. 1994. *Racial Formation in the United States,* 2d ed. New York: Routledge.

Ortony, Andrew, ed. 1979. *Metaphor and Thought,* 1st ed. New York: Cambridge University Press.

———. 1993. *Metaphor and Thought,* 2d ed. Cambridge: Cambridge University Press.

Otheguy, Ricardo. 1990. "Thinking about Bilingual Education: A Critical Appraisal." *Harvard Educational Review* 52 (3): 301–314.

Padilla, Genaro. 1999. "UC Students Finish What They Start." *San Francisco Chronicle,* June 1, p. A19.

Page, Benjamin I., and Robert Y. Shapiro. 1989. "Educating and Manipulating the Public." In *Manipulating Public Opinion: Essays on Public Opinion as a Dependent Variable,* ed. Michael Margolis and Gary A. Mauser, pp. 294–320. Pacific Grove, Calif.: Brooks/Cole Publishing Co.

Paludan, Phillip Shaw. 1994. *The Presidency of Abraham Lincoln.* Lawrence: University Press of Kansas.

Pancake, Ann S. 1993. "Exploitation of Metaphor in the Persian Gulf War." *Metaphor and Symbolic Activity* 8 (4): 281–295.

Paredes, Américo. 1958. *With a Pistol in His Hand: A Border Ballad and Its Hero.* Austin: University of Texas Press.

Paredes, Raymund A. 1973. "The Image of the Mexican in American Literature." Ph.D. diss., University of Texas, Austin.

Park, Edward J. W. 1998. "Competing Visions: Political Formation of Korean Americans in Los Angeles, 1992–1997." *Amerasia Journal* 24 (1): 41–57.

Park, Edward J. W., and John S. W. Park. 1999. "A New American Dilemma?: Asian Americans and Latinos in Race Theorizing." *Journal of Asian American Studies* 2 (3): 289–309.

Payne, Kevin I., and Bruce I. Biddle. 1999. "Poor School Funding, Child Poverty, and Mathematics Achievement." *Educational Researcher* 28 (6): 4–13.

Pearl, Arthur. 1997. "Democratic Education as an Alternative to Deficit Thinking." In *The Evolution of Deficit Thinking: Educational Thought and Practice,* ed. Richard R. Valencia, pp. 132–159. London: Falmer Press.

Peñalosa, Fernando. 1975. "Sociolinguistic Theory and the Chicano Community." *Aztlán: A Journal of the Social Sciences and the Arts* 6 (1): 1–11.

———. 1980. *Chicano Sociolinguistics.* Rowley, Mass.: Newbury House.

Pennycook, Alastair. 1994. *The Cultural Politics of English as an International Language.* New York: Longman.

———. 1998. *English and the Discourses of Colonialism.* New York: Routledge.

Perea, Juan F. 1992. "Demography and Distrust: An Essay on American Languages, Cultural Pluralism and Official English." *Minnesota Law Review* 77 (2): 269–374.

———. 1995. "Los Olvidados: On the Making of Invisible People." *New York University Law Review* 70 (4): 965–991.

———, ed. 1997. *Immigrants Out! The New Nativism and the Anti-Immigrant Impulse in the United States.* Albany: New York University Press.

Pérez-Torres, Rafael. 1997. "Refiguring Aztlán." *Aztlán: A Journal of Chicano Research* 22 (2): 15–41.

Pettit, Arthur G. 1980. *Images of Mexican Americans in Fiction and Film.* College Station: Texas A&M University Press.

Philips, Susan U. 1972. "Participant Structure and Communicative Competence." In *Functions of Language in the Classroom,* ed. Courtney Cazden et al. New York: Teachers College Press.

Phillips, Jonathan, and Paul Murray, eds., with John Crocker, assoc. ed. 1995. *The Biology of Disease.* Oxford: Blackwell Science.

Phillipson, Robert. 1992. *Linguistic Imperialism*. Oxford: Oxford University Press.

Pitha, Petr, and Petr Sgall. 1990. Review of George Lakoff's *Women, Fire and Dangerous Things: What Categories Reveal about the Mind*. *Prague Bulletin of Mathematical Linguistics*, vol. 53, pp. 55–61.

Pompa, Leon. 1990. *Vico: A Study of the "New Science,"* 2d ed. New York: Cambridge University Press.

Powell, Philip W. 1971. *Tree of Hate: Propaganda and Prejudices Affecting United States Relations with the Hispanic World*. New York: Basic Books.

Preuß, Ulrich K. 1996. "Two Challenges to European Citizenship." *Political Studies* 44 (2): 534–552.

Purcell, William M. 1990. "Tropes, Transsumptio, Assumptio, and the Redirection of Studies of Metaphor." *Metaphor and Symbolic Activity* 5 (1): 35–53.

Quinn, Naomi. 1991. *The Cultural Basis of Metaphor*. Stanford, Calif.: Stanford University Press.

Rabinow, Paul, ed. 1984. *The Foucault Reader*. New York: Pantheon Books.

Ramírez, J. David, Sandra D. Yuen, and Dena R. Ramey. 1991. *Final Report, Longitudinal Study of Immersion Strategy, Early-Exit and Late-Exit Transitional Bilingual Education Programs for Language-Minority Children*. San Mateo, Calif.: Aguirre International.

Ramírez-Berg, Charles. 1989. "Immigrants and Aliens, and Extraterrestrials: Science Fiction's Alien 'Other' as (among Other Things) New Hispanic Imagery." *CineAction!*, no. 18, pp. 3–17.

Rawls, John. 1971. *A Theory of Justice*. Oxford: Oxford University Press.

Reddy, Michael J. 1979. "The Conduit Metaphor: A Case of Frame Conflict in Our Language about Language." In *Metaphor and Thought*, 1st ed., ed. Andrew Ortony. New York: Cambridge University Press.

Reeves, Frank. 1983. *British Racial Discourse: A Study of British Political Discourse about Race and Race-Related Matters*. Cambridge: Cambridge University Press.

Ricento, Thomas. 2000. "Historical and Theoretical Perspective in Language Policy and Planning." *Journal of Sociolinguistics* 4 (2): 196–213.

Rickford, John R. 1997. "Suite for Ebony and Phonics. Reflections on the Richness and Utility of the African American English Dialect." *Discover* 18 (12): 82–87.

———. 1999. *African American Vernacular English: Features, Evolution, Educational Implications*. Malden, Mass.: Blackwell Publishers.

Ríos, Francisco Armando. 1969. "The Mexican in Fact, Fiction, and Folklore." *El Grito: A Journal of Contemporary Mexican American Thought* 2 (4): 14–28.

Roberts, Bari-Ellen, with Jack E. White. 1998. *Roberts versus Texaco: A True Story of Race and Corporate America*. New York: Avon Books.

Robinson, Cecil. 1963. *With the Ears of Strangers: The Mexican in American Literature*. Tucson: University of Arizona Press.

Rocco, Raymond. 1998. "Citizenship, Civil Society, and the Latino City: Claiming Subaltern Spaces, Reframing the Public Sphere." Manuscript. Author's personal collection, UCLA.

Rodinger, David R. 1991. *The Wages of Whiteness: Race and the Making of the American Working Class*. London: Verso.

Rodríguez, Clara E., and Héctor Cordero-Guzmán. 1992. "Placing Race in Context." *Ethnic and Racial Studies* 15 (4): 523–542.

Rodriguez, Richard. 1982. *Hunger of Memory. An Autobiography. The Education of Richard Rodriguez*. New York: Bantam Books.

Romano-V., Octavio Ignacio. 1968. "The Anthropology and Sociology of the Mexican-Americans: The Distortion of Mexican-American History." *El Grito: A Journal of Contemporary Mexican American Thought* 2 (1): 13–26.

———. 1970. "Social Science, Objectivity, and the Chicanos." *El Grito: A Journal of Contemporary Mexican American Thought* 4 (1): 4–16.

Rorty, Richard. 1989. *Contingency, Irony and Solidarity*. Cambridge: Cambridge University Press.

Rosaldo, Renato. 1996. "Surveying Law and Border." *Stanford Law Review* 48 (5): 1037–1045.

Rosin, Hanna. 1994. "Raisin Hell. (California Farmers and the Immigration Reform Initiative Proposition 187)." *New Republic* 211 (20): 15–17.

Ruíz, Vicki L. 1998. *From Out of the Shadows: Mexican Women in Twentieth-Century America*. New York: Oxford University Press.

Saenz, J. Luz. 1933. *Los méxico-americanos en la Gran Guerra: y su contingente en pró de la democracia, la humanidad y la justicia*. San Antonio, Tex.: Artes Gráficas.

Said, Edward. 1978. *Orientalism*. New York: Routledge and Kegan Paul.

Sánchez, George I. 1932a. "Group Differences and Spanish-Speaking Children—A Critical Review." *Journal of Applied Psychology,* vol. 16, pp. 549–583.

———. 1932b. "Scores of Spanish-Speaking Children on Repeated Tests." *Pedagogical Seminary and Journal of Genetic Psychology,* March, pp. 223–231.

———. 1940. *Forgotten People*. Albuquerque: University of New Mexico Press.

Sánchez, George J. 1993. *Becoming Mexican-American: Ethnicity, Culture and Identity in Chicano Los Angeles, 1900–1945*. Oxford: Oxford University Press.

———. 1999. "Nativist Response to Education, Society and Language." Lecture given as part of series entitled Education, Society and Language. University of Southern California, January 20.

Sánchez, Leo. 1973. "Treatment of Mexican Americans by Selected U.S. Newspapers, January–June 1970." Master's thesis, Pennsylvania State University.

Sánchez, Rosaura. 1983. *Chicano Discourse: Socio-historical Perspectives*. Rowley, Mass.: Newbury House.

Sanderson, Michael. 1999. *Education and Economic Decline in Britain, 1870 to the 1990s*. Cambridge: Cambridge University Press.

San Miguel, Guadalupe, Jr., and Richard R. Valencia. 1998. "From the Treaty of Guadalupe Hidalgo to Hopwood: The Educational Plight and Struggle of Mexican Americans in the Southwest." *Harvard Educational Review* 68 (3): 353–412.

Santa Ana, Otto. 1993. "Chicano English and the Chicano Language Setting." *Hispanic Journal of Behavior Sciences* 15 (1): 3–35.

———. 1999. "Like an Animal I Was Treated: Anti-immigrant Metaphor in U.S. Public Discourse." *Discourse and Society* 10 (2): 191–224.

———, ed. Forthcoming. *Tongue Tied: The Lives of Multilingual Children in Public Education.*

Santa Ana, Otto, with Juan Morán and Cynthia Sánchez. 1998. "Awash under a Brown Tide: Metaphor and the Ideology of Immigration in American Discourse." *Aztlán: A Journal of Chicano Research* 23 (2): 137–176.

Santa Ana, Otto, and Claudia Parodi. 1998. "Modeling the Speech Community: Configuration and Variable Types in the Mexican Spanish Setting." *Language in Society,* vol. 27, pp. 23–51.

Santa Ana, Otto, and Eduardo Rivas. 1999. "Saving Private Citizen: How We Talk about Politics in Public Discourse." Manuscript. Author's personal collection, UCLA.

Saragoza, Alex M., Concepción R. Juárez, Abel Valenzuela, Jr., and Oscar González. 1992. "History and Public Policy: Title VII and the Use of the Hispanic Classification." *La Raza Law Journal,* vol. 5, pp. 1–27.

Scales-Trent, Judy. 1995. *Notes of a White Black Woman.* University Park: Pennsylvania State University Press.

Schact, Richard. 1983. "Truth and Knowledge." *Nietzsche.* Boston: Routledge and Kegan Paul, pp. 52–117.

Scheurich, James Joseph, and Michelle D. Young. 1997. "Coloring Epistemologies: Are Our Research Epistemologies Racially Biased?" *Educational Researcher* 26 (4): 4–16.

Schiffman, Harold. 1996. *Linguistic Culture and Language Policy.* New York: Routledge.

Schliche, Paul, ed. 1999. *Oxford Reader's Companion to Dickens.* London: Oxford University Press.

Schön, Donald A. 1979. "Generative Metaphor: A Perspective on Problem-Setting in Social Policy." In *Metaphor and Thought,* 1st ed., ed. Andrew Ortony, pp. 137–163. New York: Cambridge University Press.

Schön, Donald A., and Martin Reim. 1994. *Frame Reflection: Toward the Resolution of Intractable Policy Controversies.* New York: Basic Books.

Searle, John. 1993. "Metaphor." In *Metaphor and Thought,* 2d ed., ed. Andrew Ortony, pp. 83–111. Cambridge: Cambridge University Press.

———. 1998. *The Philosophy of Mind.* Springfield, Va.: The Teaching Company.

Sears, David O. 1988. "Symbolic Racism." In *Eliminating Racism*, ed. Phyllis A. Katz and Dalmas A. Taylor, pp. 53–84. New York: Plenum Press.

Shannon, Sheila M. 1995. "The Hegemony of English: A Case Study of One Bilingual Classroom as a Site of Resistance." *Linguistics and Education*, vol. 7, pp. 175–200.

Sidanius, Jim, Felicia Pratto, and Lawrence Bobo. 1996. "Racism, Conservatism, Affirmative Action, and Intellectual Sophistication: A Matter of Principled Conservatism or Group Dominance?" *Journal of Personality and Social Psychology* 70 (3): 476–491.

Simón, Laura Angélica. 1997. *Fear and Learning at Hoover Elementary*, a film directed and narrated by Laura Angélica Simón, 53 minutes, sound, color. Josepha Producciones. Hohokus, N.J.: Transit Media.

Simon, Richard. 1993. "Activists for Immigrant Rights Battle Erosion of Public Support. They Are up against Polls Showing Negative Attitudes about Newcomers. Advocates' Counteroffensive Cites Economic Contributions and Calls for Compassion." *Los Angeles Times*, November 24, p. A24.

Skrentny, John David. 1996. *The Ironies of Affirmative Action: Politics, Culture, and Justice in America*. Chicago: University of Chicago Press.

Skutnabb-Kangas, Tove. 1989. "Multilingualism and the Education of Minority Children." In *Linguicism Rules Education*, ed. Robert Phillipson and Tove Skutnabb-Kangas. Cited in Ricento 2000.

Smith, Rogers M. 1998. "Citizenship." In *A Companion to American Thought*, ed. Richard Wightman Fox and James T. Kloppenberg, pp. 121–124. Malden, Mass.: Blackwell.

Smitherman, Geneva. 1986. *Talking and Testifying: The Language of Black America*. Detroit: Wayne State University Press.

Snow, Catherine E., Susan Burns, and Peg Griffin, eds. 1998. *Preventing Reading Difficulties in Young Children*. Washington, D.C.: National Academy Press.

Solórzano, Daniel G. 1998. "Critical Race Theory, Race, and Gender Microaggressions, and the Experience of Chicana and Chicano Scholars." *Qualitative Studies in Education* 11 (1): 121–136.

Sosa, Lionel. 1998. *The Americano Dream: How Latinos Can Achieve Success in Business and Life*. New York: Penguin Group.

Stanton-Salazar, Ricardo. 1997–1999. Personal communication.

Steele, Shelby. 1991. *The Content of Our Character: A New Vision of Race in America*. New York: St. Martin's Press.

Stefancic, Jean. 1997. "Latino and Latina Critical Theory: An Annotated Bibliography." *California Law Review* 85 (5): 1509–1584.

Stefancic, Jean, and Richard Delgado. 1996. *No Mercy: How Conservative Think Tanks and Foundations Changed America's Social Agenda*. Philadelphia: Temple University Press.

Street, Brian V. 1984. *Literacy in Theory and Practice*. Cambridge: Cambridge University Press.

Stubbs, Michael. 1986. *Educational Linguistics*. Oxford: Basil Blackwell.

Suárez-Orozco, Carola, and Marcelo Suárez-Orozco. 1995. *Transformations: Immigration, Family Life, and Achievement Motivation among Latino Adolescents*. Stanford, Calif.: Stanford University Press.

Sweetser, Eve E. 1990. *From Etymology to Pragmatics: Metaphorical and Cultural Aspects of Semantic Structure*. New York: Cambridge University Press.

Takaki, Ronald. 1993. *A Different Mirror: A History of Multicultural America*. Boston, New York, Toronto, and London: Back Bay Books.

Tan, Alex. 1978. "Evaluation of Newspapers and Television by Blacks and Mexican-Americans." *Journalism Quarterly,* vol. 55, pp. 673–681.

Taylor, Ronald B. 1975. *Chávez and the Farm Workers*. Boston: Beacon Press.

Tell, Carol. 1999. "Renewing the Profession of Teaching: A Conversation with John Goodlad." *Educational Leadership* 56 (8): 14–19.

Templeton, Alan R. 1998. "Human Races: A Genetic and Evolutionary Perspective." *American Anthropologist* 100 (3): 632–650.

Thorndike, Edward L. 1913. *The Principles of Teaching: Based on Psychology*. New York: Seiler.

Tollefson, James W. 1991. *Planning Language, Planning Inequality*. New York: Longman.

Turner, Bryan S. [1984] 1996. *The Body and Society: Explorations in Social Theory*. London: Sage Publications.

———. 1990. "Outline of a Theory of Citizenship." *Sociology* 24 (2): 189–217.

Turner, Ralph H. 1960. "Sponsored and Contest Mobility and the School System." *American Sociological Review* 25 (5): 855–867.

United Nations. 1996. *World Population Prospects: The 1996 Revision*. New York: United Nations.

United States Bureau of the Census. October 1993. *In-School Enrollment—Social and Economic Characteristics*. Current Population Reports, p. A26. Washington, D.C.: U.S. Department of Commerce.

Urciuoli, Bonnie. 1996. *Exposing Prejudice: Puerto Rican Experiences of Language, Race and Class*. Boulder, Colo.: Westview Press.

Vaca, Nick C. 1970a. "The Mexican-American in the Social Sciences. Part I: 1912–1935." *El Grito: A Journal of Contemporary Mexican American Thought* 3 (3): 3–24.

———. 1970b. "The Mexican-American in the Social Sciences. Part II: 1936–1970." *El Grito: A Journal of Contemporary Mexican American Thought* 4 (1): 17–51.

Valdés, Guadalupe. 1998. "The World Outside and Inside Schools: Language and Immigrant Children." *Educational Researcher* 27 (6): 4–18.

Valencia, Richard R., ed. 1997. *The Evolution of Deficit Thinking: Educational Thought and Practice.* London: Falmer Press.

Valencia, Richard R., and Daniel G. Solórzano. 1997. "Contemporary Deficit Thinking." In *The Evolution of Deficit Thinking: Educational Thought and Practice,* ed. Richard R. Valencia, pp. 160–210. London: Falmer Press.

Valenzuela, Abel, Jr. 2001. "Day Laborers as Entrepreneurs?" *Journal of Ethnic and Migration Studies* 27 (2): 335–352.

Van Besien, Fred. 1989. "Metaphors in Scientific Language." *Communication and Cognition* 22 (1): 5–22.

van Dijk, Teun A. 1985. "Introduction: The Role of Discourse Analysis in Society." In *Handbook of Discourse Analysis,* vol. 4, ed. Teun A. van Dijk, pp. 1–8. London: Academic Press.

———. 1987. *Communicating Racism: Ethnic Prejudice in Thought and Talk.* Newbury Park, Calif.: Sage Publications.

———. 1989. "Structures of Discourse and Structures of Power." *Communications Yearbook,* vol. 2, pp. 18–59.

———. 1991. *Racism and the Press.* London: Routledge.

———. 1993a. *Elite Discourse and Racism.* Newbury Park, Calif.: Sage.

———. 1993b. "Principles of Critical Discourse Analysis." *Discourse and Society* 4 (2): 249–283.

VanSlyke Turk, Judy, Jim Richstad, Robert L. Bryson, Jr., and Sammye M. Johnson. 1989. "Hispanic Americans in the News in Two Southwestern Cities." *Journalism Quarterly,* vol. 66, pp. 107–113.

van Teeffelen, Toine. 1994. "Racism and Metaphor: The Palestinian-Israeli Conflict in Popular Literature." *Discourse and Society* 5 (3): 381–405.

Vélez-Ibáñez, Carlos G. 1988. "Networks of Exchange among Mexicans in the U.S. and Mexico: Local Level Mediating and International Transformations." *Urban Anthropology* 17 (1): 27–51.

———. 1997. *Border Visions: Mexican Cultures of the Southwest United States.* Tucson: University of Arizona Press.

Vérnez, George, and Kevin F. McCarthy. 1996. *The Costs of Immigration to Taxpayers: Analytical and Policy Issues.* Santa Monica, Calif.: Rand Corporation.

Vigil, Diego James. 1998. *From Indians to Chicanos: The Dynamics of Mexican-American Culture,* 2d ed. Prospect Heights, Ill.: Waveland Press, Inc.

———. 1999. "Streets and Schools: How Educators Can Help Chicano Marginalized Gang Youth." *Harvard Educational Review* 69 (3): 270–288.

Violi, Patrizia. 1990. Review of several volumes, including George Lakoff's *Women, Fire, and Dangerous Things: What Categories Reveal about the Mind. Semiotica* 80 (3–4): 321–336.

Voss, James F., Joel Kennet, Jennifer Wiley, and Tonya Y. E. Schooler. 1992. "Experts at Debate: The Use of Metaphor in the U.S. Senate Debate on the Gulf Crisis." *Metaphor and Symbolic Activity* 7 (3–4): 197–214.

Washington, James M., ed. 1991. *A Testament of Hope: The Essential Writings and Speeches of Martin Luther King, Jr.* New York: HarperCollins.

Weber, David J., ed. 1973. *Foreigners in Their Native Land: Historical Roots of the Mexican American.* Albuquerque: University of New Mexico Press.

Wetherell, Margaret, and Jonathan Potter. 1992. *Mapping the Language of Racism: Discourse and the Legitimation of Exploitation.* New York: Columbia University Press.

Wildman, Stephanie. 1996. *Privilege Revealed.* New York: New York University Press.

Wiley, Terrence G. 1996. "English-Only and Standard English Ideologies in the U.S." *TESOL Quarterly* 30 (3): 511–535.

———. 1998. "The Imposition of World War I Era English-Only Policies and the Fate of German in North America." In *Language and Politics in the United States and Canada: Myths and Realities,* ed. Thomas Ricento and Barbara Burnaby, pp. 211–241. Mahwah, N.J.: Lawrence Erlbaum.

Williams, Fredrick, ed. 1970. *Language and Poverty.* Chicago: Markham.

Williams, Gregory Howard. 1991. *Life on the Color Line.* New York: Dutton.

Wilson, Clint C., and Felix Gutiérrez. 1985. *Minorities and Media: Diversity and the End of Mass Communication.* Beverly Hills, Calif.: Sage.

Wilson, Edward O. 1997. *Consilience: The Unity of Knowledge.* New York: Alfred A. Knopf.

Winter, Steven L. 1988. "The Metaphor of 'Standing' and the Problem of Self-Governance." *Stanford University Law Review* 40 (6): 1371–1516.

———. 1989. "Transcendental Nonsense, Metaphoric Reasoning, and the Cognitive Stakes for Law." *University of Pennsylvania Law Review* 137 (4): 1105–1237.

———. 1990. "Bull Durham and the Uses of Theory." *Stanford University Law Review* 42 (3): 639–693.

Wolfe, Alan. 1998. *One Nation, After All.* New York: Viking.

Wolfe, Paula M. 1999. "Changing Metaphors for Secondary ESL and Bilingual Education." In *So Much to Say: Adolescents, Bilingualism, and ESL in the Secondary Schools,* ed. Christian J. Faltis and Paula M. Wolfe. New York: Teachers College Press.

Wolfram, Walt. 1998. "Language Ideology and Dialect: Understanding the Oakland Ebonics Controversy." *Journal of English Linguistics* 26 (2): 106–119.

Woll, Allen L. 1977. *The Latin Image in American Film.* Los Angeles: UCLA Latin American Center Publications.

Woodward, C. Vann. 1960. *The Burden of Southern History.* Baton Rouge: Louisiana State University Press.

Woolard, Kathryn A. 1989. "Sentences in the Language Prison: The Rhetorical Structuring of an American Language Policy Debate." *American Ethnologist* 16 (2): 268–278.

Young, Iris Marion. 1989. *Justice and the Politics of Difference.* Princeton, N.J.: Princeton University Press.

Zagorin, Adam. 1997. "Charlie's an Angel?" *Time,* February 3, p. 36.

Zarefsky, David. 1999. "Lecture 22: Moving toward Emancipation." *Abraham Lincoln in His Own Words.* Springfield, Va.: The Teaching Company.

Zentella, Ana Celia. 1997. *Growing Up Bilingual: Puerto Rican Children in New York.* Oxford: Blackwell.

Zinn, Howard. 1980. *A People's History of the United States.* New York: Harper & Row.

# Permissions Acknowledgments

I would like to acknowledge that publishers have given me permission to reprint excerpts of their copyrighted material authored by the following writers:

John L. Austin, an excerpt from "A Plea for Excuses" in his *Philosophical Papers,* published by Clarendon Press, Oxford, England. Reprinted by courtesy of the editor of the Aristotelian Society, © 1961.

Peter Brimelow, excerpts from *Alien Nation: Common Sense about America's Immigration Disaster.* By permission of Random House Publishers. © 1995 by Peter Brimelow.

Joanne Brown, an excerpt from "Language" appearing in *A Companion to American Thought,* edited by Richard Wightman Fox and James T. Kloppenberg. By permission of Blackwell Publishers Ltd. © 1995.

Kitty Calavita, excerpts from "The New Politics of Immigration: 'Balanced-Budget Conservatism' and the Symbolism of Proposition 187," reprinted from *Social Problems,* vol. 43, no. 3, August 1996, pp. 284–305, by permission of the Society for the Study of Social Problems. © 1995.

*Commentary,* for excerpts from its special issue dedicated to affirmative action. Reprinted from *Commentary,* vol. 105, no. 3, March 1998, by permission; all rights reserved.

John Dewey, an excerpt from "My Pedagogic Creed," appearing in Martin S. Dworkin, *Dewey on Education,* pp. 20–22, reprinted by permission of the publisher, Teachers College Press, Columbia University. All rights reserved. © 1959 by Teachers College, Columbia University.

John F. Dovidio, an excerpt from "'Aversive' Racism and the Need for Affirmative Action," appearing in *Chronicle of Higher Education,* vol. 43, no. 46. Reprinted by permission of the author.

Christopher Edley, Jr., excerpts from chapters entitled "Introduction: The White House Review" and "Facts and Law" of *Not All Black and White: Affirmative Action and American Values.* © 1996 by Christopher Edley, Jr. Reprinted by permission of Hill and Wang, a division of Farrar, Straus and Giroux, LLC.

John Fonte, an excerpt from the March/April 1997 *American Enterprise,* vol. 8, no. 2, p. 72. Reprinted by permission of *American Enterprise.*

Paulo Freire, an extended excerpt from *Pedagogy of the Oppressed.* Reprinted by an exceptional permission of the Continuum Publishing Company. © 1970 by Paulo Freire.

Stephen J. Gould, an excerpt from his essay entitled "The Pattern of Life's History." Reprinted with the permission of Simon & Schuster from *The Third Culture,* edited by John Brockman. © 1995 by John Brockman.

Jürgen Habermas, an excerpt from *Legitimization Crisis.* German text © 1973 by Suhrkamp Verlag, Frankfurt am Main. Introduction and English translation © 1975 by Beacon Press. Reprinted by permission of Beacon Press, Boston.

# Index

California Civil Rights Initiative (CCRI), 128, 129. See also Proposition 209
California Educational Code (conflation of literacy and language in), 222
Calvinism, as template for entrepreneurial virtue, 301
Carnegie, Andrew, 298
Castro, Sal, 2
Chávez, César, 2, 275, 276, 281
Chavez, Linda, 196, 269
Chávez, Lydia, 128, 154
child: as commodity, 172; as passive object, 166; as unit of industrial production, 170
Chilton, Paul, 39, 48–49, 258, 261, 270
Chilton, Paul, and Mikhail Ilyin, 259
Churchill, Winston, 262
Cicero, 26
Cioran, Emile, 235
citizenship, 276–281; Brimeloe's proposal regarding, 280, 286–287; Governor Wilson's proposal regarding, 6, 286–287; and Latinos as non-citizens, 285–293; and naturalization, 257
citizen versus denizen, 273–281
Civil Rights Act of 1964, 105, 113, 124, 128, 186, 275; Title VI, 217; Title VII, 113–114
civil rights discourse, 108
Civil Rights Movement, 152, 275, 305; subversion of 1960s discourse of, 153–154; as war, 108
CLASSROOM AS BATTLEGROUND, 171–172; AS SAFE HAVEN, 172; AS WAREHOUSE, 172–173
Clinton, Bill, 128, 132, 149, 154, 347
codeswitching, 353
cognition, 24, 28–31
cognitive metaphor theory, critique, 44–49
cognitive science theory, 8
coherence, evaluation measure of metaphor analysis, 28, 254
Cold War, 48
colonialism, English-only, 235; and linguistic reflexes, 216
Colvin, Richard, 158–159, 162, 351
Commentary, 105, 126, 142, 343–344, 345; essayists, 133–135, 148–150, 182, 185

Common European House, 261–262. See also Chilton, Paul
COMMUNITY, in metaphor summary table, 325
Comte, Auguste, 259
conduit metaphor, 36–38, 200–202
congruence, 79; as evaluation measure of metaphor analysis, 28, 254
Conner, Bull, 153
constructivism, 27–28, 161
conventional metaphor, 42; backgrounding and foregrounding in, 36–37; contesting of, 296; inertia of, 35–36
counter-stories, 296
Craven, W. A., 86
Crawford, James, 218
CURRICULUM, in metaphor summary table, 330

Darwin, Charles, 318
Decade of the Hispanics, 3–7
Dewey, John, 307
Dickens, Charles, 157, 164, 305, 306
discourse, 8, 17–21, 43, 335; anti-Latino, 314; counter-hegemonic, 314; and critical analysis, 16–17, 335; as linguistic material, 19; of the 1960s, 114–124; as power, 11; public, 53–54; as social practice, 17, 28; as unit of critical analysis, 20
discursive formation, as linguistic versus extralinguistic practices, 17
discursive metaphor, caveat, 38–39
discursive practice, 253; of Los Angeles Times, 101–103; news media presentation of, 54–55; reciprocity in, 56; of schools, 193. See also Foucault, Michel
Dole, Bob, 138, 144, 235, 236
Douglas, William O., 41
Douglass, Frederick, 102–103, 276, 319
Dovidio, John, 110, 136
dropout, 183
Duke, David, 137, 270
Durkheim, Émile, 259
Dyer, Richard, 110–111

Eastin, Delaine, 227
economies of scale, 164

Gramsci, Antonio, 16
Grant, Madison, 274
Gratz, Jennifer, 125
Great American Experiment, 102
Great Chain of Being, 84–86
Great Society (Lyndon Johnson), 107
Griffith, James, 351

Habermas, Jürgen, 130
Haley, Margaret, 165
Hall, Stuart, 55
Hampton, James, 44
Handlin, Oscar, 256, 272, 274
*Happy Days* (television sitcom), 351
Haraway, Donna, 21
Hardin, Garrett, 267
*Hard Times* (novel by Charles Dickens),
  164, 168
Haycock, Kati, 348
Hayes-Bautista, David, 302
Headstone, Bradley, 165
hegemony, Anglo-American, 9, 148, 234–
  239, 148
Herman, Edward, and Noam Chomsky,
  52
Hernández, Guillermo, 334, 341
Hernández, Roger, 246–247
Hernández-Chávez, Eduardo, 334
Hicks, Joe, 302
Hill, Jane, 289
Himmelfarb, Gertrude, 48
Hinojosa, Raúl, 341
Hobbes, Thomas, 49, 258, 263
Holmes, Oliver Wendell, Jr., 40
Holyfield, Evander, 93
Horsman, Reginald, 274
Hussein, Saddam, 137

ideology, 18, 47
immanent order of world, 22
immigrant, 65–66, 88, 341; imagery associated with, 351; insurgent metaphors
  associated with, 300–303; as less-than-
  human, 93–103, 285–293
IMMIGRANT: AS ANIMAL, 82–89, 99–103,
  276; AS ANGEL, 284; AS BURDEN, 71,
  96, 99; AS CHILD, 98; AS CRIMINAL,
  96, 99; AS DISEASE, 71, 96, 99; AS

DISREPUTABLE PERSON, 89; AS
  ENEMY, 94, 99; AS ENTREPRENEUR,
  301; and metaphor summary table, 83;
  respecifying domains of, 297–303; AS
  RIGHTFUL RESIDENT OF NATION AS
  HOUSE, 303; AS SOLDIER, 95; AS TAX
  BURDEN, 96; AS WEED, 89, 103
IMMIGRATION, 68–81; AS DANGEROUS
  WATERS, 72–79, 239–240; insurgent
  metaphors of, 297–299; in metaphor
  summary table, 83
industrialism, 168
insurgent discourse, 296–297
insurgent metaphors, 312–313; regarding
  education, 305–313; regarding immigrants, 300–303; regarding immigration, 297–299
interpretive schema and scripts, 313–314
Iron Curtain, 261, 262

Jackendoff, Ray, 23, 46
Jackendoff, Ray, and David Aaron, 44–46
Jackson, Jesse, 139
Jim Crow laws, 125, 143
Johnson, Lyndon, 107, 108–109, 114, 115,
  119, 123, 152, 275, 304, 345
Johnson, Mark, 177

Kafka, Franz, 290
Kant, Immanuel, 169, 337
Kassenbaum, Nancy, 113
Keating, Charles, 92–94
Kennan, George, 49
Kennedy, John F., 124–125
Kerner Commission and Report (1968
  National Advisory Commission on
  Civil Disorders), 108, 111, 112, 113, 124,
  127–128, 133, 154, 189, 304
King, Martin Luther, Jr., 17, 106, 108, 111,
  114–115, 119–124, 127, 132–133, 136–
  137, 139, 152–153, 281, 282, 304, 319,
  345, 347–348; use of personification
  metaphors by, 116
King, Rodney, 95
KNOWLEDGE: AS ABODE, 160, 308; AS
  CONSTRUCT, 161, 167, 307; and TO
  KNOW IS TO SEE, 31
Kotkin, Joel, 301

Kuhn, Thomas, 21, 34
Ku Klux Klan lynchings, 143

Laclau, Ernesto, 19
Lakoff, George, 20, 21–25, 28, 29, 32, 33, 44, 46–48, 88, 96–99, 253–254; and Mark Johnson, 26–27, 285, 286; and Mark Turner, 46, 84–85, 339
La Mettrie, Julien Offray de, 35
Langacker, Ronald, 21
language: differentiated from literacy, 218–230; and hegemonic narrative, 237–239; in U.S. education discourse, 211
LANGUAGE, 38; AS BARRIER, 207–209, 217; AS CONDUIT, 201; AS FOREIGN, 211–212; AS HANDICAP, 223–224; in metaphor summary table, 325; AS PRISON, 230–233; as radial concept, 237; AS TOOLMAKER, 337, 363; AS WATER, 201–204. See also ENGLISH AS WATER
language acquisition, 208–211, 217; and confusion with literacy development, 218–221
language education, 206–207
La Opinión, 244, 245
Larsen, Yvonne, 221
Latino electorate, difference from Anglo electorate, 247
Latino public education, 156
Latinos: discourse about, 7–9; as foreign, 289–293; AS GRASSLAND ROOTSTOCK, 272; language metaphors for, 207–218; in metaphor summary table, 326; sanitization of racist public discourse about, 295; script about, for relations on national stage, 284–293
Lau v. Nichols, 217, 219
LEARNING AS BUILDING, 307–310. See also constructivism
learning theory: and behaviorism, 159; and constructivism, 27–28, 161; and forge theory, 159, 163; and mechanistic metaphors, 159; and organic metaphors, 159; and other metaphors, 158–162
Lee, James Kyung-Jin, 346
Leviathan (work by Thomas Hobbes), 49, 258

LIFE, 44; AS JOURNEY, 32–33; AS PATH, 177
Lincoln, Abraham, 262, 342
linguicism, 216, 237
linguistic competence, 220, 356
linguistic performance, 220
Lipsitz, George, 5, 346, 354
literacy, differentiated from language, 218–230
Loo, Patricia, 299
Los Angeles "riots," 95
Los Angeles Times, 54–56, 244–245; coverage of Proposition 209 in, 104; discursive practice in, 101–103; pro-Proposition 227 stance of, 243
Loury, Glenn, 114–115, 151
LOVE, 36–37; AS WAR, 26–31
Lovelock, James, 259
low-income neighborhoods, 41–45

Maastricht Treaty, 265, 315–316
Machiavelli, Niccolò, 169
Macías, Reynaldo, 241, 358, 360
Mahony, Roger, 284
mainstream, 190–191; assimilation to, 192–194. See EDUCATION AS RIVER
Makath, Keshav, 126–127
Malcolm X, 115–119, 123, 139, 152, 281, 304, 345
Mandela, Nelson, 110
Manifest Destiny, 274
Marshall, T. H., 277–278
Marshall Plan, 112
Martín-Barbero, Jesús, 52
mass media, 49–56
math curriculum, 1997 debate about, 158
McCarthy, Eugene, 269
McChesney, Robert, 51
M'Choakunchild, Mr., 165
meaning, origin of, 44
Mehan, Hugh, 94
Méndez v. Westminster School District, 234
meritocracy, 125, 142; as American Olympics, 190
metaphor: as cognitive framework for worldview, 21; constructivist, 349; conventional, 336; definition of, 26, 45, 282; and event structure, 32–33;

foundational, 31–33; higher-order cultural, 32, 321, 323, 339; in institutions, 39–41; insurgent, 296; literature on, 335–336; lower-order, 321; mapping of, 27, 336; mixing of, 340; original, 79; and physics, 34; in political action, 43; in science, 33–35; shift in, 37–38; in social policy, 41–43; subverting the conventional, 304–305; as text, 27; theories of, 21–43; as unit of discursive practice, 101; as unit of hegemonic expression, 9

metaphor analysis: and classification procedure, 57–58; and empirical diachronic method, 46–49, 59–60, 104; and empirical synchronic method, 46–49, 57–58; and evaluation measures, 28, 254; and intersubjective technique, 57; and labeling procedure, 44–45, 336

metaphor theory: cognitive, 25–44; literalist, 22–23; pragmatics, 23–25

metaphor token, 57, 58, 339

metaphysics, imaginative versus rational, 25–26

methods: empirical linguistic, 8; rationalist linguistic, 46–49

MEXICAN CULTURE AS GRASSLAND, 272

MEXICAN IMMIGRANTS AS TOOLS, 299–300. *See* immigrant

Mexicans: as impure race, 340; representation of, in Anglo-American imagination, 333. *See also* Latinos

Mexican Sleeping Giant, 1–2, 9

Miles, Robert, 100

Milosevic, Slobodan, 126, 137

Milton, John, 40

MIND, 35; AS BODY, 31; AS VINE, 311

Mio, Jeffery, 314

Morrison, Toni, vii, 361

Myrdal, Gunnar, 85, 128

Nagel, Carlos, 359

NATION, 49, 58; AS BODY, 96, 108, 124, 255–259, 342; AS CASTLE, 264; AS CITY, 263; AS FABRIC, 316; AS FAMILY, 97–99, 342–343, 359; AS HOUSE, 79–81, 108, 260–273, 342; in metaphor summary, 271–273; AS SHIP, 20–21, 265–268

National Academy of Sciences, 223

National Education Association, 165, 166

naturalization, 257

naturalized metaphor, 42, 53. *See also* metaphor

Ndebele, Njabulo, 235

neoconservative discourse: on racism, 133–135, 145–146; stratagems in, 138–151

news media, 55–56, 245–247

Newton, Isaac, 319

Nietzsche, Friedrich, 318

Oakes, Jeannie, 180

Olivas, Michael, 349

Operation Wetback, 1

Padilla, Genaro, 148

Paine, Thomas, 269

Paludan, Phillip Shaw, 343

paradigm shifts, 34

Paredes, Américo, 255

Paredes, Raymund, 333

Parodi, Claudia, 334

*Phaedrus* (work by Plato), 30

*Plan de Delano,* 275

Plato, 30, 130, 258

Plotkin and Scheureman, 96

POLITICS: in metaphor summary table, 328; AS WAR, 107–108, 131; AS WEATHER, 131

POLITY, in metaphor summary table, 326

Pons, María Cristina, 339

pop culture, 52

positivism, 16, 22–23, 28, 33–34, 161; and skepticism of cognitivist accounts, 42–43

Powell, Colin, 149–150, 154

practicality narrative in public education, 184

presupposition, definition of, 340

Preuß, Ulrich, 278, 359

Proposition 63 (1986 California referendum), 239. *See also* English-only

Proposition 187 (1994 California referendum), 67. *See also* immigrant; immigration

Proposition 209 (1996 California referendum), 128–130; color-blind language of,

140; *Los Angeles Times* coverage of, 104. *See also* affirmative action

Proposition 227 (1998 California referendum), 197–200; fallacy of, 222; hidden message in, 229–230; public opinion polls regarding, 243–245. *See also* bilingual education

public discourse. *See* discourse

PUBLIC OPINION, in metaphor summary table, 327

PUBLIC SENTIMENT, in metaphor summary table, 327

Purcell, William, 26

Quinn, Naomi, 177

racial dictatorship, 105

racism, 99–103; in affirmative action proponent's discourse, 131–133; in American discourse, 131, 151–155; aversive, 110; benign, 15, 333–334; in biblical metaphors, 118–119; civilizational, 111; classification of, 109–113, 344; covert, 110, 112; definition of, 100; foundational, 102, 111; as an individual's crime, 140–141; institutional, 110, 112, 137, 181; legislated, 112; legitimated, 127; in metaphor summary table, 328; modern, 147; in neo-conservative discourse, 133–135, 145–146; in 1960s discourse, 118–124; overt, 109–110; and personification metaphor, 152; reticence about discussing, 114–115; sanitized, 15; societal, 110, 112, 141–143; statutory, 275; white, 109, 127, 128, 139, 140, 154

RACISM: AS CANCER, 122–124, 153, 256, 282; AS DISEASE, 120–123, 139

rationalist linguistic research, 47–49

Rawls, John, 281

Reagan, Ronald, 141, 263

Reddy, Michael, 36–39, 200–201

Reeves, Frank, 102

REFERENDA, in metaphor summary table, 329

*Republic* (work by Plato), 130, 258

reverse discrimination, 127, 134

Ricento, Thomas, 356, 358

Rickford, John, 353

Riley, Richard, 228, 242

Rivas, Eduardo, 344, 359

Rockwell, George Lincoln, 152

Rohrabacher, Dana, 98

Rorty, Richard, 317–319

Rosch, Eleanor, 44

Rosenthal and Jacobson, 352

Sánchez, George I., 2, 344, 363

Sánchez, George J., 247

Sandberg, Carl, 255

Save Our State (SOS) referendum, 266, 316. *See also* Proposition 187

Scheurich, James Joseph, and Michelle Young, 109–111, 134

Schön, Donald, 41–43, 270

SCHOOL, in metaphor summary table, 331

SCHOOL ACHIEVEMENT, in metaphor summary table, 329

SCHOOL AS FACTORY, 162–171, 182, 195

Schwarz, Charles, 137

Searle, John, 35

second-language development, 210–211

self-fulfilling prophecy in education, 179

semantics, 281–284

*Shape of the River, The* (work by William Bowen and Derek Bok), 135–136

Sheltered English, 199, 204, 205, 363

Simón, Laura Angélica, 352

Skinner, B. F., 159

Skrentny, John David, 111, 281

Skutnabb-Kangas, Tove, 216

slavery, 342

social order, 18, 54, 193

social progress, 318

social science: contending paradigms in, 22–23; research liabilities of, 48; socially engaged, 16

social theory, linguistic turn in, 19, 337

social values, indices of, 15

Solórzano, Daniel, 143, 344

Sowell, Thomas, 269

Spencer, Herbert, 259

Stanton-Salazar, Ricardo, 168, 351

statistics: on California bilingual students and teachers, 225; on California demographics (1980–1990), 66–67; on California public schools (1997), 197;

on California recession (1993), 5; on Equal Employment Opportunity Commission, 113; on language and literacy of minority students, 223; on Latino education, 156, 348; on Latinos (1980), 4; on minority student achievement, 135–136, 148
Steele, Shelby, 146
St. Paul, 319
Street, Brian, 219
student: AS COMPUTER, 159; AS CREATOR, 161; as creator versus recipient of knowledge, 161–162; AS EMPTY VESSEL, 159, 160, 162, 194–195; AS KNOWLEDGE BUILDER, 195; AS MACHINE, 159; in metaphor summary table, 332; AS PLANT, 162; as raw material for factory, 164, 169; and subject positions, 193
Suárez-Orozco, Carola and Marcelo, 95–96, 256
subverted conventional metaphors, 139, 304–305
SUCCESS AS A RACE, 108, 183, 185, 190
Sweetser, Eve, 30

taboo, against discussing racism, 134, 146
Taliban government of Afghanistan, 126
teachers: as automatons, 165; as factory workers, 164. *See* school
Texaco racism, 137
Texas Ranger suppressions, 143
Thorndike, Edward, 159, 163
Title VI, 217
Title VII, 113–114
Torres, Carlos, 339
Treaty of Guadalupe Hidalgo, 65, 273–274
Truman, Harry S, 49
Turner, Bryan, 259
Turner, Ralph, 183–184
Tyson, Mike, 92–94

umbrella metaphor, 321; in metaphor summary table, 323
Unamuno, Miguel de, 60, 319, 339, 364
United Farm Workers, 275

United States: as apartheid state, 110; as nation of immigrants, 65; as racial dictatorship, 105
UNITED STATES AS HOUSE, 260, 293
United States Constitution, 218
United States/Mexico border: BORDER, militarization of, 255, 351; in metaphor summary table, 324
University of California Regents, 128, 139
Unz, Ron, 199, 200, 211, 221, 222–223, 224, 234, 248; Unz initiative, 241. *See also* Proposition 227
*Uprooted, The* (work by Oscar Handlin), 272

Valdés, Guadalupe, 352, 354, 357
Valenzuela, Abel, Jr., 301
van Dijk, Teun, 16, 17, 20, 50, 100
van Teeffelen, Toine, 99
Vico, Giambattista, 25–26, 337
Vigil, James Diego, 309, 334
Violi, Patrizia, 44
Volpe, Justin, 137
von Bismarck, Otto Eduard Leopold, 344
von Humboldt, Wilhelm, 337
Voting Rights Act of 1975, 232

Wallace, George, 152
whiteness, possessive investment in, 5
white privilege, 247
white racism, 109, 127, 128, 139, 140, 154. *See also* racism
Wiley, Terrance, 363
Wilson, Edward O., 21, 34
Wilson, Pete, 5, 24, 77, 97, 102, 128, 139, 286–287
Winter, Stephen, 39–41, 43–44, 46
Wittgenstein, Ludwig, 337
Woolard, Kathryn, 232

Young, Iris Marion, 280–281
Young, Whitney, 112
Yukawa, Hideki, 34

Zamora, David, 345